A Catalog of Music for the Cornett

Publications of the Early Music Institute

Thomas Binkley, General Editor

Accompaniment on Theorbo and Harpsichord: Denis Delair's Treatise of 1690. A Translation with Commentary by Charlotte Mattax.

Thomas Binkley and Margit Frenk. *Spanish Romances of the Sixteenth Century.*

J. P. Freillon Poncein. *On Playing Oboe, Recorder, and Flageolet.* Translated with an Introduction by Catherine Parsons Smith.

Luis Gásser. *Luis Milán on Sixteenth-Century Performance Practice.*

Robert A. Green. *The Hurdy-Gurdy in Eighteenth-Century France.*

George Houle. *Le Ballet des Fâcheux: Beauchamp's Music for Molière's Comedy.*

George Houle. *Doulce memoire: A Study in Performance Practice.*

Sterling Scott Jones. *The Lira da Braccio.*

Antoine Mahaut. *A New Method for Learning to Play the Transverse Flute.* Translated and edited by Eileen Hadidian.

Betty Bang Mather and Gail Gavin. *The French Noel: With an Anthology of 1725 Arranged for Flute Duet.*

Ockeghem's Missa cuiusvis toni: *In Its Original Notation and Edited in all the Modes.* With an Introduction by George Houle.

Monsieur de Saint Lambert. *A New Treatise on Accompaniment: With the Harpsichord, the Organ, and with Other Instruments.* Translated and edited by John S. Powell.

David Hogan Smith. *Reed Design for Early Woodwinds.*

A Catalog of Music for the Cornett

MICHAEL COLLVER

and

BRUCE DICKEY

Indiana University Press

Bloomington and Indianapolis

The paper used in this publication meets the minimum requirements of American National Standard for Information Sciences – Permanence of Paper for Printed Library Materials, ANSI Z39.48-1984.

Manufactured in the United States of America

Library of Congress Cataloging-in-Publication Data

Collver, Michael.
  A catalog of music for the cornett / Michael Collver and Bruce Dickey.
    p.   cm. – (Publications of the Early Music Institute)
  Includes bibliographical references (p.   ) and index.
  ISBN 0-253-20974-9 (pbk.)
    1. Cornett music – Bibliography. I. Dickey, Bruce. II. Title.
  III. Series.
  ML 128.C86C6   1995
  016.7889'9026 – dc20   94-44769

1   2   3   4   5   00   99   98   97   96   MN

For Thomas Binkley

CONTENTS

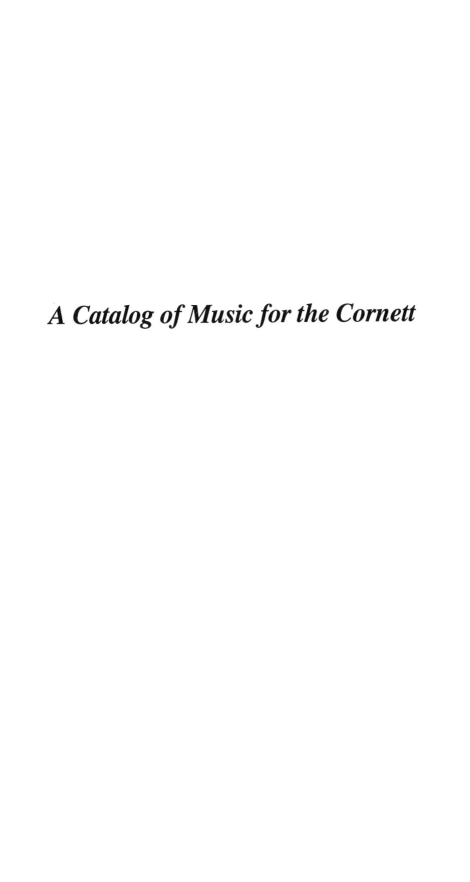

A Catalog of Music for the Cornett

INTRODUCTION

The purpose of this catalog is to list all extant music with a specified instrumentation that includes the cornett. While each year brings a significant increase in the amount of cornett music available in modern editions and facsimiles, the majority of the cornett's repertoire remains unpublished and unknown. Since the number of cornett players today is small in relation to the quantity and importance of the repertoire, this situation is not likely to change soon. The authors' purpose, therefore, is to provide a guide to this instrument's vast repertoire in original manuscripts and prints.

Despite the historical importance of the cornett – to which the present catalog amply attests – little recent scholarship has been devoted to the instrument. Georg Karstädt's pioneering dissertation of 1935,[1] though written before the modern revival of the instrument and superseded in many details, remains the only serious monographic study. Numerous local studies, particularly in Germany and Italy, of court, church and civic musical establishments provide detailed information on hundreds of cornettists, giving us the names of players, their duties and salaries, instrument purchases, etc. Unfortunately, no serious attempt has so far been made to bring this information together and to provide a composite international picture of cornett playing. Among others, Keith Polk[2] has shed valuable light on some of the earliest *virtuosi* of the instrument, yet many questions remain about how, where, and when the cornett first appeared. Similarly, the demise of the cornett continues to raise thorny questions. Why did an instrument so lavishly praised in 1600 apparently plunge into relative obscurity in the span of forty years? Are our impressions perhaps false? Each year seems to bring evidence of cornett playing at a later date and to shorten that dark span of time in which the instrument was entirely out of use.

A number of bibliographic works are of use in tracing the instrument's repertoire. Indispensable for its broad scope is the *Répertoire International des Sources Musicales* (RISM). (For details of all works cited, see the Bibliography.) The RISM bibliography of printed works is the standard source for identifying and locating them. RISM's policy of providing titles but no incipits or tables of contents, however, limits its usefulness in identifying music written for a specific instrument. For Italian printed instrumental music, this situation is mitigated by the existence of Claudio Sartori's *Bibliografia della musica strumentale italiana stampata in Italia fino al 1700*. Despite its restricted scope, Sartori's bibliography is invaluable for its detailed and laudably accurate information from prefaces and tables of contents. Unfortunately, no comparable bibliographic tools exist for Italian manuscripts. For German sacred music, Diane Parr Walker and Paul Walker have recently published the bibliography *German Sacred Polyphonic Vocal Music between Schütz and Bach,* which, although limited in the period it covers, includes instrumentations for both printed and manuscript music. For

---

[1] Dissertation, Friedrich-Wilhelms-Universität Berlin, 1935; published in a shortened version as "Zur Geschichte des Zinken und seiner Verwendung in der Musik des 16.-18. Jahrhunderts," *Archiv für Musikforschung* II (1937): 385-432.

[2] See especially, Keith Polk, *German Instrumental Music of the Late Middle Ages* (Cambridge: Cambridge University Press, 1992).

much of the repertoire, however, one must search through a plethora of individual library catalogs, thematic composer indices, and other assorted bibliographic tools of wildly varying accuracy as well as monuments and collected editions in order to obtain an overview of the repertoire of the instrument or to locate specific works.

The present catalog aims to remedy this situation. It is intended first and foremost as an aid to cornettists, but it should also prove useful to players of other instruments (in particular, violin, curtal, and trombone) whose repertoires touch upon that of the cornett, and to anyone wishing to gain an understanding of this instrument and its role in the music of the sixteenth through the eighteenth centuries.

Organization

The entries in this catalog are arranged alphabetically by composer. Each entry represents either a manuscript work (or a volume of manuscript works) specifying cornett as part of the instrumentation or a printed collection containing at least one work for the instrument. In the case of prints, the title and publication data are followed by an indented listing of all the individual pieces that mention the instrument. Each manuscript entry begins directly with an indented title (if one is present) and a listing of all the individual pieces specifying cornett that it contains. Discrepancies among title pages, indexes, and headings of pieces are noted. When there are multiple works by one composer, prints are arranged chronologically, followed by manuscript works organized alphabetically by library and then by manuscript call number (or shelf mark). (For the extensive lists of works by J.S. Bach and J.J. Fux we found it more expedient to list the manuscript works in alphabetical order by title.) Multiple works from a particular manuscript are listed in the order in which they appear there. Anonymous works are listed by library in call number order.

For practical reasons the entries are divided into separate listings of vocal and instrumental music. Sources that contain both instrumental and vocal works are placed in both lists, although only the relevant contents are cited. Instrumental pieces within the context of an opera or cantata have been left in the vocal list, but are cross-referenced when deemed substantial enough to constitute a stand-alone work. Cross-referencing is also supplied for entries in which the distinction between vocal and instrumental music is not clear. Theoretical works dealing with the cornett as well as musical works the source or location of which are currently unknown are listed in the Appendix. Lost works for which we have library source information have been kept in the main lists.

Unless otherwise noted, all information preceding the library sigla in each entry was obtained from the original source. In cases where the original was not available to us, asterisks indicate the sources upon which we have relied. For convenience SartMS and RISM reference numbers are given where applicable. Note that in the absence of an asterisk, SartMS and RISM are not the sources of the information for the entry. The library sigla follow RISM where possible. Where no RISM sigla exist, similar ones have been devised or taken from those in GroveD.

This catalog is intended as a guide to the primary source material and not to modern editions of cornett music. Nevertheless, where modern editions are readily available and of good quality, or represent the only surviving source of the music, we have listed them. The list of modern editions is not, however, intended to be comprehensive.

The present project was begun as a simple card file at the Schola Cantorum Basiliensis on the initiative of Edward H. Tarr. The present authors took over the project in the late 1970s and published a first version including only instrumental music in *Basler Jahrbuch für historische Musikpraxis* 5 (1981): 263-313. In subsequent years a number of students at the Schola Cantorum and other friends of the cornett have contributed to the growth of the catalog. The authors would particularly like to thank Douglas Kirk (McGill University), John Howard (Harvard University Library), Oscar Mischiati (Civico museo, Bologna), and Arno Paduch (Leipzig).

Cataloging the Cornett Repertoire

During its "golden age" (roughly 1550 to 1650) the cornett was played in virtually every corner of Europe. Probably heard most often in churches, it also played an important role in civic and ceremonial music, and was even heard, "to the astonishment of some and the disapproval of others,"[3] in the intimate surroundings of the chamber.

One of the goals of this catalog is to provide a picture of the repertoire played by the cornettists in question. Before considering the music contained in the catalog, however, we must reflect on some issues concerning the nature and extent of the cornett repertoire, the sources in which it is preserved, and the problems of cataloging it.

The contents of the catalog have been shaped by three principal factors: 1) our own preconceptions of where to look for cornett repertoire, 2) the way in which the repertoire has been preserved in prints and manuscripts, and 3) the varying degrees of access we had to the material in libraries and archives in various countries, either directly or through reference tools.

Conditions in each country or geographic region have influenced each of the above factors; therefore extreme care must be exercised in making regional, national, or chronological comparisons on the basis of this catalog. The significance and validity of any such conclusions are reduced by the variability in the age, methodology, and comprehensiveness of our sources of information. This variability is greater in the vocal list because of the larger number of secondary sources cited; but since secondary sources influenced which primary sources were ultimately examined, the data are far from consistent even in the instrumental list.

---

[3]A performance of the Cavaliere Luigi dal Cornetto of Ancona, in which the cornett was played in a small chamber to the astonishment of the "music-loving Gentlemen who were present," is described by Vincenzo Giustiniani (*Discorso sopra la musica dei suoi tempi* [Venice, 1628]). Vincenzo Galilei, on the other hand (*Dialogo della musica antica, et della moderna* [Florence, 1581]), maintains that "these instruments are never heard in the private chambers of judicious gentlemen, lords and princes, where only those [musicians] take part whose judgement, taste, and hearing are unsullied; for from such rooms [these instruments] are totally prohibited."

The Extent of the Cornett Repertoire

When we started compiling our lists, we had preconceptions of which period to explore for cornett music. Consequently, our most vigorous search was in primary and second-ary sources of the late sixteenth and early seventeenth centuries. We searched late seventeenth- and early eighteenth-century sources as well but concentrated on those known to be associated with the cornett. Our bias led us to expect to find fewer sources the later we went, and consequently we did not search for or expect to find any cornett indications in late eighteenth- and early nineteenth-century sources. The discovery of a few instrumental and vocal works dating from after 1750 was not sufficient impetus for us to conduct an intensive search through Rococo and Classical inventories. Nevertheless, we have ended up with information about a fair number of cornett instrumentations in isolated sources up to 1810. This situation has presented an unanticipated problem, namely, that the terms *cornetto, cornetta,* etc. appear to have been used continuously into the nineteenth century but eventually referring to different instruments. The keyed bugle was established in England by 1814 and was introduced to the Continent at Waterloo in 1815. It is likely that it did not take hold in Italy until the 1820s, when the valved cornet also made its appearance. In Italy the valved cornet and keyed bugle were often called *cornetto* and *cornetta.*[4] Because of such terminologi-cal problems, we have chosen 1815 as a cut-off date for our list. While the role of the *cornetto curvo* in late eighteenth- and early nineteenth-century music is open to debate, it does now appear to have been a tradition that persisted in some isolated areas and generated a larger repertoire than has previously been thought.

The Problem of Unspecified Instrumentation

A large amount of the music that would have been played by cornettists carries no specific instrumentation, or at least no cornett specification, because it a) predates the practice of specified instrumentation, b) falls within a period in which certain instru-mentation options were only partially indicated in the music, or c) falls into a category of music for which the tradition of performance on cornett was so strong as to make a specific indication to that effect unnecessary.

As is well known, until about 1600 instrumentation was seldom indicated in music. Instrumentalists played vocal music (or instrumental music based on vocal models), choosing the appropriate instruments according to a variety of criteria which were part of a well-established tradition. For instrumental performance, a cornettist could have made use of virtually the entire repertoire of sixteenth-century vocal music, both sacred and secular. In addition he or she[5] had available a much smaller number of instrumental pieces of unspecified instrumentation: *ricerari, canzoni da sonar,* dances, intradas, and the like. While numerous descriptions exist of individual performances with exact

---

[4] Ralph Dugeon, *The Keyed Bugle* (Metuchen, NJ & London: Scarecrow Press, 1993).

[5] There is considerable evidence that cornetts and trombones were sometimes played in convents. Indeed some of the nuns (most notably at San Vito in Ferrara) were highly praised for their virtuosity on these instruments.

instrumentations, it is only when they appear together with the music that we have included them in this catalog. Actual instrumentations do not appear in printed sources until the last decade of the sixteenth century and not much earlier in manuscripts. It would obviously be meaningless to include the entire repertoire of sixteenth-century vocal and instrumental music in a catalog of cornett music. Such a catalog must begin where instrumentation becomes specific.

Even after instrumentation was routinely indicated in musical prints and manuscripts, it was not a precise practice. It was common in the first half of the seventeenth century to indicate alternative instrumentations. Among the common alternatives, the most frequent was *"per violino overo cornetto"* (for violin or cornett). The violin and the cornett were often considered interchangeable (as were the trombone and the *viola*). This idea of interchangeability, together with the frequent inconsistencies, discrepancies, and contradictions found in title pages, headers, and tables of contents, suggests that the two instruments were often considered interchangeable even when the choice was not indicated. Indeed, a careful examination of the music reveals that the use of such indications was often careless or casual, perhaps the addition of an ignorant publisher eager to increase his market. Sometimes the pieces marked *"overo cornetto"* are no more suitable for the cornett than those marked merely *"violino,"* and occasionally they are even less so. Moreover, in the early decades of the seventeenth century we often find the general indication *per soprano,* which may appropriately be taken as synonymous with *per violino overo cornetto*. Thus, the body of music presumably played by cornettists was considerably larger than that part of it which unambiguously specified the instrument.

A similar problem is posed by the relationship of the cornett to the human voice. The sound of the cornett was often likened to that of the voice, and for that reason the instrument was often used to replace or reinforce it. The tradition of cornett *colla parte* was so strong in Germany, where a large percentage of the works specifying the instrument employ it in this way, that we may safely presume that the cornett was also used to double voices in works where it is not mentioned. Indeed, in light of the prevalence of this tradition one might even ask whether *colla parte* use of the cornett should be included in the catalog at all. Should we not limit ourselves to the more interesting *concertato* parts? In fact, the distinction between *colla parte* and concerted writing is rarely made in title pages, parts, tables of contents, or library catalogs. The only way to be sure that a cornett part is concerted or *colla parte* is to examine the music itself. Even then the situation is complicated by the fact that the same work may use the instrument *colla parte* for one section, and as an independent voice in another. In addition, sometimes the cornett can double or substitute for a voice, depending upon the requirements of a particular performance situation. Heinrich Schütz provides texted cornett parts for the highest voices in his *Psalmen Davids*, specifying that they may also be sung if boys are found with high enough voices to sing them. Ultimately we have chosen to include *colla parte* works in the catalog both for the practical reason that it has been impossible to examine each work individually, and for the historical one, that these works are a precious testimony to the importance and duration of one of the most significant traditions of cornett playing.

An additional related problem lies in the fact that the distinction between "vocal" and "instrumental" music is not always entirely clear in the sixteenth century. This problem is most apparent when vocal works exist in a textless form in sources providing instrumentations. Such is the case with a manuscript preserved in the Proske-Bibliothek in Regensburg (Hs. A.R. 775&777) containing 120 madrigals, chansons, and motets by various authors, including Orlando di Lasso. All of the works are untexted, and thirty-four of them specify cornett together with various combinations of trombones and shawms. While this manuscript undoubtedly represents the repertoire of a late sixteenth-century wind band and probably reflects the use by such bands of all sorts of vocal music for ceremonial occasions, we cannot ignore that these parts could also have been used by an instrumental group accompanying voices. Thus, while we have included these works in the instrumental list, we have also cross-referenced them in the vocal list.

Preservation and Transmission of the Music

Obviously only a part (and probably a small part) of the music specifying cornett that was originally set down in manuscript or printed form has come down to us. The way in which this surviving portion has been transmitted, however, influences what we perceive to have been the nature of the original repertoire. The essence of this influence lies in the fundamental difference between printed and manuscript music.

Musical prints and manuscripts bear different relationships to musical performance. Manuscripts, except when they form part of a collection compiled by a later hand, are usually closely tied to a specific performance situation. They generally indicate the performing forces that were available in a particular place at a particular time. Prints, on the other hand, were intended to be sold and had to be adapted to the marketplace. This process of adaptation often created a conservative bias toward instrumentation, a tendency to tailor instrumentations to the lowest common denominator.

A manuscript of a *versetto* by Giovanni Paolo Colonna in the archives of San Petronio in Bologna provides a good example of differences between printed and manuscript sources.[6] The printed version of this piece appears in the composer's *Salmi a 8 voci*, Op.1, published in Bologna in 1681. There the work appears for eight voices and two organs. The manuscript, however, provides a glimpse of how such works were performed in the vast acoustic of the church of San Petronio. In the archives we find the parts in multiple copies indicated in Table I. In addition to these parts there are three others in a later hand: one unspecified basso continuo, one part for theorbo, and one for "organo terzo." Thus while the printed version might give an impression of performance by a total of ten musicians, the manuscript implies a force of at least thirty-nine performers (and possibly more, since two singers or instrumentalists could read from one part). The huge performing forces reflected in the manuscript version are specific to the acoustics of San Petronio with its fourteen-second reverberation. In this case, the printed version represents only the essentials of the composition, to be adapted at will according to local circumstances and performance practices.

From printed music alone there is little evidence that a high level of cornett playing was maintained in Italy after 1650. Yet in the region of Bologna alone, a number of

---

[6] The authors are indebted to Marc Vanscheeuwijck for providing this information.

manuscripts by such composers as Passarini, Perti, and Bassani demonstrate that highly skilled cornettists were still active there until at least the end of the century.

Table I. Manuscript Part Instrumentations for "Memento Domine David" by Giovanni Paolo Colonna (I-Bsp ms.)

Choir I	no. of copies	Choir II	no. of copies
Soprano	4	Soprano	4
Alto	4	Alto	4
Tenor	5	Tenor	6
Bass	6	Bass	6
Alto cornett	1	Alto cornett	1
Tenor Trombone	2	Tenor Trombone	2
Bass Trombone	2	Bass Trombone	2
Violin	3	Violin	3
Viola alto/Violetta alto	3	Viola alto	3
Viola tenore	2	Viola tenore	2
Violoncino basso	2	Violoncino basso	2
Violone	2	Violone	2
Organo 1°	1	Organo 2°	1

The Changing Political Situation

A major problem we faced in compiling this catalog was the changing political situation in Europe in the wake of the fall of the "Iron Curtain." During the Second World War virtually the entire contents of the immense and priceless collection of Berlin's Prussian State Library were relocated for safekeeping in other parts of Germany and Poland. The postwar disappearance of some of these holdings and their subsequent partial resurfacing have created enormous obstacles for bibliographic research even while making fascinating reading.[7] This dispersal and retrieval can be summarized as follows:

1. The major centers of storage in the West were Marburg and Tübingen. Their holdings were gradually returned to Berlin, where they became part of the collection of the Staatsbibliothek Preussicher Kulturbesitz in West Berlin.
2. The major centers of storage in German-occupied Poland were in Silesia. Most of the holdings (the major exception being those in Cracow) were eventually returned

---

[7]See Nigel Lewis, *Paperchase: Mozart, Beethoven, Bach ... The Search for Their Lost Music* (London: Hamish Hamilton Ltd., 1981).

to Berlin, where they were incorporated into the Deutsche Staatsbibliothek in East Berlin.

3. After the reunification of Germany the East and West Berlin libraries were unified under the name Deutsche Staatsbibliothek Preussicher Kulturbesitz. The East Berlin branch has been designated *Haus 1* and the Western one, *Haus 2*. We have consequently altered the old RISM sigla **Dddr**-Bds and **Dbrd**-B to **D**-BI and **D**-BII, respectively. Since the reunification, printed works have remained in their respective libraries according to the postwar division. Manuscript works, however, are undergoing a reorganization. Their locations by call number as of May 1994 are as follows: Mus. ms. 220–23 680 in *Haus 2*; Mus. ms. 29 023–29 959 in *Haus 1*; Mus. ms. 30 001–30 444 in *Haus 1*; Mus. ms. 38 001–38 274 in *Haus 1*; Mus. ms. 40 004–40 649 in *Haus 1*.

Further complicating the situation summarized above are the cases of two Polish libraries: the Biblioteka Jagiellońska in Cracow and the Biblioteka Uniwersytecka in Wrocław (formerly Breslau). Once most of the Berlin holdings had been returned to either East or West Berlin, it became clear that a part of the collection, including some of the most valuable manuscripts of Beethoven, Bach, and Mozart, was missing. In 1976 it became generally known that these manuscripts and other material from Berlin were in Cracow. It took scholars and musicians considerably longer to realize the importance of the thousands of prints of seventeenth-century music, both sacred and secular, Italian and German, many of them *unica*, which are also currently held in Cracow. This collection of prints is kept separate from the holdings of the Jagiellonian library and, except for two file drawers of hastily and informally compiled cards, remains uncataloged. As a result, it is difficult to search these sources in a thorough way for cornett works. While the authors were able to spend some time in Cracow, there is certainly more repertoire to be found there.

A similar situation exists with regard to an important collection of manuscripts once housed in in Wrocław. These manuscripts, cataloged in the 1880s by Emil Bohn and thus generally known as the Bohn Collection, were long thought to have been lost or destroyed during the Second World War. Our conversation with the librarian at the Wrocław library in 1993 revealed her conviction that these manuscripts had been removed from Wrocław when the library there was bombed and that they had since found their way to Berlin, where they were housed, without acknowledgement, at the Deutsche Staatsbibliothek. Quite recently this situation has been openly acknowledged and the manuscripts are available for easy consultation at **D**-B$_I$. As in Cracow, these works have not been integrated into the Berlin collections but are considered holdings of the Wrocław University Library, temporarily housed in the Staatsbibliothek. We therefore list both of these collections under under the sigla of the library to which they belong, with an explanatory note about their current location; i.e., for Berlin prints **D**-B (now in **PL**-Kj), and for the Wrocław manuscripts **PL**-WRu (now in **D**-BI).

The "Missing" Repertoire

A brief glance through this catalog will reveal that it contains little music from England, France, and Spain. While this situation may be partly caused by the way the instrument was used in these countries, it is probably also linked to the way in which the music has been preserved there, and to the amount of bibliographic access we have.

In these countries the lack of a flourishing publishing industry in the seventeenth century has severely limited the amount of surviving printed music. In addition, there is strong evidence that the principal use of cornetts was to double voices in church choirs – a practice which did not necessarily lead to the indication of instrumentations on scores and parts surviving in manuscript. In Spain and Latin America, despite the lack of specific indications in the music, archival records make it clear that the cornett was widely used in cathedrals from just after the mid-sixteenth century until well into the eighteenth century, when it was gradually displaced by the more modern oboe in concerted music in the Baroque style. The sparseness of written indications of cornett in the music reflects the function of the instrument within the liturgy. The musicians scored the motets, chansons, and madrigals themselves for moments of "occasional" music within the liturgy (e.g., at the Elevation or during the Offertory). It was in the developing villancico tradition, from which the cornett is largely absent, that idiomatic instrumental parts (usually strings and later Baroque winds) are found.[8]

Likewise, very little music specifically for cornetts has survived from England. This is due in part to the fact that the cornett began its road to obsolescence about the time that it became common to specify instrumentations. The use of the cornett at the Court, in the Chapel Royal, and in the provincial and collegiate churches was widespread at least to the time of the Commonwealth. In the Chapel Royal as well as in the cathedrals at such places as Canterbury, York, and Durham, the cornetts and trombones were principally used to double the voices of a choir. Thus, a good deal of music which would have been played on cornett probably survives in sources lacking instrumental indications. Indeed, no vocal music with specific cornett indications has yet come to light. One of the most important sources which can, at least partially, be identified with the cornett and trombone ensemble is the set of five manuscript partbooks at the Fitzwilliam Museum now known as Fitzwilliam Mus. MSS 24.D.12-17. This set of books has been demonstrated to represent part of the repertoire of the royal wind music under King James I, and it comprises most of the English music contained in our catalog. The partbooks contain music of various sorts: untexted madrigals and motets by late sixteenth-century composers (Ferrabosco, Marenzio, Lasso, Anerio, Rovigio, Vecchi, etc.), a variety of Pavans, Almands, and other miscellaneous pieces (partly attributed with initials, but without instrumentations), and finally (read from the back of the volumes upside-down) a series of dances by Matthew Locke, Charles Coleman, and Nicholas Lanier labelled "5 partt things ffor the Cornets." Some of the Locke pieces are also found in an autograph score in the British Library headed "for His Majesty's Sagbutts and Cornets."

The Prints

The largest part of the repertoire in this catalog is contained in printed collections, the majority spanning a period of just over a hundred years, from 1591 to 1695. In addition

---

[8] For information on the use of the cornett in Spain we are grateful to Douglas Kirk.

to collections, there are a few so-called *Gelegenheitskompositionen*: pieces composed for special occasions and published as single works. The 247 printed collections are dominated by eighty-eight publications from the most famous Venetian presses, notably Vincenti, Amadino, Gardano, and Magni. The Venetian dominance is not surprising considering that Venice was both the major center of cornett playing until *ca.* 1630, and by far the most important center for music publishing at the time the cornett was at its peak of popularity. At the height of their production, the Venetian presses were turning out more music than all of the rest of Europe combined.[9] After 1610 Venetian music publishers were in decline, and the emerging importance of those of Rome, Florence, Bologna, and, above all, Milan is reflected in the appearance of prints of cornett music from these centers.

Outside of Italy the major centers for the publication of cornett music were also those for music and book publishing in general. Chief among them were the German cities of Leipzig, Dresden, Nürnberg, and Frankfurt, with sixteen, thirteen, ten, and nine prints, respectively. Another leading northern European publishing city, Antwerp, contributed ten prints.

Beyond Italy and Germany conditions favorable to music publishing did not exist before the end of the seventeenth century. The reasons for this are complex and involve the centralization of court activity in England and France and the lack of competition due to royal privilege. It has been pointed out that music publishing before the eighteenth century was never a very lucrative activity, and largely dependent upon the generosity of patrons who sponsored music "less with the intention of circulating a composer's repertoire, than as a demonstration of a patron's munificence and taste."[10] The large centralized courts such as London, Paris, and Vienna seem to have been less interested in such sponsorship, their lavish musical performances being perfectly well served by manuscript copies.

Graphical representation of the number of publications with cornett parts contained in this catalog reveals some significant trends. Graph 1 shows the number of prints of instrumental music specifying cornett that were issued each decade. The upward sweep of this graph between 1580 and 1620 does not necessarily represent the ascending popularity of the cornett, but rather the increasing tendency of publishers to specify instrumentation. The peak between 1620 and 1630, however, and the gradual descent to 1700 surely reflect the fortunes of the cornett in the seventeenth century. Indeed, what we may be seeing here is the virtual end of the cornett repertoire, the upward sweep being merely an artifact due to changes in the conventions of indicating instrumentation and the descent its actual decline in musical importance.

A subtler picture emerges if we separate Italian prints from those of the "Northern" presses, as shown in Graph II. Here it becomes clear that the peak in the 1620s was due primarily to Italian (actually Venetian) production. The sharp drop in production in the

---

[9] D. W. Krummel and Stanley Sadie, ed., *Music Printing and Publishing* (London: Macmillan; New York: Norton, 1990), 83.

[10] *Ibid,* 95.

1630s was almost certainly due to the devastating plague which hit Venice in 1630, reducing its population by thirty percent and producing a terrible economic slump in a publishing industry already in decline. This is supported by data[11] which show that the largest drops in production of Italian music presses (in 1577 and 1631) correspond to outbreaks of plague in Italy. The proportion of cornett music production relative to the overall music output of Italian presses is shown in Graph III. The rise in the number of printed collections for cornett in the 1590s, their peak in production (1605-1630), and the crash in production in the 1630s are all mirrored in the total music publishing output, but the publishing industry rebounded, whereas the publication of cornett music was devastated and never recovered to former levels. It is possible that the manner of indicating instrumentation begun around 1600 took a more conservative course in Italy at this time, thus eliminating the cornett alternative to violin as well as lavish instrumentations in general. The decline in production of music for cornett could also be the result of conservative hiring practices in an era of tighter city and chapel budgets. Regardless of the cause, 1630-1633 marks a turning point for the cornett in Italy from a position of prominence to one of obscurity. The 1630 slump in production is also mirrored in the northern presses, but Graph II shows that they actually reached a peak in production of cornett music some twenty years later than the Italians. Instrumental music for cornett continued to be published in small amounts in the northern countries until 1697, nearly twenty years after the last Italian collection (1679).

The number of prints of vocal music specifying cornett in each decade (Graph IV) shows similar contours, including the slump in output that we have attributed to the Venetian plague. The exception to this is in the three decades following 1630, where the total vocal output exceeds that of instrumental music. In Graph V it can be seen that this is primarily the result of the northern presses, which reach a peak in production thirty years later than do the Italian presses. The distinctly separate curves formed by the northern and Italian outputs in Graph V seem to indicate that the use of the cornett in vocal music north and south of the Alps underwent independent courses of development in the years after 1630. This is a contrast to instrumental music, where the graphs of northern and southern prints follow each other quite closely. The difference in the figures for vocal music is almost entirely accounted for by an enormous boom in the use of cornett (or at least in the frequency of its indication in prints) in Reformation church music. While the cornett was also enjoying a boom in Catholic Austria during this period, this is not reflected in prints, owing to the lack there of an equivalent publishing industry. It should be noted, by way of caution, that the differences in the figures for printed vocal music may reflect a divergence in the practice of indicating instrumentation as much as differences in actual use of the cornett. Employment records indicate that equivalent numbers of cornettists (and indeed many of the same composers) worked in Vienna and Venice,[12] but this equivalence is not reflected in print or manuscript

---

[11] Tim Carter, "Music Publishing in Italy, c. 1580-c.1625: Some Preliminary Observations," *Royal Musical Association Research Chronicle* 20 (1986-87): 19-37.

[12] See Eleanor Selfridge-Field, "The Viennese Court Orchestra in the Time of Caldara," in *Antonio Caldara: Essays on his Life and Times,* ed. Brian Pritchard (Aldershot: Scolar Press, 1987), and *Venetian Instrumental Music from Gabrieli to Vivaldi* (Oxford, Blackwell, 1975; 3rd ed., New York: Dover, 1994).

indications after 1630. Though the use of the cornett declined, its traditional role in northern sacred music continued through the time of Bach and beyond – the last printed collection dating from 1775.

It should not be assumed from these graphs that 1700 marks the end of the cornett's repertoire or lifespan any more than 1600 marks its beginning. The cornett was certainly old-fashioned by 1700, and though there must have been some excellent players, it probably presented a liability to music publishers wishing to stimulate their sales. Considering this, it is not surprising that the cornett disappears first from the pages of printed music while continuing to be played considerably longer in some musical centers.[13] It should also not be assumed that the peak in the 1620s corresponds with the high point of cornett playing. The peak represents, strictly speaking, only the high point in the currently documented publication of music specifying cornett. It is possible that the high point of cornett playing occurred earlier, before the advent of specific instrumentation. Of course, our graphs are only an indirect indication of cornett activity, and there are many more factors to consider – most importantly, the total music publishing figures as well as equivalent information on other instruments to serve as a control group. Comparing the total published music specifying cornett with the total output in Italy listed in Carter, we find a similar rise and fall of output for the period of 1600-1630. But in the period thereafter (1630-1640) this relationship changes, and music specifying cornett declines as the publishing industry begins to

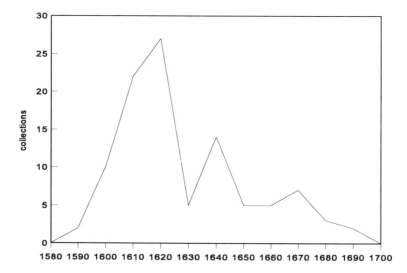

Graph I. Number of collections of instrumental music specifying cornett published each decade.

---

[13] The last accounts of cornett use are in isolated regions where the *Stadtpfeiffer* tradition continued. Johann Georg Kastner reported in his book *Les danses des morts* (1852) that in 1840 he heard an ensemble of cornetts and trombones in Stuttgart.

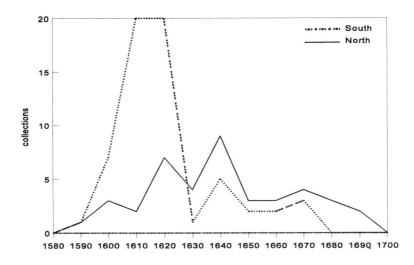

Graph II. Number of collections of instrumental music specifying cornett published each decade by "Southern" (Italian) and "Northern" presses.

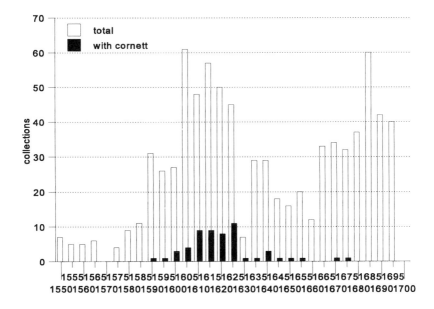

Graph III. Total collections with instrumental music issued by Italian publishers contrasted with those containing instrumental music specifying cornett (data on total output from SartMS).

Graph IV. Number of collections of vocal music specifying cornett published eac decade.

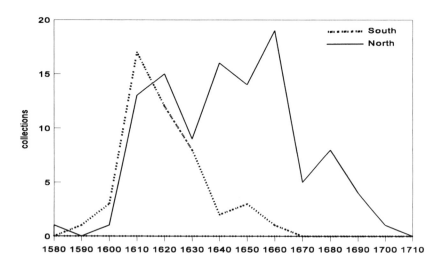

Graph V. Number of collections of vocal music specifying cornett published eac decade by "Southern" (Italian) and "Northern" presses.

recover. Obtaining comprehensive data from the latter half of the century in Italy as well as other geographical areas would allow us to draw more complete conclusions. This, along with more documentary and iconographical evidence, is needed to determine the extent to which our graphical indications of cornett publishing conform to the rise and fall of cornett playing in general.

The Manuscripts

No catalog of an instrumental repertoire can ever be complete, even within its defined limits. For the information in this catalog we have been, of course, dependent upon the bibliographic tools available. Unfortunately, fewer such tools exist for seventeenth-century manuscripts than for prints, and this catalog thus reflects a bias in the direction of printed music. Hopefully this situation will change in the near future. The RISM *Series A/II* is a database relating to manuscripts which, when completed, will be a comprehensive listing of all music manuscripts from 1600 to 1800. It is, however, a work in progress, with only a very small percentage of libraries cataloged to date.

Cataloging the cornett repertoire in manuscripts presents some special problems, since the indication of instrumentation in manuscript works is often an ambiguous and messy affair. If indications are present on a title page or at the top of a part, they may well be spotted by a thorough cataloger; but more often than not the indication "cornett" lies buried, barely legible, in the middle of a vocal or violin part. Particularly problematic for the cataloger of cornett music are opera scores. When indicated in opera manuscripts, the cornett usually appears in a symbolic context in only one or two scenes (often associated with underworld or maritime themes). Although fifteen operas are included in our catalog, the true number of operas with parts for cornett is undoubtedly higher. In opera manuscripts the title-page instrumentation usually indicates the general setting of the entire opera, leaving out "special effects" instruments like the cornett. Bibliographic sources of opera music often omit instrumentation altogether, making the detection of cornett parts all the more difficult. Morever, specific instrumentations in dramatic music may often have been left up to the last-minute discretion of the director, and treated much more like stage sets, to be discarded after a specific performance.[14]

The catalog contains over 1,000 works preserved in manuscript, of which only 233 are dated. Though the relative rarity of accurate dating makes a graphical analysis or statistical comparison with printed sources impossible, we may note that the greatest number of cornett indications in dated manuscripts occurs in the second half of the seventeenth century, when published works for the instrument were in decline. The instrument appears in limited numbers of manuscripts into the eighteenth century, long after publishing for the instrument had virtually stopped. The preponderance of "northern" vocal music among these dated manuscripts (all but twenty-six are vocal music, and only fifteen are Italian) further supports the divergence in the development of cornett music suggested in Graph IV: the decline of the cornett was more gradual north of the Alps, where the traditional role of the cornett as a church and *Stadtpfeiffer* instrument continued well into the eighteenth century.

---

[14] See entries for Francesco Corteccia, Matthew Locke, and others in the Appendix.

Though they are scattered widely among some sixty cities in seventeen countries, the vast majority of the manuscript works are contained within a small number of important manuscript collections. Because the manuscript sources are often specific to sites and events, it might be useful to reflect on the various collections that contain significant numbers of pieces specifying cornett.

The Bokemeyer Collection

This enormous collection of scores, currently divided between Haus 1 and 2 of the Deutsche Staatsbibliothek Preussischer Kulturbesitz in Berlin, is primarily the fruit of the prodigious collecting activity of Georg Österreich, a musician at the courts of Gottorf and Wolfenbüttel between 1680 and 1735. Österreich, together with a number of copyists, amassed a collection of several thousand scores, of which about 1,800 have survived. Österreich sold the collection to his friend and fellow collector Heinrich Bokemeyer, who himself added some materials to the collection and whose name has become attached to it. The collection eventually passed into the possession of the Berlin State Library, where it was arranged more or less alphabetically by composer and the individual manuscripts were bound into volumes. A detailed catalog of the collection was prepared by Harald Kümmerling in 1970.

The Bokemeyer Collection includes an important body of German Protestant vocal music of about 300 composers – the primary works in the collection that call for cornett. Included are a large number of works with cornett by Johann Rosenmüller and Johann Schelle as well as works by Samuel Capricornus, Johann and Johann Philip Krieger, Johann Kuhnau, Marco Giuseppe Peranda, Johann Theile, and others.

The Erfurt Collection

This collection of 164 sacred works, also housed in the Deutsche Staatsbibliothek Preussischer Kulturbesitz in Berlin, represents an entirely different sort of collection than the Bokemeyer. Most of these works were copied for the use of one institution, St. Michael's church and school in Erfurt. The manuscripts were transferred from the school library to the Preussischer Staatsbibliothek in Berlin in 1914, where they were integrated into the manuscript collection. A description and catalog of the collection were published in 1925 by Elisabeth Noack in *Archiv für Musikwissenschaft.*

The music in the Erfurt collection, most of it copied for the use of the cantor by Johann Christian Appelmann, a teacher at the school from 1678 to 1683, was intended for the edification of the students and the populace. It includes mostly music by central German composers, including works with cornett by Georg Ludwig Agricola, Paul Becker, Crato Bütner, Georg Calmbach, Werner Fabricius, Sebastian Knüpfer, and Johann Rosenmüller.

The Grimma Collection

Currently part of the manuscript collection of the Sächsische Landesbibliothek in Dresden, this collection of manuscript parts was also compiled to provide music for one school and church, that of the Fürstenschule in Grimma, near Dresden. The roughly 450 works which survive are only part of what was a much larger collection amassed by cantor Samuel Jacobi between 1680 and 1721. As in the Erfurt collection, the works of central German composers are best represented, including ones with cornett by Vincenzo Albrici, P. Crusius, Werner Fabricius, Sebastian Knüpfer, Marco Giuseppe

Peranda, Johann Rosenmüller, Johann Schelle, Christian Andreas Schulze, Daniel Vetter, Johann Heinrich Wilhelmi, Friedrich Wilhelm Zachow, and Johann Christoph Ziegler.

The Düben Collection

Like Georg Österreich, Gustaf Düben was an avid collector of musical manuscripts which he gathered for the purpose of study. Born in Stockholm in 1628 he was himself a composer, though his fame as a collector of 1,500 vocal and 300 instrumental works has overshadowed the importance of his own works. A much more international collector than Österreich, Düben gathered manuscripts by such composers as Dieterich Buxtehude, Kaspar Förster, Samuel Friedrich Capricornus, and Johann Heinrich Schmelzer. The collection contains a number of autograph scores as well as parts copied out by Düben and his assistants for each of the works he obtained. The collection was given to the University of Uppsala in 1732 and was cataloged in 1942 by Folke Lindberg.

The Emil Bohn Collection

The Bohn collection, consisting of holdings of the Wrocław University Library currently housed in Berlin (see above under "The Changing Political Situation"), differs from the collections described above in that it represents neither materials associated with a particular institution nor the efforts of a single collector. When in 1887 Emil Bohn undertook to catalog the manuscript holdings of the Breslauer Stadtbibliothek, the musical manuscripts there were in chaos. The cataloging effort took three years and resulted in a catalog published in 1890 under the title *Die musikalischen Handschriften des XVI. und XVII. Jahrhunderts in der Stadtbibliothek zu Breslau.*

The Bohn manuscripts contain almost exclusively parts and organ intabulations of sacred music, largely from the libraries of Wrocław's three principal protestant churches: St. Elisabeth, St. Maria Magdalena, and St. Bernhardin. In addition there are a few secular vocal pieces and a small collection of instrumental works. The earliest work dates from 1544 and the most recent from 1690. Best represented in the collection are little-known local composers such as Michael Büttner, Sebastian Lemle, Matthaeus Apelles von Löwenstern, Martin Mayer, Johannes Phengius, and Tobias Zeutschner. In addition there are a number of manuscripts, some of them autographs, by better-known composers such as Crato Bütner, Erasmus Kindermann, Johann Hermann Schein, Johann Schop, Giovanni Valentini, and Johann Vierdanck.

Despite the efforts of Bohn, the materials in this collection still present many difficulties. Many works are incompletely or badly preserved and in many cases the incomplete or contradictory labelling of parts makes a reconstruction of the intended instrumentation difficult. Owing to the limited amount of time which we had available to spend with the original materials, we have had to rely largely on Bohn's catalog in compiling our entries. We are aware that in many cases the instrumentations taken from that are inaccurate. We have, however, verified the present existence in Berlin of all the works listed in our catalog.

The Liechtenstein Music Collection

The Liechtenstein Music Collection dates from the reign of Karl Liechtenstein-Castelcorn (1664-1695) as Prince Bishop of Olmütz and comprises part of the musical archives of the Collegiate Church of St. Maurice in Kroměříž, Czech Republic. Besides maintaining a first-rate musical cappella of his own, the Prince Bishop had close ties to the Imperial court in Vienna. The musical collections which he acquired contain nearly 1,000 compositions by composers active both at the Kroměříž court (most notably Biber and Vejvanovsky) and at the Imperial court (including Valentini, Bertali, and Schmelzer).

The Music Collection of the Austrian State Library
     The music collection of the Austrian State Library in Vienna contains undoubtedly the largest collection of music specifying cornett. Compiled during the reigns of five Hapsburg emperors (1619-1740), the collection stands as a monument to an unbroken cornett tradition in the Viennese *Hofkapelle*, which employed cornettists as late as 1746. The library contains twenty-nine compositions that include the cornett by two of the emperors, Ferdinand III (*r.* 1637-1657) and Leopold I (*r.* 1657-1705). The *Hofkapell-meister* represented in the collection by manuscript works with cornett include Antonio Bertali, Antonio Draghi, Johann Josef Fux (116 vocal works), Giovanni Priuli, Giovanni Felice Sances (at least twenty-three works), Giovanni Valentini, and Marc'Antonio Ziani.

Observations on the Repertoire

Instrumental Music
Although cornettists undoubtedly improvised on soprano lines of motets and chansons, music for a solo soprano instrument and basso continuo specifying cornett is relatively uncommon compared with the other settings in which the instrument appears. Of the fifty-three works for solo cornett and basso continuo, forty-eight specify the violin as the first choice; the cornett is uniquely specified in only two. This tendency to desig-nate cornett as an alternative, usually second choice, is reflected in larger instrumental works as well. Specifically, there are 235 pieces that designate "violin or cornett"; 112 pieces, "cornett or violin." It is difficult to judge what importance should be given to this distinction. The specification of alternate instrumentations is mostly associated with printed music rather than manuscripts, and largely represents an attempt to make music adaptable to the largest number of situations. If the market for violin music was greater than for cornett music, there must always have been financial pressure to list the violin first, regardless of the intentions of the composer. Moreover, the appearance of cornett and violin together in the same piece seems to have been an exception. Only thirty-eight pieces specify cornett *and* violin, but the exceptional character of this specification becomes more apparent when we consider that in sixteen the instruments are segregated by pairing (i.e., 2Ctto, 2V) or placement in different choirs.

     Probably the most important instrumental medium for cornett music from Gabrieli (1597) through Reiche (1696) was the ensemble of cornett(s) and trombones. This "homogenous" instrumental consort is represented by 233 published pieces in the catalog, although it must be admitted that fully 117 of these works come from two collections by Pezel (1670 and 1685). Cornetts and trombones appear less often (thirty pieces) in mixed instrumental ensembles.

     Basso continuo instruments are seldom indicated for individual pieces in printed collections. More often they are mentioned on the title pages or as the name of a partbook, such as *Basso per l'organo*. When an instrument is mentioned, it is most often the organ. Of the published instrumental pieces for cornett with basso continuo, 229 do not specify an instrument, 94 specify organ, 57 specify lute (chitarrone or theorbo), and only 2 specify *cembalo* (harpsichord or *spinetto*). The larger number of basso continuo parts for the organ is not surprising considering the instrument's widespread use in the church and chamber music of the seventeenth century, but the insignificant number of basso continuo parts for the harpsichord seems to indicate that harpsichord and cornett were seldom intended to be heard together. It might also be of interest to point out that the lute, chitarrone, and theorbo are specified not only for the basso continuo, but in twenty-five pieces as separate parts both figured (as in Kapsberger, 1615) and unfigured (as in Ferro, 1649). In general, however, our information is not consistently detailed enough to distinguish basso continuo parts from concerted bass parts. The most frequent bass instrument other than the trombone associated with the instrumental music of the cornett is the *fagotto*, represented in sixty-nine pieces.

Sonata, canzona, and *sinfonia* are by far the most common designations encountered for instrumental pieces in the cornett repertoire. These terms, all of which originated in the sixteenth century, stood in a complicated and confusing relationship throughout much of the seventeenth century. At the beginning of the seventeenth century independent instrumental music was in its infancy. These terms, arriving from different directions, often touched upon each other, and were sometimes used synonymously, as the genres to which they were attached gradually found their identities. Indeed Stefano Bernardi calls his pieces *sonate* on the title page and *canzoni* on the individual pieces. Yet more often than not composers seem to have had a tangible distinction in mind, even if their ideas did not necessarily agree with those of other composers or theorists. It is common to find such titles as Nicolò Corradini's *Partitura del primo libro de canzoni francese à 4. & alcune suonate*, where the two types are clearly set apart. Similarly, *sinfonia, sonatella,* and *sonatina* sometimes referred to short binary dance pieces, but at other times were used for extended works for which the terms *sonata* and *canzona* would seem equally appropriate.[15]

The cornett is featured in all the popular instrumental genres of the seventeenth century, including the *canzona, sonata, sinfonia, ricercar, fantasia, fuga,* and *capriccio* as well as numerous dance forms, according to the numerical distribution shown in Table II. Setting aside dance forms, we see the clear numerical predominance of the *sonata,* followed by the *canzona* and *sinfonia*. Although the *canzona* and *ricercar* appear to be the dominant solo forms (s and s, Bc) for the cornett, those terms fell into disuse after 1630. In contrast, the *sonata* continued to be developed and the term was, by 1650, the preferred designation for large ensemble works, especially in northern countries. While the *canzona, sonata,* and *sinfonia* encompassed a wide variety of settings, dance-related forms in the cornett repertoire appeared mostly in large settings for five or more instruments. These works are mostly associated with the *Stadtpfeiffer*

---

[15] For further discussion of the relationship of these terms, see William S. Newman, *The Sonata in the Baroque Era*, 4th ed. (New York: Norton, 1983), 17-32.

tradition, which fostered the production of many collections of short sonatas and dances in the latter half of the seventeenth century.

Table II. Distribution of Instrumental Genres

	Canzon	Sonata	Sinfonia	Ricercar	Fuge/Fantasia	Capriccio	Dance
s				8			
sBc	17	16	2				
sbBc	29	21	21	4	2		1
ssBc	12	27	13		1	4	
ssbBc	15	13	36		3	1	46
à4	10	38	14		16	2	5
≤ à5	16	104	10		1	1	125
other	4	6	4		27	11	7
Total	103	225	100	12	60	30	184

Vocal Music
On both sides of the Alps, despite sporadic (and largely symbolic) appearances in opera and regular employment for civic functions, the cornett was first and foremost a church instrument. In sacred music there were four principal functions for the cornett: 1) playing obbligato parts (often together with or in place of the violin) in small-scale works; 2) playing obbligato parts within a cornett and trombone ensemble in large-scale, usually polychoral works; 3) playing *colla parte* in an ensemble of cornetts and trombones in large-scale works; and 4) playing pairs of obbligato parts in alternation with pairs of other instruments (violins, recorders, trombones, viols).

1. Obbligato cornett parts in small-scale sacred works
     The first four decades of the seventeenth century in Italy saw the publication of a large number of *concerti ecclesiastici* for a few voices and a few instruments in which the cornett was a frequent participant. The instrumental parts typically contain *sinfonie* and *ritornelli* as well as sections of concerted writing in which the instruments partici- pate in the imitative vocal texture. While one or two cornetts are frequently alternatives to violins, in other cases a cornett and a violin are specified, as in the *Concerti sacri scielti* of Stefano Bernardi (1621). Bernardi's motets (for which he provided secular *contrafacta* in a separate publication) combine two or three voices with a similar number of instruments, including violin, cornett, trombone, lute, and theorbo. Both Amadio Freddi and Orazio Tarditi composed Vespers psalms featuring a violin and a cornett, while Paolo Tarditi used a violin and a cornett as the first voices of two otherwise vocal choirs. The cornett also appears in an obbligato role in small-scale works by composers as Lorenzo Agnelli, Giovanni Antonio Bertola, Nicolò Corradini,

Archangelo Crotti, Ignatio Donati, Paolo Funghetto, Michel'Angelo Grancini, Pietro Lappi, Leone Leoni, Tarquino Merula, Sante Petrucci, Benedetto Ré, and Francesco Usper. In a relatively late example of the idiom, Sisto Reina includes in his 1660 collection an extended and dramatic setting of *De profundis* for bass solo and two cornetts. After 1640 such instrumental *obbligati* were normally given to two violins in what became a convention indicated by the phrase *con i suoi violini*. In 1685 Giovanni Battista Bassani combined the conventional violins with a solo cornett in his oratorio *La morte delusa*. Here the old-fashioned cornett echoes each aria to the accompaniment of violins, in one of the cornett's last stellar notes in Italian music.

In German-speaking countries, despite a clear preference for using cornetts in large-scale polychoral works, a significant number of *geistliche Konzerte* for smaller numbers of voices also feature the instrument. Heinrich Schütz's first book of *Symphoniae sacrae* is directly indebted to the Italian tradition and contains unsurpassed masterpieces of the genre, employing the cornett alone with four singers and in numerous combinations of other wind instruments. He employs two cornetts (almost certainly mute cornetts are intended) along with two tenors in the powerfully expressive setting of *Anima mea liquefacta est*. Samuel Capricornus, *Kapellmeister* at the Württemberg court in Stuttgart, employed both the *cornetto* and the *cornettino* in a virtuoso manner in small settings.[16] Other composers working in Germany and Austria who use the cornett in a significant way in few-voiced sacred concertos include Vincenzo Albrici, Giovanni Martino Cesare, Andreas Hammerschmidt, Johann Albrecht Kress, Samuel Michael, Marco Giuseppe Peranda, David Pohle, Johann Rosenmüller, and Johann Rubert.

2. Obbligato parts for the ensemble of cornett and trombones

Both in Italy and in northern countries, from the time that instrumentation began to be indicated in printed music to around 1640, cornett and trombone parts in large-scale church music seldom display truly independent instrumental writing. In this respect certain works with instrumental *obbligati* of Giovanni Gabrieli (and of Michael Praetorius) are exceptional. More often cornetts (and/or violins) and trombones play from texted parts which sometimes carry indications of tutti or *ripieno* and solo or *istromento*, to show where voices or instruments play together or alone. The presence of a text underlay in a part, however, does not necessarily indicate that a voice was intended. Numerous examples exist from this period in which all voices are texted, yet one or two parts (usually one per choir) are clearly marked *"voce"* and others *"cornetto"* or *"trombone."* Examples of this practice are seen in the works of Sulpitia Cesis, Heinrich Schütz (particularly in the *Psalmen Davids*), Christoph Strauss, and Francesco Usper. While such indications sometimes indicate a definitive instrumentation, at other times they reveal a flexible approach, leaving great latitude to the *maestro*

---

[16] On 11 May 1657, the cornettist David Böddecker and other musicians made a formal complaint against Kapellmeister Capricornus for the unusually difficult parts he asked them to play. Böddecker claimed that these parts and the fact that he was required to play the *cornettino* were harming his health. It seems more likely, however, that the dispute arose from the fact that Capricornus won out over Böddecker's brother, court organist Philipp Friedrich Böddecker, in the competition for the post of Kapellmeister (cited in Friend Robert Overton. *Der Zink* [Mainz: Schott, 1981], 149).

di cappella to adapt them to local circumstances. Thus the *Salmi Boscarecci* of Ignatio Donati can be performed in six different ways accommodating ensembles of from six to twenty-four elements.

In Italy we also find a number of works in which the cornetts (or violins) play obbligato parts while the trombones are used as optional ripieno instruments doubling voices. In some cases the trombones are eliminated altogether (or their presence was a convention unnecessary to indicate in the music) while cornetts and violins combine in various ways with voices (see works by Ruggiero Giovanelli, Ortensio Polidori, and Paolo Tarditi). In the second half of the seventeenth century, it is more common to find cornetts without trombones in Italy. Indeed, their function seems to converge with that of trumpets, with which they often dialogue or for whom they sometimes substitute. In the works of Giacomo Perti, Alessandro Stradella, and above all Francesco Passarini, cornett and *clarino* writing are hardly to be distinguished.

In northern countries the cornett's principal role in sacred music after *ca.* 1640 was within the cornett and trombone ensemble, which could have either an obbligato or a *colla parte* function as a component in large-scale polychoral compositions. In their most typical configuration, such works also include a string group (sometimes with a *fagotto* as bass), solo singers, a ripieno choir, two or more trumpets, and a continuo group of *violone* and one or more organs. Such works are extremely numerous in the Bokemeyer, Düben, Grimma, and Liechtenstein collections. In Austria we find polychoral works by such composers as Antonio Bertali, Heinrich Ignaz von Biber, Andreas Hofer, Georg Muffat, Johann Schmelzer, and Jan Křtitle Tolar (who makes use of no fewer than sixteen solo singers in his *Missa Viennensis*). Works in such settings were also much cultivated in Germany, especially in Leipzig (e.g., Johann Caspar Horn, Sebastian Knüpfer, Johann Rosenmüller, and Thomas Schelle) and Dresden (e.g., Vincenzo Albrici, Christoph Bernhard, Marco Giuseppe Peranda, and Christian Ritter).

3. The *colla parte* cornett and trombone ensemble

Everywhere the cornett was played, one of its major functions was to support the human voice. The practice of doubling voices with cornetts and trombones was extremely widespread and goes far beyond the pieces included in this catalog, which serve only to document the practice where it was specified in the music. While the practice was certainly common in Italy, we find it more meticulously notated in Germany and Austria, probably because a greater portion of the repertoire in these countries is preserved in manuscript, where performance indications are more complete. In many cities, particularly Vienna, an ensemble of cornett, two trombones, and *fagotto* became a standard ensemble for doubling an SATB choir. In the catalog, this formation is documented 111 times in the works of composers associated with the Imperial Court – seventy-seven times in the works of Fux alone.

In seventeenth and early eighteenth-century Germany the practice of doubling voices with cornetts and trombones was virtually universal in the performance of music in *stile antico*, the classical sixteenth-century style still much used in German Lutheran churches as late as the eighteenth century. A manuscript in the Berlin Staatsbibliothek which preserves, partly in the hand of J.S. Bach, a group of instrumental and vocal parts to Palestrina's *Missa sine nomine a 6* bears witness to the prevalence and persistence of this practice in Leipzig. Bach's instrumentation of this mass includes two cornetts and four trombones, as well as a basso continuo group of organ, harpsichord, and *violone*. In addition Bach follows the practice of the time in using cornett and trombones as a *colla parte* ensemble in a dozen of his cantatas.

4. Alternating obbligato instruments

Many of the cornett parts in German sacred music from the second half of the seventeenth century display a common characteristic: a pair of cornetts alternates playing obbligato parts and *sinfonias* with pairs of other instruments, usually violins, violas, trombones, recorders, and trumpets. Since these are all instruments which the *Stadtpfeiffer* would know how to play (see the test piece for *Stadtpfeiffer* by Johann Gottlieb Görner), these alternating instrumental parts were most likely meant to be played by a single pair of musicians.

Nomenclature

Instrumental nomenclature was considerably more complex and inconsistent in the seventeenth and eighteenth centuries than it is today. The listing of instrumentations has, therefore, required a certain amount of interpretation. Sometimes sources employ idiosyncratic terminology or abbreviations which are difficult to decipher. We have tried, for the most part, to "translate" these indications into standard abbreviations, in doubtful cases leaving the original terms unabbreviated and untranslated. The following points require further clarification:

1. All historical terms clearly referring to the cornett (*cornet, cornetto, corneto, cornone, Zink, Zinck, Zing,* etc.) in both singular and plural forms have been abbreviated as "Ctto." No attempt has been made to modify this abbreviation with range indications (i.e., aCtto or tCtto) unless this is specified in the original part designation, although some parts marked *cornetto* are in tenor clef and clearly require a larger instrument. Terms which normally refer to the horn family (*corno, cornu, cornio*) can sometimes create confusion. The cornett is, of course, a small horn, and the diminutive forms by which it was known in romance languages did not become standard until the sixteenth century. After 1600, however, the non-diminutive form almost certainly refers to natural horns rather than cornetts. Confusion can be created, however, by the terms *corne., corn., cornio,* etc. when used as abbreviations of *cornetto* (or the term *corn.i* as an abbreviation of *cornetti*). In the late seventeenth and eighteenth centuries, the term *corno* occasionally appears on parts which, because of their musical characteristics (*colla parte* function, use of chromatic notes, etc.), appear to be for cornett. Only when the musical reasons are obvious and compelling have we included such pieces in the catalog.

2. In addition to the terms mentioned above, which are used in a generic sense to refer to the whole family of cornetts, as well as to the standard cornett in *a*, two terms designating different instrument types are met with frequently in the catalog: *cornettino* (Cttino) and *cornetto muto* (Ctto muto).

Cornettino is a term which appears to have been used almost exclusively in northern countries, particularly Germany and Poland. Of the 199 works in the catalog specifying *cornettino*, 16 are from Poland (including transcriptions by cantor Gottfried Nauwerck of works by Italian composers), 5 from Austria, 1 from Italy, and 177 from Germany (including 9 works from the Düben collection by composers working in Germany). The *cornettino* is strongly represented in the Bokemeyer and Grimma collections (twenty-eight works). Whether the *cornettino* was unknown or little used outside the areas in which the term appears must remain an open question. Despite the small number of indications for the instrument in Austria and Italy, the extremely high tessitura of certain works from these areas would suggest its use in pieces which carry the indication *cornetto*.[17] It is possible in these cases that the term *cornetto* is being used in a generic sense, as seems to have been the case with some tenor-clef parts. Just as often, the parts marked *cornettino* do not display ranges that are higher than that typically encountered in the cornett repertoire. It cannot be determined whether in these cases the *cornettino* was preferred because of its special tone color or because of some other technical consideration.

Similar questions are posed by the use of the term *cornetto muto*, which occurs with less frequency (thirty-nine works) but more equally divided between Germany (twenty-one) and Austria (eighteen). The term never occurs in the Italian works in this catalog, although a madrigal of Giovanni Gabrieli in a German manuscript carries the indication. Since there is ample evidence of many types (treatises, surviving instruments, descriptions of performances) for the use of the mute cornett in Italy in the sixteenth century, we must assume that the instrument either went out of fashion by the time instrumentation began to be indicated in music, or that the generic term *cornetto* could also include the mute cornett. The internal evidence of the music presented in this catalog is not sufficient to make a decision on this point. The mute cornett seldom occurs in instrumental music (we have located only six such works) and is seen most often in a *colla parte* function.

3. We have used the abbreviation "Fl" to indicate *flauto* or *flautino* (recorder), and "Trav" to indicate *traverso*. The historical terminology, however, is by no means as clear-cut as this might imply, and entries which derive from secondary sources may be unreliable in distinguishing between the two instruments.

4. Although we have used the abbreviation "Va" to indicate *viola* and *viole*, historically "viola" was used to indicate a variety of stringed instruments. If *viola da braccio* appears in the original, we have cited "VaBr," and similarly with *viola da gamba* ("VaG"). Neither primary nor secondary sources, however, always distinguish between the two.

5. The abbreviation "Vo" is used to indicate *violone*, regardless of what instrument this might have designated. Some of the parts marked *violone*, particularly in the first half of the seventeenth century, are concerted bass parts and were certainly intended for an 8' bass instrument of the violin family (the term *violoncello* was not in use until later in the century). Other parts are clearly continuo parts probably intended for a 16' instrument.

---

[17] See in particular the *Missa in labore requies* of Georg Muffat, which frequently ascends to *e'''*, and the opera *La Camilla trionfante* of Giovanni Bononcini, which has soloistic passages ascending even to *f#'''*.

6.   The abbreviation "Tpt" is used to indicate all trumpet types regardless of whether they are in *principale* or *clarino* ranges.   When the ranges of the trumpet parts are known, they are so indicated.

7.   The terminology for bassoon-type instruments in the seventeenth and eighteenth centuries is not as straightforward as today.   Consequently, our abbreviation "Fag," designating *fagotto*, could denote a "Baroque bassoon," *chor-fagott*, or *dolzaina*, as well as the curtal ("two-keyed dulcian") which is commonly associated with the seventeenth-century cornett repertoire.

8.   The abbreviation "Lt," designating the lute, may be taken in some instances as a generic term denoting theorbo or chitarrone.

ABBREVIATIONS

1.perf	first performance	ms, mss	manuscript(s)
a	alto (instrument)	no., nos.	number(s)
A	alto (voice)	nr.	near
acc.	accompaniment	o	or
ad lib	*ad libitum*	Ob	oboe
ad plac	*ad placitum*	Org	organ
b	bass (instrument)	p., pp.	page(s)
b	born	princ	*principale*
bapt.	baptised	Q	quintus
B	bass (voice)	*r*	*recto*
Bc	basso continuo (unspecified)	*rip*	*ripieno*
Bomb	*bombarda*	rit.	ritornello
Br	*braccio*	s	soprano (instrument)
cap	cappella	S	soprano, canto (voice)
cat	catalog	t	tenor (instrument)
Cemb	*cembalo*, harpsichord	T	tenor (voice)
cent	century	tab	tablature
Ch	choir	Timp	timpani, *Pauken*
Chit	*chitarrone*	Tior	theorbo, *tiorba*
ca	*circa*, about	Tpt	trumpet (*clarino*, *tromba*,
compl	complete		*trombetta*)
conc	*concertato*	Trav	*traverso*
Cttino	*cornettino*	Trb	trombone, sackbutt
Ctto	cornett, *cornetto, Zink*	Tpt	*clarino, tromba, trombetta*
Ctto muto	*cornetto muto, stiller Zink*	*v*	*verso*
d	died	v	voice (unspecified)
f., ff.	folio(s)	V	violin, *violino*
facs.	facsimile	Va	viola, *viole*
Fag	bassoon, *fagotto*	VaBr	viola *da braccio*
fl	flourished	VaG	viol, *viola da gamba*
Fl	recorder, *flauto, flautino*	Vc	violoncello
G	*gamba*	Vo	violone
Hp	harp	vol(s)	volume(s)
incompl	incomplete	Vtta	*violetta*
inst	instrument, instrumentation,	W	work, *Werke*
	instrumental	WWII	World War II
Lt	*liuto*, lute	[?]	missing part
mvmt	movement		

N.B. For the holdings of parts in modern libraries, we also have adopted the following RISM abbreviations:

A	alto
A1	alto 1
AI	alto of choir I
AII	alto of choir II
B	bass
Bar	baritone
BI	bass of choir I
BII	bass of choir II
C	canto
C1	canto 1
C2	canto 2
Ex.	exemplar
S	soprano
S1	soprano 1
SI	soprano of choir I
SII	soprano of choir II
S2	soprano 2
T	tenor
T1	tenor 1
TI	tenor of choir I
TII	tenor of choir II
v1	voice 1
v2	voice 2
1, 2, etc.	1st voice, 2nd voice, etc.

BIBLIOGRAPHY

In the text the following abbreviations are used to indicate secondary sources:

AdlerMW   Adler, Guido. *Musikalische Werke der Kaiser Ferdinand III., Leopold I. und Joseph I.* Vienna: Artaria, 1892-93. Reprint, Westmead: Gregg International, 1972.

AIM   American Institute of Musicology

BernC   Bernstein, Harry. "A Study of the Cornettino and its Music in the Seventeenth and Eighteenth Centuries." Master's thesis, University of Chicago, 1978.

BernS   Bernstein, Harry. "Alessandro Stradella's serenata *Il Barcheggio*." D.M.A. dissertation, Stanford University, 1979

BmB   *Bibliotheca musica Bononiensis*

BohnD   Bohn, Emil. *Bibliographie der Musik-Druckwerke bis 1700, welche in der Stadtbibliothek, der Bibliothek des Academischen Instituts für Kirchenmusik und der Königlichen und Universitäts-Bibliothek zu Breslau aufbewahrt werden.* Berlin: Commissions-Verlag von A. Cohn, 1883. Reprint, Hildesheim: Georg Olms, 1969.

BohnH   Bohn, Emil. *Die musikalischen Handschriften des XVI. und XVII Jahrhunderts in der Stadtbibliothek zu Breslau.* Breslau: Commissions-Verlag von J. Heinauer, 1890.

BrownIM   Brown, Howard Mayer. *Instrumental Music Printed Before 1600, A Bibliography.* Cambridge, MA: Harvard University Press, 1965.

BrownSCI   Brown, Howard Mayer. *Sixteenth-Century Instrumentation: The Music for the Florentine Intermedi.* AIM, 1973.

BuchW   Buch, Hans-Joachim. *Die Tänze, Lieder und Konzertstücke des Werner Fabricus.* Thesis, Bonn, 1961.

BuxtW   *Dietrich Buxtehudes Werke.* Ugrino: Ugrino Verlag, 1925-   Reprint, New York: Broude International Editions, 1977-

BWV   Wolfgang Schmieder. *Thematisch-systematisches Verzeichnis der musikalischen Werke von Johann Sebastian Bach.* Leipzig: 1950. (Bach Werke Verzeichnis)

ChafeCM   Chafe, Eric Thomas. *The Church Music of Heinrich Biber.* Studies in Musicology, 95. Ann Arbor, MI: UMI Research Press, 1987.

CMM   *Corpus mensurabilis musicae.* Rome: AIM, 1947-

DdT   *Denkmäler deutscher Tonkunst,* Ser. 1. Leipzig: Breitkopf & Härtel, 1892-1931.

DTB   *Denkmäler deutscher Tonkunst,* Ser. 2: *Denkmäler der Tonkunst in Bayern.* Leipzig: Breitkopf & Härtel, 1900-20; Augsburg: Filser, 1924-31.

DTÖ   *Denkmäler der Tonkunst in Österreich.* Vienna: Universal Edition, 1894-1938.

EcorPBN   Ecorcheville, Jules. *Catalogue du fonds de la musique ancienne de la Bibliothèque Nationale.* Paris: Publications annexes de la Société internationale de musique, 1910-14. Reprint, New York: Da Capo Press, 1972.

EdM   *Das Erbe deutscher Musik.* Leipzig, etc., 1935-

EinSC   Einstein, Alfred. Manuscript in the Smith College Music Archives, Northampton, MA, 1935.

EitQ   Eitner, Robert. *Biographisch-bibliographisches Quellen-Lexikon der Musiker und Musikgelehrten der christlichen Zeitrechnung bis zur Mitte des neunzehnten Jahrhunderts.* 10 vols. Leipzig: Breitkopf & Härtel, 1900-1904. Reprint in 6 vols., Graz: Akademische Druck- und Verlagsanstalt, 1959.

EngelKH   Engelbrecht, Christiane. *Die Kasseler Hofkapelle im 17. Jahrhundert und ihre anonymen Musikhandschriften aus der Kasseler Landes-bibliothek.* Kassel: Bärenreiter, 1958.

FuxW   Johann Joseph Fux*, Sämtliche Werke.* Kassel: Bärenreiter, 1959-

GraupnerF   Graupner, Friedrich. *Das Werk des Thomaskantors Johann Schelle (1648-1701).* Altenburg: F.A. Kunzsch, 1929.

GreveBR   Greve, Werner. *Braunschweiger Stadtmusikanten.* Braunschweig: Stadtarchiv und Stadtbibliothek Braunschweig, 1991.

GroveD   *The New Grove Dictionary of Music and Musicians.* London: Macmillan: Washington, DC: Grove's Dictionaries of Music, 1980.

HaberOB   Haberkamp, Gertraut. *Die Musikhandschriften der Benediktiner-Abtei Ottobeuren.* München: G. Henle, 1986.

Hamel   Hamel, Fred. "Die Psalmkompositionen Johann Rosenmüllers." Dissertation, University of Strassburg, 1933. Strassburg: Heitz, 1933. Reprint, Baden-Baden: Koerner, 1973.

HändelW   *The Works of G.F. Händel.* Leipzig: Breitkopf & Härtel, 1859-1902.

HardML   Harding, Rosamond E.M. *A Thematic Catalogue of the Works of Matthew Locke.* Oxford: author; distrib. Blackwell, 1971.

HowardL   Howard, John Brooks. "The Latin Lutheran Mass of the Mid-Seventeenth Century." Ph.D. dissertation, Bryn Mawr, 1983.

HM   *Hortus Musicus.* Kassel: Bärenreiter, 1936-

HughesBM   Hughes-Hughes, Augustus. *Catalogue of Manuscript Music in the British Museum,* Vol. III. London: Trustees of the British Museum, 1909. Reprint, London: British Museum, 1966.

HuysBR   Huys, Bernard. *Catalogue des imprimés musicaux des XVe, XVIe e XVIIe siècles (Bibliothèque Royal de Belgique, Bruxelles).* Brussels: Bibliothèque Royal, 1965..

KämpS   Kämper, Dietrich. *Studien zur instrumentalen Ensemblemusik des 16. Jahrhunderts in Italien.* Köln & Wien: Bohlau, 1970.

Köchel	Köchel, Ludwig Ritter von. *Johann Josef Fux. Hofcompositor und Hofkapellmeister der Kaiser Leopold I., Josef I., und Karl VI. von 1698 bis 1740.* Vienna: A. Holder, 1872. Reprint, Hildesheim: Georg Olms, 1974.
KellnerK	Kellner, Altman. *Musikgeschichte des Stiftes Kremsmünster.* Kassel: Bärenreiter, 1956.
KrauseK	Krause, David W. "The Latin Choral Music of Sebastian Knüpfer with a Practical Edition of the Extant Works." Ph.D. dissertation, The University of Iowa, 1973.
KriegerW	Inventory – Krieger Weissenfels 1685 (in DdT 53).
Krummacher	Krummacher, Friedhelm. *Die Überlieferung der Choralbearbeitungen in der frühen evangelischen Kantate.* Berlin: Merseburger, 1965.
KümmerKB	Kümmerling, Harald. *Katalog der Sammlung Bokemeyer.* Kassel: Bärenreiter, 1970.
LD	Johann Andreas Herbst, *Drei mehrchörige Festkonzerte für die Freie Reichsstadt Frankfurt.* Kassel: Bärenreiter, 1937.
LeonardT	Leonard, Charlotte. "The Rôle of the Trombone and its *Affekt* in the Music of the Lutheran Church of Seventeenth-Century Saxony and Thuringia." Dissertation, Wake Forest University, NC, sched. 1996.
MAB	*Musica Antiqua Bohemica.*
MackeyT	Mackey, Elizabeth. "The Sacred Music of Johann Theile." Ph.D. dissertation, University of Michigan, 1968.
MagginiLB	Maggini, Emilio. *Lucca, Biblioteca del seminario; catalogo delle musiche stampate e manoscritte del fondo antico.* Milano: Istituto editoriale italiano, 1965.
MAM	*Musik der alten Meister.* Graz: Akademische Druck- und Verlagsanstalt, 1954-
McCredieM	McCredie, Andrew D. "Nicholas Matteis – English Composer at the Habsburg Court," *Music & Letters* 48 (1967): 127-137.
MBE	*Musica barroca española.*
MeyerMS	Meyer, Ernst H. *Die mehrstimmige Spielmusik des 17. Jahrhunderts in Nord- und Mittel-Europa.* Kassel: Bärenreiter, 1933.
ML	*Music & Letters*
MitUB	Mitjana, Rafael. *Catalogue critique et descriptif des imprimés de musique des XVIe et XVIIe siècles, conservés à la Bibliothèque de l'Université royale d'Uppsala.* 3 vols. Uppsala: Amlqvist & Wiksell, 1911-51.
MonteverdOP	Malipiero, Gian Francesco, ed. *Tutte le opere di Claudio Monteverdi.* Vienna: Universal Edition, 1926-42. Rev. ed., 1968.
MQ	*The Musical Quarterly.* New York, 1915-

MüllerK Müller, Joseph. *Die musikalischen Schätze der Königlichen- und Universitäts-Bibliothek zu Königsberg in Preussen.* Bonn, 1870. Reprint, Hildesheim: Georg Olms, 1971.

NoackE Noack, Elisabeth. "Die Bibliothek der Michaeliskirche zu Erfurt." *Archiv für Musikwissenschaft* VII (1925): 65-116.

OttoS Otto, Craig A. *Seventeenth-Century Music from Kroměříž, Czecho-slovakia: A Catalogue of the Liechtenstein Music Collection on Microfilm at Syracuse University.* Syracuse, NY: Syracuse University Libraries, 1977.

PraetW Michael Praetorius, *Gesamtausgabe der musikalischen Werke.* Berlin: Georg Kallmeyer, 1928-41.

RimbachK Rimbach, Evangeline Lois. "The Church Cantatas of Johann Kuhnau." Ph.D. dissertation, Eastman School of Music, University of Rochester, 1966.

RISM *Répertoire international des sources musicales publiés par la Societé internationale des bibliothèques musicales.*

RISM AII *RISM Serie A/II: Musikhandschriften 1600-1800,* Munich: K. G. Saur, 1995. (annual updates)

RRMBE *Recent Researches in the Music of the Baroque Era.* New Haven, CT; Madison, WI: AR Editions, 1964-

SamuelN Samuel, Harold E. *The Cantata in Nuremberg During the Seventeenth Century.* Studies in Musicology, 6. Ann Arbor, MI: UMI Research Press, 1982. (Originally, Ph.D. dissertation, Cornell University, 1963.)

SartMS Sartori, Claudio. *Bibliografia della musica strumentale italiana stampata in Italia fino al 1700.* 2 vols. Firenze: Leo S. Olschki, 1952-68.

ScheidtW *Samuel Scheidts Werke.* Hamburg: Ugrino/Abteilung Verlag, 1923-53.

ScheinW Johann Hermann Schein, *Neue Ausgabe sämtlicher Werke.* Kassel: Bärenreiter, 1963-

SchützGA Heinrich Schütz, *Sämtliche Werke.* Leipzig: Breitkopf & Härtel, 1885-1927. Reprint, Wiesbaden: Breitkopf & Härtel, 1968-74.

SchützW Heinrich Schütz, *Neue Ausgabe sämtlicher Werke.* Kassel: Bärenreiter, 1955-.

SeiffertL Seiffert, Max. "Die Chorbibliothek der St. Michaelisschule in Lüneburg zu Seb. Bach's Zeit." *Sammelbände der Internationale Musik-Gesellschaft* 9 (1907-08): 593-621.

SEM *University of California, Santa Barbara, Series of Early Music,* 1960-

SKMB   *Süddeutsche Kirchenmusik des Barock.* Altötting: A. Coppenrath, 1974-

SMd   *Schweizerische Musikdenkmäler.* Basel: Bärenreiter, 1955-

SMw   *Studien zur Musikwissenschaft,* 1913-34, 1955-66, 1977-

SorensenS   Sorensen, Soren. *Diderich Buxtehudes vokale Kirkemusik.* Copenhagen: E. Munksgaard, 1958.

SPES   *Studio per Edizioni Scelte.*

SpielmannZ Spielmann, Markus. "Der Zink im Instrumentarium des süddeutsch-österreichischen Raumes 1650 bis 1750." In *Johann Joseph Fux und die barock Bläsertradition.* Kongreßbericht Graz, 1985. Alta Musica, 9. Tutzing: Hans Schneider, 1987, 121-55.

SüssKM   Süss, Carl. *Kirchliche Musikhandschriften des XVII. und XVIII. Jahrhunderts in der Stadtbibliothek Frankfurt am Main,* Berlin & Frankfurt am Main: Frankfurter Verlags-Anstalt, 1926.

VogEinB   Vogel, Emil, Alfred Einstein, et al. *Bibliografia della musica italiana vocale profana pubblicata dal 1500 al 1700.* 3 vols. Pomezia: Minkoff, 1977.

WalkerSB   Walker, Diane Parr, and Paul Walker. *German Sacred Polyphonic Vocal Music Between Schütz and Bach.* Warren, MI: Harmonie Park Press, 1992.

WDMP   *Wydawnictwo dawnej muzyki polskiej.* Warzawa/Kraków: PWM Edition, 1928-

WE   *Wellesley Edition.* Wellesley College, MA, 1950-

WelterRL   Welter, Friedrich. *Katalog der Musikalien der Ratsbücherei, Lüneburg.* Lippstadt: Kistner & Siegel, 1950.

WernerZ   Werner, Arno. *Städtische und fürstliche Musikpflege in Zeitz bis zum Anfang des 19. Jahrhunderts.* Buckeburg & Leipzig: Siegel, 1922.

WoodwardP   Woodward, Henry. "A Study of the Tenbury Manuscripts of Johann Pachelbel." Ph.D. dissertation, Harvard University, 1952.

LIBRARY SIGLA

A–ÖSTERREICH (AUSTRIA)

Gmi	Graz, Musikwissenschaftliches Institut der Universität
HE	Heiligenkreuz, Zisterzienserstift
Iu	Innsbruck, Universitätsbibliothek
KR	Kremsmünster, Benediktiner Stift Kremsmünster, Regenterei oder Musikarchiv
Sca	Salzburg, Salzburger Museum Carolino Augusteum, Bibliothek
Sd	— Dom-Musikarchiv
SP	St. Pölten, Diözesanarchiv
Wgm	Wien, Gesellschaft der Musikfreunde in Wien
Wn	— Österreichische Nationalbibliothek Musiksammlung
Ws	— Schottenstift
WIL	Wilhering, Zisterzienserstift, Bibliothek und Musikarchiv

B–BELGIQUE/BELGIË (BELGIUM)

Bc	Bruxelles, Conservatoire Royal de Musique, Bibliothèque
Br	— Bibliothèque Royale Albert 1er
Lc	Liège (Luik), Conservatoire Royal de Musique, Bibliothèque

CH–SCHWEIZ (SWITZERLAND)

Bm	Basel, Musikakademie der Stadt Basel, Bibliothek
Bu	— Öffentliche Bibliothek der Universität Basel, Musiksammlung
BEsu	Bern, Stadt- und Universitätsbibliothek
E	Einsiedeln, Kloster Einsiedeln, Musikbibliothek
Zz	Zürich, Zentralbibliothek, Kantons-, Stadt-, und Universitätsbibliothek

CS–ČESKA REPUBLIKA (CZECH REPUBLIC, formerly Czechoslovakia)

KRa	Kroměříž, Státní zámek a zahrady
Pdobrovského	Praha, Národní muzeum, Dobrovského knihovna
Pu	— Státní knihovna ČSR – Universitní knihovna hudební oddělení

D-DEUTSCHLAND (GERMANY)

As	Augsburg, Staats- und Stadtbibliothek
BI	Berlin, Deutsche Staatsbibliothek preussischer Kulturbesitz Haus 1 (formerly Deutsche Staatsbibliothek, East Berlin)
BII	— Deutsche Staatsbibliothek preussischer Kulturbesitz Haus 2 (formerly Staatsbibliothek preussischer Kulturbesitz, West Berlin)
Bhm	— Staatliche Hochschule für Musik und Darstellende Kunst
Bu	— Universitätsbibliothek der Freien Universität
BAs	Bamberg, Staatsbibliothek
BAUk	Bautzen, Stadt- und Kreisbibliothek

BD	Brandenburg/Havel, Domstiftsarchiv und Musikbibliothek der Katharinenkirche
BFa	Burgsteinfurt, Gymnasium Arnoldinum
BNu	Bonn, Universitätsbibliothek
BS	Braunschweig, Stadtarchiv und Stadtbibliothek
BSÄ	Bad Säckingen, Trumpet Museum [a non-RISM siglum]
BÜ	Büdingen (Hessen), Fürstlich Ysenburg- und Büdingisches Archiv und Schloßbibliothek
Cm	Coburg, Moritzkirche, Pfarrbibliothek
DS	Darmstadt, Hessische Landes- und Hochschulbibliothek
Dl(b)	Dresden, Sächsische Landesbibliothek, Musikabteilung
DI	Dillingen/Donau, Kreis- und Studienbibliothek
DIp	— Bischöfliches Priesterseminar, Bibliothek
DIP	Dippoldiswalde, Kirchenbibliothek und Musikbibliothek des Evangelisch-Lutherischen Pfarrarchivs
DO	Donaueschingen, Fürstlich Fürstenbergische Hofbibliothek
DT	Detmold, Lippische Landesbibliothek
EB	Ebrach, Katholisches Pfarramt, Bibliothek
EF	Erfurt, Wissenschaftliche Allgemeinbibliothek, Musiksammlung
EIl	Eisenach, Landeskirchenrat, Bibliothek
ERu	Erlangen, Universitätsbibliothek
F	Frankfurt/Main, Stadt- und Universitätsbibliothek, Musik- und Theaterabteilung Manskopfisches Museum
FBsk	Freiberg, Stadt- und Kreisbibliothek
FRIts	Friedberg (Hessen), Bibliothek des Theologischen Seminars der Evangelischen Kirche in Hessen und Nassau
Gs	Göttingen, Niedersächsische Staats- und Universitätsbibliothek
GAU	Gauernitz-Constappel, Pfarrbibliothek
GRu	Greifswald, Universitätsbibliothek der Ernst-Moritz-Arndt-Universität (formerly Bibliotheca Acad. Kgl. Universitätsbibliothek), Musiksammlung
GOa	Gotha, Augustinerkirche
GOl	— Forschungsbibliothek (formerly Landesbibliothek)
Hs	Hamburg, Staats- und Universitätsbibliothek, Musikabteilung
HAh	Halle/Saale, Händel-Haus
HAmk	— Marienbibliothek
HAu	— Universitäts- und Landesbibliothek Sachsen-Anhalt, Musiksammlung
HEu	Heidelberg, Universitätsbibliothek
HVl	Hannover, Niedersächsische Landesbibliothek
JE	Jever, Marien-Gymnasium, Bibliothek
Kdma	Kassel, Deutsches Musikgeschichtliches Archiv
Kl	— Murhard'sche Bibliothek der Stadt Kassel und Landesbibliothek
KA	Karlsruhe, Badische Landesbibliothek, Musikabteilung
KIl	Kiel, Schleswig-Holsteinische Landesbibliothek
KMs	Kamenz, Stadtarchiv
KNu	Köln, Universitäts- und Stadtbibliothek

Lr	Lüneburg, Ratsbücherei und Stadtarchiv der Stadt Lüneburg, Musikabteilung
LA	Landshut, Bibliothek des Historischen Vereins für Niederbayern
LEb	Leipzig, Bach-Archiv
LEbh	— VEB Breitkopf & Härtel, Verlagsarchiv
LEm	— Musikbibliothek der Stadt Leipzig
LEsm	— Museum für Geschichte der Stadt Leipzig, Bibliothek
LEt	— Thomasschule, Bibliothek
LEu	— Universitätsbibliothek der Karl-Marx-Universität, Fachreferat Musik
LR	Lahe, Lehrerbibliothek des Scheffel-Gymnasiums
LUC	Lucau, Archiv der Nikolaikirche
LÜh	Lübeck, Bibliothek der Hansestadt Lübeck Musikabteilung
Mbs	München, Bayerische Staatsbibliothek
Mu	— Universitätsbibliothek
MGmi	Marburg/Lahn, Betriebseinheit Musikwissenschaft im Fachbereich Geschichts-wissenschaften der Phillips-Universität Marburg
MGu	— Universitätsbibliothek der Phillips-Universität
MLHr	Mühlhausen, Blasiuskirche, Archiv
MÜs	Münster, Santini-Bibliothek (incorporated into Bibliothek des Bischöflichen Priesterseminars: MÜp)
MÜG	Mügeln, Pfarrarchiv
MZs	Mainz, Stadtbibliothek
Ngm	Nürnberg, Bibliothek des Germanischen National-Museums
Nst	— Stadtbibliothek
NA	Neustadt/Orla, Pfarrarchiv
NEhz	Neuenstein, Kreis Öhringen Hohenlohe-Zentralarchiv
NOk	Nordhausen, Kirchenbibliothek St. Blassii-Petri
OB	Ottobeuren, Bibliothek der Benediktiner-Abtei
OLl	Oldenburg, Landesbibliothek
PR	Pretzschendorf über Dippoldiswalde, Pfarrarchiv
Rp	Regensburg, Bischöfliche Zentralbibliothek
	— Universitätsbibliothek
ROu	Rostock, Universitätsbibliothek
ROST	Rothenstein, Pfarrarchiv
Sl	Stuttgart, Württembergische Landesbibliothek
SAh	Saalfeld, Heimatmuseum, Bibliothek
SWl	Schwerin, Wissenschaftliche Allgemeinbibliothek
SWsk	— Schloßkirchenchor (Evangelisch-Lutherische Pfarre der Schloßkirche, Pfarrarchiv)
Tu	Tübingen, Universitätsbibliothek der Eberhardt-Karls-Universität
Us	Ulm, Stadtbibliothek mit Stadtarchiv
UDa	Udestedt über Erfurt, Pfarrarchiv, Evangelisch-Lutherisches Pfarramt
V	Villingen (Baden-Württemberg), Städtische Sammlung (Stadtarchiv)
W	Wolfenbüttel, Herzog-August-Bibliothek, Musikabteilung
WA	Waldheim, Stadtkirche St. Nikolai Bibliothek

WF	Weißenfels, Heimatmuseum, Bibliothek (mit Bibliothek des Vereins für Natur- und Altertumskunde)
WRiv	Weimar, Institut für Volkmusikforschung (formerly Volksliedforschung)
WRl	— Staatsarchiv (formerly Landeshauptarchiv)
ZI	Zittau, Stadt- und Kreisbibliothek "Christian Weise-Bibliothek"
ZZ	Zeitz, Heimatmuseum

DK–DANMARK (DENMARK)

| A | Århus, Statsbiblioteket i Århus |
| Kk | København, Det kongelige Bibliotek |

E-ESPAÑA (SPAIN)

C	Córdoba, Archivo de la Catedral
LPA	Las Palmas de Gran Canaris, Archivo catedralicio [a non-RISM siglum]
VAcp	Valencia, Colegio y capilla del Corpus Christi
Zac	Zaragoza, Archivo de música del Cabildo

EIRE–IRELAND

| Dm | Dublin, Marsh's Library |

F–FRANCE

BO	Bordeaux, Bibliothèque municipale
Pa	Paris, Bibliothèque de l'Arsenal
Pc	— Conservatoire National de Musique (in F-Pn)
Pn	— Bibliothèque nationale
Psg	— Bibliothèque Sainte-Geneviève
Sim	Strasbourg, Institut de musicologie de l'Université
Ssp	— Bibliothèque du Séminaire protestant

GB–GREAT BRITAIN

Cfm	Cambridge, Fitzwilliam Museum
Ckc	— Rowe Music Library, King's College
DRc	Durham, Cathedral Library
Ge	Glasgow, Euing Musical Library
Lbl	London, The British Library
Lcm	— Royal College of Music
Lwa	— Westminster Abbey Library
Mp	Manchester, Central Public Library
Ob	Oxford, Bodleian Library
Och	— Christ Church Library
Ouf	— Oxford University, Faculty of Music Library
T	Tenbury, St. Michael's College Library

H–MAGYARORSZÁG (HUNGARY)

Bb	Budapest, Bartók Béla Zeneüvészeti Szakközépiskola Könyvtára
Bl	— Liszt Ferenc Zenemüvészeti Föiskola Könyvtára
Bn	— Orzágos Széchényi Könyvtár, with Magyar Zenemüvészek Szövetsége
Gc	Györ (Raab), Püspöki Papnevelö Intézet Könyvtára
P	Pécs (Fünfkirchen), Székesegyhaázi Kottatár
PH	Pannonhalma, Szent Benedek Rend Központi Fökönyvtára

HR–RVATSKA (CROATIA, fomerly YU–YUGOSLAVIA)

Dsmb	Dubrovnik (Ragusa), Knjižnica samostana Mala Braća

I–ITALIA (ITALY)

Baf	Bologna, Archivio dell'Accademia filarmonica
Bam	— Biblioteca Raimondo Ambrosini (presso la Cassa Risparmio)
Bc	— Civico Museo Bibliografico-Musicale
Bof	— Biblioteca dell'Oratotio dei Filippini
Bsf	— Archivo del Convento di San Francesco
Bsp	— Archivio di San Petronio
BRd	Brescia, Museo Diocesano di Arte Sacra Chiostri di S. Giuseppe
CEc	Cesena, Biblioteca comunale Malatestiana
Fa	Firenze, Archivio dell'Annunziata
Fc	— Biblioteca del Conservatorio di Musica "L. Cherubini"
Fn	— Biblioteca Nazionale Centrale
FEc	Ferrara, Biblioteca comunale Ariostea
FELd	Feltre, Archivo del Capitolo Metropolitano, Duomo
FZac	Faenza, Archivo capitolare
Ls	Lucca, Biblioteca del seminario arcivescovile presso la Curia
Mb	Milano, Biblioteca nazionale Braidense
Mc	— Biblioteca del Conservatorio "Giuseppe Verdi"
Mcap	— Cappella musicale del Duomo
Mdemicheli	— Private collection Demicheli
Muc	— Università Cattolica
MOe	Modena, Biblioteca Estense
Ps	Padova, Biblioteca del seminario vescovile
PCd	Piacenza, Archivio del Duomo
Ras	Roma, Archivio di Stato
Rc	— Biblioteca Casanatense
Rdp	— Archivo Doria Pamphili
Rsc	— Biblioteca Musicale governativa del Conservatorio di Santa Cecilia
Rsg	— Archivio di San Giovanni in Laterano
Rvat	— Biblioteca Apostolica Vaticana
REm	Reggio-Emilia, Archivo di Stato

Sac	Siena, Biblioteca dell'Accademia Musicale Chigiana
Sd	— Archivo Musicale dell'opera del Duomo (with Bibl. Piccolomini)
SPd	Spoleto, Archivio del Duomo
SPE	Spello, Archivo di Santa Maria Maggiore
Tn	Torino, Biblioteca nazionale universitaria
TRbmf	Trento, Biblioteca Musicale Laurence K.J. Feininger
TRc	— Biblioteca Communale
TSmt	Trieste, Civico Museo Teatrale di fondazione Carlo Schmidl
TSsc	— Fondazione Giovanni Scaramangà di Altomonte
Vgc	Venezia, Biblioteca e istituto della Fondazione Giorgio Cini
Vsm	— Archivio della Procuratoria di San Marco
VCd	Vercelli, Archivio del Duomo
VEcap	Verona, Biblioteca capitolare

L–LITHUANIA (formerly USSR)

| KA | Kaliningrad (Königsberg), Oblastnaja biblioteka |

N–NORGE (NORWAY)

| T | Trondheim, Det Kongelige Norske Videnskabers Selkab, Biblioteket |

NL–NEDERLAND (THE NETHERLANDS)

At	Amsterdam, Toonkunst-Bibliotheek
DHgm	Den Haag, Gemeente Museum
DHk	— Koninklijk Huisarchief

P–PORTUGAL

| PC | Coimbra, Biblioteca Geral da Universidade |

PL–POLSKA (POLAND)

Furstenstein	[a non-RISM siglum]
GD	Gdańsk (Danzig), Biblioteka Gdańska Polskiej Akademii Nauk
GDj	— St. Johanneskirche Bibl. [a non-RISM siglum]
GDs	— Staatsarchiv [a non-RISM siglum]
Kj	Kraków (Cracow), Biblioteka Jagiellońska
LEtpn	Legnica, Biblioteka Towarzystawa Przyjaciół Nauk
Tm	Toruń, Książnica Miejska im. M. Kopernika
Tu	— Biblioteka Uniwersytecka
Wn	Warszawa, Muzeum Narodowe, Biblioteka
Wu	— Biblioteka Uniwersytecka
WRu	Wrocław (Breslau), Biblioteka Uniwersytecka

R–ROMANIA
Sb   Sibiu, Biblioteca Muzeului Bruckenthal

SL–SLOVENIJA (SLOVENIA, formerly YU–Yugoslavia)
Lsa   Ljubljana (Laibach), Biblioteka slovenske akademije znanosti in umetnosti
Lu   — Narodna in univerzitetska knjižica

S–SVERIGE (SWEDEN)
L   Lund, Universitetsbiblioteket
Sk   Stockholm, Kungliga Biblioteket
Skma   — Kungliga Musikaliska Akademiens Bibliotek
STr   Srängnäs, Roggebiblioteket (formerly Stifts- och Läroverksbiblioteket)
Uu   Uppsala, Universitetsbiblioteket
V   Västerås, Stifts- och Landsbiblioteket
VX   Växjö, Stifts- och Landsbiblioteket

US–UNITED STATES OF AMERICA
AA   Ann Arbor, MI, University of Michigan, Music Library
Bp   Boston, MA, Boston Public Library, Music Department
BE   Berkeley, CA, University of California, Music Library and Bancroft Library
Cn   Chicago, IL, Newberry Library
CA   Cambridge, MA, Harvard University, Music Libraries
Eu   Evanston, IL, Northwestern University Libraries
Lu   Lawrence, KS, University of Kansas Libraries
MSu   Minneapolis, MN, University of Minnesota, Music Library
Nsc   Northampton, MA, Smith College, Werner Josten Music Library
NH   New Haven, CT, Yale University, The Library of the School of Music
NYp   New York, NY, New York Public Library at Lincoln Center
Pu   Pittsburgh, PA, University of Pittsburgh, Music Library
PHu   Philadelphia, PA, University of Pennsylvania Music Library
R   Rochester, NY, Sibley Music Library, Eastman School of Music, University of Rochester
SM   San Marino, CA, Henry E. Huntington Library & Art Gallery
U   Urbana, IL, University of Illinois, Music Library
Wc   Washington, DC, Library of Congress, Music Division
Ws   — Folger Shakespeare Library
WI   Williamstown, MA, Williams College, Chapin Library
WS   Winston-Salem, NC, Moravian Music Foundation, Peter Memorial Library

INSTRUMENTAL MUSIC SPECIFYING CORNETT

ABRAN [Ebram] (*fl* 1543-64)

    71. Tant vous alles doux, Guillemette à 6: 2Ctto, 3Trb.
Ms contains 120 untexted vocal pieces by various authors, 34 of which specify cornett(s). See also composers Corteccia, F., Gabrieli A., Gosswin, A., Lange, G., Lasso, O., Monte, P., Ruffo, V., Striggio, A., Utendal, A., Wert, G.
D-Rp Hs. A.R. 775&777

ADSON, John (*b ca* 1586; *d* London, 1640)

Courtly masquing ayres, composed to 5. and 6. parts, for violins, consorts, and cornets. . . . London: T. Snodham for John Brown, 1621.
    Airs 19, 20, 21 à 5: 2Ctto, 3Trb.
The only headings concerning instrumentation are on the pages containing airs 19, 20, & 21. The headings read: *For Cornets & Sagbuts.*
EIRE-Dm (incompl); **GB**-Lbl (incompl), -Lcm (incompl), -Och, -Ob   RISM A326
Facs. edition: Amsterdam: Teatrum Orbis Terrarum

AICHINGER, Gregor (*b* Regensburg, 1564/5; *d* Augsburg, 1628)

Cantiones ecclesiasticae, trium et quatuor vocum cuivis cantorum sorti accomodatae, cum basso generali & continuo in usum organistarum. . . . Dillingen: Adam Meltzer, 1607.
    Canzon con 2 cornetti sive cornetto e violino: 2Ctto o Ctto e V, Bc[Org].
A-Wn (S,A,Bc); **D**-Rp (S,A,T,Bc)   RISM A538
Edition: RRMBE 13

ANONYMOUS

    Sonata à 8 Istrumenti con tromba: Tpt o Ctto, 2Ctto o 2V, 2V, aVa, tVa, Vc, Vo, Tior, Fag, Org.
A-Wn   *card catalog

    Sonata à 6: 2Cttino, Tpt, 3Trb, Org.
The alternative of *cornetti* is implied by the heading on the second cornettino part: *Cornett: 2o*
CS-KRa B IV 36(1)   OttoS

    Sonata à 7: 2Tpt, 2Ctto, 3Trb, Org.
CS-KRa B IV 99 (dated 1670, Trb part missing)   OttoS

    Sonata à 13: 2V, 2Ctto, Org (other parts missing).
CS-KRa B IV 133 (incompl)   OttoS

    Sonata per là camera è chiesa, Sonata–Courenta–Gavotte: 2V, 2Ctto, 3Va o 3Trb, Org.
CS-KRa B IV 162 (dated 1670)   OttoS

Sonata à 9: ChI 2V, Vtta, Vtta o VaG; ChII Ctto o V, 2Trb; Fag o VaG, Org.
CS-KRa B IV 179   OttoS

Sonata cum tubis in pleno: 2V, 3Va, 2Tpt o 2Ctto, 3Trb, Vo, Org.
CS-KRa B IV 77   OttoS

Sonata: 2V, 2Tpt o Ctto é Tpt, 3Trb, Timp, Org.
Cornetts are omitted from the title; however, the Tpt parts are marked *cornetto é clarin*.
CS-KRa B IV 98   OttoS

123a. Canzone à 3 "di l'Contessa": 2Ctto, b, Bc.
D-Rp Ms. 732

   69. Occhi perchè si lieti oltra à 7: 2Ctto, 5Trb.
   86. Deus misereatur à 8: 2Ctto, 2"Pumart," 4Trb.
   103. Salve rex Regnum pater misericordiae à 6: 2Ctto, 3Trb, " Pumart."
   118. Christus resurgens a [*recte* ex] mortius à 6: 2Ctto, 4Trb.
   119. Apervit Christus mentem discipulos à 6: 5Ctto, Trb.
D-Rp Hs. A.R. 777&777 (see under ABRAN)

Chorale. Af hoeleyden oprunden er: Ctto, 2Trb, Org.
DK-A R110 (ms from *ca* 1765 by H.E. Grossman[?])   *RISM AII 203352

Recueil de plusieurs vieux airs. . . .
XXVI. Pavane la petite guaire fait pour les cornete en oboi en 1601: s,s,a,t,t,b
XCIX. Passemeze fait pour le hautbois et cornets en 1615: s, b.
F-Pc F494 (ms dated 1690; copyist André Philidor)

Sonata à 5 Tromba e Cornetto con Violini e B.C.
The instrumentation is from the title page; parts are marked *Tromba p^a* and *Tromba I*.
The piece was once attributed to Giovanni Paolo Colonna, but has now been relegated
to anonymous.
I-Bsp L. C. LVI

De la sol re. Principale ottave e cornetto e violoncello: [Ctto, Vc], Org.
The indication of cornett could also be an organ registration.
I-Mdemicheli MSS. Mus 121   *RISM AII 96665

Sonata cornettino solo: Cttino, Bc.
This work is preserved in a manuscript score together with a sonata for Fag and Bc.
After the title of the cornett piece is written *A'g 16:86 M:S*. At the end of the piece are
found the initials *SR* .
I-MOe ms. mus. e 316. (dated 1686)

Echo in violino over Cornetto
PL-WRu ms. 114 (lost)   *BohnH

Sonata prima à 6: 2Ctto, 2Tpt, 3Trb, Bc.
Sonata seconda à 5: 2V, 2Ctto o Fl, Fag, Bc.
S-Uu Inst. Mus. i hs 11:17

Sonatina (Adagio) – Intrada – Intrada: 2Ctto, 3Trb.
The ms also contains two sonatas of Pezel that exist in *Hora decima*. The works listed
are quite similar to those from *Hora decima* and may also be by Pezel.
S-Uu Inst. Mus. i hs 11:26d   RISM AII 85908

Sonatella: 2Ctto, 3Trb.
S-Uu Inst. Mus. i hs 11:27 – 11:27a These are two slightly different versions of the
same piece, and may also be by Pezel (as in ms 11:7).   RISM AII 85884

Sonata à 2. cornetto con basso continuo: 2Ctto, Bc.
At the bottom of the ms title page is the name Andreas Düben with the date *17 Octobris
Anno 1692*.
S-Uu Inst. Mus. i hs 13:9 (dated 1692)

Sinfonia à 5: 2Ctto, 3Trb.
S-Uu Inst. Mus. i hs 65:24 (missing Trb2)

BALDASSARE, Pietro (*b* Rome, before *ca* 1690; *d* after 1768)

Sonata per il Cornetto: Ctto, [2V, Va, Org].
Sonata con Cornetto: Ctto, 2V, Va, Org.
A-Wn ms 97a,b
Edition: Musica Rara 1,526/7

BANCHIERI, Adriano (Bologna, 1568-1634)
*Moderna armonia di canzoni alla francese, opera vigesima sesta . . . per suonare con
facilità tutte nell'organo, ò clavacimbalo et dentrovi (piacendo) concertare uno & due
stromenti acuto e grave. . . .* Venice: Amadino, 1612.
15 Canzoni à 2 (Prima-Quintadecima): s, b, Org.
Prima Fantasia con quatro Stromenti uniti: s, a, t, b.
Seconda Fantasia con quatro Stromenti a dui Chori: s, a, t, b.
Magnificat del sesto tuono: 2s, 2t, Org.
The foreword contains the following instrumentation and transposition suggestions:
*Seconda, si possono in occorenza dentrovi concertare uno, & dui strumenti, semplici
ò congiunti come piace, Acuto & Grave, come al dire Violino & Violone, overo
Trombone e Cornetto. Terza, non si devono trasportare, ne alla Quinta, ne alla
Quarta, ma si bene ne gli proprij termini assignati all'Acuto, & Grave.* The partitura
contains only the basso continuo of the Magnificat.
I-Bc (partitura)   SartMS I 1612a; RISM B837

*Vezzo di perle musicali modernamente conteste alla regia sposa effigiata nella sacra
cantica; opera ventesima terza . . . accomodata, che sopra il basso seguente si può
variare un'istesso concerto in sei modi, con una & dui parti, così voci, come stromenti.*
Venice: Riccardo Amadino, †1610, ∞1616.

21 motets

Following the last page of music, the author gives the following table of the six ways in which the motets may be performed: *Gli Concerti à dui Parti Uguali si possono variare in sei modi. 1. Dui Soprani Voci. 2. Dui Violini overo Cornetti. 3. Un Soprano voce l'altro Violino. 4. Un Soprano voce, qual piu piace. 5. Un Tenore solo, qual piu piace. 6. Dui Tenori un'ottava sotto. Gli Concerti à dui Parti Inuguali si possono variare in sei modi. 1. Basso & Soprano voci. 2. Trombone & Violino Stromenti. 3. Basso voce sola. 4. Soprano voce sola. 5. Basso Voce & Soprano Violino. 6. Basso Trombone & Soprano voce.*

†I-Bc; **D**-Rp (Org); ∞ **D**-B (3 partbooks, now in **PL**-Kj), -Rp (missing Org part and last page of all other parts)   RISM B805/806

BECKER, Dietrich (Hamburg, 1623-1679)

Musicalische Frühlings-Früchte bestehend in drey- vier- und fünff-stimmiger Instrumental-Harmonia, nebenst dem Basso Continuo. Hamburg: Georg Rebenlein, 1668.

    28. Canzon à 4: 2V, 2Ctto, "Viol" o Fag, Bc.

D-B (5 partbooks, now in **PL**-Kj), -KIl; **GB**-Lbl; **S**-Uu, -V   RISM B1525

BELLI, Giulio (*b* Longiano nr. Forlì, *ca* 1560; *d* ?Imola, in or after 1621)

Concerti ecclesiastici a due et a tre voci. Venice: Bartolomeo Magni, †1613; Frankfurt: Nikolaus Stein, ∞1621.

    16. Canzone à 2: Ctto o V, Trb, Bc.

    29. Canzone à 3: 2Ctto o 2V, Trb, Bc.

For Canzona 16., only cornett and trombone are specified in the *tavola*, but the heading in the canto partbook specifies *Cornetto ò Violino.*

†**A**-Wn; **I**-Bc, -Bsp; **PL**-WRu (missing Bc); ∞**D**-Dlb (B,Bc); **F**-Pc (missing B); **I**-FA (Bc); **PL**-WRu (S2)   SartMS I&II 1613b; RISM B1771

BERLIN, Johan Daniel (*b* Memel, Prussia, 1714; *d* Trondheim, 1787)

    Sinfonia à 5: Ctto, 2V, Va, Bc.

N-T XM 23

Facs. edition: *Basler Jahrbuch für historische Musikpraxis* V (1981): 405-420; Edition: Noton N8917-A

BERNARDI, Stefano (*b* Verona, *ca* 1585; *d* Salzburg?, 1636)

Madrigaletti a due et a tre voci con alcune sonate a tre per due violini overo, cornetti, & un chitarrone, trombone, overo fagotto . . . opera duodecima . . . libro secondo. Venice: Alessandro Vincenti, †1621, ∞1627.

    7 canzonas à 3 (Canzon Prima-Settima): 2V o 2Ctto, Tior o Fag o Trb, Bc.

The alternatives Tior o Fag o Trb are given in the *tavola* for all seven canzonas; but the *basso* partbook differs, giving only *fagotto* for canzon no. 4, and *liuto o fagotto* for canzon no. 5. The basso continuo part was added later in the 1627 print.

†**A**-Wn; ∞†**I**-Bc; ∞**F**-Pn   RISM B2069/2070

Edition: Ars Antiqua Editions (all seven canzonas)   SartMS I 1612f, 1627f

Il terzo libro de madrigali a sei voci concertati con alcune sonate accommodate per ogni sorte d'istromenti . . . opera decimaterza. Venice: Alessandro Vincenti, 1624.

Sonata terza: V, Ctto, a, t, t, b, Bc.

Sonata ottava à 12: ChI 4V; ChII 4Ctto; ChIII 4Trb; Bc.

This print also contains one vocal work specifying cornett (see vocal list).

D-Kl (missing S), -Rp (B)   SartMS I&II 1624c; RISM B2071

BERTALI, Antonio (*b* Verona, 1605; *d* Vienna, 1669)

Sonata secunda: 2V, 2Ctto, 2Trb, Vo, Org.

The part headings indicate 2V, 2Cttino, Va, VaG, Org.

CS-KRa B IV 65   OttoS

Sonata S. Leopoldi à 14: 2V, 2Cttino, 2Tpt, 3Vtta, Ctto muto, 4Trb, Org.

The mute cornett part is marked *cornetto muto con tromboni.*

CS-KRa B IV 111,138 (dated 1662); 2nd version: BIV 138 (dated 1672, incompl, &
has an added Vo part.)   OttoS

Edition: Musica Rara

Sonata S. Placidi: 2V, 4Va, 2Tpt, 2Ctto, 3Trb, Vo, Org.

CS-KRa B IV 102   OttoS

Edition: Musica Rara

Sonata à 13: 2V, 2Ctto, 2Tpt, 3Va, 3Trb, Fag, Org.

CS-KRa B IV 113 (dated 1669, missing V2, Tpt1, Org)   OttoS

Sonata à 13: 2V, 2Va, 2Ctto, 4Tpt, 3Trb, Org.

CS-KRa B IV 94 (dated 1669)   OttoS

Edition: Musica Rara

6 Sonatas: 2V, 2Va, [Vo]; o 2Ctto, 3Trb; Bc.

S-Uu instr. mus. i hs 1:6

*Edition: Musica Rara 1,525

BISMANTOVA, Bartolomeo (*fl* 1677; *d* 1694)

Preludio per Cornetto: Ctto solo.

D-BSÄ

BOLLIUS, Daniel (Sinfonias: see *Repraesentatio harmonica conceptionis* in vocal list)

BONDIOLI, Giacinto (*b* Quinzano nr. Brescia, 1596; *d* Brescia, 1636)

Soavi fiori colti . . . laudi, motetti, magnificat, e canzoni concertati a 2 voci. . . .
Venice, 1622.

7 canzoni: V o Ctto, Trb o Fag, Org.

1. La Quinzana   5. La Giuppona
2. La Gagliarda   6. La Finetta
3. La Dieda   7. La Giusta
4. La Scarpa

The cornett part in "La Quinzana" indicates *Cantus* on the *C* part, but the indication *Violino over Cornetto* is found in the *tavole* and on the *B* part.
D-B (C, B, Org, now in **PL**-Kj)

In: Biagio Marini, *Affetti musicali . . . opera prima.* Venice: Bartholomeo Magni, 1617.
    La Hiacinta, Canzona à 2: V o Ctto, Trb, Bc.
The composer of Canzona "La Hiacinta" is given as: *Hiacinto Bondioli Zio del Autore.*
PL-WRu; **US**-Nsc (in ms EinSC compl)   RISM M657
Facs. edition: SPES   SartMS I&II 1617c

BORSARO, Arcangelo (*b* Reggio Emilia; *fl* 1587-1616)

Odorati fiori, concerti diversi a una, due, et tre voci, con altri da concertate con voci & stromenti . . . & il basso per l'organo, opera duo decima. . . . Venice: Ricciardo Amadino, 1615.
    30. La Matusaleme à tre: 2V o 2Ctto, Trb, Org.
D-Rp (T,B,Org)   SartMS II 1615o; RISM B3782

BOTTI, G. F. [Antonio?]

    One work: Ctto, Bc.
HR-Dsmb 10/244 (18th-cent ms)   *RISM AII 500052639

BRUCKNER, Hen. [Brückner, Brikner]

    Sonata Solemnis à 20: 4Tpt ("tubae campestres"), 2V, 2Ctto, 2Fl, 4Vtta, 4Trb, "basseto," [Timp].
CS-KRa B IV 206   OttoS

    Sonata à 4: 2V, 2Ctto, Bc.
CS-KRa B IV 59   OttoS
*Edition: Musica Rara[18]

BRUNELLI, Antonio (Pisa, 1575-1630)

Varii esercitii . . . per una, e due voci . . . e per esercitio di cornetti, traverse, flauti, viole, violini, & simili strumenti, con alcuni ruggieri à dua soprani per sonare. Opera undecima. Florence: Zanobi Pignoni e Comp., 1614.
    Aria di Ruggiero per sonare: 2s, b.
Also contained in the print are 2 exercises for s, b, and 3 sets of exercises for 2s, Bc.
I-Fn   SartMS I 1614g; RISM B4647
Edition: Pelikan 976

---

[18] The editor states that the instrumentation is given on the title page of the work as *2 Violini e 2 Cornetti* but not in the parts. Our microfilm copy was missing the title page.

BUONAMENTE, Giovanni Battista (*b* Mantua, late 16th cent; *d* Assisi, 1642)

Sonate et canzoni a due, tre, quattro, cinque et a sei voci . . . libro sesto . . . con il suo basso continuo. Venice: Alessandro Vincenti, 1636.
Sonata Quarta à 2: V & Ctto o 2V, Bc.
Sonata Quinta à 2: V & Ctto o 2V, Bc.
Canzon à 5: 2V o 2Ctto, 3Trb, Bc.
Sonata à 5: V, Ctto, 3Trb, Bc.
Sonata à 6: V, Ctto, 3Trb, Tior, Bc.
Sonata à 6: 2V o 2Ctto, 4Trb o 4VaBr, Bc.
The headings in the V2 partbook for Sonata quarta and Sonata quinta specify *Cornetto ò Violino Secondo*, while the *tavola* indicates *cornetto e violino*. In Canzon à 5, the heading in the V2 partbook specifies *Violino ó Cornetto secondo*.
GB-Ob; **D**-Kdma, -Kl; **PL**-WRu (missing V2); **US**-Nsc   RISM B4943
Edition: Musica Rara 1,518 (of the canzon à 5)   SartMS I&II 1636

CAROUBEL, Pierre Francisque (*b* Cremona; *d* Paris, 1611)

In: Michael Praetorius, *Terpsichore, musarum aoniarum quinta. Darinnen allerley frantzösische Däntze und Lieder. . . .* Wolfenbüttel: Fürstl. Druckerei, 1612.
CCLXXXVIII. Passameze pour les cornetz [à 6]: 6 unspecified parts.
D-Hs; **F**-Pn   RISM P5366
Edition: PraetoriusW 15

CASTELLO, Dario (*fl* Venice, early 17th cent)

Sonate concertate in stil moderno per sonar nel organo overo clavicembalo con diversi instrumenti. A 1. 2. 3. & 4. voci . . . libro secondo. . . . Venice: Bartolomeo Magni, †1629, ∞1644; Antwerp: Pierre Phalèse, ‡1656.
Sonata decima settima à 4. In ecco: 2Ctto, 2V, Org o Cemb.
†**PL**-WRu (incompl); ∞**GB**-Ob; ∞**I**-Fn (missing part 3); ‡**GB**-Lbl (missing parts 1,2&3)
Facs. edition: SPES; Edition: RRMBE 24   RISM C1462/1463/1464
      SartMS I&II 1629f, 1644e

CAZZATI, Mauritio (*b* Luzzara nr. Reggio Emilia, *ca* 1620; *d* Mantua, 1677)

Sonate a due istromenti cioè violino, e violone . . . opera XXXXXV. Bologna: n.p., 1670.
12 Sonatas: V o Ctto, Vo, Org o Tior.

La Pelicana. Sonata prima	La Moranda. Sonata settima
La Prata. Sonata seconda	La Muzzia. Sonata ottava
La Pelina. Sonata terza	La Machiavella. Sonata nona
La Cagnola. Sonata quarta	La Casarenga. Sonata decima
La Gaetana. Sonata quinta	La Nanna. Sonata undecima
La Silvestra. Sonata sesta	La Zoppia. Sonata duodecima

The title page of the Canto partbook specifies *Violino ò Cornetto,* whereas the headings of individual sonatas indicate only violin.
I-Bc   SartMS I 1670a; RISM C1656

CECCHINO, Tomaso (*b* Verona, *ca* 1580; *d* Hvar, 1644)

Cinque messe a due voci . . . con otto sonate per gl'istrumenti, bassi & soprani; & con la partitura . . . opera vigesima terza.   Venice: Alessandro Vincenti, 1628.

Sonata prima: [V o Ctto], Org.   Sonata quinta: [V o Ctto], Org.
Sonata seconda: [V o Ctto], Org.   Sonata sesta: [V o Ctto], Org.
Sonata terza: [V o Ctto], Org.   Sonata settima: [V o Ctto], Org.
Sonata quarta: [V o Ctto], Org.   Sonata Ottava: 2V o V, Ctto, Org.

For the first seven sonatas the title page indicates a generic soprano instrument. The above instrumentations are derived from the *tavola: Tutti li Soprani de le Sonate che sono in quest'Opera, possono esser sonati con l'Organo da un solo Violino, ò vero Cornetto, senza altro Istrumento Basso, se piace; eccetto l'ultima che deve esser sonata con due Violini ò vero un Violino & un Cornetto.*

D-BII; -**B** (3 partbooks, now in **PL-**Kj); **PL-**WRu (missing S2,T)   RISM C1677
SartMS I 1628e

CESARE, Giovanni Martino (*b* Udine, *ca* 1590; *d* Munich, 1667)

Musicali melodie per voci et instrumenti à una, due, tre, quattro, cinque, e sei. . . . Munich: Nicolaus Heinrich, 1621.

La Foccarina: Ctto o V, Org.
La Giorgina: Ctto o V, Org.
La Massimiliana à 2: 2Ctto o 2V, Org.
La Joannina à 2: 2Ctto o 2V, Org.
La Augustana à 2: Ctto, Trb, Org.
La Costanza à 3: 2Ctto o 2V, Trb, Org.
La Famosa à 3: 2Ctto o 2V, Trb o Va, Org.
La Gioia à 3: 2Ctto o 2V, Trb, Org.
Ecco à 3: 3Ctto o 3V, Org.
La Monachina à 4: 3Ctto, Trb, Org.
La Fenice à 4: 2Ctto, 2Trb, Org.
La Vittoria à 6: 3Ctto, 3Trb, Org.

This print also contains two vocal works specifying cornett (see vocal list).

D-Rp, -**F** (part 2); **US-**Nsc (in ms EinSC compl)   RISM C175
Edition: Musikverlag Max Hieber   SartMS I 1621b

CIMA, Giovanni Paolo (*b ca* 1570; *fl* Milan until 1622)

Concerti ecclesiastici a' una, due, tre, quattro voci . . . & sei sonate, per instrumenti à due, tre, e quattro . . . con la partitura per l'organo.   Milan: Simon Tini & Filippo Lomazzo, 1610.

Sonata: Ctto o V, Trb o Vo, Org.
Sonata à 3: V, Ctto, Vo, Org.
Capriccio d'Andrea Cima à 4: V, Ctto, Vo, Trb, Org.

D-B (now in **PL-**Kj); **I-**Bc, -**VEcap**   RISM C2229
Edition: Sikorski, Ed. no. 472 (1&2); Facs. edition: SPES   SartMS I&II 1610d

CLAVIUS, Christophorus (*b* in or nr. Bamberg, *ca* 1538; *d* Rome, 1612)

97. Laudate Dominum in sanctis eius à 8: 2Ctto, 2"Pumart," 4Trb.
D-Rp Hs. A.R. 775&777 (see under ABRAN)

COLEMAN, Charles (*b ca* 1605; *d* London, 1664)

From: 5 "Partt things ffor the Cornetts":
8. Almand: 2Ctto, 3Trb.
9. Courant: 2Ctto, 3Trb.
10. Shortt Almand: 2Ctto, 3Trb.
11. Saraband: 2Ctto, 3Trb.
GB-Cfm ms. mus. 734 (dated 1661, missing partbook 3)
Edition: Peter Holman, ed. (London: Nova Music, 1982)

COLERUS, Valentin

Neue, lustige liebliche und artige Intraden, Täntze und Gagliarde mit vier und fünff Stimmen auff allerley Seitenspiel . . . (wie auch etliche auff vier Zincken) . . . zugebrauchen. Jena: Johann Weidner, 1605.
GB-Lbl (T)   *RISM C3302

COPRARIO, John (*b ca* 1570/80; *d* London, *ca* 1626)

"A Verse for the Organ, A Sagbot & Cornute"
US-NYp Drexel 5469 (Org partitura only)

CORRADINI, Nicolò (*d* Cremona, 1646)

Partitura del primo libro de canzoni francese à 4. & alcune suonate. Venice: Bartolomeo Magni, 1624.
Suonata à 2 Cornetti in risposta. La Golferamma: 2Ctto, Bc.
The print also contains 9 canzoni à 4, 1 sonata à 4, 1 sonata à 3 & 1 sonata à 2, all without specific instrumentation.
I-Bc   SartMS I 1624a; RISM C3955

CORTECCIA, Francesco (Florence, 1502-1571)

62. Guardan [e] almo pastore à 6: Ctto, 5Trb.
D-Rp Hs. A.R. 775&777 (see under ABRAN)

DRAGHI, Antonio (Sinfonia: see vocal list)

FARINA, Carlo (*b* Mantua, *ca* 1600; *d ca* 1640)

Il terzo libro delle pavane, gagliarde, brand: mascherata, arie franzese, uolte, corrente, sinfonie, à 3. 4. voci con il basso per sonare. Dresden: Gimel Bergen, 1627.
6 Sinfonias (nos. 28-33): 2V o 2Ctto, Bc.
D-Kl, -Kdma   SartMS I 1627c; RISM F99

FERRO, Marco Antonio (*d* Vienna, 1662)

Sonate à due , tre, & quatro . . . opera prima. Venice: Gardano, 1649.
    Sonata 5. à 3: V, tVaG, VaG; o Ctto, Trb, Tior; Bc.
    Sonata 7. à 4: 2V, VttaBr, VaG; o 2Ctto, VttaBr, Fag; Bc.
    Sonata 8. à 4: 2V, VttaBr, VaG; o 2Ctto, Trb, Fag; Bc.
    Sonata 11. à 4: 2V, VttaBr, VaG; o 2Ctto, Trb, Fag; Bc.
    Sonata 12. à 4: 2V, VttaBr, VaG; o 2Ctto, VttaBr, Tior; Bc.
PL-WRu (missing Bc); **US**-Nsc (EinSC compl)   SartMS I&II 1649e; RISM F543

FONTANA, Giovanni Battista (*b* Brescia; *d* Padua, *ca* 1630)

Sonate a 1. 2. 3. per il violino, o cornetto, fagotto, chitarone, violoncino o simile altro istromento. . . . Venice: Bartolomeo Magni, 1641.
    Sonata prima: V o Ctto, Bc.
    Sonata seconda: V [o Ctto], Bc.
    Sonata terza: V [o Ctto], Bc.
    Sonata quarta: V [o Ctto], Bc.
    Sonata quinta: V [o Ctto], Bc.
    Sonata sesta: V [o Ctto], Bc.
    Sonata settima: 2V o 2Ctto, Bc.
    Sonata ottava: 2V [o 2Ctto], Bc.
    Sonata nona: V o Ctto, Fag o Chit o Vo, Bc.
    Sonata decima: V [o Ctto], Fag [o Chit o Vo], Bc.
    Sonata undecima: 2V [o 2Ctto], Bc.
    Sonata duodecima: V [o Ctto], Fag [o Chit o Vo], Bc.
    Sonata terza decima: 2V o 2Ctto, Fag [o Chit o Vo], Bc.
    Sonata quarta decima: 2V [o 2Ctto], Fag [o Chit o Vo], Bc.
    Sonata quinta decima: 2V [o 2Ctto], Fag [o Chit o Vo], Bc.
    Sonata sesta decima: 3V [o 3Ctto], Bc.
    Sonata decima settima: 2V [o 2Ctto], Fag [o Chit o Vo], Bc.
    Sonata decima ottava: 2V [o 2Ctto], Fag [o Chit o Vo], Bc.
Instrumentations are given on the title page and on the headings of the following pieces in the partbooks indicated below:
    CI partbook (Sonata prima): *Violino primo ò cornetto*; CII partbook (Sonata settima): *Violino secondo ò cornetto*; B partbook (Sonata nona): *Fagotto ò Chitarone ò Violonzono: con Violino ò cornetto*; B partbook and *Partitura* (Sonata terza decima): *con fagotto e due Violini ò cornetti.*
Each of these headings appears on the first piece in a partbook and not on the pieces which follow. Both the consistency of this practice and the title of the print suggest that the alternative use of the cornett is not restricted to those pieces in which it is specifically mentioned.
GB-Ob; **I**-Bc, -Fn; **PL**-WRu (missing partitura)   RISM F1475
Facs. edition: SPES   SartMS I 1641b

FÖRSTER, Kaspar (*b* Danzig, bapt. 1616; *d* Oliva nr. Danzig, 1673)

    Sonata a. 7. instrom: 2V, 2Cttino, [Va]Br, Fag, Vo, Bc.
S-Uu inst. mus. i hs 3:8   Edition: Hänssler 28.002; Musica Rara 1,949a/b

FRANZONI, Amante (*b* Mantua, *fl* 1605-1630)

Concerti ecclesiastici a una, due, et a tre voci col basso continuo per l'organo . . . libro primo. Venice: Ricciardo Amadino, 1611.
 Canzon francese. La Bernareggia: Ctto, 2Trb, Org.
For this piece the *tavola* reads: *a due Trombone, e Cornetto*, and the headings read: *a doi Tromboni, e Cornetto.*
A-Wn (missing T)   SartMS I 1611a; RISM F1812

FRESCOBALDI, Girolamo (*b* Ferrara, 1583; *d* Rome, 1643)

Il primo libro delle canzoni ad una, due, trè, e quattro voci. Accomodate, per sonare ogni sorte de stromenti. Rome: Giovanni Battista Robletti, 1628.
 Canzon prima, violino solo: cornetto: V o Ctto, Bc.
 Canzon seconda, violino solo over cornetto: V o Ctto, Bc.
 Canzon terza, violino solo over cornetto: V o Ctto, Bc.
Of the three editions of this print, only that of 1628 supplies instrumentations.
D-Lr (missing Bc); I-Bc (missing Bc), -Ps (incompl Bc); PL-WRu (missing S2); US-Wc (missing S2)   RISM F1868
Edition: London Pro Musica, GF1   SartMS I&II 1628j

FRISONE, Lorenzo

In: *Flores praestantissimorum virorum a Philippo Lomatio bibliopola delibati unica, binis, ternis, quaternisque vocibus decantandi.* Milan: Filippo Lomazzo, 1626.
 Canzon quinta à 3: 2V o 2Ctto, b *come piace*, Org.
(see also Francesco Rognoni in the instrumental list and Ignatio Donati in the vocal list for other pieces in this print)
I-CEc (S, A, T); US-R (S, A, B, Partitura ad Organum)   SartMS II 1626n

FROMM, Andreas (*b* Pänitz nr. Wusterhausen, 1621; *d* Prague, 1683)

Actus musicus (Es war ein reicher Mann) de divite et Lazaro, das ist musicalische Abbildung der Parabel vom reichen Manne und Lazaro, Lucae 16. Mit gewissen Persohnen . . . und allerley Instrumenten als Orgel, Clavi-cymbel, Laut, Violigam, Trompeten, Paucken, Dulcian, Cornetten, Posaunen, Geigen, & Flöten . . . . Stettin: Jeremias Mamphrasen [Georg Gloetzke], 1649.
 Symphonia: 2Ctto, Bc.
PL-WRu (missing 5 v/inst parts, Bc)   RISM F2039
Edition: Bärenreiter 919

FURCHHEIM, Johann Wilhelm [Forcheim] (*b ca* 1635/40; *d* Dresden, 1682)

 Sonata à 5: 2V, 2Ctto, Fag, Bc.
S-Uu inst. mus. i hs 3:16 (has a second unfigured Bc part); D-Kdma
Edition: Organum iii/26

FUX, Johann Joseph (*b* Hirtenfeld, Styria, 1660; *d* Vienna, 1741)

 Sonata à 4: V, Ctto, Trb, Fag, Org.
D-Dl (ms by J. D. Zelenka, *Collectaneorum musicorum libri 4* . . . [1717-18])
Edition: DTÖ 19 (Jg. IX) *[Köchel 347]

FUX, Vinzenz [FUXIO, Vincenzio]

Canzon pro tabula à 10: 2Ctto, 2V, Va, 3Trb, Org.
A-KR ms. L14   *Edition: MAM 51

GABRIELI, Andrea (Venice, *ca* 1510-1586)

105. Exultate justi in Domino à 10: Ctto, 5Trb, 4"Pumart."
106. Laudate Dominum à 10: Bassus, 4Trb, 4"Pumart," 2Ctto.
D-Rp Hs. A.R. 775&777 (see under ABRAN)

GABRIELI, Giovanni (Venice, *ca* 1553/6-1612)

Sacrae symphoniae, Joannis Gabrieli . . . senis, 7, 8, 10, 12, 14, 15, & 16, tam vocibus,
quam instrumentis. . . . Venice: Angelo Gardano, 1597.
Sonata pian, & forte à 8: ChI Ctto, 3Trb; ChII V, 3Trb.
Canzon duodecimi toni à 10: ChI Ctto, s, a, t, b; ChII s, a, t, t, b.
Canzon in ecco duodecimi toni à 10: ChI 4Ctto, Trb; ChII 4Ctto, Trb.
Canzon sudetta accomodate per concertar con l'Organo: ChI 4Ctto, Trb; ChII 4Ctto,
Trb, [Org].
Canzon quarti toni à 15: ChI Ctto, 4Trb; ChII Ctto, 4Trb; ChIII V, 4Trb.
For "Canzon sudetta" there is no specified part for the Organ.
A-Wn; **D-B** (8 partbooks, now in **PL-Kj**), -Rp, -As (missing S); I-FEc, -BRd (missing
10-12), -PCd   BrownIM 1597₅; SartMS I&II 1597e; RISM G86
Edition: IMAMI (compl); *Collegium Instrumentale*, Hänssler,16.012[1], 16.020[2]

Canzoni e sonate del signor Giovanni Gabrieli . . . a 3. 5. 6. 7. 8. 10. 12. 14. 15. & 22.
voci. per sonar con ogni sorte de instrumenti. Venice: Gardano, 1615.
Canzon IV à 6: 2V, Ctto, s, 2Trb, Org.
Canzon X à 8: ChI 2V, a, b; ChII 2Ctto, a, b; Org.
Canzon XI à 8: ChI 2Ctto, b, b; ChII 2V, b, b; Org.
Canzon XIV à 10: ChI V, Ctto, a, b, b; ChII V, Ctto a, b, b; Org.
Canzon XV à 10: 2V, 2Ctto, s, a, t, t, b, b, Org.
Canzon XVII à 12: ChI V, Ctto, b, b; ChII V, Ctto, b, b; ChIII V, Ctto b,b; Org.
Sonata XVIII à 14: ChI 2Ctto, 3Trb; ChII 2Ctto, 3Trb; ChIII 4Trb; Org.
Sonata XX à 22: ChI s, s, a, t, 2Trb; ChII s, a, t, b, [?]; ChIII a, t, b, b; ChIV Ctto, a,
t, b; ChV s, a, t, b; Org.
CS-Pu (Org); **D-As** (missing B), -B (13 partbooks, now in **PL-Kj**), -Kl; I-Bc (T
incompl), -Rsc (A, T, B, 5)   SartMS I&II 1615f; RISM G88
Edition: Le Pupitre 27; Musica Rara 1,574, 1,580, 1,583, 1,586, 1,587, 1,589, 1,590,
1,592

GIOVANELLI, Ruggiero (2 sinfonias: see vocal list)

GÖRNER, Johann Gottlieb (*b* Penig, Saxony, *bapt.* 1697; *d* Leipzig, 1778)

Test piece for the musicians in Zeitz: Tpt, aTrb, Ctto, Horn, V, Ob; 2V, Va, Vc.
This piece contains one section for each wind instrument with string accompaniment.
D-ZZ (dated 1743)   *GroveD

GOSSWIN, Anton (*b* Liège? *ca* 1546; *d* 1597/98)

80. Ad te levavi oculos meos [à ?]: [vocal part?], 2Ctto, 3Trb, "Pumart."
81. Letatus sum in his quae [à ?]: [vocal part?], 2Ctto, 3Trb, "Pumart."
D-Rp Hs. A.R. 775&777 (see under ABRAN)

GRANCINI, Michel'Angelo (See vocal list: *Sacri fiori concertati*, 1631, for an alternative instrumental setting of "Trium puerorum cantemus hymnû.")

GRANDI, Alessandro (sinfonia: see *Raccolta Terza di Leonardo . . .* in vocal list)

GREMBOSZEWSKI, Martin (*d* Danzig, 1658)

Aria voce sola per un cornetto: Ctto, Bc.
Canzonetto à 2 voci: Ctto, Fag, Org.
PL-GDs sign. 300, 36/58 (dated 1629)
Edition: Franz Kessler, ed., *Danziger Instrumental-Musik des 17. und 18. Jahrhunderts* (Neuhausen-Stuttgart: Hänssler, 1979)

HAKE, Hans

Ander theil neuer Pavanen, Sonaten, Arien, Balletten, Brandlen, Couranten, und Sarabanden, mit 2. 3. 4. 5. & 8. Instrumenten mit dem Basso continuo. Stade: [Elias Holwein], 1654.
Arias 37, 38, 39, 40: 2Ctto, 3Trb, Bc.
GB-Lbl (voce1&3, Bc); **D-Rp** (voce1, b); **S-VX** (voce1&2, b, Bc), -Uu (missing 3&4)
RISM H1895

HAMMERSCHMIDT, Andreas (sinfonias: see *Missae, V. VI. VII. . . .* [1643] in vocal list)

HAUSSMAN, Valentin (*b* Gerbstedt nr. Eisleben, *ca* 1565/70; *d ca* 1614)
Neue Intrade, mit sechs und fünff Stimmen auff Instrumenten, fürnemlich auff Fiolen lieblich zugebrauchen . . . . Nürnberg: Paul Kauffmann, 1604.
Passameza à 5, in 6 Variations: V, Ctto, a, t, b.
Galliarde à 5: V, Ctto, a, t, b.
D-B (3 partbooks, now in **PL-Kj**), -BAUk; **PL-Wn** (A,T), -WRu   *RISM H2397
*Edition: DdT 16

HESSEN, Moritz Landgraf von (*b* 1572; *d* Eschwege, 1632)

Intrada à 4, a Cornetti: s, s, s, s.
Paduana d'Eccelio à piffaro, [?] , corneto, trombone, dolzano: s, s, a, t, b.
Pauana Francisco Segario à 5 Stromenti, cioè Fiauto, cornetto muto, trombone sordono, et Viola di Gamba: s, s, a, t, b.
Pavana dell'Ottone Landgravio H[essiae] a5 stromenti diversi, cioè Violino et viola soprano [*sic*], cornetto et cornetto muto, trombone: s, s, a, t, b.

The ms in which these pieces survive was copied at Kassel in 1887 by F. Liebling, oboist of the 83rd Regiment. The pieces were either composed or arranged after 1615 by Moritz Landgraf von Hessen.

GB-Lbl Add. Ms. 33295   *HughesBM

Editions: EdM 2. Reihe, 1; 2nd pavane in *Pavanen und Gagliarden*, ed. Manfred Harras (Zürich: Pan, 1981)

HINGESTON, John (*b* York?, early 17th cent; *d* London, 1688)

>   Fantasia: 2Ctto, Trb, [Org].
>   Fantasia: Ctto, Trb, [Org].

GB-Ob   *GroveD

*Edition: Musica Rara 1,267, 1,268

HORN, Johann Caspar (*b* Feldsberg, Lower Austria, *ca* 1630; *d* Dresden, *ca* 1685)

Parergon Musicum . . . bestehend in allerhand lustigen Intraden, Gagliarden, Couranten, Balletten, Sarabanden, Chiquen, &c . . . mit zwey Chören auff Violen, Cornetten, Schalmeyen, Flöten &c. nach Belieben in 5.7.10.11. und 12. Stimmen . . . auffgesetzt und . . . in diesem sechsten Theil zusammen getragen. . . . Leipzig: G. H. Frommann, 1676.

>   1. Intrade a 5: 2V, 2Cttino, Fag o Trb, Bc.
>   2. Gagliarda a 5: 2V, 2Cttino, Fag o Trb, Bc.
>   3. Intrade a 7: 2V, 2Cttino, 2Va, Fag o Trb, Bc.
>   4. Intrade a 7: 2V, 2Cttino, 2Va, Fag o Trb, Bc.
>   5. Gagliarda a 7: 2V, 2Cttino, 2Va, Fag o Trb, Bc.
>   6. Sarabande fugue a 7: 2V, 2Cttino, 2Va, Fag o Trb, Bc.
>   7. Intrade a 10: 2V, 2Cttino, 2Trb, 2Va, Fag, Vo, Bc.
>   8. Intrade a 10: 2V, 2Cttino, 2Trb, 2Va, Fag, Vo, Bc.
>   9. Courante a 10: 2V, 2Cttino, 2Trb, 2Va, Fag, Vo, Bc.
>   10. Ballo a 10: 2V, 2Cttino, 2Trb, 2Va, Fag, Vo, Bc.
>   11. Ballo a 10: 2V, 2Cttino, 2Trb, 2Va, Fag, Vo, Bc.
>   12. Intrade a 10: 2V, 2Cttino, 2Trb, 2Va, Fag, Vo, Bc.
>   13. Courante a 10: 2V, 2Cttino, 2Trb, 2Va, Fag, Vo, Bc.
>   14. Ballo a 10: 2V, 2Cttino, 2Trb, 2Va, Fag, Vo, Bc.
>   15. Chique a 10: 2V, 2Cttino, 2Trb, 2Va, Fag, Vo, Bc.
>   16. Sarabande a 10: 2V, 2Cttino, 2Va, Fag o Trb, Bc.
>   17. Intrade a 11: 2V, 2Cttino o 2Fl, 3Trb, 2Va, Fag, Vo, Bc.
>   18. Allemande a 11: 2V, 2Cttino o 2Fl, 3Trb, 2Va, Fag, Vo, Bc.
>   19. Courante a 11: 2V, 2Cttino o 2Fl, 3Trb, 2Va, Fag, Vo, Bc.
>   20. Gagliarda a 11: 2V, 2Cttino o 2Fl, 3Trb, 2Va, Fag, Vo, Bc.
>   21. Ballo a 11: 2V, 2Cttino o 2Fl, 3Trb, 2Va, Fag, Vo, Bc.
>   22. Chique a 11: 2V, 2Cttino o 2Fl, 3Trb, 2Va, Fag, Vo, Bc.
>   23. Sarabande a 11: 2V, 2Cttino o 2Fl, 3Trb, 2Va, Fag, Vo, Bc.
>   24. Intrade a 12: 2V, 3Va, 3Fl o 3Cttino, 2Trb, Fag, Vo, Bc.
>   25. Courante a 12: 2V, 3Va, 3Fl o 3Cttino, 2Trb, Fag, Vo, Bc.
>   26. Ballo a 12: 2V, 3Va, 3Fl o 3Cttino, 2Trb, Fag, Vo, Bc.

27. Sarabande a 12: 2V, 3Va, 3Fl o 3Cttino, 2Trb, Fag, Vo, Bc.
28. Intrade a 12: 2V, 3Va, 3Cttino, 2Trb, Fag, Vo, Bc.
29. Gagliarda a 12: 2V, 3Va, 3Cttino, 2Trb, Fag, Vo, Bc.
30. Sarabande a 12: 2V, 3Va, Cttino, 2Trb, Fag, Vo, Bc.

The preface *An den Musik-Liebenden* provides valuable information on the choice of instruments in these pieces:

Das Directorium kan zwar nach Gelegenheit der Personen und Instrumenten eingerichtet werden. Es is aber zu erinnern weil diese Musicalia benebenst den Violen zugleich auff blasende Instrumenta gesetzet sind daß 1. an statt der Cornettinen auch gar füglich Trombetten, (iedoch nur die ersten 6. Stücke) ingleichen Schalmeyen oder auch Flautinen können gebraucht werden; Doch ist solcher gestalt der Violen-Chor desto vollstimmiger anzuordnen. Was 2. die Mittelstimmen anbelanget kan man solche nach Belieben und Gelegenheit Bestellen oder auslassen; biß auff die letzten 3. Stücke worinnen die Mittel-Partien sich alleine hören lassen und also nothwendig so viel möglich besetzet seyn müssen. Ebenfalls 3. so kan auch der Violon ausgelassen werden wenn der Fagott (oder an statt dessen eine Trombone) bestellet ist. Wenn aber der Fagott gar nicht darbey seyn kan so soll auch der Violon nicht à part, sondern aus dem Basso Continuo mitgespielet werden. Schließlichen: Je mehr Partien, je besser Gratie. Hermit lebe wohl!

D-B (V1, V2, Cttino1, Cttino2, Fag, Bc, now in **PL**-Kj); **GB**-Lbl (V1, V2)
Edition: Carl Nef, *Geschichte der Sinfonie und Suite* (Leipzig: Breitkopf & Härtel, 1921)   RISM H7415

HÜBER, Vendelini

Sonata quarta à 6: 2V, 2Ctto, 2Trb, Org.
CS-KRa BIV 6   OttoS

JELIĆ, Vincenz [Jelich] (*b* Fiume, Yugoslavia, 1596; *d* Zabern, Alsace, *ca* 1636)

Parnassia militia, concertuum unius, duarum, trium et quatuor vocum: tam nativis quam instrumentalibus vocibus, ad organum concinendarum . . . opus primum. Straßburg: Paul Ledertz, 1622.
Ricercar primo, del primo tono: Ctto, Trb, Bc[Org].
Ricercar secundo, del 5. tono: Ctto Trb, Bc[Org].
Ricercar tertio: Ctto, Trb, Bc[Org].
Ricercar quarto: Ctto, Trb, Bc[Org].
In the print these ricercars appear without Bc. A ms basso continuo part is found in D-F.
A-SP (A); **D**-F; **GB**-Lbl (missing S); **PL**-WRu (S)   RISM J520
Edition: (without ms Bc) Zagreb: Jugoslavenska Akademija Znanosti Umjetnosti, 1957

Arion secundus, psalmorum vespertinorum, tam de tempore, quam de Beata Maria Virgini, quatuor vocibus, alternatim ad organum concinendorum adjunctis Magnificat, Salve Regina, et octo tonis ad omnia instrumenta accomodatis . . . opus tertium. Straßburg: Paul Ledertz, 1628.
The print contains 11 vocal works and "Octo variationis Tonorum" for instruments.
II Secundo Ton. Violin overo Cornet: 4V o 4Ctto, Org.
VIII Octavo Ton. Violin overo Cornetto: 4V o 4Ctto, Org.

D-Mbs (S[incompl], A); **F**-Pn (A, B, Org)   RISM J522
Edition: *Monuments of the Croatian Past*, III

JEUNE, Henry Le

In: Marin Mersene, *Harmonie universelle contenant la thèorie et la pratique de la musique.* . . . Paris: Sebastian Cramoisy, 1636.
Phantasie à cinq parties composée par le sieur Henry le Jeune, pour les cornets: 5Ctto (premier dessus, second dessus, haut-contre, taille, basse).
F-BO, -Pc
Facs. edition: Paris: Centre National de la Recherche Scientifique, 1965
The piece occurs without attribution as "Symph. cu 4 cornibus vulgo *Cornetti*, una cu dulcino, sive vulgò Fagotto instituenda" in Athanasius Kircher, *Musurgia universalis sive ars magna consoni et disoni.* . . . (Rome: Francisci Corbelletti, 1650). **A**-Wn; **D**-Rp; **F**-Pn; **GB**-Lbl; **US**-NYp; Facs. edition: Hildesheim: Georg Olms, 1970

KAPSBERGER, Johann Hieronymus (*b* Venice, *ca* 1580; *d* Rome, 1651)

Libro primo di sinfonie a quattro con il basso continuo. . . . Rome: Giovanni Battista Robletti, 1615.

Sinfonia 1: s, s, a, b, b, Bc.	Sinfonia 10: s, s, b, b, Bc.
Sinfonia 2: s, s, b, b, Bc.	Sinfonia 11: s, s, a, b, b, Bc.
Sinfonia 3: s, b, Bc.	Sinfonia 12: s, s, Bc.
Sinfonia 4: s, Org.	Sinfonia 13: s, Org.
Sinfonia 5: s, s, b, b, Bc.	Sinfonia 14: s, s, b, b, Bc.
Sinfonia 6: s, s, b, b, Bc.	Sinfonia 15: s, s, a, b, Bc.
Sinfonia 7: s, s, b, b, Bc.	Sinfonia 16: s, s, a, b, b, Bc.
Sinfonia 8: s, s, a, b, Bc.	Sinfonia 17: s, s, a, b, b, Bc.
Sinfonia 9: s, s, b, b, Bc.	Sinfonia 18: s, s, b, b, Bc.

An *Avertimento* supplies the following directions: *Per primo & secundo basso s'intende qual si voglia strumento che suoni in consonanza, come sarebbe Lauto Chitarrone, Cimbalo, Arpa, & suoi simili. Per primo & Secundo canto, Violino, Cornetto, & suoi simili.* Thus "s" parts are intended for violin or cornetto (or other), "b" parts for lute, chitarrone, harpsichord or harp. All parts indicated "b" are figured and the indication *Basso per l'Organo* occurs twice (sinfonias 4 and 13) in the Bc part.
Sinfonia 15 is also found, though without any instrumentation or bass figures, in Athanasius Kircher, *Musurgia universalis* (Rome: Francisci Corbelletti, 1650).
GB-Lbl (S1, B, Bc [incompl]); **I**-Rvat/barberini   RISM K187

KEMPIS, Nicolaus A (*b ca* 1600; *d* Brussels, 1676)

Symphoniae unius, duarum, et trium violinorum. . . . Antwerp: Pierre Phalèse, 1644.
Symphonia 1: V o Ctto, Va o Fag, Bc.
Symphonia 2: V o Ctto, Va o Fag, Bc.
Symphonia 3 supra ut re mi fa sol la: V o Ctto, Va o Fag, Bc.
Symphonia 4: V o Ctto, Va o Fag, Bc.
Symphonia 5: V o Ctto, Va o Fag, Bc.
Symphonia 6: V o Ctto, Va o Fag, Bc.
Symphonia 7: V o Ctto, Va o Fag, Bc.

Symphonia 8: V o Ctto, Va o Fag, Bc.
D-Kl (missing parsII); **F-Pn** (parsII)   SartMS I 1644a; RISM K377

Symphoniae unius, duorum, trium, IV. et V instrumentorum adjunctae quatuor instrumentorum & duarum vocum . . . operis secundi liber primus. . . . Antwerp: Magdalène Phalèse, 1647.
Symphonia Prima: V o Ctto, bVa o Fag, Bc.
Symphonia Secunda: V o Ctto, bVa o Fag, Bc.
Symphonia Tertia: V o Ctto, bVa o Fag, Bc.
Symphonia Quarta:V o Ctto, bVa o Fag, Bc.
Symphonia Quinta: V o Ctto, bVa o Fag, Bc.
Symphonia prima à 3: V, Ctto o V, Trb, Bc.
Symphonia tertia à 4: 2V, Ctto, bVa, Bc.
Only symphonias 4 & 5 à 2 specify *violino* in the headings of the first partbook, but the index gives the cornett as an alternative for all five symphonias à 2.
GB-Lbl, **-DRc** (pars I-V, Bc)   SartMS I 1647; RISM K378

Symphoniae unius, duorum, trium, IV, et V instrumentorum adjunctae quatuor instrumentorum & duarum vocum . . . opus tertium et ultimum. . . . Antwerp: Magdalène Phalèse, 1647.
Symphonia Prima: V o Ctto, bVa o Fag, Bc.
Symphonia Secunda: V o Ctto, bVa o Fag, Bc.
Symphonia Tertia: V o Ctto, bVa o Fag, Bc.
Symphonia Quarta: V o Ctto, bVa o Fag, Bc.
Symphonia Quinta: V o Ctto, bVa o Fag, Bc.
Symphonia secunda à 3: V, Ctto, Trb, Bc.
Symphonia quarta à 3: 2V, Ctto o V, Bc.
Symphonia tertia à 4: 2V, Ctto, bVa, Bc.
Only symphonias 1-4 specify *violino* in the headings of the first partbook, but the index gives the cornett as an alternative for all five symphonias à 2.
GB-Lbl   SartMS I 1649c; RISM K379

KERTZINGER, Augustino

Sonata ab 11: 2V o 2Ctto, 2Va, VaG, 4Trb, Fag, Vo, Org.
CS-KRa B IV 80   OttoS

KINDERMANN, Johann Erasmus (Nürnberg, 1616-1655)

Deliciae studiosorum von allerhand Symphonien, Arien, Sonaten, Intraden, Balleten, Sonetten, und Rittornellen, auf allerhand blasenden Instrumenten als: Cornettn Posaunen, Flöten, Fagotten . . . Dritter Theil. Nürnberg: Wolfgang Endter, 1643.
1. Symphonia: 2Ctto o 2V, Trb o Fag o Vo, Bc.
2. Symphonia: 2Ctto o 2V, Trb o Fag o Vo, Bc.
3. Symphonia: 2Ctto o 2V, Trb o Fag o Vo, Bc.
5. Sonata: 2Ctto o 2V, Trb o Fag o Vo, Bc.
6. Symphonia: 2Ctto o 2V, Trb o Fag o Vo, Bc.
7. Symphonia: 2Ctto o 2V, Trb o Va, Bc.

9. Symphonia: 2Ctto o 2V, Trb o Fag o Vo, Bc.
15. Symphonia: 2Ctto o 2V, Trb o Fag o Vo, Bc.
16. Sonata: 2Ctto o 2V, Trb o Fag o Vo, Bc.
18. Symphonia: 2Ctto o 2V, Trb o Fag o Vo, Bc.
19. Symphonia: 2Ctto o 2V, Trb o Fag o Vo, Bc.
20. Sonata: 2Ctto o 2V, Trb o Fag o Vo, Bc.
21. Ritornello: 2Ctto o 2V, Trb o Fag o Vo, Bc.
22. Symphonia: 2Ctto o 2V, Trb o Fag o Vo, Bc.
25. Ballet: 2V o 2Ctto, [Vo], Bc.
29. Ritornello: 2Ctto o 2V, Trb o Fag o Vo, Bc.
30. Symphonia: 2Ctto o 2V, Trb o Fag o Vo, Bc.
31. Ballet: 2Ctto o 2V, Trb o Fag o Vo, Bc.
35. Intrada: 3Ctto o 3V, Trb o Va, Trb o Fag o Vo, Bc.
36. Symphonia: 2Ctto o 2V, 3Fag o 3Trb o 3Vo, Bc.

The index of the partbooks lists Symphonia no. 3 as a Sonata. For Symphonia no. 7, cornetts are specified in the partbooks, but violins are specified in the headings. In the index, Symphonia no. 18 is listed as an Aria. For Ballet no. 25, the index indicates 3 "Viol." and the headings indicate *Cornetto ó Violino & Violino*.
I-Bc; **D**-B (1 partbook dated 1644, now in **PL**-Kj), -Kdma, -Ngm   RISM K555
Edition: DTB 24 (Jg. XIII)

LANGE, Gregor (*b* Havelberg, Brandenburg, *ca* 1540; *d* Breslau, 1587)

102. Laetatis sum à 8: 2Ctto, 4Trb, 2 "Pumart."
104. Nisi dominus à 8: 3Ctto, 3Trb, 2 [?] "Pumart."
D-Rp Hs. A.R. 775&777 (see under ABRAN)

LANIER, Nicholas (London, *bapt.* 1588; *d* 1666)

From: "5 partt things ffor the Cornetts":
12. Almand: 2Ctto, 3Trb.
13. Sarabande: 2Ctto, 3Trb.
GB-Cfm mus. ms. 734 (missing partbook 3)
Edition: Peter Holman, ed. (London: Nova Music, 1983)

LAPPI, Pietro (*b* Florence, 1575; *d* Brescia, 1630)

Rosario musicale, una Messa a 2 cori con 3° coro aggiunto, tutti i salmi dei vespri con 2 motetti litanie, 2 motetti Te Deum, una canzona con alcuni introiti. Venice: Bartolomeo Magni, 1629.
[Canzona] "L'Anconitana" à 8: Trb o Ctto o V all'ottava.
I-BRd   *SartMS; *RISM L699

LASSO, Orlando di (*b* Mons, Hainaut, 1532; *d* Munich, 1594)

70. Concupiscendo concupiscit à 6: 2Ctto, 4Trb.
77. Domine quid multiplicati sunt à 6: 2Ctto, 2"Pumart," 2Trb.
78. Cantate Domino canticum novum [à 5]: 2Ctto, "Pumart," 3Trb.
79. Deus in adiutorium meum indende [à 8]: 2Ctto, 3"Pumart," Trb.

90. Laudate pueri à 7: 2Ctto, 2"Pumart," 3Trb.
91. Decantabat populus à 7: 6Ctto, Trb.
92. Domine, quid multiplicati sunt à 6: 2Ctto, 2"Pumart," 2Trb.
93. Laudate Hierusalem dominum à 6: 2Ctto, 2"Pumart," 2Trb.
95. Omnia tempus habent à 8: Ctto, "Pumart," 4Trb.
116. Surge propera à 6: 2Ctto, 4Trb.
120. Angelus Domini descendit de coelo à 6: 2Ctto, "Pumart," 3Trb.

D-Rp Hs. A.R. 775&777 (see under ABRAN)

LEGRENZI, Giovanni (*b* Clusone nr. Bergamo, *ca* 1626; *d* Venice, 1690)

Sonate a due, tre, cinque, e sei stromenti . . . libro terzo, opera ottava. Venice:
Francesco Magni, †1663, ∞1664; Bologna: Monti, ‡1671.
    La Buscha à 6: 2V, 2Ctto o 2V, VaBr, Fag o Vo, Bc.
This instrumentation is found in the partbook headings. The *tavola* specifies *Due
Violini, e Violone, due Canti, e Fagotto.*
†**I**-Baf, -Bc; **F**-Psg, **PL**-WRu; ∞**F**-Psg; ‡**I**-Bc (V1), -Baf (Org), -Bsp, -FEc; **US**-BE
(missing V1, Org)   RISM L1619/1620/1621
Edition: Musica Rara   SartMS I&II 1663b, 1671b

LICHTLEIN, Wilhelm

    Capriccio di cornetti à 6: 6Ctto.
D-Tu mus. ms. 40028 (dated 1599)   *MeyerMS
Edition: Musikverlag Hans Gerig 530

LOCKE, Matthew (*b* Devon, 1621/2; *d* London, 1677)

    "ffor his Majesty's Sagbutts & Cornetts"
    Ayre à 5; Courante à 5; Pavan-Almand à 6; Saraband à 4; Canon. 4 in 2
    Canon 4 in 2. A Plaine Song given by Mr. William Brode of Hereford
GB-Lbl Add. ms. 17801 f. 62 (Ayre and Courante); ff. 63*v*-64 (Pavan-Almand); f. 65
(saraband); f. 63 (Canon); ff. 64*v* (Canon . . . Plaine Song)
Edition: Oxford University Press (together with "5 partt things . . . "; see next entry)

    From: "5 Partt things ffor the cornetts"
    1. Ayre: 2Ctto, 3Trb. (same as GB-Lbl 17801)
    2. Courantt: 2Ctto, 3Trb. (same as GB-Lbl 17801)
    3. Almand: 2Ctto, 3Trb.
    4. Saraband: 2Ctto, 3Trb.
    5. Almand: 2Ctto, 3Trb.
    6. Corantt: 2Ctto, 3Trb.
    7. Almand: 2Ctto, 3Trb.
GB-Cfm mus. ms. 734 (missing partbook 3)
Edition: Ed. Anthony Baines (London: Oxford University Press, 1951; a reconstructed
edition under the title *Music for his Majesty's Sackbuts and Cornetts*)

LOOSEMORE, Henry (*b* Devon; *d* 1670)
"A Verse for y Organ A Sagbot Cornute & Violin."
US-NYp Drexel 5469 (Org partitura only)
Reconstructed edition: Ian Payne, *The Provision and Practice of Sacred Music at Cambridge Colleges and Selected Cathedrals, c.1547– c.1646* (New York: Garland, 1993)

LÖWE VON EISENACH, Johann Jacob (*b* Vienna, *ca* 1629; *d* Lüneburg, 1703)
Sonaten, Canzonen, und Capriccen a II. Instrumentis. Jena: Franz Mohr [Johann Jacob Bauhofer], 1664.
  Canzon I à 2: V, Cttino, Bc.
  Capricci X à 2: 2Cttino o 2V, Bc.
S-Uu   *RISM L2752
Edition: Musica Rara 1,128

MAFFIOLETTI, Giovanni Battista (1725-1800)
  Sonata per Cornetta. Allegro, Andante, Allegro: Ctto, 2V, Vo, Clarinet, Fag.
The date estimate for this ms may be too early, in which case there is a likelihood that the intended instrument is a keyed bugle or valved cornet.
I-FELd ACFM 99 (mid 18th-cent ms)   *RISM AII 34535

MAGINI, Francesco (*fl* 1700-1712)
  Sonate due del . . . Maestro del Senatorie e Conservatori di Roma nel anno 1700 al 1712. Propria per li Senatori di fiato, e Concerto de Tromboni, Cornetti etc. di Costel d'Angelo.
  2 Sonatas: 2Ctto, 4Trb.
D-BII Mus. ms. L 155 (dated 1710)   *EitQ

"Sonate di Francesco Magini per il Campidoglio 1713"
  1. Sonata La Balama: adagio, allegro, grave: 2Ctto, 4Trb (attb).
  2. Sonata La Corsina: adagio, allegro, adagio: 2Ctto, 4Trb (attb).
  3. Sonata La Bolognetti: adagio, allegro, adagio: 2Ctto, 4Trb (attb).
  4. Sonata La Saccetti: adagio, allegro, grave: 2Ctto, 4Trb (attb).
  5. Sonata La Teodola: grave, allegro, grave: 2Ctto, 4Trb (attb).
  6. Sonata La Albana: allegro, adagio, allegro: 2Ctto, 4Trb (attb).
  7. Sonata La Riviera: adagio, allegro, [unspec. mvmt], adagio: 2Ctto, 4Trb (attb).
D-MÜs SANT Hs 2436 (19th-cent ms by Fortunato Santini)   *RISM AII 75899

MALVEZZI, Cristofano (Sinfonia à 6: see *Intermedii et Concerti* [1591] in vocal list)

MARINI, Biagio (*b* Brescia, *ca* 1587; *d* Venice, 1663)
Affetti musicali . . . opera prima nella quale si contiene, symphonie, canzon, sonate balletti, arie, brandi, gagliarde & corenti. à 1.2.3. acomodate da potersi suonar con violini corneti & con ogni sorte de strumenti musicali. . . . Venice: Bartholomeo Magni, 1617.

Il Vendramino, Balletto o Sinfonia à 3: 2V o 2Ctto, b, Bc.
La Albana, Sinfonia breve à 2: 2V o 2Ctto, Bc.
La Candela, Sinfonia breve à 2: 2V o 2Ctto, Bc.
La Zorzi, Sinfonia grave à 3: 2V o 2Ctto, b, Bc.
La Cornera, Sinfonia à 2: 2V o 2Ctto, Bc.
La Martinega, Sinfonia à 2: 2V o 2Ctto, Bc.
La Ponte, Sonata à 2: V o Ctto, Bc.
La Giustiniana, Sinfonia à 3: 2V o 2Ctto, Trb, Bc.
La Bemba, Canzon à 2: 2V o 2Ctto, Bc.
La Foscarina, Sonata à 3 con il tremolo: 2V o 2Ctto, Trb o Fag, Bc.
[La Hiacinta, Canzona à 2: V o Ctto, Trb, Bc.]
La Gambara, Sinfonia à 3: 2V o 2Ctto, b, Bc.
La Marina, Canzone à 3: V o Ctto, 2Trb, Bc.
La Orlandina, Sinfonia à 1: V o Ctto, b *se piace*, Bc.
La Gardana, Sinfonia à 1: V o Ctto, Bc.

For Sinfonia "La Zorzi"only 2V è Basso are specified in the *tavola*. The composer of Canzona "La Hiacinta" is given as: *Hiacinto Bondioli Zio del Autore*. (See entry: Bondioli, Giacinto)

PL-WRu; **US**-Nsc (in ms EinSC compl)   RISM M657
Facs. edition: SPES   SartMS I&II 1617c

Madrigali et symfonie a una 2. 3. 4. 5 . . . opera seconda. . . . Venice: Bartolomeo Magni, 1618.
La Rizza. Canzon à 4: V, Ctto, Trb, Fag, Bc.
La Bombarda. Canzon à 2: V, Ctto, Bc.

D-B (B, now in **PL**-Kj); **I**-Bc (S1); **GB**-Lbl (S2)   SartMS I&II 1618d; RISM M658

Sonate, symphonie canzoni, passemezzi, balletto, corenti, gagliarde, et ritornelli, a 1. 2. 3. 4. 5. & 6. voci, per ogni sorte d'instrumenti . . . opera ottava. Venice: Bartolomeo Magni, 1626.[19]
Sonata seconda: 2V o 2Ctto, Bc.
Sonata terza: 2V o 2Ctto, Bc.
Sonata quarta: 2V o 2Ctto, Bc.
Sonata quinta: 2V o 2Ctto, Bc.
Sonata sesta: 2Fl o 2Ctto, Bc.
Sonata senza cadenza decima terza: 2V o 2Ctto, Bc.
Sinfonia terza: 2Ctto, Trb, Bc.
Sinfonia quarta: 2Ctto, Trb, Bc.
Canzone prima: 4V o 4Ctto, Bc.
Canzone terza à 4: 4Trb o Va[G] [o Ctto, 3Trb; o V, 3VaG], Bc.
Canzone quarta à 4: Et si può Sonare anco à 2: 2V o 2Ctto, 2Trb *ad lib*, Bc.
Canzone sesta à 4: 2Ctto, 2Trb *ad lib*, Bc.
Canzone decima à 6: 2V o 2Ctto, 4Va o 4Trb, Bc.

---

[19] In this print the date *MDCXXVI* has been altered by hand to read *MDCXXVIIII*.

Sonata prima: V o Ctto, Bc.

Sonata per l'Organo: V o Ctto, Trb *ad lib* [o V o Ctto], Org.

For "Sonata quarta" the heading in partbook *C I* specifies 2V.

For "Sonata quinta" the heading in partbook *C I* specifies *a doi soprani,* whereas the *tavola* and the *C II* partbook specify *doi Violini ò Cornetti.*

For "Sonata sesta" the headings in the Canto partbooks specify *Flautini,* whereas the *tavola* specifies *Flauti.*

For "Sinfonia terza" and "Sinfonia quarta" the instrumentation is found in the *tavola,* whereas the headings in the *C I* partbook specify only *Canto Primo.*

For "Canzone terza" the sub-heading in the *C I* partbook reads: *questa parte può esser Sonata da un Corneto, ò Violino al'Octava.* The Va[G] alternative may be implied by the fact that *Viole* is indicated in the *tavola,* and that *Violino* is given as a substitute for the *canto viole.*

For "Canzone quarta" the instrumentation is found in the *tavola,* whereas the headings in the Canto partbooks specify *Soprani soli.*

For "Canzone sesta" the instrumentation is found in the *tavola,* whereas the heading in the *C I* partbook reads: *Et si può sonare due parti Solamente cioue le 2. Soprani overo li 2 Bassi.*

For the "Sonata per l'Organo" the sub-heading of the Trb *ad lib* part in the *CII* partbook reads: *Può esser anco Sonata, da Un Violino o Cornetto al'Octava.*

PL-WRu S1 (incompl), S2, T, B (incompl), 5/6; **US**-NSc (in ms EinSC compl)

SartMS I&II 1629g; RISM M663

Corona melodica ex diversis sacrae musicae floribus. . . . Antwerp: Pierre Phalèse, 1644.

4 Sonatas: 2V o 2Ctto, Bc.

B-Br (Bc)   *BernC   SartMS I 1640c; RISM M666

Per ogni sorte d'istromento musicale diversi generi di sonate, da chiesa, e da camera, a due, trè, & à quattro . . . libro terzo, opera XXII. . . . Venice: Francesco Magni, 1655.

Sonata per due violini: 2V o 2Ctto, Bc.

Sonata violino e basso: V o Ctto, b, Bc.

For the "Sonata per due violini," cornett is indicated only in the *tavola* of the partbooks. For the "Sonata violini e basso," cornett is indicated only in the *tavola* of the Bc partbook.

I-Bc; **GB**-Ob; **PL**-WRu (missing V1)   RISM M671

Facs. edition: SPES   SartMS I&II 1655a

MAZZOCCHI, Virgilio (see vocal list for "Beatum Franciscum à 16," which contains a Sinfonia: 2Ctto, 2V, 2Trb, Vo, Org.)

MEDER, Johann Valentin (ritornelli: see "Die Beständige Argenia" in vocal list)

MELANI, Jacopo (ritornelli: see "Ercole in Tebe" in vocal list)

MERULA, Tarquinio (1594/5-1665)

Il primo libro de motetti, e sonate concertati a due, tre, quattro, e cinque voci, co'l basso per l'organo . . . opera sesta. . . . Venice: Alessandro Vincenti, 1624.

Sonata prima: V o Ctto, [b], Org.

Sonata seconda: V o Ctto, [b], Org.
For both sonatas the *tavola* specifies *Canto, & Basso.*
I-Bc (missing B)   RISM M2338
Edition: Ars Antiqua Editions (both sonatas)   SartMS I 1624d

MISEROCA, Bastiano

*I pietosi affetti . . . a una, due, tre, & quattro voci, con le letanie della Beata Vergine
a sei . . . libro terzo.* Venice: Giacomo Vincenti, 1618.
    Canzon à 3: 2Ctto o 2V, Trb, Bc[Org].
D-Rp (S, T, B, Org); I-Bc; US-NSc (in ms EinSC)   RISM M2877

MOLTER, Johann Melchior (*b* Tiefenort nr. Eisenach, 1696; *d* Karlsruhe, 1765)

    Sinfonia [F major]: 2Tpt, 5Timp, 2Trav, Ctto, 2V, Vtta, Vc, Cemb.
Cornett is indicated in the score, but the part is marked *hautbois.*
D-KA Mus. ms. 615 (score and parts)

MONTE, Phillippe de (*b* Mechlin, 1521; *d* Prague, 1603)

    73. Ho sempre in teso, dir che nel'inferno: 2Ctto, 2"Pumart," 2Trb.
    74. [L]a dolce vista à me si dolcemente à 6: 2Ctto, 2"Pumart," 2 Trb.
    75. Cantai un tempo/Misero que spaerava esser in via à 6: 2Ctto, 3"Pumart," Trb.
D-Rp Hs. A.R. 775&777 (see under ABRAN)

MONTEVERDI, Claudio (sinfonias: see *L'Orfeo* [1607] in vocal list)

MORANDI, Pietro? (1745-1815)

    Concerto di Morandi Ripieno misto, Pte. Flauto, e Cornetto: Fl, Ctto, Pianoforte.
The apparent date of this ms places it in a position of near-overlap with the keyed bugle
and other brass instruments that were often designated by the term *cornetto.* Therefore,
there is some doubt that it is intended for the *cornetto curvo.*
HR-Dsmb 10/259 (ms from 18th/19th cent)   *RISM AII 500052848

MUSSI, Giulio

*Il primo libro delle canzoni per sonar a due voci . . . opera quinta con il basso per
l'organo et nel fine una toccata in ecco a doi soprani. . . .* Venice: Alessandro
Vincenti, 1620.
    [canzona] L'Amaltea: 2V o 2Ctto *in ecco,* Org.
The *tavola* specifies *doi Canti in Ecco.*
D-Mbs; I-Bc   SartMS I 1620i; RISM M8226

NERI, Massimiliano (*b* Brescia? *ca* 1615?; *d* Bonn, 1666)

Sonate da sonarsi con varij stromenti a tré sino a dodeci opera seconda. . . . Venice:
Francesco Magni, 1651.
    Sonata ottava à 6: 2Ctto, Fag, 3Trb, Bc.
    Sonata undecima à 9: 2V, Va, 2Ctto, Fag, 3Trb, Bc.
    Sonata decimaquarta à 12: 2Ctto, Fag, 3Trb, 2V, Va, Tior o Va, Bc.

The preface contains the following remark regarding the flexibility of instrumentation in these sonatas: *Amico Lettore resta contento ch'io t'avverta, che se bene nella sopradita tavola per ciascheduna Sonata vanno assegnati gl'instromenti, tuttavia resta alla dispositione di chi vorrà servirsene cambiarli à proportione sodisfacendo al proprio gusto, & havendo riguardo alla commodità.*
A ms transcription by Emil Bohn of the "Sonata decimaquarta" is in **PL**-WRu.
PL-WRu (missing A, T, B, *5*)   SartMS I&II 1615b; RISM N403

PASINO, Stefano (*b* Brescia, early 17th cent; *d* Lonato? nr. Brescia, after 1679)

Sonate a 2. 3. 4. instrumenti de quali, una è composta in canone, & un'altra ad immitatione di verse sogliono fare diversi animali brutti opera ottava. . . . Venice: Francesco Magni, 1679.
      Sonata duodecima detta la Savolda à 4: 2Ctto, 2Trb, Bc.
GB-Ob; **I**-Bc (V2, bVa, Bc)   SartMS I&II 1679b; RISM P970

PATTARINA, Maria
      124. Canzone "di Maria Pattarina" à 3: 2Ctto, Trb o Va, Bc.
D-Rp Ms. 732

PEZEL, Johann Christoph (*b* Glatz, Silesia, 1639; *d* Bautzen, 1694)
Hora decima musicorum Lipsiensium, oder musicalische Arbeit zum Abblasen, im 10. Uhr Vormittage in Leipzig, bestehend in 40. Sonaten mit 5. Stimmen, als 2. Cornetten und 3. Trombonen. Leipzig: Georg Heinrich Frommann [Johann Koler], †1670, ∞1674.
      40 Sonatas à 5: 2Ctto o 2V, 2Trb o 2Va, bTrb o Vo, Bc.
Stringed instruments are specified only in the 1674 edition entitled *Supellex sonatarum selectarum. . . .* It is identical to the 1670 edition but gives the following alternative instrumentation in the partbook headings: Ctto o VI, Ctto o VII, Trb o VaI, Trb o VaII, bTrb o Vo, Bc.
†**CH**-Zz; †**S**-V (missing title page); ∞**D**-B (5 partbooks, now in **PL**-Kj) , -OB; (2 sonatas in ms **S**-Uu instr. mus. i hs 11:26 a-b)   RISM †P1692, ∞P1694
Editions: Musica Rara 1,107/1,111; DdT 63 (12 sonatas)

Bicinia variorum instrumentorum ut à. 2. violinis, cornet. flautinis. clarinis. clarino. et fagotto. . . . Leipzig: Autor, 1675.
      8 Sonatinas (nos. 61-68) à 2 Cornett: 2Ctto, Bc.
A-Wn; **S**-Uu   RISM P1695
Editions: Musica Rara 1,273 (nos. 61,62,65,66) & 1,537 (nos. 63,64,67,68); DdT 63

Fünff-stimmigte blasende Music, bestehend in Intraden, Allemanden, Balleten, Courenten, Sarabanden und Chiquen, als zweyen Cornetten und dreyen Trombonen. Frankfurt: Balthasar Christoph Wust, 1685.
      Contains 76 Dance pieces: 2Ctto, 3Trb (40 Intradas, 12 Sarabanden, 10 Balleten, 4 Allemanden, 3 Arien, 5 Couranten, 1 Gagliard, 1 Chique)

1-16. Intrade	20. Aria	24. Ballet
17. Allemande	21. Sarabande	25. Sarabande
18. Courante	22. Bal	26. Gagliard
19. Sarabande	23. Sarabande	27. Allemande

28. Courente	40. Intrade	52-59. Intrade
29. Bal	41. Intrade	60. Allemande
30. Sarabande	42. Sarabande	61. Courente
31. Allemande	43. Intrade	62. Ballet
32. Courente	44. Aria	63. Sarabande
33. Bal	45. Ballet	64. Gigue
34. Saraband	46. Sarabande	65. Intrade
35. Intrade	47. Ballet	66. Aria
36. Courente	48. Sarabande	67. Intrade
37. Bal	49. Ballet	68. Sarabande
38. Sarabande	50. Intrade	69-76. Intrade
39. Intrade	51. Ballet	

D-BNu, -Rp; **F**-Pc; **GB**-Lbl   RISM P1697
Edition: Musica Rara 1,210, 1,105, 1,106; DdT 63

PICCHI, Giovanni (*fl* 1600-25)

Canzoni da sonar con ogni sorte d'istromenti a due, tre, quattro, sei, & otto voci, con il suo basso continuo. Venice: Alessandro Vincenti, 1625.
    Canzon prima: 2V o 2Ctto, Org.
    Canzon seconda: V o Ctto, Fag, Org.
    Canzon quarta: 2V o 2Ctto, Org.
    Canzon quinta: 2V o 2Ctto, Org.
    Canzon undecima: 2Ctto, 2Trb, Org.
    Canzon decima terza: 2Ctto, 2Trb, Org.
    Canzon decima quarta: 2V o 2Ctto, 4Trb, Org.
The heading of "Canzon seconda" specifies *violino*.
I-Bc; **PL**-WRu   SartMS I 1625b; RISM P2042
Facs. edition: SPES

PIETRAGRUA, Gasparo [GRUA, PIETRA GRUA] (*b* Milano, 16th cent; *d* after 1651)

Concerti, et canzon francese à una, due, tre, e 4. voci . . . opera prima. . . . Milan: Giorgio Rolla, 1629.
    Canzone detta la Viana, voce sola: V o Ctto, Bc.
    Canzone detta l'Appiana, voce sola: V o Ctto, Bc.
    Canzone à 2, detta la Nozente: V o Ctto, Vo o Trb, Bc.
    Canzone à 2, detta la Bianchina: 2V o 2Ctto, Bc.
I-Mcap, -Muc   SartMS I 1629c; RISM P2345

POGLIETTI, Alessandro (*b* Tuscany ? early 17th cent; *d* Vienna, 1683)

    Sonata à 3: Ctto, Fl, Fag, Org.
CS-KRa B IV 191   OttoS
Edition: Musica Rara 1,987

PORTA, Ercole (*b* Bologna, 1585; *d* Carpi, 1630)

Vaga ghirlanda di soavi, & odorati fiori musicali, à 1. 2. 3. 4. & 5. voci . . . opera terza. . . . Bologna: heredi di Gio. Rossi, 1613.
   La Luchina, canzon in risposta: V, Ctto, 2Trb, Bc.
I-Bc (T)   *SartMS I 1613c; RISM P5193

Sacro convito musicale ornato di varie et diverse vivande spirituali a una, due, tre, quattro, cinque, & sei voci . . . opera settima. Venice: Alessandro Vincenti, 1620.
   La Caporale: 2V o 2Ctto, Bc.
D-F; I-Bc   SartMS I 1620a; RISM P5194

PUGLIANI, Francesco (18th cent)
   Sonata per Organo Pieno Con Cornetta: Ctto, Org.
I-Mdemicheli MSS. Mus 4 (ms from 2nd half 18th cent)   *RISM AII 96145

PULITI, F. Gabriello (*b* Montepulciano, *ca* 1575; *d* Istria, 1641/4)

Fantasie scherzi et capricci da sonarsi in forma di canzone, con un violino solo o vero cornetto con il basso principale . . . opera decemanona. . . . Venice: Alessandro Vincenti, 1624.
   11 pieces: V o Ctto, Bc.

1. La Michiela	5. La Diana	9. La Dionisia
2. La Bonzia	6. La Gabriella	10. La Bidigna
3. La Monica	7. La Pulita	11. La Battaglia
4. La Maria	8. La Capricciosa	

I-TSsc (missing Bc)   SartMS II 1624l; RISM P5659

REICHE, Gottfried (*b* Weissenfels, 1667; *d* Leipzig, 1734)

Vier und Zwanzig neue Quatricinia mit einem Cornett und drey Trombonen vornehmlich auff das so genannte Abblasen auff den Rathhäusern oder Thürmen mit Fleiß gestellet. . . . Leipzig: Johann Rölern, 1696.
   24 pieces: Ctto, 3Trb.

1. Sonatina à 4	9. Sonatina à 4	17. Fuga à 4
2. Fuga à 4	10. Sonatina à 4	18. Fuga à 4
3. Sonatina à 4	11. Fuga à 4	19. Fuga à 4
4. Fuga à 4	12. Fuga à 4	20. Sonatina à 4
5. Fuga à 4	13. Fuga à 4	21. Fuga à 4
6. Fuga à 4	14. Fuga à 4	22. Fuga à 4
7. Sonatina à 4	15. Sonatina à 4	23. Fuga à 4
8. Sonatina à 4	16. Sonatina à 4	24. Sonatina à 4

D-B (now in **PL-Kj**)
Edition: Merseburger 1308

RICCIO, Giovanni Battista (Venice, *fl* 1609-21)

Il terzo libro delle divine lodi musicali . . . et alcune canzone da sonare a una 2. 3. et 4. stromenti. Venice: Bartolomeo Magni, 1620.

Canzon: "Flautin" o Ctto, Org.
Canzon La Rubina à 3: 2V o 2Ctto, Trb, Org.
D-F   SartMS I 1620b; RISM R1285
Facs. edition: SPES

ROGNONI TAEGGIO, Francesco (*b* ?Milan; *d* before 1626)

In: *Flores praestantissimorum virorum a Philippo Lomatio bibliopola delibati unica, binis, ternis, quaternisque vocibus decantandi.* Milan: Filippo Lomazzo, 1626.
Canzon prima: 2V o 2Ctto, Org.
Canzon seconda: 2V o 2Ctto, Bc.
I-CEc (S, A, T); **US-R** (C, A, B, Partitura)   SartMS II 1626n

ROSSI, Salomone (Mantua, *ca* 1570-1630)

Il primo libro delle sinfonie et gagliarde a tre, quatro, & a cinque voci . . . per sonar due viole, overo doi cornetti, & un chittarrone o altro istromento da corpo. . . . Venice: Ricciardo Amadino, 1607.
Sinfonia prima. Va sonata alla quarta alta. à 3: [2V o 2Ctto], [b, Chit].
Sinfonia seconda. à 3: [2V o 2Ctto], [b, Chit].
Sinfonia tertia. à 3: [2V o 2Ctto], [b, Chit].
Sinfonia quarta. à 3: [2V o 2Ctto], [b, Chit].
Sinfonia quinta. à 3: [2V o 2Ctto], [b, Chit].
Sinfonia sesta. à 3: [2V o 2Ctto], [b, Chit].
Sinfonia settima. à 3: [2V o 2Ctto], [b, Chit].
Sinfonia ottava. à 3: [2V o 2Ctto], [b, Chit].
Sinfonia nona. à 3: [2V o 2Ctto], [b, Chit].
Sinfonia decima. Va sonata alla quarta alta. à 3: [2V o 2Ctto], [b, Chit].
Sinfonia undecima. à 3: [2V o 2Ctto], [b, Chit].
Sinfonia duodecima. à 3: [2V o 2Ctto], [b, Chit].
Sinfonia tertiadecima. à 3: [2V o 2Ctto], [b, Chit].
Sinfonia quartadecima. à 3: [2V o 2Ctto], [b, Chit].
Sinfonia quintadecima. à 3: [2V o 2Ctto], [b, Chit].
Sinfonia à 4: [V o Ctto], a, t, [b, Chit].
Sinfonia à 4. Su la quarta alta: [V o Ctto], a, t, [b, Chit]
Gagliarda à 4. detta Venturino: [V o Ctto], a, t, [b, Chit]
Gagliarda à 4. detta Marchesino: [V o Ctto], a, t, [b, Chit]
Sonata à 4: [V o Ctto], a, t, [b, Chit].
Sinfonia à 5 & à 3. si placet con doi Soprani, & il chittarrone: [2V o 2Ctto], a, t, [b], Chit.
Sinfonia grave à 5: [2V o 2Ctto], a, t, [b, Chit].
Gagliarde à 5 & à 3. si placet detta L'Andreasina: [2V o 2Ctto], a, t, [b, Chit].
Sinfonia à 5 & à 3. si placet: [2V o 2Ctto], a, t, [b, Chit].
Gagliarde à 5 & à 3. si placet detta la Norsina: [2V o 2Ctto], a, t, [b, Chit].
Gagliarde à 5 detta la Massara: [2V o 2Ctto], a, t, [b, Chit].
Passegio d'un balletto à 5 & à 3. si placet: [2V o 2Ctto], a, t, [b, Chit].

The only indications of instrumentation are those found on the title page as given above, excepting the specification of chitarrone in the title of the first Sinfonia à 5 & à 3. The Sonata à 4 is called *Sinfonia* in the heading of the *Tenore* partbook.

D-As; I-Bc (C1); US-Nsc (in ms EinSC)   RISM R2763
Edition: Mercury Music Corp.; Facs. edition: SPES   SartMS I 1607c

ROVETTA, Giovanni (Venice, *ca* 1595-1668)

Salmi concertati a cinque et sei voci . . . et alcune canzoni per sonar à tre è quatro voci con basso continuo . . . opera prima. . . . Venice: Bartolomeo Magni, ∞1626, †1641.
    Canzon seconda à 3: 2V o 2Ctto, Trb, Bc.
†A-Wgm; **GB**-Lbl; ∞I-Bc (S,A,T,B,5,V1,Bc); **PL**-WRu   RISM R2962/2963
Edition: Ars Antiqua Editions   SartMS I 1626a, 1641e

    Canzona a 4 Voc: Ctto, 3[Trb], Org.
A-KR L 13 (ms from 1633-39)   *RISM AII 600153419

RUFFO, Vincenzo (*b* Verona, *ca* 1508; *d* Sacile, 1587)

    115. Vespere autem sabbati à 6: 2Ctto, 4Trb.
D-Rp Hs. A.R. 775&777 (see under ABRAN)

SCHEIDT, Samuel (*bapt.* 1587; *d* Halle, 1654)

Paduana, galliarda, couranta, alemande, intrada, canzonetto, ut vocant, quaternis, & quinis vocibus, in gratiam musices studiosorum, potissimum violistarum concinnata una cum basso continuo. Hamburg: Michael Hering [Paul Lange], 1621.
    18. Canzon cornetto à 4 voc: 4Ctto, Bc.
It is also interesting to note that in the foreword, no. 21 "Gagliard battaglia," is dedicated to *Zachariae Hartelio, Musico Instrument. Cornet.*
D-EF (T), -UDa (S incompl, Bc); -W (missing Bc); **PL**-WRu (missing B, Bc); **S**-Uu (Bc)
Edition: ScheidtW 2-3.   RISM S1349

SCHEIN, Johann Hermann (*b* Grünhain nr. Annaberg, 1586; *d* Leipzig, 1630)

Banchetto musicale newer anmutiger Padouanen, Gagliarden, Courenten und Allemenden à 5. auff allerley Instrumenten, bevoraus auff Violen. . . . Leipzig: A. Lamberg & C. Klosemann, 1617.
    Intrada à 4: Ctto, V, Fl, b.
D-B (1 partbook, now in **PL**-Kj), -Kl, -Mbs (5); -UDa (S)   RISM S1376
Edition: ScheinW 9

SCHMELZER, Johann Heinrich (*b* Scheibbs, L. Austria, *ca* 1620/3; *d* Prague, 1680)

Sacro-profanus concentus musicus fidium aliorumque instrumentorum. Nürnberg: Michael Endter, 1662.
    Sonata II a otto, due cori: V, 3Va, Cttino, 3Trb, Org.
    Sonata XII a sette: 2Cttino, 2Tpt, 3Trb, Org.

A-Wn (missing parsIV); **D-**W; **F-**Pn; **S-**Uu; **US-**Wc; (Sonata XII also in ms **S-**Uu inst mus i hs 8:16; (also in ms **CS-**KRa B IV 34 (incompl) & B IV 78).   RISM S1658
Editions: DTÖ 111-112; Brass Press (sonata XII); Musica Rara (both sonatas)

    From Draghi's *Il trionfator de' centauri* (1674)
    Balletto di centauri, ninfe et salvatici à 3 chori . . . per la festa A. Schonbrun: ChI
    5 "Viole radopiati"; ChII 3 "Piffari," Fag; ChIII 2Ctto muto, 3Trb; Org.
A-Wn; **CS-**KRa B XIV 29 (dated 1674)   OttoS
Edition: DTÖ 56

    Sonata à 4 detta la Carioletta: V, Ctto, Trb, Fag, Bc.
CS-KRa B IV 213 (dated 1669)   OttoS
Edition: Musica Rara 1,703

    From the Theaterfestspiel *La flecha del amore* (1672)
    Balletto de spiritelli (Sonatina, Intrada Aria, Retirada): V "Piffarato," 2Ctto muto
    o 2Va "piffaro," 2V, 2Va, Vo, 3Trb, Org.
A-Wn ms. 16583, no. 91; **CS-**KRa B XIV 25
Edition: DTÖ 56

SELLE, Thomas (sinfonias: see entries in vocal list)

SIEFERT, Paul (Danzig, 1586-1666)
Psalmorum Davidicorum, ad Gallicam melodiam arte compositorum musicali, qui diversis sistuntur partibus, à 4. 5. 6. 7. 8. vocibus . . . pars secunda. . . . Danzig: Autor Typgrphèo Rhetanio, 1651.
    16. Canzon à 8 *ad placitum*; ChI 3V o 3Ctto, Trb; ChII 3Trb, Trb "grosso"; Org.
The print also contains 11 vocal works with symphonias specifying cornett (see vocal list).
S-Uu   MitUB
*Edition: Franz Kessler, *Danziger Instrumental-Musik des 17. und 18. Jahrhunderts* (Neuhausen-Stuttgart: Hänssler, 1979)

SPEER, Daniel (*b* Breslau, 1636; *d* Göppingen, 1707)
Recens fabricatus labor, oder neugebachene Taffel-Schnitz von mancherley lustigen Rencken und Schwencken . . . mit 1. 2. 3. Sing-Stimmen und 2. Violinen . . . Item . . . Stücklein mit underschiedlichen Instrumenten insonderheit vor die Kunst-Pfeiffer zum Auffwarten bequem, mit Trompeten, Cornetten, Trombonen, und Fagotten, samt einer Party mit 5. Violen. . . . Frankfurt: n.p., 1685.
    13. Aufzug à 6: 6Tpt o 6 Ctto & Trb.
    14. Aufzug à 6: 6Tpt o 6 Ctto & Trb.
    15. Sonata à 5: 2Ctto, 3Trb, Bc.
    16. Sonata à 5: 2Ctto, 3Trb, Bc.
    18. Sonata à 4: Tpt o Ctto, 3Trb, Bc.
    19. Sonata à 4: Ctto, 3Trb, Bc.

CH-Zz (missing V2, Vo); **D**-F (V2, Vo); **F**-Pn; **R**-Sb (V2)   RISM S4070
Editions: EdM 1. Reihe, 14; Schott BLK 104

Musicalisch-Türckischer Eulen-Spiegel . . . mit Ungarisch- Griechisch- Moscowitisch-Wallachisch- Kosakisch- Rusnakisch- und Pohlnisch-lustigen Balleten mit ihren Proportionibus, auch andern nützlichen blasend- und geigenden Sonnaten. . . . Güntz: n.p., 1688.
    25. Sonata à 5: 2Ctto, 3Trb, Bc.
    29. Sonata à 5: 2Ctto, 3Trb, Bc.
    30. Sonata à 5: 2Ctto, 3Trb, Bc.
For Sonata 29. the heading in the canto I partbook specifies *Clarin I*; the canto II partbook specifies *Cornetto II*.
D-W; **US**-Wc   RISM S4072

Grund-richtiger, kurtz-leicht- und nöthiger, jetzt wol-vermehrter Unterricht der musicalischen Kunst. . . . Ulm: Georg Wilhelm Kühne, 1697.
    6 pieces: 2Ctto, Trb.
B-Bc; **D**-B; -LEm; **F**-Pn; **GB**-Lbl, -Lcm; **S**-Sk (incompl); **US**-NYp, -Wc
Facs. edition: Peters

SPIEGLER, Matthias (*b* Markdorf, Baden, *ca* 1595; *d* after 1631)

Olor solymaeus nascenti Iesu, moriturus ipse, praecinens. . . . Ravensburg: Johann Schöter, 1631.
    Canzon à 2: Cttino, Fag, Org.
    Canzon à 3: 2V o 2Cttino[o 2Ctto], Fag, Org.
    Canzon à 3: 2V o 2Cttino, Fag, Org.
    Capriccio à 3: 2V o 2Cttino, Fag, Org.
The partbook heading of the first Canzon à 3 indicates *Doi Violini, o Cornetti*. This print also contains 56 vocal pieces, two of which are with instruments.
D-Rp; **PL**-WRu (S2 incompl, T, Org)   RISM S4097
Editions: EdM 1. Reihe, 14; Musica Rara 1,830 (Canzon à 2)

STADEN, Sigmund Gottlieb (*bapt.* Kulmbach, *ca* 1607; *d* Nürnberg, 1655)

In: Georg Philipp Harsdörffer, *Frauenzimmer Gesprechspiele . . . fünfter Theil.* Nürnberg: Wolfgang Endter, 1645.
    Der VII Tugenden, Planeten, Tone oder Stimmen. Aufzug. In kunst-zierliche Melodien gesetzt. Symphonia vor dem 1. Aufzuge: [2Ctto], Org.
The instrumentation for the Symphonia is given as *3 Corneten oder Zincken, und einem Positif.* This may, however, be an error, since the piece has two voices in soprano clef and one voice in bass clef with figures.
CH-Zz; **D**-DI, -ERu, -HEu (2X), -HVl, -KNu, -Mbs (2X), -MZs, -Ngm (2X), -Nst, -NEhz, -OLl, -Tu, -Us, -W; **GB**-Lbl; **US**-Cn, -NH   RISM S427
Edition: AIM, *Studies and Documents* 14

STÖRL, Johann Georg Christian (*b* Kirchberg an der Jagst, 1675; *d* Stuttgart, 1719)

    6 Sonatas: Ctto, 3 Trb.

D-BI (lost)

*Edition: EdM 1. Reihe, 14

STRADELLA, Alessandro (*b* Rome, 1644; *d* Genoa, 1682)

    Sonata à 4. due violini, e due cornetti divisi in due chori: ChI 2V, Bc; ChII 2Ctto; Bc.

In the Torino ms the title appears as above and the *partitura* gives the following instrumentation: "P. Ch°." – "Violini," "2°. Ch°." – "Cornetti." In the Modena ms only the title "[Sinfonia à] 2V solo" appears.

I-MOe ms. mus. F. 1129, pp. 1-13; -Tn ms. Foà 11, f. 84-92

Edition: Edward H. Tarr, ed., *Archives de la musique instrumentale*, 11 (Paris: Costallat, 1968)

STRAUSS, Christoph (sinfonias: see *Missae . . . octo, novem* [1631] in vocal list)

STRIGGIO, Alessandro (Mantua, *b ca* 1540; *d* 1592)

    76. Ecco ch'io lass'il core à 6: 2Ctto, 3Trb, "Pumart."

D-Rp Hs. A.R. 775&777 (see under ABRAN)

TELEMANN, Georg Philipp (*b* Magdeburg, 1681; *d* Hamburg, 1767)

    Sinfonia [F major]: Fl, VaG, V, Ob, 2Va, Vo, Ctto, 3Trb, Bc.

D-DS ms. 1034/43   RISM AII 10096

Edition: Schott 5687

THORETTE, Pierre (*b ca* 1620; *d* Liège, 1684)

    Chasse de St. Hubert: 2V, 2Ctto o 2Fl, 2Corno da caccia, Fag, Bc.

B- Lc   *GroveD

TOLAR, Jan Křtitel [Johannes Baptista Dolar] (fl Bohemia/Moravia, late 17th cent)

    Sonata à 13: 2V, 2Va, 2Tpt, 2Ctto, 4Trb, Fag, Vo, Org.

CS-KRa B IV 71

Edition: MAB 40, no. 5

URBANO, Gregorio

Sacri armonici concentus singulis, binis, ternis, quaternis vocibus concinendi nec non, & symphonia tribus instrumentis. . . . Venice: Bartolomeo Magni, 1640.

    Simphonia La Barbisona: 2Ctto, Trb, Org.

PL-WRu (C2,A/B,Org; missing Ctto1 of sinfonia) SartMS I&II 1640d; RISM U102

USPER, Francesco [SPONGA] (*b* Parenzo, Istria, before 1570; *d* Venice, 1641)
Compositioni armoniche nelle quali si contengono motetti sinfonie sonate canzoni &
capricci a 1. 2. 3. 4. 5. 6. 7. & 8. voci . . . opera terza. . . . Venice: Bartolomeo Magni,
1619.
    Sonata à 8 con quattro soprani: 2V, 2Ctto, 4Trb, Bc.
There are no instrumental indications on the cornett or violin parts, but a heading on the
basso continuo says: *Con quattro soprani & doi cornetti.* The print also contains 2
vocal pieces specifying cornett (see vocal list).
D-B (compl, now in **PL**-Kj); **US**-Nsc (in ms EinSC)   SartMS I&II 1619a

UTENDAL, Alexander (*b* Netherlands, *ca* 1530-40; *d* Innsbruck, 1581)
    96. Adesto dolori meo à 6: 2Ctto, Trb, 3"Pumart."
    117. Plangent eum à 6: 2Ctto, 3Trb, "Pumart."
D-Rp Hs. A.R. 775&777 (see under ABRAN)

UTRECHT, Heinrich (*b* Minden; *d* 1634 or later)
Concertatio musicalis etlicher Toccaten, Ricercare, Padovanen, Galliarden, auff ein
Cornet Fagot oder Violino und Viola di Gamba mit zwo Stimmen neben einem General
Baß gesetzet. Celle: E. Holwein, 1631.
    19 pieces: Ctto o V, Fag o VaG, Bc.
D-Kdma (microfilm of S-V); **S**-V (C,2ª vox incompl)   *GroveD   RISM U129

VALENTINI, Giovanni (*b* Venice, 1582/3; *d* Vienna, 1649)
    Canzon à 2: Ctto, Trb, Org Bc.
A-KR L 13 (ms from 1633-39)   RISM AII 600153161

    Sonata: 2Ctto.
    Sonata: 2Ctto muto, Va, VaG.
A-Wn ms. 19421

    Sonata à 4: V, Cttino, Trb, Fag, Org.
D-Kl ms. 60q; -Kdma

    Sonata à 5: 2V, 2Ctto, Trb, Bc.
PL-WRu (lost)   *BohnH

VEJVANOVSKÝ, Pavel Josef (*b* Hukvaldy, *ca* ?1633/39; *d* Kroměříž, 1693)
    Sonata à 6: 2V, 2Ctto, Tpt, Vo, [Org].
CS-KRa B IV 177   OttoS
Edition: MAB 49, part 3

    Sonata Ittalica à 12: 3V, 2Ctto, 3Tpt, 4Va[G], Org.
CS-KRa B IV 53 (dated 1668)   OttoS
Edition: Musica Rara

VIADANA, Lodovico (*b* Viadana nr. Parma, *ca* 1560; *d* Gualtieri nr. Parma, 1627)

Cento concerti ecclesiastici a una due, a tre, & quattro voci. Con il basso continuo per sonar nell'organo . . . opera duodecima. Venice: Giacomo Vincenti, ∞1602, 1603, 1604, †1605, ‡1607, 1608, 1610, 1612, §1615.
    3. Fratres ego enim, Canto solo o Tenore: S o T o Ctto, Org.
    4. Accipite et manducate, seconda parte, Canto solo over Cornetto: S o Ctto, Org.
    104. Canzon Francese in risposta: V, Ctto, 2Trb, Org.
The following instructions for an alternative instrumental setting are in the basso continuo partbook for "Fratres ergo enim" and "Accipite et manducate": *Sonando questo Concerto co'l Cornetto l'Organista Sonara la quarta alto. . . .*
∞**D**-Rp (T); †**I**-Bc; **D**-As; ‡**GB**-Lbl; **D**-Rp; **I**-R (A); §**D**-B (now in **PL**-Kj)
            SartMS I&II 1602a, I 1605i, 1607h, 1612d; RISM V1360/V1367
Edition: Bärenreiter, 1964-

Centum concertum ecclesiasticorum I. II. III. IV. vocum. . . . Frankfurt: N. Stein, 1609.
(The contents are the same as the above.)
A-Wn (SATB)   SartMS I 1609c; RISM V1394

VIERDANCK, Johann (*b ca* 1605; *d* Stralsund, 1646)

Erster Theil newer Pavanen, Gagliarden, Balletten und Correnten. . . . Greifswald: J. Jeger, 1637. Rostock: †Johann Hallevord, 1641.
    11 suites (Pavane, Gagliarde, Ballo, Corente): 2V, Vo o VaG; o 2Cttino, Fag; Bc.
The preface reads: *Alß erinnere ich frendliche hierbey, Daß diese Pavanen und Gagliarden eigentlich auff keine andere Instrumente alß Geigen gerichtet seyn, da die zween Discant auff Violinen, der Bass auff einem Violen oder Viola di Gamba. . . . Doch stehets einem jedwedern frey, ob er an statt einer oder aller beyder Discant Geigen, Cornettini, oder QuartZincken nebenst einem Fagott gebrauchen wil. . . .*
F-Psg (B); †**D**-Bi (V1); **D**-B (4 partbooks, now in **PL**-Kj), -Kdma [3/1966]   MGG 13, 1606   RISM V1458/1459
Edition: *Organum*, 3. Reihe, 4 (one suite)

Ander Theil darinnen begriffen etliche Capricci, Canzoni und Sonaten. mit 2. 3. 4. und 5. Instrumenten ohne und mit dem Basso Continuo. . . . Rostock: Johann Richel, 1641.
    1. Capriccio à 2: 2Ctto o 2V.
    2. Capriccio à 2: 2Ctto o 2V.
    3. Capriccio à 2: 2Ctto o 2V.
    5. Sonata: 2Ctto.
    6. Sonata: 2Ctto.
    7. Capriccio à 3: 3Ctto o 3V.
    8. Capriccio à 3: 3Ctto o 3V.
    9. Capriccio à 3: 3Ctto o 3V.
    10. Capriccio à 3: 3Ctto o 3V.
    11. Capriccio à 3: 3Ctto o 3V.
    12. Capriccio à 3: 3Ctto o 3V.
    13. Capriccio à 3: 3Ctto o 3V.
    14. Capriccio à 3: 3Ctto o 3V.

17. Capriccio mit zwey Cornettinen, oder Violinen, sonderlich darzu gerichtet, ob sich zwey Musici in einer Orgel oder anderen Corpore alleine wolten horen lassen: 2Ctto o 2V, Org.
18. Capriccio (as for no. 17): 2Ctto o 2V, Org.
19. Capriccio (as for no. 17): 2Ctto o 2V, Org.
26. Capriccio: 3Ctto, "grossen Fagott," Bc.
27. Sonata: Ctto, 3Trb, Bc.
28. Sonata: Ctto, 3Trb, Bc.
29. Sonata: 2Ctto, 2V, Bc.
31. Sonata worin die Melodia des Liedes: Als ich einmahl Lust bekam etc. enthalten: 2Ctto, 3Trb, Bc.

D-B (compl, now in **PL**-Kj), -Kdma [3/1967], -W (prima vox)　　　RISM V1460
Partial edition: HM 21

VIRGILIANO, Aurelio (*fl ca* 1600)

Del dolcimelo . . . libro secondo. Dove si contengono ricercate fiorite; e madrigali con canzoni diminuite, per sonar uagamente con ogni sorte d'instrumento.
1. Ricercar facile di Flauto: Cornetto: Violino: Traversa e simili.
4. Ricercata per Cornetto: Violino: Traversa et altri Instrumenti.
6. Ricercata per Traversa: Violino: Cornetto et altri Instrumenti.
7. Ricercata per Flauto: Cornetto: Violino: Traversa; e simili in battaglia.
8. Ricercar come di sopra.
9. Ricercar come di sopra.
10. Ricercar come di sopra.
12. Ricercar di Flauto: Cornetto: Violino: Traversa; e simili.
14. Ricercar di Flauto: Cornetto: Violino: Traversa; e simili.
16. Ricercar di Cornetto: Violino: Traversa; e simili.

I-Bc
Facs. edition: SPES; Edition: London Pro Musica REP 1

WALTER, Johann (*b* Kahla, Thuringia, 1496; *d* Torgau, 1570)

Fugen auf die acht tonos zwei- und dreistimmig sonderlich auf Zinken.
2 Fugen: sb.　　　6 Fugen: ss.　　　2 Fugen: bb.　　　1 Fuge: ssb.
4 Fugen: bbb.　　10 Fugen: sss.　　2 Fugen: stb.

D-LEu Cod Mus. 50 (dated 1542)
Partial editions: *Johann Walter Sämtliche Werke* 4 (Kassel: Bärenreiter, 1973); HM 63

WECKMANN, Matthias (*b* Niederdorla nr. Mühlhausen, *ca* 1619; *d* Hamburg, 1674)

1. Sonata à 4: Cttino, V, Trb, Fag, Bc.
2. Sonata à 4: V, Cttino, Trb, Fag, Bc.
3. Sonata à 4: V, Cttino, Trb, Fag, Bc.
4. Sonata à 4: V, Cttino, Trb, Fag, Bc.
5. Sonata à 4: Cttino, V, Trb o VaBr, Bomb o Fag, Bc.
6. Sonata à 4: V, Cttino, Trb, Bomb o Fag, Bc.
7. Sonata à 4: V, Cttino, Trb, Fag o Bomb, Bc.

   8. Sonata à 3: Cttino o V, V, Fag, Bc.
   9. Sonata à 4: V, Cttino, Trb, Fag o Bomb, Bc.
   10. Sonata à 3: Cttino o V, V, VaG o Trb, Bc.
D-Lr K.N. 207/14   WelterRL
Editions: EdM 2. Reihe (Schleswig-Holstein), 4; Musica Rara 1,698 (one sonata à 4)

WEICHMANN, Johann (sinfonia: see *Der CXXXIII Psalm* [1649] in vocal list)

WERT, Giaches de (*b* Weert nr. Antwerp, 1535; *d* Mantua, 1596)

   84. Iaus_rt iam alla__It [Text unreadable] à 8: 2Ctto, 2"Pumart," 4Trb.
   94. Adesto dolori meo à 6: 2Ctto, 2"Pumart," 2Trb.
D-Rp Hs. A.R. 775&777 (see under ABRAN)

WHYTHORNE, Thomas (*b* Ilminster, 1528; *d* London, 1596)

*Cantus. Of duos or songs for two voices . . . The Second which doth begin at the XXIII.
song, are made for two children to sing. Also they may be aptly made for two treble
Cornets to play or sound: or otherwise for voices or Musical Instruments that be of the
lyke compasse or distance in sound.* London: Thomas Este, the assigne of William
Byrd, 1590.
   15 Songs (nos. 23-37): SA o 2Ctto.
GB-Lbl, -Ob (B)   BrownIM 159011; RISM W993
Edition: Walter Bergman, ed. (London: Schott, 1955)

ZIELEŃSKI, Mikolaj (*fl* 1611)

*Communiones totius anni, quibus in solennioribus festis Sanctae Romanae Ecclesiae
uti consuevit ad cantum organi per unam, duas, tres, quattuor, quinque, & sex voces
tum instrumentis musicalibus, & vocis resolutione, quam itali gorgia vocant,
decantanda . . . & tres fantasiae instrumentis musicalibus accommodatae. . . .* Venice:
Giacomo Vincenti, 1611.
   23. Fantasia: Ctto e Fag, o V e Va"grossa."
   27. Fantasia: 2Ctto e Fag, o 2V e Va"grossa."
   28. Fantasia: 2Ctto e Fag, o 2V e Va"grossa."
PL-Kc (partitura pro organo), -WRu (CAT) [RISM says 8 St., org]   RISM Z 200

VOCAL MUSIC SPECIFYING CORNETT

ABRAN, [EBRAM] (see instrumental list)

AGNELLI, Lorenzo (1610-1674)
Il secondo libro de motteti. . . .   Venice: Alessandro Vincenti, 1638.
   Plateae tuae: ST, Ctto, Fag, Bc.
I-Bc (incompl: S,A,Bc); **PL**-WRu (incompl: S,T,Bc)

AGRICOLA, Georg Ludwig (*b* Grossfurra, Thuringia,1643; *d* Gotha, 1676)
   Gott, man lobet dich in der Stille: SATB *conc & cap*, 2V, Ctto, 2Tpt, 3Trb, Org Bc.
The composer may be Frieddrich Heinrich Agricola.
D-BII Mus. ms. 365 (Erfurt collection, parts dated 1682) NoackE RISM AII 150087

AHLE, Johann Rudolph (Mühlhausen, 1625-1673)
Neu-gepflantzter thüringischer Lustgarten, in welchen XXVI Neue geistliche
musicalische Gewächse mit 3.4.5.6.7.8.10. und mehr Stimmen . . . mit und ohne
Instrumenten, mit und ohne Capellen, auch theils mit und ohne General Bass zu
brauchen versetzet. . . . *Theil I.* Mühlhausen: Johann Hueter, 1657.
   24.   Magnificat, Anima mea Dominum ab 8: SATB, Ctto o V, 2Trb o 2Va, Vo o
      Trb, Bc.
   25.   Wie ein lieber Buhle: ChI&II SATB; 2Tpt o 2Ctto *ad plac.*
A-Wgm; **D**-BI (3), -B (9 partbooks now in **PL**-Kj), -BD, -BÜ (1,2,3,4,5,7,8,Bc), -Dlb
(1,2,3,7,8), -EII (1,2,3), -FBsk (2,3,5,Bc), -GOI (2,4,5,6), -HAmk, -Kl, -MLHr, -SAh
(1,2,3,4,5,Bc), -UDa (2,7), -W; **GB**-Lbl, -Lcm (incompl); **PL**-Tu (1), -WRu (2,4,5,6
7,8,Bc); **S**-Uu; **US**-NYp (8)   MitUB   RISM A485
Edition: DdT 5

Neugepflantzen thüringischen Lustgartens Nebengang, in welchem X neue geistliche
musicalische Concertgewächse, mit 3.4.5.6.7.8.10 und mehr Stimmen zu dem Basso
Continuo . . . versetzet. Mühlhausen: Autor (Johann Hüter); Erfurt: Johann Bircker,
1663.
   8.   Sie ist fest gegruendet a 7 & 12: SSATB, cappella à 5, 2V, Bc; 2Trb, 2Tpt,
      2Ctto, e 2Fl *si placet.*
D-Dlb (1,2,3,Bc), -EII (1,2,3), -MLHr (1,2,4,5,6,Bc), -SAh (1,2,3,4,5); **PL**-WRu
(1,2,3,5,6,Bc); **S**-Uu (1,2/3,4/5, instrumentum 1,2,Bc)   RISM A488

ALBRICI, Vincenzo (*b* Rome, 1631; *d* Prague, 1696)
   Domine Deus exercituum rex à 9 o à 20: ChI SATB, 2V, 2Va, Fag, Org; ChII
   SATB, 2Ctto, 3Trb, Bc.
   Aurora lucis emicat: SATB, SATB, 2V, 2Va, Fag, 2Cttino, 2Trb, Bc.
This ms, entitled *XIX lateinische Kirchenstücke von Albrici*, contains 19 works by
Albrici in various instrumentations.
D-BII Mus. ms. 501 (Bokemeyer collection, score), -Kdma [2/1692] [2/1696]
KümmerKB   RISM AII 150313

Omnis Caro foemum: SATB, Cttino, V, Trb, Fag, Org.
D-Dlb Mus. ms. 1821 E 502   *BernC; SeiffertL

In convertendo Dominus captivitatem à 10, 14, 15, o 20: SSATB, 2V, 2Va, Fag, 2Cttino, 2Trb, Org.
D-Dlb Mus. ms. 1821 E503

Amo te laudo te à 6: SS, 2Cttino, Fag, "spinetta," Org.
The *spinetta* and organ parts are not identical; the *spinetta* is only specified for the *sinfonie* and *ritornelli*. SeiffertL lists a piece with identical name and setting but with *cornetti* instead of *cornettini*.
S-Uu Vok. Mus. i hs 47:4 (parts), 82:2 (score)

Benedicte Domine Jesu à 6: SSB, 2V o 2Ctto, Fag o VaG, b, Org.
S-Uu Vok. Mus. i hs 1:4 (parts, missing Ctto2); 81:54 ff. 54-56 (score dated 1665)
                                                                    RISM AII 86052

ALDROVANDINI, [Giuseppe Antonio Vincenzo] (Bologna, 1672/3-1707)

Chirie, è Gloria à 4 con stru:ti Anno 1708 li 28 Aprile: SATB *conc & cap*, 2V, Va, Ctto, Trb, Vo, Bc.
The score indicates oboe instead of cornett, and there is no indication of trombone.
I-Bof ms. 3 (score and parts)

ALTENBURG, Michael (*b* Alach nr. Erfurt, 1584; *d* Erfurt, 1640)

Der dritte Theil. Christlicher, lieblicher und andächtiger newer Kirchen und Hauß Gesänge. . . . Zweene newe Intraden 10. voc. zu 2. Choren, da der erste auff Geigen, der ander auff Zincken und Posaunen geruchtet, oder nur auff das Orgelwerck, darein ein ChoralStimm . . . kan gesungen werden. . . . Erfurt: J. Röhstock, †1620, ∞1621.
    21. Intrada 10 voc. Gleich wie sich sein ein Vögelein: ChI 5 "Geigen"; ChII S[*cap*], "[1] Zincken und [3] Posaunen" o Org.
    22. Intrada 10 voc. Ein feste Burg ist unser Gott: ChI 5 "Geigen"; ChII S[*cap*], "[1] Zincken und [3] Posaunen" o Org.
The soprano vocal part, a simple chorale tune, is designated as a "*General Diskant vor die Schulmäglein.*"
†**D**-B (8 partbooks: S,A,T,B,5,6,7,8, now in **PL**-Kj), -DLb (S,A,B), -Kdma, -NA, -SAh (S,A,B); **GB**-Lbl (S); ∞**D**-SAh (T,B,5,6,7,8), -HAh (B)   RISM A889/890

ANERIO, Giovanni Francesco (*b* Rome, *ca* 1567; *d* Graz, 1630)

Teatro armonico spirituale di madrigali a cinque, sei, sette, & otto voci concertati con il basso per l'organo. . . . Rome: G. B. Robletti, 1619.
    Due figli un padre avea à 6: SSATTB *conc & cap*, V, V o Ctto, Ctto, Lt, Tior, Org. (with sinfonia)
    Eccone al gran Damasco à 8: SATB, SATB, 2V, Lt, Ctto, Tior, Org. (with sinfonia: "Combattimento con l'instrumenti")
D-B (1 part, now in **PL**-Kj), -Rp (T,6,7); **F**-Pc (S1,S2,A,T,B,6,8,Org); **I**-Rc (S2,T, 6,7,Org), -Rsc, -Sac (7)   RISM A1123

Edition: In Howard Smither, Concentus Musicus, 7, *Oratorios of the Italian Baroque I* (Laaber: Laaber-Verlag, 1985)

ANONYMOUS (arranged by library and call number)

Hymn de Ss.ma Trinitate: O lux beata: SAB, V, V o Ctto, Ctto, Fag, Org.
A-KR L 13   *RISM AII 600153431

Messe: Ch[?], 2V, Va, 2Ob, Fag, Ctto, 2Tpt, 2Tpt[princ], 2Trb, Timp, Vc, Org.
A-Wn mus hs 1769 (ms from mid-18th cent)   *card catalog

Missa ultimum vale: 8v *conc & cap*, 2V, 2Va, 2Ctto, 3Trb, 4Tpt, Vo, Org.
CS-KRa B I 86   OttoS

Missa Rubra: 8v, 2V, 3Va, 2Tpt, 3Trb, [2Ctto, Timp], Vo, Org.
CS-KRa B I 168[20]   OttoS

Missa absque nomine: 8v *conc*, 4v *cap*, 2V, 2Va, 2Ctto, 5Tpt, 3Trb, Timp, Vo, Org.
CS-KRa B I 226   OttoS

[Missa]: ATTBB *conc*, 8v *cap*, 2V, 3Va, 2Ctto, 4Trb, Fag, bVa, Vo.
CS-KRa B I 278 (missing S,S,A)   OttoS

[Missa]: 8v, 2V, 4Va, 2Ctto 3Trb, Vo, Org.
CS-KRa B I 280   OttoS

[Missa]: 8v, 2V, 2Ctto, 4Tubae, Org, Bc.
CS-KRa B I 283   OttoS

Exaltabo in te Domine: SATB *conc & cap*, 2V, Trb, [Ctto], 3Trb *ad lib*, Vo, Org.
CS-KRa B II 9   OttoS

Offertorium de Ascensione Domini. Ascendit Deus in jubilo: 8v, 2V 2Ctto, 4Tpt *in conc*, Bc.
CS-KRa B II 128   OttoS

O venerabile: AA, 2Ctto, bVa, Org.
CS-KRa B II 273 (possibly identical to Capricornus, O venerabile)   OttoS

Regnum mundi et omne ornamentum: 5v *conc & cap*, 2V, 2Ctto, 3Trb *ad lib*, Vo, Org.
CS-KRa B II 317 (dated 1672, missing Trb parts)   OttoS

---

[20] The inscription "*G.Z.G. 8 bris 1674*" appears at the end of the organ part.

Litaniae Laurentanae: 5v *conc*, 4v *cap*, 2V, 2Ctto, [Bc].
CS-KRa B V 63 (dated 1666)   OttoS

Salve Regina à 12: SSATB, 2V, 2Ctto, 3Trb, [Bc].
CS-KRa B VI 30 (dated 1666)   OttoS

Ich will euch mir vertrauen: SATB, V, 2V, Va, 2Tpt, 2Ctto, Fag, Vo, Timp, Bc.
D-BI   *NoackE

Magnificat: ChI&II SATB; 2V, 2Vtta, 2Ctto, 3Trb, Fag, Bc.
D-BI Mus. ms. anon. 30240 (Bokemeyer collection, score)   *KümmerKB

Herr, der König freuet sich: SSATB *conc & rip*, 2V o 2Ctto, 2Trb, Trb o Fag o Vo,
Org, Bc.
D-BII Mus. ms. anon. 648 (Erfurt coll., parts dated 1677, attrib. to "M.B." on ms)
*NoackE; *WalkerSB

Seht euch vor, für den falschen Propheten: ATTB *conc*, SATB *cap*, 2V o 2Ctto,
2Va o 2Trb, Vo o Trb, Bc.
D-BII Mus. ms. anon. 1011 (dated 1680, ms by J.C. Appelman)   *NoackE

Allein Gott in der Höh (missa in F): SSATTB, 2V, 2Fl, 2Ctto, 2Va o 2Trb, Trb o
Fag, Bc.
Missa ex F: SSATTB, 2V, 3Va, 2Fl, 2Ctto, Trb o Fag, Bc.
It is possible that these are the same work, listed under different titles with different
instrumentations by their respective secondary sources.
D-BII Mus. ms. anon. 1037   *NoackE; *WalkerSB

Ich weiß daß mein Erlöser lebet: SSATB *conc & cap*, 2V o 2Ctto, 2Tpt, Bc.
D-BII Mus. ms. anon. 1203 & 1204 (Erfurt, score and parts dated 1680)   *NoackE

Christ lag in Todesbanden: 5v *conc & rip*; Cttino, V*piccolo*, 3 Viol, 3 Bomb, Bc.
This could be the same piece as D-Dlb 1825 E 525 by Kuhnau.
D-Dl [?] Dresden Fürstenschule (Grimma U 335/N34)
*Friedhelm Krummacher, "Zur Sammlung Jacobi der ehemalige Fürstenschule
Grimma," *Die Musikforschung* 16, no. 4 (Oct.-Dec. 1963): 346.

Dancket dem Herrn: SSATB *conc & rip*, 2V o 2Ctto, 2Tpt, 2Va o 2Trb, Fag o Trb,
Bc.
D-Dlb mus. ms. 2 E 511 (Grimma U 510/T48; Grimma U 320/N7, parts)   *WalkerSB

Die Engel sind allzumal dienstbare Geisten: SATB, 2V, Va, 2Ctto, Bc.
D-Dlb mus. ms. 2 E 601 (Grimma a.5./T56, score & parts)   *WalkerSB

Jubilate Deo omnis terra: SSATB, 2V, 2Ctto, 2Tpt, 2Trb, Fag, Bc.
D-F   *SüssKM

Dies ist der Tag: SSATB, 2V, 2Fl, 2Ctto, 2Tpt, Vo, Org.
D-F ms. Ff. mus. 6   *SüssKM

Lob, Ehr sei Gott: SSATB, 2V, 2Fl, Ctto, 2Tpt, Vo, Bc.
D-F ms. Ff. mus. 7   *WalkerSB

Jauchzet Gott alle Land: SATB, 2V, 2Tpt, 2Ctto, 2Hn, Bc.
D-F ms. Ff. mus. 16   *WalkerSB

Wohl dem der den Herrn fürchtet: ATB, 2V, 2Va, 2Ctto, 2Tpt, Fag, Vo, Org.
D-F ms. Ff. mus. 34   *SüssKM

Veni Sancte Spiritus: ATB, 2V, Bc (the tenor is designated for cornett in the ms).
D-Kl mus. ms. 2° 51h   *EngelKH

Dulcis Jesu: ChI TTTB, Ctto, V; ChII STTB, Ctto, V; ChIII
D-Kl mus. ms. 2° 53/0   *EngelKH

Ich bin eine Blume zu Saron: SSATB, 2V, 2Ctto, Fag, Bc.
D-Kl mus. ms. 2° f. 58b   *EngelKH

Komm Gott Hymen gib Gedeyen à 10: SSATTB, 2V, Cttino, Fag o Vo, Bc.
D-Kl mus. ms. 2° 58d (missing Cttino part)   *EngelKH

Philothea. Id est: Anima deo chara, comoedia sacra anno 1643 & 1658. . . . Münich:
Johann Wagner (Johann Jaecklin), 1669.
    11v; 3V, 4Va[G], 3Ctto, 4Trb.
D-Mbs; **F**-Pn (missing V4/Trb4)   *RISM AN2139

2. O Jesulein Zart à 10: S[S]AT[B], 2Ctto o 2V, 2Trb, o 2Va, [?], Org.
3. O Jesulein o Gottes Sohn: S[S]AT[B], 2Ctto o 2V, 2Trb, o 2Va, [?], Org.
4. Kleine Kinder große Kinder à 10: S[S]AT[B], 2Ctto o 2V, 2Trb, o 2Va, Org.
5. Ein kleines Kinderlein à 10: S[S]AT[B], 2Ctto o 2V, 2Trb, o 2Va, [?], Org.
D-Rp Hs. A.R. 589-592 (incompl)

D-Rp Hs. A.R. 775&777 (see instrumental list under ABRAN)

17. Dixit Dominus: S[?]AATTB [?], with Ctto & V in ripieno
D-Rp Hs. A.R. 988 (incompl)

Martin Wincklers . . . Anno 1701. Domin.1. post Trinitatis in der St. Michaelis
Kirche abgelegtes Proben Stücke.
Aria "Was du tust sobedenke das Ende": T, V, Cttino, Trb, Org o Vo.
Ritornello post V. 1.: Cttino, Org o Vo.
Ritornello post V. 2.: V, Org o Vo.
Ritornello post V. 3.: Trb, Org o Vo.

Post V. 4. Sonata da capo und Was du tust et claudatur
D-ZZ (dated 1701)   *WernerZ

Christian Dilesii Anno 1704 abgelegtes Proben Stücke
Ich will den Herrn loben: B, V, Ob, Tpt, Ctto, Trb, Vo o Fag, Org.
D-ZZ (dated 1704)   *WernerZ

Se pur ti guardi: Ctto [other voices?]
DK-Kk (R135) (ms from *ca* 1556)   *RISM AII 203009

Laudate Dominum à 8: [AAAABBBB], 4Ctto, 4Trb.
Partbooks containing this piece bear the stamped date *1541*. Each partbook has the handwritten inscription *mit 4 zincken und 4 pusaun* for this piece. The ranges of the cornett parts are g – g'. The vocal assignments are editorial, as all partbooks are untexted. More information is needed to determine whether this piece and others of the manuscript represent autonomous instrumental versions or instrumental parts to double a choir.
DK-Kk ms. Gl. Kgl. Samling 1872, 4° (index no. 158)
Edition: Ed. Henrik Glahn, *Music from the Time of Christian III*, Dania Sonans, Part 3, No. 12 (Copenhagen: Egtved, 1986)

Buccinate geminate: SSATB, 2V, 2Va, 4Tpt o 4Ctto, Fag, Org.
The score indicates *clarini* but the parts are labeled "cornettino 1 and 2 concertate and ripeini."
F-Pc mus. Vm¹ 1179

Sequentia del Corpus Domini: SATB *conc & cap*, 2V, Ctto, V, Org.
I-Bof ms. 42

[Salmo, Beatus vir]: ChI SATB; ChII SATB; 2V, Ctto, Trb, Tior, Org.
I-Bof ms. 80

Confitebor à 4. fugato: SATB *conc & cap*, [2V?], Ctto, Trb, Bc.
I-Bof ms. 82

Confitebor à 8 Pieno, è Breve: SATB, SATB, 2V, Ctto, Trb, Vo, Org.
One violin part is in soprano clef, but the other is in tenor clef.
I-Bof ms. 83

Messa à 5 Concer:a con V.V. e ripieni: SATB *conc & cap*, 2V, Va, Ctto, Trb, Vo, Bc.
I-Bof ms. 94

Domine ad adiuvandum: ChI,II,&III SATB; 2Ctto, 2V, Fag, Vo, Tior, Org.
I-FZac ms. Cart. 47'''x (missing T,B of ChII)

Al arma al arma: SSAT, 2Ctto, Bc.

Hola Hau Pastorcillos: ChI SSST; ChII SATB; TT; 2Ctto, "tenorete," Bc.

P-C (M M 238)

*Edition: Manuel Carlos de Brito, ed., *Vilancicos do seculo XVII*, Portugaliae Musica, series A, vol 40 [*recte* 43] (Lisbon: Fundação C. Gulbenkian, 1983)

Gross ist der Herr und hochberümbt à 8: SS, 2Ctto (only two parts survive)

PL-WRu (Bohn collection Ms. mus. 38, now in **D**-BI, parts dated 1624)   *BohnH

3. Warumb betrübstu dich mein Hertz: SSAATTB *conc & cap*; 2Ctto, 4Trb, Bomb., Vo, Org

PL-WRu (Bohn collection Ms. mus. 51, now in **D**-BI, parts and tab)

17. Canzon super. An wasserflüssen Babylons à 7: 2Ctto o 2V, 2Tpt o 2Ctto, 3Trb o 3Va, Bc.
20. Kom Heiliger Geist Herre Gott: ChI SS with 2Ctto, S with Fiffaro o V, S; ChII AATB; ChInst SAA, Fl o V, 2Trb o 2VaBr, Trb o Fag, Vo, Bc.
26. Unndt es war eine stille in dem Himmell à 28: ChI AB, s, a, Va[G], b; ChII S, 2V, Va, Vo; ChIII 4Trb; ChIV SATTB, Ctto, Fag; Bc.

PL-WRu (Bohn collection Ms. mus. 59, now in **D**-BI, parts)

2. Benedicite Domino omnes Angeli à 8: ChI&II SATB; 2Ctto, Vo, Bc.

PL-WRu (Bohn collection Ms. mus. 71, now in **D**-BI, parts and tab)   *BohnH

2. Lobet den Herren ihr seine Engel à 12: ChI SATB *conc*; ChII SATB, Ctto, 3Trb; ChIII 2Ctto o 2V, 2Trb o 2Va; Vo, Bc.

PL-WRu (Bohn collection Ms. mus. 77, now in **D**-BI, parts)   *BohnH

2. Herr ich trawe auff dich à 8: ChI&II SATB; 2V o 2Ctto, Org.

PL-WRu (Bohn collection Ms. mus. 81, now in **D**-BI, parts)   *BohnH

1. Es ist gewisslich an der Zeit à 4: ATB, Ctto, Vo, Org.

PL-WRu (Bohn collection Ms. mus. 83, now in **D**-BI, parts and tab)   *BohnH

1. Exiit edictum a Caesare Augusto à 12: SSAATTBB, 2Ctto e Fag, 2V e Vo, o 2Fl e "Flautone."

PL-WRu (Bohn collection Ms. mus. 87, now in **D**-BI, parts)   *BohnH

Benedicam Dominum in omni tempore à 10: SSATTB, 3V, Vo; Cap: SAT[T?]B, Ctto, b; Bc.

PL-WRu (Bohn collection Ms. mus. 217, now in **D**-BI, parts)   *BohnH

Das alte Jahr ist nun vergahn à 15: ChI B; ChII SSSA, 2Ctto, Trav; ChIII S, 3Trb, Bomb; ATTB cap; 2V, Va, Vo, Bc.

PL-WRu (Bohn collection Ms. mus. 222, now in **D**-BI, parts)   *BohnH

Das ist mir lieb, daß der Herr meine Stimme: SATTB *conc & cap*, Ctto, 4Trb, Vo, Org.
PL-WRu (Bohn collection Ms. mus. 224, now in **D**-BI, parts)   *BohnH

Der Herr segne euch auß Zion: STTB, 2V, 2Va, Vo; CapI S o Ctto, ATB; CapII SATB, Ctto, 3Trb; Bc.
PL-WRu (Bohn collection Ms. mus. 226, now in **D**-BI, parts and tab)   *BohnH

1. Domine ad adjiuvandum / 2. Laudate Dominum omnes gentes: SSATB *conc*, SATB *cap*; 2V, 3Trb, 2Tpt o 2Cttino, 2Tpt, Org.
PL-WRu (Bohn collection Ms. mus. 230, now in **D**-BI, parts)   *BohnH

Du Hirte Israel höre: SSATT *conc*, SSATTB *cap*, with 2Ctto, 4Trb, Bomb; Vo, Org.
PL-WRu (Bohn collection Ms. mus. 236, now in **D**-BI, parts)   *BohnH

Duo Seraphim clamabant à 12: ChI SSTB, 2Ctto o 2V; ChII SATB, 2Trb; Bc.
PL-WRu (Bohn collection Ms. mus. 238, now in **D**-BI, parts)   *BohnH

Frewet euch des Herrn ihr gerechten à 9: ChI SSAB; ChII STTB, 4Trb; 2Ctto, Bc.
PL-WRu (Bohn collection Ms. mus. 244, now in **D**-BI, parts)   *BohnH

Gott fähret auff mit Jauchtzen à 8 (with sinfonia): ChI SATB, Ctto, 3Trb; ChII SATB, Trb; Vo, Org.
PL-WRu (Bohn collection Ms. mus. 248, now in **D**-BI, parts)   *BohnH

Gott mein Ruhm, schweige nicht à 10: ChI SATB, 2V, Va; ChII S, Ctto, 5Trb; SSTTTB *cap*; Org.
PL-WRu (Bohn collection Ms. mus. 251, now in **D**-BI, parts)   *BohnH

Haec est dies quam fecit Dominus à 8: ChI SSTB; ChII SATB *cap*; 2Ctto, Vo, Org.
PL-WRu (Bohn collection Ms. mus. 252, now in **D**-BI, parts and tab)   *BohnH

Halleluja, Ave Maria gratia plena: SSTT *conc*, ATTB *cap*, V, Va, 2Ctto, 2Trb, Vo, Bc.
PL-WRu (Bohn collection Ms. mus. 254, now in **D**-BI, parts)   *BohnH

Halleluja. Es stehe Gott auf: ChI 2V; ChII&III SATB; ChIV, 2Tpt o 2Ctto, 3Trb; Vo, Org.
PL-WRu (Bohn collection Ms. mus. 256, now in **D**-BI, parts)   *BohnH

Halleluja. Gegrüsset seystu Holdselige (with sinfonia): T *conc*; SSATB *rip*, 2Ctto, 3Trb; Bc.
PL-WRu (Bohn collection Ms. mus. 257, now in **D**-BI, parts and tab)   *BohnH

Halleluja. In dulci jubilo: SSATTB *conc, rip, & cap,* 2Ctto, 4Trb, Vo, Bc.
PL-WRu (Bohn collection Ms. mus. 259, now in **D**-BI, parts and tab)   *BohnH

Herr Gott ich rufe zu dir à 10: ChI SSATB, 2Ctto, Bc; ChII SATB, 4Trb, Bc.
PL-WRu (Bohn collection Ms. mus. 266, now in **D**-BI, parts)   *BohnH

Herr mein Gott ich wil dir dancken: SATBB *conc*, 2V, 2Ctto, 5Trb; ST *cap*, Ctto, Trb, Va; Vo, Bc.
PL-WRu (Bohn collection Ms. mus. 269, now in **D**-BI, parts and tab)   *BohnH

Ich habs gestalt ins Herrn gewalt à 12: ChI T, 3V, Vo; ChII S, 2Ctto, 4Trb; Org.
PL-WRu (Bohn collection Ms. mus. 278, now in **D**-BI, parts)   *BohnH

Ich hebe meine Augen auf zu den Bergen à 16: STB *conc*; ChI S[S]AT[T]B; ChII S, 4Trb; Cappella: SSAT[T]B; 2V, Ctto,Va, Vo, Bc.
PL-WRu (Bohn collection Ms. mus. 279, now in **D**-BI, parts and tab)   *BohnH

Jubilate Deo omnis terra / Uns ist ein Kind geboren: SSATTBB; Ctto, 2Trb, Bomb; SSSSAT[B]BB *cap*, Ctto, 2Trb; Vo, Bc.
Kommet herzu, last uns dem Herren frolocken: ChI SSTB, 3V, 2Ctto; ChII STTB, 4Trb; Vo, Bc. [lost?]
PL-WRu (Bohn collection Ms. mus. 286 , now in **D**-BI, parts)   *BohnH

Komm Heiliger Geist, Herre Gott à 12: ChI&II SATB; V, 2Va, Vo, Ctto, 3Trb, Bc.
PL-WRu (Bohn collection Ms. mus. 287, now in **D**-BI, parts and tab)   *BohnH

Lobet den Herren alle Heyden: ChI SSATTB; ChII AB, Trb; Cappella: ST, 2Ctto o 2V, 3Trb, Trb o Vo; Bc.
PL-WRu (Bohn collection Ms. mus. 295, now in **D**-BI, parts)   *BohnH

Magnificat II toni: ChI&II SATB; S, 2Ctto, 4Trb; Vo, Bc.
PL-WRu (Bohn collection Ms. mus. 299, now in **D**-BI, parts)   *BohnH

Magnificat super: Heut triumphiret Gottes Sohn à 8: ChI&II SATB, Ctto, Bc.
PL-WRu (Bohn collection Ms. mus. 301, now in **D**-BI, parts and tab)   *BohnH

Magnificat super: Lobet den Herren alle Heyden: SSATTB *conc*; S[S][A] A[T]T[B]B *cap*, 2Ctto, [3?]Trb; 2V, Vo, Org.
PL-WRu (Bohn collection Ms. mus. 302, now in **D**-BI, parts)   *BohnH

Magnificat à 8: ChI SATB *conc*; ChII STTB *rip* [V, Ctto, 3Trb]; Vo, Org.
PL-WRu (Bohn collection Ms. mus. 304, now in **D**-BI, parts)   *BohnH

Magnificat à 16: ChI SSTB; ChII SATB, 2Tpt, Ctto, c, t; ChIII S, 4Trb; SATB *cap*; S[A?]TB *cap*; Vo, Bc.
PL-WRu (Bohn collection Ms. mus. 305, now in **D**-BI, parts and tab)   *BohnH

Meine Seel erhebet den Herren: ChI SSAB *conc*, 2Ctto, Trb, Fag; ChII STTB, with 4Trb; SAAT*cap*; Vo, Bc.
PL-WRu (Bohn collection Ms. mus. 307, now in **D**-BI, parts and tab)   *BohnH

Missa super: Bonum est: ChI SSAB, Ctto muto with A; ChII ATTB, with 2Trb, Vo o Fag; 2Ctto; 2Bc.
PL-WRu (Bohn collection Ms. mus. 311, now in **D**-BI, parts)   *BohnH

Missus est angelus Gabriel: SATB, 2Ctto, 4Trb, Bc.
PL-WRu (Bohn collection Ms. mus. 315, now in **D**-BI, parts)   *BohnH

Mit fried und frewd ich fahr dahin à 14: SSATTB *conc*, SATB *cap*, Ctto, 2Trb, Bomb, Vo, Bc.
PL-WRu (Bohn collection Ms. mus. 316, now in **D**-BI, parts)   *BohnH

Nun preiset alle Gottes Barmhertzigkeit: STT *conc*, SATB *cap*, 2V, 2Ctto, 3Trb, Vo, Bc.
PL-WRu (Bohn collection Ms. mus. 321, now in **D**-BI, parts)   *BohnH

Psallite Domino exultate Deo à 10: SATB *conc*, 2V, 3Trb; SATB *rip*, Ctto; Bc.
PL-WRu (Bohn collection Ms. mus. 329a, now in **D**-BI, parts)   *BohnH

Selig sind, die da geistlich arm sind (with sinfonia): SSATB *conc & cap*, 2Ctto, 3Trb, Vo, Bc.
PL-WRu (Bohn collection Ms. mus. 331, now in **D**-BI, parts and tab)   *BohnH

Singet dem Herrn ein newes Lied: ChI ST*conc*, AB, 3Trb; ChII ATB, 2Ctto, 3Trb; Cappella: S with Ctto; Vo, Org.
PL-WRu (Bohn collection Ms. mus. 333, now in **D**-BI, parts)   *BohnH

Singet dem Herrn ein newes Lied: SSATTB *conc*; SATTB *cap* with Ctto, 4Trb; 2V, Vo, Org.
PL-WRu (Bohn collection Ms. mus. 334, now in **D**-BI, parts)   *BohnH

Singet dem Herrn ein newes Lied: ChI [SS]TB, 2Ctto; ChII SATB, 4Trb; Ch"di violini" SSAB; 2Tpt; Vo, Bc.
PL-WRu (Bohn collection Ms. mus. 335, now in **D**-BI, parts and tab)   *BohnH

Singet löblich und lobet den Herren à 10 o 16: SSAATB, 2V, Ctto, Trb, Vo, Bc.
PL-WRu (Bohn collection Ms. mus. 336, now in **D**-BI, parts and tab)   *BohnH

Veni Sancte Spiritus et emitte: ChI SSATB; ChII SATB, Ctto, 3Trb; Cappella: SATB, 2V o 2Cttino; Vo, Bc.
PL-WRu (Bohn collection Ms. mus. 344 now in D-BI, parts)   *BohnH

Von Himmel hoch da komm ich her à 8 o 16: ChI SSSB; ChII SATB; 3V, Vo; Ctto, 4Trb; Vo, Bc.
PL-WRu (Bohn collection Ms. mus. 348 now in D-BI, parts) (A second version exists in parts and tablature as Ms. mus. 348a, highly ornamented but without cornetto.) *BohnH

Wem Gott der Herr ein Tugendsahmes Weib: SSTT*conc*; ATTB, 2V, 2Fl, 2Ctto, 4Trb; Cappella: SB, Ctto; Vo, Bc.
PL-WRu (Bohn collection Ms. mus. 349 now in D-BI, parts)   *BohnH

Laudabo nomen dei à 6: TTB, 2Cttino, Fag, Bc.
S-Uu Vok. Mus. i hs 69:13

Siehe, wie fein und lieblich ist: SATB, 2V, 2Cttino, Bc.
S-Uu 70:11   *WalkerSB

ARNOLD, Georg (*b* Feldsberg, Lower Austria; *d* Bamberg, 1676)
Operis secundi liber I. missarum: psalmorum: et magnificat a quinque vocibus & duobus violinis e viola in concerto: trombonis aut violis pro libitu ad concertantes voces quatuor. Nec non altero choro ac binis cornetis ad placitum. Cum speciali basso pro organo. . . . Innsbruck: Michael Wagner, 1656.
   1. Domine ad adjuvandum me festina [& Missa]: SSATB, 2V, 2Ctto, Vo, Bc.
   2. Dixit Dominus & Missa à 9 vel 14 applicari potest: SSATB, 2V, "& 2 clarinis vel cornetis necessarijs sine reliquis instrumentis & vocibus," bVa, Org.
   3. Confitebor tibi Domine: SSATB, 2V, 2Ctto, Vo, Bc.
   4. Beatus vir [& Missa]: SSATB, 2V, 2Ctto, Vo, Bc.
   5. Laudate pueri: SSATB, 2V, 2Ctto, Vo, Bc.
   6. Laudate Dominum, omnes gentes: SSATB, 2V, 2Ctto, Vo, Bc.
   7. Laetatus sum: SSATB, 2V, 2Ctto, Vo, Bc.
   8. Nisi Dominus: SSATB, 2V, 2Ctto, Vo, Bc.
   9. Lauda Jerusalem Dominum: SSATB, 2V, 2Ctto, Vo, Bc.
   10. Credidi propter quod locutus sum: SSATB, 2V, 2Ctto, Vo, Bc.
   11. In convertando: SSATB, 2V, 2Ctto, Vo, Bc.
   12. Domine probasti me: SSATB, 2V, 2Ctto, Vo, Bc.
   13. Magnificat sexti toni: SSATB, 2V, 2Ctto, Vo, Bc.
   14. Magnificat octavi toni à 7 vel 14 applicari posunt: SSATB, "& 2 Violinis absque secundo Choro, Trombonis, Cornetis, sive Violinis," Org.
D-BAs (S2,A1 *rip*,T1,B1), -Rp (A1); **GB**-Lbl (ATTBB, V1, Vo); **S**-Uu (SSATB *conc*, V1,V2, ATTB *rip*, Ctto1,Ctto2,Vo)   MitUB; *WalkerSB   RISM A2162

Nulla scientia melior est illa à 7: SSATB, 2V *conc*; [2V], 3Va, 2Cttino, 3Trb *cap*; Vo, Bc.

S-Uu (copied from *Liber Secundus Sacrum Cantione*. . . . [Innsbruck, 1661] by Gustav Düben; ms dated 1663)
Edition: DTB 10 (without cornettino and trombone parts)

BACH, Johann Michael (*b* Arnstadt, 1648; *d* Gehren, 1694)

Das Blut Jesu Christi: SATTB, with Ctto, 4Trb, Bc.
D-Berlin Altbachisches Archiv; Bibl. der Singakadamie (lost, but WalkerSB lists it as being in **D-GOa**)
*Edition: EdM 1 (Altbachisches Archiv, I. Teil)

BACH, Johann Sebastian (*b* Eisenach, 1685; *d* Leipzig, 1750)

In alphabetical order by title:

   Ach Herr, mich armen Sünder: ATB *conc*, SATB *cap*, Ctto, 2Ob, Trb, 2V, Va, Bc
   (Ctto, Ob, V, col soprano in mvmt 6).
D-LEm f. 15f (1.perf: 25 June 1724)   BWV 135

   Also hat Gott die Welt geliebt: SB *conc*, SATB *cap*, Horn, Ctto, 3Trb, 2Ob, Ob da
   caccia, Vc *piccolo*, 2V, Va, Bc (Ctto col soprano in mvmt 5).
D-LEt (1.perf: 21 May 1725)   BWV 68

   Christ lag in Todesbanden: SATB *conc & cap*, 2V, 2Va, Ctto, 3Trb, Bc (Ctto col
   soprano in mvmts 2,3,8).
D-LEb St. Thom.   BWV 4   RISM AII 200020889

   Christum wir sollen loben schon: SATB *conc & cap*, Ctto, 3Trb, Ob d'amore, Ob
   da caccia, 2V, Va, Bc (Ctto, Ob d'amore, V, col soprano in mvmts 1 & 6).
D-LEb St. Thom. (1.perf: 26 Dec. 1724)   BWV 121   RISM AII 200020921

   Christus, der ist mein Leben: STB *conc*, SATB *cap*, Horn, Cttino, 2Ob, 2Ob
   d'amore, 2V, Va, Bc (Cttino, Ob, col soprano in mvmts 1 & 6).
The ms indicates *Corñio* for the cornettino part.
D-BI (1.perf: 12 Sept. 1723)   BWV 95

   Du wahrer Gott und Davids Sohn: SAT *conc*, SATB *cap*, 2Ob d'amore, Ctto, 3Trb,
   2V, Va, Bc (Ctto col soprano in mvmt 4).
D-BI (Cornett appears only in the B minor "Zwischen" version, first performed in Zwischen, 20 Feb. 1724)   BWV 23

   Es ist nichts gesundes an meinem Leibe: STB *conc*, SATB *cap*, Ctto, 3Trb, 3Fl,
   2Ob, 2V, Va, Bc (Ctto, 3Trb in mvmts 1,6).
D-BI (1.perf: 29 Aug. 1723)   BWV 25

Gottlob! Nun geht das Jahr zu Ende: SATB *conc & cap*, Ctto, 3Trb, 2Ob, "Taille,"
2V, Va, Bc (Ctto, Ob, V, col soprano in mvmts 2,6).
D-BI (1.perf: 30 Dec 1725)   BWV 28

Ich freue mich in dir: SATB *conc & cap*, Ctto, 2Ob d'amore, 2V, Va, Bc (Ctto col
soprano in mvmts 1,6).
D-BI 3 in: Am. B.44; -LEb St. Thom. (1.perf: 27 Dec. 1724)   BWV 133
RISM AII 200021022 & 200020930

Missa sine nomine (Palestrina): SSATTB, 2Ctto, 4Trb, Vo, Cemb, Org.
This is a manuscript copy of the Palestrina *Missa sine nomine à 6*, partially in the hand
of J. S. Bach, including Bach's instrumentation and figures.
D-BI Mus. ms. 16714

Nimm von uns, Herr, du treuer Gott: SATB *conc & cap*, Ctto, 3Trb, Trav, 2Ob, Ob
da caccia (Taille), 2V, Va, Bc (Ctto col soprano in mvmts 1,7).
D-LEb St. Thom. (1.perf: 13 Aug. 1725)   BWV 101   RISM AII 2000020914

O Jesu Christ, mein's Lebens Licht: SATB, 2"Litui," Ctto, 3Trb.
D-LEbh mus. ms. 5   BWV 118

Sanctus [D major]: SATB, Ctto, 2V, Va, Org Bc (Ctto col soprano).
D-LEbh mus. ms. 11 (1.perf: 25 Dec. 1723)   BWV 238

Sehet welch eine Liebe: SAB *conc & cap*, Ctto, 3Trb, Ob d'amore, 2V, Va, Vc, b,
Org (Ctto, V, col soprano in mvmts 1,2,4,8).
D-BI 3 in: Am.B.44 (1.perf: 27 Dec. 1723)   BWV 64   RISM AII 200021017

BANCHIERI, Adriano (Bologna, 1568-1634)
(See *Vezzo di perle musicali. . . .* [1610, 1616] in the instrumental list which contains
21 motets with various alternatives for vocal performance.)

BASSANI, Giovanni Battista (*b* Padua, *ca* 1657; *d* Bergamo, 1716)
La Morte Delusa, "Oratorio à cinque voci cioè Canto due Alti, Tenore & Basso con
corneto violini, e choro di anime suffragate": SAATB *conc & cap*, 2V, 2Va, Ctto
[o V], Bc.
A note in the ms indicates that 3 violins can be used instead of 2 violins & cornett.
I-MOe mus. F60 (1.perf: 1686)

Magnificat: SATB (with V, 2Va, Fag); V [o?] Ctto, Bc.
The instrumental line bears the marking "Violino 1. Corn:".
D-BII Mus. ms. 1161 (Bokemeyer collection, score) Only the name Bassani appears on
the score but KümmerKB lists [Giovanni Battista] Bassani as the author.

BEAULIEU, Lambert de (*fl* 1576-1590)[21]

Balet comique de la Royne. . . . Paris: Adrian le Roy, Robert Ballard & Mamert Patisson, 1582.

For voices and instruments including: Lt, Lira da Br, Lira da G, Va da Lyra, Fl, Hp, Trb, Ctto, Ob, Org.

The instrumentation is not specific within the structure of the *Balet* but in the preface there is the following description for the beginning of the drama: " . . . *le silence ayant esté imposé, on ouit aussi tost derrriere le chasteau une note de hauts-boys, cornets, sacquebouttes, et autres doux instruments de musique: desquels l'harmonie" estant cessee, le sieur de la Roche.* . . . " (Also of interest in this work is an splendid engraving of 8 Satyrs playing cornetts.)

A-Wn; B-Br; F-Pc, -Pn; I-Tn; NL-DHgm; S-Uu; US-Lu, -U   RISM B1448

Edition: *Chefs d'oeuvre classiques de l'opéra français* (Paris, 188?; reprint, New York: Broude, 1971)

BECCARI, Fabio

Il secondo libro de sacri concenti a 2. 3. 4. 5. e 6. voci. Milan: Melchiore Tradate, 1611.

Laudate Dominum: Sinfonia di Quattro voci, con Cornetto e Trombone (incompl).

A-Wn (Bc); D-Mbs (B); I-PCd (Bc)   RISM B1507

BECKER, Paul (*ca* 1615-1697)

Wohl dem, der den Herrn fürchtet: SSATB *conc* & *cap*, 2V, 2Ctto[o Cttino], 2Va o Trb, Vo o Fag, Bc.

The possible use of cornettino instead of cornett is implied by the word *Cornettin,* which appears occasionally in the violin parts.

D-BII Mus. ms. 1227 (Erfurt collection, score and parts dated 1674)   NoackE

BEER, Johannes (*b* St. Georg, Upper Austria, 1665; *d* Weissenfels, 1700)

Missa S. Marzellini à 19 o 22: 8vv *conc*, 2V, 3Va, 2Tpt, Timp, Ctto muto, 3Trb *rip*, Org, Vo.

A-KR   *SpielmannZ

BERCKELAERS, Johannes

Cantiones natalitiae IV. vocum et IV. instrument. Antwerp: héritiers de Pierre Phalèse, 1667.

Noyt en vasser soeter macht: 4v, 2Ctto e 2Tpt, Bc.

NL-DHgm (B, V1); US-CA (A, T)   RISM B1982

Cantiones natalitiae duabus, quatuor & quinquè tam vocibus, quam instrumentis, decantandae . . . *liber secundus.*   Antwerp: héritiers de Pierre Phalèse, 1670.

---

[21] Fétis claimed that he wrote the music to the *Balet comique de la Royne,* but Mersenne attributed it to Girard de Beaulieu. *GroveD

Last nu alle droefheyt vluchten: 4v, 2Tpt o 2Ctto, Bc (incompl).
NL-DHgm (T, B praecentus, V1); **US-CA** (A)   RISM B1983

BERNARDI, Stefano (*b* Verona, *ca* 1585; *d* Salzburg?,1636)

*Il terzo libro de madrigali a cinque voci concertati con il basso continuo per sonare . . .
opera decima.* Venice: Giacomo Vincenti, †1619; Alessandro Vincenti, ∞1622.
   Ecco il mio cor: AT, V, Ctto, Trb o Lt, Bc.
   Deh girate: AT, V, Ctto, Trb o Lt, Bc.
   Bellezze amate. Dialogo à 2 amante: ST, V, Ctto, "tiorba o chitarrone," Bc.
   Hor se non dai: AT, V, Ctto, b "per le sinfonie," Bc.
   Mentre pomposa te ne stai, rosa: SAT, V, Ctto, Bc.
†**I-TSmt**; ∞**I-Bc**; **-VCd** (S, A, T, Bc)   RISM B2067/2068

*Concerti sacri scielti, & trasportati dal secondo, & terzo libro de madrigali a cinque
voci, con il basso per l'organo. . . .* Venice: Alessandro Vincenti, 1621.
   Quam pulchri sunt – "Ecco il mio cor": AT, V, Ctto, Trb o Lt, Org.
   Indica mihi – "Deh girate": AT, V, Ctto, Trb o Lt, Org.
   O quam suavis – "Bellezze amate": ST, V, Ctto, "tiorba o chitarrone," Org.
   O quam tu pulchra – "Mentre pomposa": SAT, V, Ctto, Org.
D-F (SATB, 5, Bc); **I-Bam**, **-Bc**, **-FEc**, **-Sac**(S,T), **-SPE**, (Bc), **-VCd**   RISM B2056

*Il terzo libro de madrigali a sei voci concertati con alcune sonate accomodate per ogni
sorte d'istromenti . . . opera decimaterza.* Venice: Alessandro Vincenti, 1624.
   O mare, o cielo, o secretari: [SA]TB, V, Ctto, Bc.
This print also contains two instrumental works (see instrumental list).
D-Kl (missing S), **-Rp** (B)   SartMS I 1624c; RISM B2071

*Encomia sacra. Binis, ternis, quaternis, quinis, senisque vocibus concinenda . . . opus
decimum quintum.* Salzburg: Gregor Kyrner, 1634.
   Natus est Christus: S, 2Ctto o 2V, Bc.
   Da pacem Domine: BBBB, 2Ctto o 2V, Bc.
D-Rp   RISM B2060

BERNHARD, Christoph (*b* Kolberg, Pomerania, 1628; *d* Dresden, 1692)

   4. Tribularer si nescirem misericordias: ChI SSATB, 2V, 2Vtta, Fag; ChII
      SSATB, 2Ctto, 3Trb *ad lib*; Bc (dated 1693).
   8. Herr, nun läßestu deinen Diener à 10: ChI SSATB, 2V, 2Va, Vo o Fag; ChII
      SSATB, 2Ctto, 3Trb *ad lib*; Org.
D-Bl Mus. ms. 30096 (Bokemeyer collection, score), **-Dlb** f 571 (lost)   KümmerKB
Edition: DdT 6

   Benedic, anima mea: ChI&II SATB; 2[Ctto], 4Trb, 2V, 2Va, Fag, Org.
The [Ctto] parts are listed as *Corne* in the ms
S-Uu vok. mus. i hs 82:6a (tab, dated 1674)
Edition: EdM 90

BERTALI, Antonio (*b* Verona, 1605; *d* Vienna, 1669)

Missa mixta: [2(SATB)], 2V, 4Va, 4Trb, 2Tpt, 2V, Vo, Bc (in the "Crucifixus," 2Ctto col soprano are indicated).
A-KR Kasten C fasc 7 no. 654, -Wgm [?]   *SMw IV (18); *GroveD; WalkerSB [no ctto listed]

Maria Magdalena: SSTT, V, 4Va, 2Ctto, Trb, Bc.
A-Wn ms. 16010   *WalkerSB

In the opera *Pazzo amor* (dated 1664, for the birthday of Kaiserin Eleonora).
A-Wn Mus. Hs. 16.861, ff. 6v-8r.   *SpielmannZ

Missa Archiducalis: SSATTB *conc & rip*, 2V, 2Ctto, 2Vtta, 2Va, Tpt, 4Trb, Org.
CS-KRa B I 6 (dated 1669)   OttoS

Missa Nihil: SATB *conc & cap*, 2V, 3Va, 2Ctto, 4Trb, Vo, Org.
CS-KRa B I 12 (missing 2Va, 2Ctto, 4Trb & 4 *cap* parts)   OttoS

Missa Resurrectionis (in Kyrie and Gloria): SSAATTBB, 2V, 4Vtta, 2Ctto, 2Tpt, 5Trb, [Bc].
CS-KRa B I 13 (dated 1669)   *WalkerSB; OttoS

Missa Omnium Sanctorum: SSAATTBB *conc & cap*, [2V, 2Va, 3Va o 3Trb, 2Ctto, Fag o Trb], Vo, Org.
CS-KRa B I 46   *WalkerSB; OttoS

Missa Cellensis à 19v: SSAATTBB, 2V, 4Va, 2Ctto, 3Trb, Vo, Org.
CS-KRa B I 137   OttoS

Missa Consecrationis à 26: SSSAATTTBB, 2V, 2Va, 2Ctto, 5Tpt, 4Trb, Vo, Org.
CS-KRa B I 184

Missa S. Spiritus: SATB SATB *conc & cap*, 2V, 2Va, VaBr, 2Ctto, 2Tpt, 4Trb, Fag, Vo, Org.
The cornett parts are marked *Cornettino i è Cornetto muto conc.*
CS-KRa B I 185   OttoS

Missa Redemptoris: SSAATTBB, 2V, 4Va, 2Ctto, 5Trb, Org.
CS-KRa B I 234 (dated 1677)   OttoS

Vidi Luciferum. de S. Michäele: SSAATTBB, 2V, 2Ctto, 2VaG, 3Trb, Vo, Org.
CS-KRa B II 282   OttoS

BERTOLA, Giovanni Antonio [same as bassoonist Bertoli] (*fl* 1639-1645)

Salmi intieri che si cantano alli vespri di tutte le feste, e solemnità dell'anno, a cinque voci con il basso continuo. Venice: Alessandro Vincenti, 1639.
 Salve Regina: STB, Ctto o V, V, Bc.
 Alma redemptoris: SAT, Ctto o V, V, Bc.
 Ave regina: SAB, Ctto o V, V, Bc.
For all of the above pieces, 2V are specified in the *tavola*, but the headings indicate V o Ctto, V.
I-Bc, -Rsg; **PL-**WRu (missing A)   BohnD   RISM B2161

BIBER, Heinrich Ignatz Franz von (*b* Wartenberg, 1644; *d* Salzburg, 1704)

Vesperae longiores ac breviores unacùm litaniis Lauretanis a IV. vocibus, II. violinis et II. violis in concerto, Additis 4. vocibus in cappellâ atque tribus trombonis ex ripienis desumendis ad libitum. Salzburg: Johann Baptist Mayr, 1693.
 SATB *conc & cap*, 2V, 2Va, Ctto, 3Trb, Org.
A-Gmi (ATB, V1, V2, Org); **D-**Mbs (with parts also in ms; according to ChafeCM, only the Munich version specifies cornett), -Kdma [3/213 ms] [3/26 print], -OB (SATB *conc*, V1, V2, Va, Org); **US-**NH (9 pts)   RISM B2613

 Missa Alleluia: ChI&II SATB *conc & cap*, 2V, 3Va, Vo, 2Ctto, 3Trb, 6Tpt, Timp, Tior, Org.
A-KR ms. C/8, 661 (dated 1698); **CH-**E ms. 438,8 (score dated 1698; copied by Sigismund Keller, 1871)

 Missa [now known as "Salisburgensis"]: ChI SSAATTBB *conc*, Org; ChII 2V, 4Va; ChIII 2Ob, 4Fl, 2Tpt [?]; ChIV 2Ctto, 2Trb [?]; ChV SSAATTBB *conc*; ChVI 2V, 4Va; "LocoI" 4 Tpt, Timp; "LocoII" 4Tpt, Timp; Org, Bc.
 Plaudite Tympana: ChI&IISSAATTBB, 4V, 8Va, 4Fl, 2Ob, 2Ctto, 4Tpt, 4Trb, 2Org, Bc.
A-Sca Hs. 751 (dated 1628);[22] **B-**Br ms. I 3864   *ChafeCM;[23] WalkerSB
Facs. edition: ed. Laurence Feininger, *Horatii Benevoli operum omnium*, VIIa, VIIb (Salzburg: Universitätsverlag Anton Pustet, 1969); Edition: DTÖ 20 (of the "Missa" attributed to Benevoli)

 Missa Bruxellensis: SATB, SATB *cap*, 4Tpt, Timp, 2Ctto, 3Trb, 2V, 3Va, Bc.
B-Br ms. II 3862
Edition: ed. Laurence Feininger, *Horatii Benevoli operum omnium*, VIIa (Salzburg: Pustet, 1970)

 Missa Christi resurgentis: [SATB, SATB, 2V, 2Va, 2Ctto, 2Tpt, 3Trb, Vo, Org.]
CS-KRa B I 103   OttoS

---

[22] Chafe believes 1628 to be a mistake for 1682. At any rate, 1628 is clearly an error.

[23] The original attribution to Benevoli is put into question by Chafe, who attributes the works to Biber.

A.M.D.G.B.M.V. Assumptae H Vesperae à 32: SATB *conc,* SATB *cap,* 4"Viol.,"
2Ctto, 4Tpt, 3Trb, Timp, "basso di viola," 4Bc.
CS-KRa B III 89 (autograph copy, dated 1674) and B III 97   OttoS

BILDSTEIN, Hieronymus (*b* Bregenz, *ca* 1580; *d ca* 1686)
Orpheus Christianus, seu symphoniarum sacrarum prodomus 5.6.7.& 8. vocum cum basso generali. Ravensburg: Johann Schröter, 1624.
    11. Sanctus Jacobus à 7: SAT, V o Ctto, a, t, b, Bc (Org).
D-B (3 partbooks, now in **PL-Kj**), -F; **F-Pn**   RISM B2641
Edition: DTÖ 122

BÖDDECKER, Philipp Friedrich (*b* Hagenau, Alsace, 1607; *d* Stuttgart, 1683)
Melosirenicum, 2 cant. alt. 2 ten. bass. 2 violin. et fagott. cum 3 tromb. et capella a 6 concinnatum. . . . Straßbourg: Johann Heinrich Mittel, 1655.
    SSATTB *conc,* 2V, 3Trb, Fag; SATB *cap* with instruments, 2Cttino.
F-Pn vm¹ 986   *EscorPBN   RISM B3264

BÖHM, Georg (*b* Hohenkirchen nr. Ohrdruf, 1661; *d* Lüneburg, 1733)
    Jauchzet Gott alle Land: SSATB, 2V, 2Va, 2Ctto, 3Trb, Fag, Bc.
D-Bl Mus. ms. 30099 (Bokemeyer collection, score)   KümmerKB
Edition: Harald Kümmerling, ed., *Vokalwerke,* Georg Böhm Sämtliche Werke, Bd. I
(Wiesbaden: Breitkopf & Härtel, 1963)

BOLLIUS, Daniel (*b* Hechingen, Württemberg, *ca* 1590; *d* Mainz, *ca* 1642)
    Repraesentatio harmonica conceptionis et nativitatis S. Johannis Baptistae . . .
    composita modo pathetico sive recitativo.
    prima symphonia: 2Ctto, Fag.
    quarta symphonia: Ctto, V, Fl, b.
    [quinta symphonia: 2Ctto, Fag.]
We were only able to locate two symphonias, however a third (quinta sinfonia) is listed
in BohnH.
PL-WRu (Bohn collection Ms. mus. 129, now in **D-Bl**, score)

    Psalmus CXXXIII [Ecce nunc Benedicte] concertatus à 9: SSAAT, 2Ctto, Fag, Tior
    o Lt, Bc.
PL-WRu (Bohn collection Ms. mus. 129b, now in **D-Bl**, parts)

    Dialogus harmonicus: SSB, Ctto, Fag, Tior o Lt, Bc.
PL-WRu (Bohn collection Ms. mus. 129c, now in **D-Bl**, parts)   *BohnH

BONONCINI, Giovanni Maria (*bapt.* Modena, 1670; *d* 1747)
    Missa brevis à 2 cori con stromenti aggiunti da Harrer: Ch I&II SATB, 2V, Va, Ctto,
    3Trb, 2Ob, Bc (unfigured), "Basso ripieno," Cemb, Org.
D-Bll Mus. ms. 2183 (ms by Johann Gottlob Harrer, 1752)   RISM AII 152392

In the opera *La Camilla Trionfante* (1697):
Act II Scene 17: Tiranna Gelosia: S [2V], Ctto, [Va], Bc (top instrumental part says "Unisoni, Corneto solo").
Act III Scene 13: Tutto armato: S [2V], Ctto, [Va], Bc (first part says "Cornetti" and later "Corneto solo").
D-BII Mus. ms. 2184 (ms from *ca* 1760)   RISM AII 152393

BORLASCA, Bernardino (*b* Gavio Genovese, *ca* 1560; *d* after 1631)
Scala Iacob, octonis vocibus, et varijs instrumentis omnibus anni solemnitatibus decantanda . . . opus sextum. Venice: Giacomo Vincenti, 1616.
Preparate corda vestra Domino: ChI SATB, [Ctto, 3VaBr o 3VaG, Hp, Lirone, etc.]; ChII SATB, [Ctto, V, 2Trb].
Isti sunt: ChI SATB, [Ctto, 3VaBr o VaG, Hp, Lirone, etc.]; ChII SATB, [Ctto, V, 2Trb].
Clama ne cesses quasi turba: ChI SATB, [Ctto, 3VaBr o 3VaG, Hp, Lirone, etc.]; ChII SATB, [Ctto, V, 2 Trb].
Regna terrae: ChI SATB, [Ctto, 3VaBr o 3VaG, Hp, Lirone, etc.]; ChII SATB, [Ctto, V, 2Trb].
Magnificat Sexti Toni: ChI SATB, [Ctto, 3VaBr o 3VaG, Hp, Lirone, etc.]; ChII SATB, [Ctto, V, 2Trb].
Magnificat Octavi Toni: ChI SATB [Ctto, 3VaBr o 3VaG, Hp, Lirone, etc.]; ChII SATB, [Ctto, V, 2Trb]. (with sinfonias in the "Magnificat" and "Esurientes" sections having the instrumentation: ChI T, [Ctto, 2VaBr o 2VaG, Hp, Lirone, etc.]; ChII [Ctto, V, 2Trb].)
Fit porta Christi *Prima pars*: ChI SSA, [Ctto, 2VaBr o 2VaG, Hp, Lirone, etc.]; ChII SAQTB, [Ctto, V, 3Trb].
Genus superni *Secunda pars:* ChI SSA, [Ctto, 2VaBr o 2VaG, Hp, Lirone, etc.]; ChII SAQTB, [Ctto, V, 3Trb].
Honor matris *Tertia pars*: ChI SSAT, [Ctto, 3VaBr o 3VaG, Hp, Lirone, etc.]; ChII SAQTB, [Ctto, V, 3Trb].
Haec dies: ChI SATB, [Ctto, 3VaBr o 3VaG, Hp, Lirone, etc.]; ChII SATB, [Ctto, V, 2Trb].
Salve Regina à 16: Ch I&III SATB, [Ctto, 3VaBr o 3VaG, Hp, Lirone, etc.]; ChII&IV SATB, [Ctto, V, 2Trb].
A preface by the printer Vincenti explains "the will of the author": "the first choir is to consist of four principal parts with a soprano and a castrato or pleasant falsetto, accompanied by a body of diverse stringed instruments such as viole da braccia or da gamba, a large harp, a lirone, or other similar instruments as are common today, especially at the Bavarian court; indeed His Serene Highness has examples of every kind of instrument of this sort, as well as men of exquisite excellence. Moreover, where the letter *V.* is found, the voice should sing; at the word *Sinfonia* the instruments should play, and at the letter *T.* the voices and instruments should play together. The second choir should, like the first, also consist of the same voices, but of different instruments.

For, if in the first are found plucked instruments or strings, in the second should be placed wind instruments, such as cornetts and trombones, and pleasingly tempered by a violin playing the contralto part an octave above. In this same way in the first choir a cornett playing the same part, if it is a choir of viols, is such a different instrument that by following these instructions one will be assured of obtaining lovely and delightful harmony."

The above works contain *V* and *T* markings at frequent intervals, whereas the earlier titles in this print are Mass movements which do not contain such markings. The only *Sinfonia* indications are in the second Magnificat, where only the Ch1 tenor part is texted.

D-B (T1, now in **PL**-Kj), -Mbs (compl)   RISM B3757

BREHMER, Johann Daniel ? (18th cent)

    Aria: Herrscher jener Himmelshöhen: SATB, 2V, Va, Fl, Ctto, 3Trb, Org.
    Aria: Lobe Zion in der Stille: SATB, 2V, Va, Fl, Ctto, 3Trb, Org.

D-MÜG Mus. ant. 378 (18th-cent ms)   *RISM AII 230021573

BRIEGEL, Wolfgang Karl (*b* Königberg nr. Coburg, 1626; *d* Darmstadt, 1712)

Geistlichen musikalischen Rosengartens erster Theil. . . . Gotha: Johann Michael Schall, 1658.
    12. Lobet ihr Knechte: with symphonia 2Ctto, [3Trb, Bc].
    14. Nun lob, meine Seele: SSTB, 2Ctto, 3Trb, Bc.

A-Wgm; **CH**-Zz; **D**-GOl (2), -FBsk (2,3, V1, Bc), -SAh (1,2 3,5, V1, Bc); **GB**-Lbm
(1,2,4, V1, Bc)   *WalkerSB   RISM B4468

Erster Theil evangelischer Gespräch. . . . Mühlhausen: T.M. Gotz, 1660.
    1. Lieber Herr Gott à 6: SSB; 2Va, Vo; 2V, Va, Fl; 2Ctto, Trb o Fag; Bc.
    6. Fürchtet euch nicht à 9: STTB, 2V, 2Va, 2Ctto, Bc.
    7. Von Himmel hoch à 6: SATB, V, Ctto, Bc.

A-Wgm; **CH**-Zz; **PL**-WRu   RISM B4472
Karl Friederick Hirschmann, *Wollfgang Carl Briegel 1626-1712* (Giessen: O. Kindt, 1934).

Ander Theil evangelischer Gespräch. . . . Mühlhausen: T.M. Gotz, 1662.
    12. Dialogus à 5: STB, 2V, 2VaG, 2Fl, 2Ctto.

A-Wgm; **CH**-Zz; **F**-Ssp; **PL**-WRu   RISM B4471/4472

Herrn Pfarrers Johann Samuel Kriegsmanns evangelisches hosianna . . . mit 1. 2. 3. 4. und 5. Singstimmen beneben zweyen Instrumenten, und einem Generalbass . . . Frankfurt: Albert Otto Faber (Balthasar Christoph Wust), 1677.
    8. Ein anders: A[?]TB with ritornello 2Ctto, Bc.
    33. Auffs Fest der Himmelfahrt: SA[?]TB with ritornelli 2Ctto, Bc.

No. 8. "Ein anders" refers to the previous piece called *Am h. Neu-Jahrs-Tag.*

A-Wn (missing S2); **D**-DS, -F, -GOl (S1), -Mbs (S1,inst1), -UDa (inst2,Bc), -WA (missing S2), -WRiv (S1,S2,A,T,inst1); **PL**-WRu (missing A)   RISM B4481

Musikalisher Lebens-Brunn gequollen aus den fürnehmsten Kern-Sprüchen Heil. Schrifft . . . meistentheils Gesprächs-Weiss eingerichtet, mit 4. Sing-Stimmen (auch 4 Instrumenten pro complemento) sambt dem General-Bass. . . . Darmstatt: Otto Faber (Henning Muller), 1680.

77. Ich bin eine Blume zu Saron: SATB; SATB *cap*, 2Tpt o 2Ctto, 2Trb; Bc.

A-Wgm; D-FRIts, -LUC (missing vocal parts), -ROST (Va1); F-Pn (SAB, V2, Va1,Va2, Bc); GB-Lcm (incompl); PL-GD (missing Va1); S-Skma (SAT, V2, Va1,Va2), -Uu *MitUB   RISMB4484

Christian Rehefelds evangelischer Psalmen-Zweig. . . . Frankfurt: Johann David Zunner (Darmstadt: Henning Müller), 1684.

19. Der Tod ist verschlungen in den Sieg: SATB, 2V, Ctto, Trb, Bc.

D-BI (S1 incompl,S2,Bc), -Dlb, -F, -KMs (SATB, V1,Va1,Va2,Vo,Bc), -LEm (S1,S2,A incompl,B,Vo), -NA (ATB,V1,Va2,Bc incompl), -SAh (S1,AT,Bc), -V (SSATB, V1,V2,Vo,Bc)   RISM B4485

20. Friede sey mit euch: Altus Continuus, STB *cap*, Ctto, 2V, Va, Vo, Bc.
26. Herr lehre mich thun: Altus Continuus, Cappella SSATB, 2s, 2V, Va, Vo, 2Ctto, 2Trb, Bc.

PL-WRu (Bohn collection Ms. mus. 130, now in D-BI, parts)   *BohnH

BRUNELLI, Antonio (Pisa, *ca* 1575-1630)

Scherzi, arie, canzonette, e madrigali a una, due, e tre voci per sonare e cantare con ogni sorte di stromenti . . . Libro secondo, Opera decima. Venice: Giacomo Vincenti, 1614.

Cinto il crin di biond'oliva Aria a 3: SS o TT, B, [2V o 2Ctto], Bc.

A cantar in altri modi Aria a 3: SSB, [2V o 2Ctto], Bc.

Scenda quella dal canoro Aria a 3: SS o TT, B, [2V o 2Ctto], Bc.

O soave dolore Canzonetta a 3: SS o TT, B, [2V o 2Ctto], Bc.

Qual dolor qual martire Aria a una: S o T, [V o Ctto], Bc.

La pastorella mia Aria a 3: SS o TT, B [2V o 2Ctto], Bc.

Son arcieri Aria a una, o due voci se piace: S o T, B, [V o Ctto], Bc.

Donzelletta Aria a 3: SSB, [2V o 2Ctto], Bc.

Vezzosetta pastorella Aria a 2: S o T, B, [V o Ctto], Bc.

Accorta lusinghiera Aria a 2: SS o TT, [V o Ctto], Bc.

Bella donna mia Scherzo a una voce: S o T, [V o Ctto], Bc.

Pur si rupp'il fero laccio Scherzo a una voce: S o T, [V o Ctto], Bc.

Care luci Scherzo a una: S o T, [V o Ctto], Bc.

Non havea febo Aria a una: S o T, [V o Ctto], Bc.

O dell'alto Appenin a una Prima parte: T, [V o Ctto], Bc.

A cosi dolci, e si soave Seconda parte: T, [V o Ctto], Bc.

Ne men farai Terza parte: T, [V o Ctto], Bc.

The soprano instrumentation [V o Ctto] is contained in the foreword: *Mandando fuorè questo secondo libro de miei scherzi, arie, canzonette, e madrigali a una, due, e tre*

*voci, & avendo composti alcuni ritornelli, non ho volsuto mancare di avvertirli, che
ne i componimenti a tre voci, dove saranno i ritornelli a due soprani sarà ben fatto
sonare solamente il primo soprano, con il basso sopra l'instrumento di tasti, percioche
apporterà maggior comodo, e vaghezza, ma porgendosi occasione di altri strumenti
come Violini, Cornetti, e simili potranno sonarsi ambidue i soprani, perche renderanno
ottima armonia.*
B-Br; **CS-**Pdobrovského; **I-**Fc, -Vsm; **US-**C   SartI 1614f; RISM B4646

BÜTNER, Crato (*b* Gotha or Sonneberg, Thuringia, 1616; *d* Danzig, 1679)
Te Deum laudamus. . . . Danzig: Ludwig Knaust (David Friedrich Rheten), 1662.
    SSATB, SATB, ATTB, 2V, Va, 2Ctto, 2Tpt, Timp, 4Trb, Vo, Bc.
D-Kdma [2/45], -LEm   RISM B4915

    Ex Psalmo 47, Frolocket mit Händen alle Völcker A 8 voci con li stromenti, e 5
    capella è Trombetti ô Cornetti con basso continuo: SSSA, ATTB, 2V, 2Tpt o 2Ctto,
    4Trb, 6v *cap*, Bc.
***D-**Kdma [2/1725]; **S-**Uu Vok. Mus. i hs. 5:10

    Missa Germanica: O Vater, allmächtiger Gott: SATB *conc & cap*, V, Ctto, 3Va o
    3Trb, Bc.
D-BII mus. ms. 2627 (Erfurt collection, score and parts dated 1674)   *NoackE

    Deus in adjiutorium meum intende à 7, 12: SSATB *conc & rip*, (*ripieni* may be
    replaced by 2Ctto and 3Trb), 2V, 2Cttino, 2Va, b Va, Bomb grosso.
    Siehe, es hat überwunden à 14, 18: SSATTB *conc*, SATB *rip*, 2V, 2Cttino, 2Tpt,
    3Trb, b Va, Bomb grosso.
PL-GD ms. 406 (recopied by Cantor Gottfried Nauwerck, *ca* 1689)   *BernC

    Gott ist unser Zuversicht und Stärke: SSATTB, 2V, 2Ctto, Fag, Bc.
S-Uu Vok. Mus. i hs. 41:16 (anon: attrib. by Krummacher)   *WalkerSB

BÜTTNER, Michael
    Der Herr gebe euch vom Thaw des Himmels à 11: SSAT *conc*; 3V̇; SATTB *rip*,
    Ctto, 4Trb; 3V; Bc (Symphonia 3V; Symph. 4Trb).
PL-WRu (Bohn collection Ms. mus. 132, now in **D-**BI, parts)

    Hosianna dem Sohne David/Lobet alle Gott unsern Herren à 16: ChI SSAA; ChII
    ATBB; Cappella: SSAATTB, Ctto; 2V, Va, Vo, 4Trb, Org, Cemb.
    The cornett belongs in the "Cappella," but not *colla parte*.
PL-WRu (Bohn collection Ms. mus. 132a, now in **D-**BI, parts and tab)

    Ich dancke dem Herren umb seiner Gerechtigkeit willen à 8 o 12: ChI&II SATB;
        Cappella: ST[AB lost?], Ctto & V, 3Trb & "viole," Bc (with 2 symphonie)
There are two sets of parts: one set is labeled "cornetto," and "trombone" while the
other set is labeled "viol. è cornetto" and "trombone è viole".
PL-WRu (Bohn collection Ms. mus. 132b, now in **D-**BI, parts dated 1637)

Kommet her zue mir alle: ChI&II SATB; Ctto, 3Trb; 2V, Vo, Org (cornetto and trombones *colla parte* with second choir).
PL-WRu (Bohn collection Ms. mus. 132c, now in **D**-BI, parts and tab)

Lobet alle Gott den Herren à 16: SATBB, 2V, 4Trb; Cappella: SAATTB, Ctto; Vo, Bc (Cornett in cappella but not *colla parte*; *sinfonie* with violins and trombones).
PL-WRu (Bohn collection Ms. mus. 132d, now in **D**-BI, parts and tab)

BUXTEHUDE, Dieterich (*b* Oldesloe ? *ca* 1637; *d* Lübeck, 1707)
Ihr Lieben Christen freut euch nun: SSATB, 3V, 2Va, 3Ctto, 2Tpt, 3Trb, Fag, Org (with symphonia: 3Ctto, 3Trb).
A-Wgm ms. 30288; **D**-LÜh A373 (now in -BII) A312a, -Dl mus. 1832 E/1   BuxWV 51
Edition: DdT 14

Gott fähret auf mit Jauchzen: SSB, 2V, Va, 2Tpt, 2Ctto, 2Trb, Fag, Bc.
D-Kdma [2/424]; **S**-Uu Vok. Mus. i hs 82:43   BuxWV 33
Edition: BuxtW 5

Benedicam Dominum in omni tempore à 24: ChI 2V, Vo; ChII 4Tpt, Trb, Bomb o bTrb; ChIII SSATB; ChIV 2Ctto, Fag; ChV 3Trb; SATB *cap*; Bc.
D-Kdma [2/2156]; **S**-Uu Vok. Mus. i hs 50:6   BuxVW 113
Edition: BuxtW 4

Nun dancket alle Gott: SSATB, 2V, 2Ctto, 2Tpt, Fag, Vo, Bc.
D-Dl 1832 e1; **D**-LÜh mus. A373 (now in -BII) A312a; **S**-Uu Vok. Mus. i hs 82:89
BuxWV 79; *SorensenS

Wie wird erneuet wie wird erfreuet: SSATTB, 3V, 2Va, 3Ctto, 3Tpt, 3Trb, Vo, Cemb, Org.
D-LÜh mus. A373 tab   BuxWV 110; *SorensenS

Ich bin die Auferstehung: B, 2V, 2Va, 2Ctto, 2Tpt, Fag, Bc.
S-Uu Vok. Mus. i hs 82:43,3   BuxWV 44
Edition: BuxtW 2

Mein Gemüt erfreuet sich: SAB, 4V, 2Tpt, 2Fl, 2Ctto, 3Trb, 3Fag, Bc.
S-Uu Vok. Mus. i hs 85:5 f. 9   BuxWV 72
Edition: BuxtW 7

CALDARA, Antonio (*b* Venice, *ca* 1670; *d* Vienna, 1736)

Dixit Dominus: SATB *conc & cap*, 2V, 2Va, [Ctto], 2Trb, 2Tpt, Timp, Vo, Org.
A-KR E 38/206 (mid 18th-cent ms)   *RISM AII 600171822

Magnificat: SATB *conc & cap*, 2V, 2Va, [Ctto], 2Trb, 2Tpt, Timp, Vo, Org.
A-KR E 38/207 (ms from *ca* 1750)   *RISM AII 600171822

Missa: 4v *conc* [SATB], 2V *conc*, Vc, Vo, Ctto, 2Trb, Fag.
A-Wn HK 1075   *card catalog

Credo: 4v *conc & rip* [SATB], 2V *conc*, Vc, Vo, Ctto, 2Trb *conc*, Fag, 2Tpt, "Trombe," Timp, Org.
A-Wn HK 1082   *card catalog

Te Deum: SATB *conc & cap*, 2V, 2Va, Ctto, 2Trb, Fag, 2Tpt, Timp, Vc, Vo, Org.
D-BII Mus. ms. 2753 (dated 1734 but ms from *ca* 1840[!])   *RISM AII 150829

CALMBACH, Georg (*fl* 1675)

Actus Musicus in Dominic: ChI SSAATTB, 2V, 2Ctto, 2Tpt, 2Fl, Vo, Trb o Fag, Org; ChII T, 2VaG, Vo; ChIII BB *conc*, SATB *cap*; Vo, Org o Regal.
D-BII mus. ms. 2796 (Erfurt collection, score and parts dated 1675)   *NoackE

CAPRICORNUS, Samuel Friedrich (*b* Schertitz, 1628; *d* Stuttgart, 1665)

Opus musicum, ab 1.2.3.4.5.6.7.8. vocibus concertantibus, & variis instrumentis, adjuncto choro pleniori, sive, ut vocant, in ripieno concinnatum. Nürnberg: Christoph Gerhard, 1655.
    2. Kyrie [Mass]: ChI SATB *conc*; ChII SATB *rip*, 2V, 2Ctto, 3Trb, Bc.
    18. O venerabile sacramentum: AA, 2Ctto o 2V, Bc.
    20. Judica Domine: SS, V, Ctto, Bc.
A-Wgm (missing A2 *rip*), -Wn[?]; **CH-Zz**; **D-B** (now in **PL-Kj**), -Rp (missing A1 *conc*); **GB-Lbm**; **H-Bl** (T1 *rip*); **S-Uu** (ms version of "Judica Domine" in S-Uu Vok. Mus. i hs 84:58, ff. 3-6 partitura). (A ms version of "O venerabile" is in **D-BII** Mus. ms. 2980, and possibly also in **CS-KRa**.)   MitUB   RISM C928

Dritter Theil Geistlicher Harmonien, mit drey Stimmen und beygefügten Instrumenten. Stuttgart: Johann Weyrich Rösslin, 1664.
    16. Praeparate: ATB, V, Ctto, Trb, Org.
    18. Paratum cor meum: SSB, Ctto, Org.
D-B (now in **PL-Kj**), -F, -HAmk; (Paratum cor meum in ms dated 1665: S-Uu Vok. Mus. i hs 10:9[24])   RISM C935

---

[24] This ms of "Paratum cor meum" has a *cornettino* part instead of a *cornetto* part.

Opus Aureum Missaru. . . . Frankfurt: Johann & Caspar Bencard, 1670.
   3. Kyrie eleison e Gloria in excelsis Deo, tertii toni à12: SSAATTBB, 2V, 2Ctto, Org.
The print also has an engraving of an ensemble performing the "Kyrie" consisting of organ, cornett, viol, and triangle.
F-Pn; US-CAe   RISM C940

   Der Herr ist mein Hirte: SSATTB, 2Cttino, 2V, 4Trb o 3Va e Fag, Bc.
D-BII ms. 2980 (Bokemeyer collection, score; also contains "O venerabile": see *Opus musicum,* 1655); **D-Kdma** [2/2206]   *KümmerKB

   Judica Domine: SS, Ctto, V, Bc.
S-Uu Vok. Mus. i hs 10:1

   Surrexit pastor bonus: A, Cttino, Org.
SeiffertL lists a piece with identical name and setting but with *Violino solo* instead of *cornettino.*
S-Uu vok. mus, i hs 10:14   RISM AII 95106

CAZZATI, Mauritio (*b* Luzzara nr. Reggio Emilia, *ca* 1620; *d* Mantua, 1677)
   3. Deus in Adjutorium meum intende à 7 vel 12: ChI SATTB; ChII SATTB *rip,* doubled by Ctto, 4Trb; 2V, doubled by 2Cttino *ad plac;* bVa *ad plac,* doubled by Bomb; Fag; Org.
PL-GD mus. ms. 406, vol 2 (recopied from *Op. 1, Salmi e messa* [1641] by Cantor Gottfried Nauwerck in 1688)   BernC

CESARE, Giovanni Martino (*b* Udine, *ca* 1590; *d* Munich, 1667)
Musicali melodie per voci et instrumenti a una, due, tre, quattro, cinque, e sei voci . . . prima parte. Munich: Nicolaus Heinrich, 1621.
   10. Jubilate Deo à 4: SSB, Ctto, Org.
   13. Benedicam Dominum à 5: SST, 2Ctto, Org.
This print also contains twelve instrumental works (see instrumental list).
D-F (part 2), **-Kdma. -Rp**   SartMS I 1621b; RISM C175

CESIS, Sulpitia (*b* Modena, 1577; *d* after 1619)
Motetti spirituali[. . . .] Modena: Giuliano Cassiani, 1619.
   Hodie gloriosus Pater Augustinus a 8: SAT, Vo; Ctto, 2Trb, "Arciviolone."
This motet is indicated *alla quarta bassa* with the three vocal parts originally notated in soprano, mezzosoprano, and alto clefs. In addition, the alto part of the first choir and the cornetto part carry the indication *all'ottava alta.*
GB-Lbl (A1,B1); **I-MOe**   RISM C1764

CESTI, Antonio (*b* Arezzo, 1623; *d* Florence, 1669)
   In the opera *Il pomo d'oro*:
   Act 1 scene 1, "Reggia di Plutone": SB "Proserpine & Pluto," 2Ctto, 3Trb, Fag, Regal.

Act 2 scene 6 and 7, "Bocca d'Inferno": B "Caronte," 2Ctto, 3Trb, Fag, Regal.
A-Wn ms. 16844
Edition: DTÖ 6, 9.

CHINELLI, Giovanni Battista (*b* Moletolo nr. Parma, 1610; *d* Parma, 1677)

Il quarto libro de motetti a 2 e 3 voci con alcune cantilene nel fine a 3 voci con violini et altri stromenti ad libitum . . . opera nona. Venice: Alessandro Vincenti, 1652.
Psallite Domino: TTB, 2V o 2Ctto; "e parte per ripieni *ad lib*" aVa, bVa; o 2Trb; Bc.
I-Bc, -FEc (S2, A,T,B); **PL**-WRu (Bc, S2 missing, T incompl)   RISM C2066

CLAVIUS, Christophorus (see instrumental list)

COBALEDA, Alonso de

Miserere à 10: ChI SSAT; ChII SATB, Ctto muto, Tpt; ChIII STB; Hp, Cemb.
The tiple part of choir II says "*tiple de 2° coro y muta*" (i.e., Ctto muto), with music (consisting of both untexted and texted sections) marked "*tiple para la muta cuando cantan solo.*" The alto part of choir II is marked "*alto e clarin.*"
E-Zamora, Archivo Musical de la catedral sign 2/8 (dated 1712)

COLOMBINI, Francesco (*b* Carrara, 1573; *d* after mid-1630s)

Laudate Dominum à 8: SATTB, V, 2Va, Ctto o V, Trb o Va, Lt o Va; Tior, Org.
A-KR L13 (ms from *ca* 1633-39)   *RISM AII 600153404

COLONNA, Giovanni Paolo (Bologna, 1637-1695)

Memento Domine David: ChI&II SATB *cap*, each choir doubled by 3V, aCtto & 2aVa, 2tTrb& 2tVa, 2 bTrb& 2 bVioloncino; Vo, Tior, 3Org.
I-Bsp ms. L.C. Lv. 4 (Versetto from *Salmi a 8 voci,* Op. 1 [1681] in ms version with instrumentations)

COMES, Juan Battista (Valencia, 1582-1643)

Dixit Dominus à 17: ChI with Harp; ChII with Org; ChIII with Org & Vihuelas; ChIV [?]Ctto, [?]Trb, Fag.
Al Misterio "La iglesia de Dios" à 3 Chori: ChI,II&III SATB; T, Ctto, 2"Bajonito," "Bajon."
E-VAcp
*Edition: Juan Battista Guzmán, ed., *Obras musicales del insigne maestro espagñol del siglo XVII* (Madrid: Colegio Nacional de Sordo-Mundos y de Ciegos, 1888)

CONRADI, Johann Georg (*d* Oettingen, 1699)

Allein Gott in der Höh sei Ehr: SSATTB, 2V, 2Va, 2Ctto, 2Fl, Trb, Org.
D-F ms. Ff. Mus. 169 (missing Fl parts)   *SüssKM

CORRADINI, Nicolò (*d* Cremona, 1646)

Motetti a una, due, tre, e quatro voci fra quali ve ne sono alcuni concertati con instromenti, & con il basso continuo per l'organo. Libro primo. Venice: Stampa del Gardano, 1624.

Spargite flores a 3: S, V o Ctto, Vo o Trb "doppio," Org.

Cantate Domino a 3: "Nella Stessa maniera"

D-B (S,T,Org now in **PL-Kj**); **I-PCd** (compl) RISM C3953

CORTECCIA, Francesco (Florence, 1502-1571)

Musiche fatte nelle nozze dello illustrissimo Duca di Fierenze il signor Cosimo de' Medici et della illustrissima consorte sua mad. Leonora da Tolleto. Venice: Antonio Gardano, 1539.

Ingredere felicissimis auspiciis à 6: SSAATTBB, 4Ctto, 4Trb.

Gardane almo pastore à 6: 6 "Storte" (crummhorns), [Ctto].

Bacco bacco euoe à 4: SATB, [Ctto, Ctto diritto, ribecchino, pipe and tabor, 2Crummhorns, Tromba torta, Harp, Tamb].

From the CANTUS partbook *tavola* is the following description of "Ingredere felicissimis auspiciis": *Ingredere a otto voci di Franc. Corteccia cantato sopra l'arco del portone della porta al prato da vinti quatro voci da una banda, et da l'altra da quattro tromboni, et quatro cornetti nella entrada della Illustrissima Duchessa. . . .* Additional descriptions of instrumentation by Giambulari (Florence, 1539) suggest the use of cornetts in "Gardane almo pastore" and in "Bacco, bacco, euoe." The Gardano print indicates the use of crummhorns only for "Gardane almo pastore," and no instrumentation is given for "Bacco, bacco, euoe." Also of interest in this description is the staging of "Sacro e Santo Hymeno" where the muses held the following instruments (presumably they were not played during the performance): *Thalia*: Trombone, *Euterpe*: Dolziana, *Erato*: Violone, *Melpomene*: Piffaro, *Clio*: Flauto, *Terpsichore*: Liuto, *Polyma*: Crummhorn, *Urania*: Cornetto, and *Calliope*: Ribecchino.

A-Wn *BrownSCI

Edition: Forni

(One piece in D-Rp Mus. ms A.R. 775&777; see instrumental list)

C[ROATTI], F[rancesco] (*b* Ferrara; *fl* 1607-08)

Missa à 4 voci e 6 stromenti con 4 ripieni: SATB, 2Cttino, 3Trb, Bomb grosso, 4Va[G], Bc.

PL-GD Mus. ms. 401 *BernC

CROTTI, Arcangelo (*fl* Ferrara, 1608)

Il primo libro de' concerti ecclesiastici a1. a2. a3. a4. & a5. parte con voci sole, & parte con voci, & instrumenti. Venice: Giacomo Vincenti, 1608.

Sonata sopra Sancta Maria: S, 2V o 2Ctto, Trb, Org.

O gloriosa Domina: S, V o Ctto, Fag, Org.

O sacrum convivium: S, Ctto, Trb, Org.

Congratulamini: S, Ctto, Trb, b, Org.

Pater peccavi: S, Ctto, 3Trb, Org.

The heading of "O gloriosa Domina" in the *canto secondo* partbook reads *Cornetto overo Violino,* but cornett is not specified in the *tavola.*
B-Br; **I**-Bc   RISM C4552

CRÜGER, Johannes (*b* Gross-Breesen, Lower Lusatia, 1598; *d* Berlin, 1662)

Geistliche Kirchen-Melodien . . . in vier Vocal und zwey Instrumental-Stimmen als Violinen oder Cornetten übersetzet. Leipzig: Daniel Reichel (Timotheus Ritzsch), 1649.
    1. Aus meines Herzens Grunde: SATB, 2V o 2Ctto, [Org] Bc.
    2. Du o schönes Welt gebäude: SATB, 2V o 2Ctto, [Org] Bc.
    3. O du Jesu Christ dein Kripplein: SATB, 2V o 2Ctto, [Org] Bc.
    4. Nun laßt uns gehn: SATB, 2V o 2Ctto, [Org] Bc.
    5. Nun Kömm der Heiden Heiland: SATB, 2V o 2Ctto, [Org] Bc.
    6. Christ lag in Todesbanden: SATB, 2V o 2Ctto, [Org] Bc.
    7. Komm, Heiliger Geist, Herre Gott: SATB, 2V o 2Ctto, [Org] Bc.
    8. Nun lob, mein Seel, den Herren: SATB, 2V o 2Ctto, [Org] Bc.
    9. Allein Gott in der Höh sei Ehr: SATB, 2V o 2Ctto, [Org] Bc.
    10. Was mein Gott wil, das gscheh allzeit: SATB, 2V o 2Ctto, [Org] Bc.
    11. Aus meines Herzens Grunde: SATB, 2V o 2Ctto, [Org] Bc.
    12. Wach auf mein Herz, und singe: SATB, 2V o 2Ctto, [Org] Bc.
    13. Die Sohn hat sich mit ihrem Glanz gewendet: SATB, 2V o 2Ctto, [Org] Bc.
D-HAu (T,Bc,V1 incompl), -SAh (SAT,V1,V2,Bc); **GB**-Lbl (T); **PL**-WRu (S,A,V2);
US-PHu   *RISM C4571
*Partial editions: Hänssler Verlag no. 189 (nos. 1-4); Bärenreiter no. 1114 (nos. 5-13)

CRUSIUS, P. (*fl* mid 17th cent.)

    Erhebe dich, mein froher Mund: SATB, 2V, Va "Tamb," Ob o "clarinetti"[!], 2Ctto, 2Trb, Bc.
D-Dlb 3347 E 500 (Grimma LSGr 110/T16, score)   *WalkerSB

D[EYEN] (or Degen?), J[ohann] B[aptiste]

    Missa clementina: 4v *conc,* 8v *cap,* 2V, 3Va, 2Tpt, 2Ctto *in defectu Clarinorum,* 3Trb *ad lib,* Vo, Org.
CS-KRa B I 163 (missing 4v *cap* and Trb parts)   OttoS

DÍAZ [Bessón], Gabriel (*b* Alcalá de Henares, before 1590; *d* Madrid, 1638)

    Lauda Ierusalem a 11 con instrumentos: ChI SSA, Org; ChII T, Ctto, Trb, "Baxon"; ChIII SSAB.
E-C ms (*ca* 1620-30)
*Edition: MME 41

DONATI, Ignatio (*b* Casalmaggiore, nr. Parma, *ca* 1575; *d* Milan, 1638)

Salmi Boscarecci concertati a sei voci, con aggiunta, se piace, di altre sei voci, che servono per concerto . . . con il basso principale per sonar nell'organo. Op 9. Venice: Alessandro Vincenti, †1623, ∞1639.

All: ChI SSATTB; ChII SSATTB *rip*, 3V o 3Ctto, 3Trb o 3Fag; Org.

Domine ad adiuvandum	Lauda Hierusalem
Dixit Dominus	Credidi propter quod
Confitebor tibi Domine	Magnificat anima mea. Sexti toni
Beatus vir qui temet Dominum	Dixit Dominus Domino meo
Laudate pueri Dominum	Laudate pueri Dominum
Laudate Dominum omnes gentes	Magnificat anima mea. Primi toni
In exiter Israel de Aegipt	Missa primi toni
Laetatus sum	Missa secundi toni
Nisi Dominus	

†I-Bc, -Bsp, -FEc, -VCd (missing 5, Trb), -Sac (incompl); **PL**-WRu (missing SB, Trb); ∞**I**-SPd (missing S); **S**-Uu (missing ST *rip*)   *MitUB   RISM D3396/3397

In: *Flores praestantissimorum virorum a Philippo Lomatio bibliopola delibat unica, binis, ternis, quaternisque vocibus decantandi. . . .* Milan: Filippo Lomazzo, 1626.
   Concerto terzo, O gloriosa Domina: SS o TT, (S o T, V o Ctto), Org, "over una voce e instrumento à modo di ecco."
I-CEc (SAT); **US**-R (SAB, partitur)   SartMS II 1626n; RISM 1626[5]

DRAGHI, Antonio (*b* Rimini, 1634/35; *d* Vienna, 1700)
   Missa Assumptionis: SSATB *conc & cap*, 2Ctto, 4Trb, 2V, 4Va, Vo, Org.
A-KR ms. 642 (dated 1684)
*Edition: DTÖ 46

Festspiel "Il Pelegrinaggio delle Gratie," "am 22. April 1691 zum Namensfest der regierenden Kaiserin Eleonora Magdalena Theresa aufgefuert."
   "Sinfonia con stromenti da fiato": 2Ctto, 3Trb, Fag.
A-Wn   *SpielmannZ

   In the [opera] *L'Amore per virtù*: Ctto is specified
A-Wn Mus. Hs. 16.851 (dated 1697)   *SpielmannZ

   In the opera *La tirannide abbattuta dalla virtù*: Ctto is specified
A-Wn Mus. Hs. 18.886 (dated 1697)   *SpielmannZ

DURÓN, Diego (*b* Brihuega, *ca* 1658; *d* Las Palmas, 1731)
   Cantada de corpus. Resuene el orbe: A, 2Ctto, Fag, Vo, Hp.
E-LPA ms. CXIV, 43 (dated 1725)
*Edition: MBE 35

EBNER, Wolfgang (*b* Augsburg, 1612; *d* Vienna, 1665)
   Missa Contrapuncto: SATB, Ctto, 3Trb, Vo, Org.
CS-KRa B I 164 (dated 1674)   OttoS

ERLEBACH, Philipp Heinrich (*bapt.* Esens, 1657; *d* Rudolstadt, Thuringia, 1714)

Fürchtet euch nicht: SATB, 2V, 2Va, Ctto, 2Tpt, 3Trb, Vo, Timp, Bc (Fag mentioned on title page).

D-F *SüssKM

EULENHAUPT, Johann Ernst

Laudate Dominum omnes gentes: TB, Cttino o V, Trb, Bc.

D-Dl Mus. ms. 1820-E-500 *LeonardT

FABB[RINI], Gius[eppe] (*b* Siena?; *d* Siena, 1708)

Introito a Capp.a A quattro, con VV e ripieni per la Madonna dei dolori: SATB, 2V, Ctto, Cor di Bassetto, Tior, Vo, Org.

I-Sd 2753/18 (dated 1700 in Siena)   *RISM AII 174801

Missa Sancti Angeli Custodis: ChI&II SATB; 2V, Ctto, Cor di Bassetto o Tromba, Tior, Org.

I-Sd 2759/4 (dated 1707 in Siena)   *RISM AII 174803

Patrem omnipotentem *Pieno, e Breve*: ChI&II AB; 2V, 2Ctto *ad lib*, Org.

I-Sd 2782/48 (dated 1693)   *RISM AII 182433

FABRI, Stefano (Rome, *ca* 1606-1658)

Magnificat 8v a 2 cori: ChI&II SATB; V, Ctto, Tior, Lt, Org.

I-TRbmf   *La Biblioteca musicale Lawrence K.J. Feininger* (Trent: Provincia autonoma di Trento, 1985)

FABRICIUS, Werner (*b* Itzehoe, Holstein, 1633; *d* Leipzig, 1679)

Geistliche Arien Dialogen und Concerten. . . . Leipzig: Johann Bauer, 1662.
      3. Surrexit Christus hodie: SSATTTTB, 2V, 2Va, 2Ctto, 2Trb, "cum tubis et Timp." [2Tpt & timp].
      6. Schaffe in mir, Gott: SATB, 2 Schryari o 2 Ctto, 2Trb.

A-Wn, -Wgm; **B-Br**; **D-B** (now in **PL-Kj**), -BD, -W; **GB-Lbl**; (a ms version of no. 6 is contained in **S-Uu** i. hs. 81:128)   *Buch   RISM F35

Jauchzet ihr Himmel: SSATB *conc & cap*, 2V, 2Tpt o 2Ctto, Bc.

D-BII Mus. ms. 5755 (Erfurt collection, parts dated 1674)   *NoackE

Jesu, liebster Seelen Freund: SATB *conc & rip*, V o Ctto, 3Trb, Vo, Bc.

D-Dlb 1899 E-500 (Grimma U108/V2, parts)

FERDINAND III (*b* Graz, 1608; *d* Vienna, 1657)

Hymnus de Nativitate Domini. Jesu redemptor omnium: SATB *conc*, 3Fl, 3Tpt; SATB *rip* with Ctto, 2Trb, 2V, Fag; Vc, Vo, Tior, Org.

A-Wn   *AdlerMW

Deus tuorum militum: SB, Ctto, Fag, Bc.
Humanae salutis sator: SATB *conc & rip*, 2V, 2Ctto, [2?]Trb, Org.
D-Lr mus. ant. prac. K.N.28 (Humanae salutis sator dated 1650)   *WelterRL

FINATTI, Giovanni Pietro (*fl* mid-17th cent)

Missae motetta, litaniae B. Virginis, cum quatuor, eius solennibus antiphonis, duabus, tribus, quatuor, & quinque vocibus, cum instrumentis & suis replementis ad libitum, opus secundum. Antwerp: Magdelène Phalèse, 1652.
    Regina coeli: STTB, 2V o 2Ctto, Org.
CH-Zz; **F**-Pn; **I**-PCd   RISM F802

FISCHER, Ferdinand (1723-1805)

"Cantate zur unterthänigsten Feyer des Höchsten Geburts-Festes des Durch-lauchigsten Herzogs und Herrn CARL AUGUST Regierenden Herzogs zu Weimar und Eisenach &c. &c. . . .": SAT *conc*, SATB *cap*, 2Clarinetti, 2Horn, 2Tpt, Ctto, 3Trb, Timp.
D-WRl HMA 3907 (ms dated 1801)   *RISM AII 250000120

FLIXIO, Johann Joseph [FLIXIUS]

Magnus Dominus à 12: SSATBB, 2V, Ctto, 3Trb, Org
CS-KRa B II 308   OttoS

FRANCK, Johann Wolfgang (*b* Unterschwaningen, *bapt.*1644; *d ca* 1710)

Te Deum laudamus te: SSATB, 2Tpt, 2Ctto, 2V, 2Va, Bc.
Conturbatae sunt gentes: SSATBB, 4Tpt, 2Ctto, 2V, 2Va, Timp, Bc.
D-BI Mus. ms. 30298 (Bokemeyer collection, score)   KümmerKB

FRANCK, Melchior (*b* Zittau, *ca* 1579; *d* Coburg, 1639)

Halleluja. Ich fahre auf zu meinem Vater: T *conc*, AT *rip*, 2Ctto, 3Trb, Bc (with sinfonia).
PL-WRu (Bohn collection Ms. mus. 140a, now in **D**-BI, parts)

FRANZONI, Amante (*b* Mantua, *fl* 1605-1630)

Concerti ecclesiastici a una, due, et a tre voci col basso continuo per l'organo . . . libro primo. Venice: Ricciardo Amadino, 1611.
    Sopra l'aria d'Ruggiero "Lauda syon salvatorum": TT, 2V o 2Ctto, Bc.
A-Wn (missing T)   SartMS I 1611a; RISM F1812

FREDDI, Amadio (*b* Padua, *fl* 1594-1634)

Messa vespro et compieta a cinque voci col suo basso continuo aggiuntovi un violino, e corneto per le sinfonie. . . .   Venice: Ricciardo Amadino, 1616.
    Nisi Dominus: SATTB, V, Ctto, Org.
    Laetatus sum: SATTB, V, Ctto, Org.

Magnificat: SATTB, V, Ctto, Org.
I-Bc   RISM F1829

FREISSLICH, Johann Balthasar Christian (*bapt.* Immelborn, 1687; *d* Danzig, 1764)
Ehre sey Gott in der Höhe: ChI SATB, 2Tpt, Trav, 2V, Va, Vc, Timp, Bomb; ChII
SATB, Cttino, Ob, Org *pro directore*.
PL-GD Ms. 2   *BernC

Erthönt ihr Hütten der Gerechten: ChI&II; with Ctto part marked "Cornetto pro
Direct[ore]"
The ms is said to contain three other cantatas with Ctto as a ripieno instrument in ChII.
PL-GDj Ms. 31   *BernC

FROMM, Andreas (*b* Pänitz nr. Wusterhausen, 1621; *d* Prague, 1683)
*Actus musicus de divite et Lazaro, das ist musicalische Abbildung der Parable vom
reichen Manne und Lazaro, Lucae 16. mit gewissen Persohnen . . . und allerley
Instrumenten als Orgel, Clavicymbel, Laut, Violdigam, Trompeten, Paucken, Dulcian,
Corneten, Posaunen, Geigen, & Flöten. . . .* Stettin: Jeremias Mamphrasen [Georg
Göttzke], 1649.
    10. Symphonia, 2Ctto, Bc.
    13. SATTB, 2Tpt, Ctto, Fl, Bc.
    15. SSATTB, 2Tpt, 2Ctto, Bc.
PL-WRu (missing Bc & 5 vocal/inst parts)   RISM F2039
*Edition: Bärenreiter 919

FUNCKE, Friedrich (*b* Nossen, Saxony, 1642; *d* Römstedt, nr. Lüneburg, 1699)
Danck- und Denck-Mahl, über den starcken und unverhofften Donnerschlag. . . .
Hamburg: Georg Rebenlein, 1666.
    Gelobet sei der Herr aus Zion: 2(SATB), 2V o 2Ctto, 2Va o 2Trb, Fag, Bc.
D-Lr   *WalkerSB   RISM F2100

FUNGHETTO, Paolo [FONGHETTO] (*b* Verona, *ca* 1572; *d ca* 1630)
*Missa, psalmi omnes ad vesperas, complectorium motecta, et concentus, cum duobus
Magnificat, ut vocant, octonis vocibus concinenda. Una cum basso continuo ad
organum . . . nunc primum omnia. . . .* Venice: Giacomo Vincenti, 1609.
    Motette, Osculetur me osculo oris sui: SSB, V, V o Ctto, 2Va, b, Bc.
The print also contains two canzonas with no specified instrumentation.
I-BRd   SartMS I 1609e; RISM F1472

FURCHHEIM, Johann Wilhelm [Forcheim] (*b ca* 1635-40; *d* Dresden, 1682)
Lobe den Herrn meine Seele: SATB, 2Tpt, 2Cttino, Fag, Bc.
D-Bl Mus. ms. 30298 (Bokemeyer collection, score)   *EitQ; *KümmerKB

FUX, Johann Joseph (*b* Hirtenfeld, Styria, 1660; *d* Vienna, 1741)
In alphabetical order by title:

Alma redemptoris: SATB, 2V, (Ctto, 2Trb, Fag) *rip*; Vc, Vo, Org.
A-Wn ms.   *[Köchel 200]

Ave mundi spes Maria [Mottetto de B.M.V.]: SAT, 2V, Vc, Vo, Ctto, 2Trb, Fag, Org.
A-Wn ms. (AN.65 A.12 vol VI no. 11)   *[Köchel 171]

Ave pia stella Maris [Motetto della Madonna SS.]: S, 2V, Fag *conc*; SATB, Ctto, 2Trb *rip* ; Vc, Vo, Org.
A-Wn ms. 17394   [Köchel 173]
*Edition: FuxW series 3 vol 1

Ave Regina à 4: SATB, 2V, Va, Vc, Vo, Ctto, Trb, Fag, Org.
A-Wn ms. 16374   *[Köchel 223]; card catalog

Ave Regina à 4 a Cappella: SATB, 2V, Va, bVa, Vc, Vo, Ctto, 2Trb, Fag, Org.
A-Wn ms. 16376   *[Köchel 226]; *card catalog

Beatus vir: SATB, 2V, Va; (Ctto, 2Trb, Fag) *rip*; Vc, Vo, Org.
A-Wn ms. 17353 (AN.65 A.12 vol II no. 6)   *[Köchel 80]

Beatus vir – Laudate pueri: SATB, 2V; (Ctto, 2Trb, Fag) *rip*; Vc, Vo, Org.
A-Wn ms. 16415   *[Köchel 82]

Celebremus cum gaudio [Mottetto de quovis Sancto]: ST, 2V *in conc*; SATB, Ctto, 2Trb, Fag, Vc, Vo, Org.
A-Wn ms. 17387   [Köchel 181]; *card catalog

Christe, fili summi patris [Mottetto de B.M.V.]: SATB *conc & rip*; 2V, 2Trb *conc*; (Ctto, Fag) *rip*; Vc, Vo, Org.
A-Wn ms. 17391   [Köchel 175]
*Edition: FuxW series 3 vol 3

Completorium: SATB, 2V, Vc, Vo, Ctto, 2Trb, Fag, Org.
A-Wn ms.   *[Köchel 128]

Concussum est mare [Mottetto de S. Michaele Arch.]: SATB *conc & rip*; 2V; (Ctto, 2Trb, Fag) *rip*; Vc, Vo, Org.
A-Wn ms. 17398 [Köchel 177]   *Edition: FuxW series 3 vol 3

Credidi, propter quod: SATB, 2V; Vc, Vo, Ctto, 2Trb, Fag, Org.
A-Wn ms. (AN.65 A.12 vol II no. 3)   *[Köchel 231]

Cum invocarem à 4. In te Domine à 3: SATB, 2V; Ctto, 2Trb, Fag, Vc, Vo, Org.
A-Wn ms. 17358 (AN.65 A.12 vol II no. 11)   *[Köchel 130]

Dies Irae à 5: SSATB *conc & rip*; 2V, Va, Trb *conc*; (2Ctto muto, Trb, Fag) *rip*;
Vc, Vo, Org.
A-Wn ms. 16353   [Köchel 52]
*Edition: FuxW series 1 vol 7

Dixit Dominus: SATB, 2Tpt, 2V; Ctto *rip*, 2Trb, Fag, 2"Trombe," Timp, Vc, Vo,
Org.
A-Wn ms. 17344 (AN.65 A.12 vol I no. 40)   *[Köchel 70]

Dixit Dominus à 8: SSAATTBB, 2V, Va, *conc*; Ctto, 2Trb, Fag, Vc, Vo, Org.
A-Wn ms. 17347 (AN.65 A.12 vol I no. 13)   *[Köchel 72]

Dixit Dominus à 4: SATB, 2V, Vc, Vo, Ctto, 2Trb, Fag, Org.
A-Wn ms. 17346? (AN.65 A.12)   *[Köchel 74]

Dixit Dominus à 6: SATTBB, 2V, Va, 2Trb, 2Tpt; Ctto *rip*, Fag, Timp, Vc, Vo,
Org.
A-Wn ms. 17345 (AN.65 A.12 vol I no. 11)   *[Köchel 75]

Dixit Dominus – Confitebor: SATB, 2V, Vc, Vo, Ctto, 2Trb, Fag, Org.
A-Wn ms. 17399 (AN.65 A.12 vol IV no. 1b)   *[Köchel 76]

Dixit Dominus – Confitebor: SATB, 2V, Vc, Vo, Ctto, 2Trb, Fag, Org.
A-Wn ms. 17369 (AN.65 A.12 vol IV no. 1a)   *[Köchel 77]

Domine Jesu Christe à 5: SSATB *conc & rip*; 2V, Va *conc*; (2Ctto muto, 2Trb, Fag)
rip; Vc, Vo, Org.
A-Wn ms. 1635   [Köchel 53]
*Edition: FuxW vol 7

Domine probasti me: SATB, 2V; Vc, Vo, Ctto, 2Trb, Fag, Org.
A-Wn ms. 17351 (AN.65 A.12 vol II no. 4)   *[Köchel 234]

Estote fortes [Offertorium de Apostulis]: SATB *conc & rip*, 3Va; (Ctto, 2Trb, Fag)
rip; Vc, Vo, Org.
A-Wn ms. 17342   [Köchel 159]
*Edition: FuxW series 3 vol 3

In convertendo Dominus: SATB, 2V; Vc, Vo, Ctto, 2Trb, Fag, Org.
A-Wn ms. 17355   [Köchel 242]; *card catalog

In exitu Israel: SATB, 2V; Vc, Vo, Ctto, 2Trb, Fag, Org.
A-Wn ms. 17352 (AN.65 A.12 vol II no. 5)   *[Köchel 243]

Intractus pro Feria VI Quator Temporum Pentecostes
In te Domine speravi: SATB, Ctto, Va, 2Trb, Fag, Vc, Vo, Org.
Repleatur os meum laude tua alleluja: SATB, Ctto, 2Trb, Fag, Vc, Vo.
A-Wn ms. 15.820
*Edition: DTÖ 3

Introitus: In justitia tua: SATB, 2V, Va, Vc, Vo, Ctto, 2Trb, Fag.
A-Wn ver. arch. 2817   *[Köchel 282]

Laetatus sum: SATB, 2V, (Ctto, 2Trb, Fag) *rip*; Vc, Vo, Org.
A-Wn ms. 17348   *[Köchel 102]; *card catalog

Laetatus sum à 4: SATB, 2V, Va, Tpt; Ctto *rip*, Tpt, Fag, Vc, Vo, Org.
A-Wn ms. 17349   *[Köchel 104]; *card catalog

Laetatus sum. Nisi Dominus: SATB, 2V, Vc, Vo, Ctto, 2Trb, Fag, Org.
A-Wn ms. 16972   *[Köchel 106]; *card catalog

Lauda Jerusalem: SATB, 2V *conc;* (Ctto, 2Trb, Fag) *rip*; Va, Vc, Vo, Org.
A-Wn ms. 16963 [?]   *[Köchel 112]

Lauda Jerusalem: SATB, 2V, Vc, Vo, Ctto, 2Trb, Fag, Org.
A-Wn ms. 16964 [?]   *[Köchel 113]

Lauda Jerusalem. Magnificat: SATB, 2V; (Ctto, 2Trb, Fag) *rip*; Vc, Vo, Org.
A-Wn ms. 16965   *[Köchel 114]

Laudate Dominum: SATB, 2V, Va, Vc, Vo, Ctto, 2Trb, Fag, Org.
A-Wn ms. 17370   [Köchel 91]
*Edition: FuxW series 2 vol 3

Laudate Dominum à 4 da cappella: SATB, 2V, Va, Vc, Vo; (Ctto, 2Trb, Fag) *rip*;
Org.
A-Wn ms. 16968   [Köchel 92]
*Edition: FuxW series 2 vol 3

Laudate Dominum. Magnificat: SATB, 2V; (Ctto, 2Trb, Fag) *rip*; Vc, Vo, Org.
A-Wn ms. 16966   *[Köchel 93]

Laudate Dominum. Magnificat: SATB *conc & rip*; 2V *conc*; (Ctto, 2Trb, Fag) *rip*;
Vc, Vo, Org.
A-Wn ms. 16967   [Köchel 94]   *Edition: FuxW series 2 vol 3

Laudate pueri à 4: SATB, 2V, Vc, Vo, Ctto, 2Trb, Fag, Org.
A-Wn ms. 16416   *[Köchel 86]

Laudate pueri: SATB, 2V, Va, Vc, Vo, Ctto, 2Trb, Fag, Org.
A-Wn ms. 16417   *[Köchel 87]

Laudate pueri: SATB, 2V, Vc, Vo, Ctto, 2Trb, Fag, Org.
A-Wn ms. 16961   *[Köchel 88]

Laudate pueri: SATB, 2V; (Ctto, 2Trb, Fag) *rip*; Vc, Vo, Org.
A-Wn ms. 16962   *[Köchel 89]

Lettioni da Morto: SATB, 2V; Ctto, 2Trb, Fag, Vc, Vo, Org.
A-Wn ms. 17338 (AN.65 A.12 vol I no. 4)   *[Köchel 288]

Litaniae Laurentanae: SATB, 2V; (Ctto, 2Trb, Fag) *rip*; Vc, Vo, Org.
A-Wn ms. 17365 (AN65 A12 vol III no. 5)   *[Köchel 115]; *card catalog

Litaniae Laurentanae: SATB, 2V, 2Tpt, Timp *in conc*; Ctto, 2Trb, Fag, Tior, Vc, Vo, Org.
A-Wn ms. 17361 (AN.65 A.12 vol III no. 1)   *[Köchel 116]

Litaniae Laurentanae: SATB, 2V, Vc, Vo, Ctto, 2Trb, Fag, Org.
A-Wn ms. 17362 (AN65 A12 vol III no. 2)   *[Köchel 117]; *card catalog

Litaniae Laurentanae à 4: SATB, Vtta, 2Va, Vc, Vo, Ctto, 2Trb, Fag, Org.
A-Wn ms. 17368 (AN.65 A.12 vol III no. 8)   *[Köchel 118]

Litaniae Laurentanae. Mater Divinae Gratiae: SATB, 2V, 2Tpt, Timp; Ctto, 2Trb, Fag, Tior, Vc, Vo, Org.
A-Wn ms. 17366 (AN.65 A.12 vol III no. 6)   *[Köchel 122]

Litaniae. Mater Salvatoris: SATB, 2V; Ctto, 2Trb, Fag, Vc, Vo, Org.
A-Wn ms. 17364 (AN.65 A.12 vol III no. 4)   *[Köchel 123]

Litaniae. Sancta Dei genitrix: SATB, 2V, 2Tpt, Timp, 2Trb *in conc*; Ctto, 2Trb, Fag, Tior, Vc, Vo, Org.
A-Wn ms. 17363 (AN65 A12 vol III no. 3)   *[Köchel 120]; *card catalog

Litaniae. Sancta Maria: SSATB, 2V, 2Trb, 2Tpt *in conc*; Ctto, 2Trb, Fag, Tior, Vc, Vo, Org.
A-Wn ms. 17367 (AN65 A12 vol III no. 7)   *[Köchel 121]; *card catalog

Magnificat à 4: SATB *conc & rip*; 2V *conc*; (Ctto, 2Trb, Fag) *rip*; Vc, Vo, Org.
A-Wn ms. 16971   [Köchel 97]   *Edition: FuxW series 2 vol 3

Magnificat à 4: SATB *conc & rip*; 2V, Va, 2Tpt, 2Trb, Fag *conc*; (Ctto, Vc*) rip*;
Vo, Org.
A-Wn ms. 16970 [Köchel 98]
*Edition: FuxW series 2 vol 3

Magnificat: SATB *conc & rip*; 2Tpt, 2V, 3Va *conc*; (Ctto, 2Trb, Fag) *rip*; Tior, Vo,
Org.
A-Wn ms. 16969 [Köchel 99]
*Edition: FuxW series 2 vol 3

Magnificat: SATB *conc & rip*; 2V *conc*; (Ctto, 2Trb, Fag) *rip*; Vc, Vo, Org.
A-Wn ms. 17354 [Köchel 100]
*Edition: FuxW series 2 vol 3

Magnificat: SATB *conc & rip*; 2Va, Ctto, 2Trb, Fag, Vo, Org.
A-Ws [Köchel 101]
*Edition: FuxW series 2 vol 3

Mater facta, sed intacta [Hymn]: SATB, 2V, 2Trb; Ctto *rip*, Fag, Vc, Vo, Org.
A-Wn ms. 16404 *[Köchel 248]

Missa: SATB, 2V, Va, Vc, Vo, Ctto, 2Trb, Fag, Tpt[?], Timp, Org.
A-Wn ms. (AN.46 A.102) *[Köchel 47]

Missa Benjamin: SATB, 2V, Vc, Vo, Ctto, 2Trb, Fag, Org.
A-Wn ms. 16119 *[Köchel 3]; *card catalog

Missa Brevis Solemnitatis: SATB, 4Tpt, Ctto, 2Trb, 2V, Vo, Timp, Fag, Org.
A-Wn sign. cod. 19193 [Köchel 5]
Edition: FuxW series 1 vol 3

Missa Brevium ultima: SATB, 2V, Vc, Vo, Ctto, 2Trb, Fag, Org.
A-Wn ms. 16999 *[Köchel 6]; *card catalog

Missa Constantiae: SATB, 2V, 2Va, bVa, Vc, Vo, Ctto, Fag, 2Trb, Org.
A-Wn ms. (AN.43 A.95) *[Köchel 9]

Missa Corporis Christi: SATB *conc & rip*; 2Tpt, 2V, 2Trb, Fag *conc*; Va, Ctto *rip*;
Vc, Vo, Org.
A-Wn ms. 16996; **F**-Pc res. f1058 [Köchel 10]
*Edition: FuxW series 1 vol 1

Missa Dies mei sicut umbra: SATB *conc & rip*; 2V *conc*; (Ctto, 2Trb, Fag) *rip*; Vc,
Vo, Org.
A-Wn ms. 16136 [Köchel 12] Edition: SKMB 21

Missa Ferventis orationis: SATB, 2V, Vc, Vo, Ctto, 2Trb, Fag, Org.
A-Wn ms. 16116   *[Köchel 14]; *card catalog

Missa Fuge perversum mundum: 2(SATB), 2V, 3Va, Vc, Vo, Ctto, 2Trb, Fag, Org.
A-Wn ms. 16117   *[Köchel 16]; *card catalog

Missa Humilitatis: SATB *conc & rip*; 2V *conc*; (Ctto, 2Trb, Fag) *rip*; Vc, Vo, Org.
A-Wn ms. 19013   [Köchel 17]
*Edition: FuxW series vol 6

Missa In fletu solatium: SATB, 2V, Va, Vc, Ctto, 2Trb, Fag, Org.
A-Wn ms. 19011   *[Köchel 18]; *card catalog

Missa Post modicum non videbitis me: SATB, 2V, Vc, Vo, Ctto, 2Trb, Fag, Org.
A-Wn ms. 16133   *[Köchel 23]; *card catalog

Missa Preces tibi Domine laudis offerimus: SATB, 2V, Vc, Vo, Ctto, 2Trb, Fag, Org.
A-Wn ms. 16995   *[Köchel 24]; *card catalog

Missa Quid transitoria: SATB, 2V, Vc, Vo, Ctto, 2Trb, Fag, Org.
A-Wn ms. 16134   *[Köchel 30]; *card catalog

Missa Reconvalescentiae: SSATB, 2V; (Va, Vc, Vo, 2Ctto, 2Trb, Fag) *rip*, Org.
A-Wn ms. 16997   *[Köchel 31]; *card catalog

Missa S. Caroli: SATB, 2V, Va, Vc, Vo, Ctto, 2Trb, Fag, Org.
A-Wn ms. 16131   *[Köchel 33]; *card catalog

Missa S. Joannis: SATB, 2V, 3Va (a,t,b), Vc, Vo, Ctto, 2Trb, Fag, Org.
A-Wn ms. 19012   *[Köchel 34]; *card catalog

Missa S. Josephi: SATB, 2V; (Vc, Vo, Ctto, 2Trb, Fag) *rip*, Org.
A-Wn ms. 19014   *[Köchel 35]; *card catalog

Missa Temperantiae: SATB, 2V, Vc, Vo, Ctto, Fag, Org.
A-Wn ms. 17000   *[Köchel 40]; *card catalog

Missa Tempus volat: SATB, 2V, Trb; Ctto *rip*, Trb, Tior, Fag, Vc, Vo, Org.
A-Wn ms. 17001   *[Köchel 41]; *card catalog

Missa Una ex duo decim: SATB, 2V, Vc, Vo, Ctto, 2Trb, Fag, Org.
A-Wn ms., -KM; D-BII Mus. ms. 6800 (dated 1733)   *[Köchel 42]

Nisi Dominus aedificaverit. Beatus vir: SATB, 2V, Vc, Vo, Ctto, 2Trb, Fag, Org.
A-Wn ms.   *[Köchel 107]

Nisi Dominus à 4: SATB, 2V, Va; Ctto *rip*, 2Trb, Fag, Vc, Vo, Org.
A-Wn ms.   *[Köchel 109]

Nunc dimittis: SATB, 2V; Ctto, 2Trb, Fag, Vc, Vo, Org.
A-Wn ms. 17360 (AN.65 A.12 vol II no. 13)   *[Köchel 134]

Nunquam ira, nunquam dira [hymn]: SATB, 2V; (Ctto, 2Trb, Fag) *rip*, Vc, Vo, Org.
A-Wn ms. 16407   *[Köchel 249]

O ignis coelestis [Mottetto de Spiritu Sancto]: SATB *conc & rip*; 2V, Fag *conc*; (Ctto, 2Trb) *rip*; Vc, Vo, Org.
A-Wn ms. 17388   [Köchel 170]
Edition: FuxW series 3 vol 3

Omnes laudent, unde gaudent [hymn]: SATB, 2V; Vc, Vo, Ctto, 2Trb, Fag, Org.
A-Wn ms. 16400   [Köchel 250]

Omni die dic Mariae [Hymnus St. Casimiri]: SATB, 2V; Vc, Vo, Ctto, 2Trb, Fag, Org.
A-Wn ms. 16399   *[Köchel 251]

Omnis terra adoret [Mottetto à 5]: SATB *conc & rip*; 2V *conc*; Ctto, 2Trb, Fag, Vc, Vo, Org.
A-Wn ms. 17397 (AN65 A12 vol VI no. 18)   *[Köchel 183]; *card catalog

Per te mundus laetabundus [hymn]: SATB, 2V, 2Trb; Ctto *rip*, Fag, Vc, Vo, Org.
A-Wn ms. 16403   *[Köchel 252]

Plaudite Deo nostro [motet]: SATB *conc & rip*; 2V, Fag *conc*; (Va, Ctto, 2Trb) *rip*; Vc, Vo, Org.
A-Wn ms. 17383   [Köchel 167]
Edition: FuxW series 3 vol 1

Ponis nubem ascensum [Mottetto de Ascensione Domini]: SATB, 2V, Vc, Vo, Ctto, 2Trb, Fag, Org.
A-Wn ms. 17389 (AN.65 A.12 vol VI no. 10)   *[Köchel 169]; *card catalog

Quamvis muta, et polluta [hymn]: SATB, 2V; Ctto *rip*, 2Trb, Fag, Vc, Vo, Org.
A-Wn ms. 16402   *[Köchel 254]

Qui habitat in adjutorio à 4 pleno Coro: SATB, 2V; Ctto, 2Trb, Fag, Vc, Vo, Org.
A-Wn ms. 17359 (AN.65 A.12 vol II no. 12)   *[Köchel 131]

Reges Tharsis [Mottetto in Epiph. Domini]: SATB *conc & rip*; 2V, Ctto, 2Trb, Fag, Vc, Vo, Org.
A-Wn ms. 17395   [Köchel 168]
*Edition: FuxW series 3 vol 3

Requiem et Kyrie: SSATB *conc & rip*; 2V, Va; 2Ctto muto, 2Trb, Fag *rip*; Vc, Vo, Org.
A-Wn ms. 19015 (dated 1720)   [Köchel 51]
*Edition: FuxW series 1 vol 7

Sacris solemniis juncta [Offertorium de Venerabili]: SATB *conc & rip*; 2V *conc*; (Ctto, 2Trb, Fag) *rip*; Vc, Vo, Org.
A-Wn ms. 17341   [Köchel 160]
*Edition: FuxW series 3 vol 3

Salve Regina à 3: SATB, 2V; Vc, Vo, Ctto, 2Trb, Fag, Org.
A-Wn ms. (AN.65 A.12 vol I no. 9)   *[Köchel 263]

Salve Regina à 4: STB, 2V, Vc, Vo, 2Tpt, Ctto, 2Trb, Fag, Org.
A-Wn ms.   *[Köchel 259]

Salve Regina à 4: SATB, 2V; Vc, Vo, Ctto, 2Trb, Fag, Org.
A-Wn ms.   *[Köchel 264]

Salve Regina: SATB, 2V, 2Va, Ctto, 2Trb, Vc, Vo, Org.
A-Wn ms.   *[Köchel 265]

Salve Regina à 5: SSATB; (2V, Va, Ctto, 2Trb, Fag) *rip*, Vc, Vo, Org.
A-Wn ms. 16392   *[Köchel 266]

Stabat Mater: SATB, 2V, Va; Ctto, 2Trb, Fag, Vc, Vo, Org.
A-Wn ms. 16414   *[Köchel 268]

Te Deum: ChI&II SATB, (Ctto, 2Trb col SAT), 2V, 2Tpt, Fag, Vo, Org.
H-Bn mus. ms 2776
Edition: FuxW series 2 vol 1

Te Deum laudamus à 4: SATB *conc & rip*; 2Tpt, 2Tpt *princ*, Timp; 2V, Va *conc*; (Ctto, 2Trb, Fag) *rip*; Vc, Vo, Org.
A-Wn ms. 16408   [Köchel 270]
*Edition: FuxW series 2 vol 2

Te Deum laudamus à 5: SSATB, 4Tpt, Timp, 2V, 3Va; 2Ctto *rip*, 3Trb, Fag, Tior, Vo, Org.
A-Wn ms. 16409   *[Köchel 271]; *card catalog

Ut sim castus, blandus dulcis [hymn]: SATB, 2V; (Ctto, 2Trb, Fag) *rip*; Vc, Vo, Org.
A-Wn ms. 16405   *[Köchel 274]

Veni Creator spiritus [hymn]: SATB, 2Vtta, Va, Vc, Vo, Ctto, 2Trb, Fag, Org.
A-Wn ms.16411   *[Köchel 275]

Vesperae de B.M.V.: SATB, 2V, Vc, Vo, Ctto, 2Trb, Fag, Org.
A-Wn ms. 17371 (AN.46 A.12 vol IV no. 3)   *[Köchel 65]; *card catalog

Vesperae de B.M.V.: SATB, 2V, Vc, Vo, Ctto, 2Trb, Fag, Org.
A-Wn ms. 17378   *[Köchel 66]; *card catalog;

Vesperae de Confessore: SATB, 2V, Va, Vc, Vo, Ctto, 2Trb, Fag, Org.
A-Wn ms. 17377   *[Köchel 59]; *card catalog

Vesperae de Confessore: SATB, 2V; (Ctto, Fag, 2Trb) *rip*; Vc, Vo, Org.
Vesperae de Confessore: SATB, 2V, Vc, Vo, Ctto, 2Trb, Fag, Org.
Vesperae de Confessore: SATB, 2V, Vc, Vo, Ctto, 2Trb, Fag, Org.
A-Wn mss. 17373, 17374, 17375   *[Köchel 58, 60, 61]

Vesperae de Confessore à 4 pieno Coro: SATB, 2V, Vc, Vo, Ctto, 2Trb, Fag, Org.
A-Wn ms. 17376   *[Köchel 62]; *card catalog

Vespro del Sabbato: SATB, 2V, Vc, Vo, Ctto, 2Trb, Fag, Org.
A-Wn ms. 17379   *[Köchel 67]; *card catalog

Victimae paschali laudes [hymn]: SATB, 2V, 3Tpt *rip*, Timp, Ctto, Fag, Vc, Vo, Org.
A-Wn ms. 16410   *[Köchel 276]

Virgo gaude, quod de fraude [hymn]: SATB, 2V; (Ctto, 2Trb, Fag) *rip*; Vc, Vo, Org.
A-Wn ms. 26406   *[Köchel 277]

Vitae forma, morum norma [hymn]: SATB, 2V, 2Trb; Ctto *rip*, Fag, Vc, Vo, Org.
A-Wn ms. 16401   *[Köchel 278]

FUX, Vinzenz [FUXIO, Vincenzio]

Missa S. Xaverii: 8v *conc*, 2Tpt *ad lib*, 2Ctto, 2V, Va, 5Trb, Fag, Bc.
A-KR L14 (1645/49) p. 196

Missa S. Ignatij: SSAATTBB, 2V, 4Va, 2Tpt, 2Ctto, 4Trb, VaG, Vo, Org.
CS-KRa B I 45 (dated Aug. 1668)   OttoS

Missa Augusta: 8v, 2V, 2Ctto, 4Trb.
CS-KRa B I 67 (dated 1668, all parts missing)   OttoS

Missa à.7. in honoren S.a Barbarae: SSATB, 2Cttino, Org.
S-Uu Vok. Mus. i hs 54:14 (dated 1671)

GABRIELI, Andrea (see instrumental list)

GABRIELI, Giovanni (Venice, *ca* 1553/6-1612)
Symphoniae sacrae . . . liber secundus, senis, 7, 8, 10, 11, 12, 13, 14, 15, 16, 17, & 19,
tam vocibus, quam instrumentis, editio nova. Venice: Bartolomei Magni, 1615.
    Surrexit Christus, 11 vocum: ATB, 2Ctto, 2V, 4Trb, Org.
    Quem vidistis, pastores, 14 vocum: AAT, TTT, 2Ctto, 3Trb, 3 unsp. insts, Org.
    In ecclesiis, 14 vocum: ChI SATB *conc*; ChII SATB *cap*; ChIII 3Ctto, V, 2Trb; Org.
D-As (missing B), -B (compl, now in **PL-Kj**), -Kl (14 parts of 15), -Ls; **GB-Lbl** (9),
-Lcm (A,7,8,9,11); **I-Vgc**, -Bc (5), -Ls (14 parts of 15); **PL-WRu** (14 parts); **S-Skma**
(6,7,8)   RISM G87
Edition: CMM 3&4

    Udite chiari e generosi figli: ChI "di Tritoni" SSSATTTBB (Ctto muto with S1);
    ChII "di Sirene" SSATTB, "Basso grande."
D-Kl mus. ms. 2°

    Dulcis Jesu, sonata con voce à 20: ChI A, Ctto, Va, t,t,t,b; ChII t,Va, t,t,b; ChIII
    SATB, s,s,b; Org.
A Kassel court inventory of 1638 lists "Dulcis Jesu patris Imago à 20 G. G.," and the
attribution to Giovanni Gabrieli, clear from the context of the inventory, has generally
been accepted.
D-Kl 2° ms. 53 O (parts only, without attribution)

GALLERANO, Leandro (*b* Brescia; *fl* 1615-32)
    Missa a 8. Vocum cum 3 Instrumenta: SSATTB, Ctto (col S2); SATB *rip*; 2V, Vo,
    Org.
PL-WRu (Bohn collection Ms. mus. 142, now in **D-BI**, parts: S2 col Ctto defective)

GARTHOFF, Heinrich David (*fl* 1698-1708)
    Alleluia, lobet mit Freuden: SATB, 2V, Ctto, Bc.
S-L M48 (Wenster collection)   *WalkerSB

GIOVANELLI, Ruggiero (*b* Velletri, nr. Rome, *ca* 1560; *d* Rome, 1625)
    Messa à 12 voci: ChI SATB, V, Lt, Org; ChII SATB, Ctto, Tior, Org; ChIII SATB
    (including 2 *Sinfonie* with Ctto):

Sinfonia à 2 "doppo il Christe": Ctto, Tior, Org.

Sinfonia a 4 "doppo l'ultima Kyrie con tutti gli istrumenti": Ctto, V, Lt, Tior, Org.

I-FZac(d) ms. Cart. 60a

GLETLE, Johann Melchior (*b* Bremgarten, nr. Zürich, 1626; *d* Augsburg, 1683)

Expeditionis musicae classis II . . . Op. II. Augsburg: Andreas Erfurt, 1668.

39 Psalmi Breves: SSATB *conc & cap*, 2V o 2Cttino, 2Va o 2Trb, Fag o Trb, Vo, Org.

1. Domijne ad adjuvandum	21. Beatus vir
2. Dixit Dominus	22. Laudate, pueri
3. Confitebor	23. Laudate Dominum, omnes
4. Beatus vir	24. Laetatus sum
5. Laudate, pueri	25. Nisi Dominus
6. Laudate Dominum, omnes	26. Lauda Jerusalem
7. Laetatus sum	27. Credidi
8. Nisi Dominus	28. Magnificat
9. Lauda Jerusalem	29. Domijne ad adjuvandum
10. Credidi	30. Dixit Dominus
11. In convertendo	31. Confitebor
12. Domine probasti me	32. Beatus vir
13. De profundis	33. Laudate, pueri
14. Memento	34. Laudate Dominum, omnes
15. Beati Omnes	35. Laetatus sum
16. Confitebor . . . quoniam audisti	36. Nisi Dominus
17. Magnificat	37. Lauda Jerusalem
18. Domijne ad adjuvandum	38. In exitu
19. Dixit Dominus	39. Magnificat
20. Confitebor	

CH-Zz; **D**-B (1 partbook, now in **PL**-Kj), -F (missing AB *rip*), -OB (missing Fag, S1,A,T,B *rip*); **F**-Pn (missing Org); **PL**-WRu (missing B, V1, tVa, A *rip*, Org); **S**-Kma (missing Org)   *WalkerSB   RISM G2617

Expeditionis musicae classis V . . . Op.VI. Augsburg: Johann Jakob Schonigk, 1681.

   1. Litaniae Lauretanae: SSATB, 2V o 2Cttino, 2Trb o 2Va, Trb o Fag, Vo, Bc.

   4. Litaniae Lauretanae: SSATB, 2V o 2Ctto, 2Trb o 2Va, Trb o Fag, Vo, Bc.

   9. Litaniae Lauretanae: SSATB, 2V o 2Ctto, Vo, Bc.

  11. Litaniae Lauretanae: SSATB, 2V o 2Ctto, 2Trb o 2Va, Trb o Fag, Vo, Bc.

  13. Litaniae Lauretanae: SSATB, 2V, 2Tpt o 2Cttino, 2Va o 2Trb, Fag o Trb, Vo, Bc.

  14. Litaniae Lauretanae: SSATB, 2V, Tpt, Tpt o Cttino, 2Va o 2Trb, Vo, Bc.

  15. Litaniae Lauretanae: SSATB, 2V o 2Ctto, 2Va o 2Trb, Fag o Trb, Vo, Bc.

[?]. Kyrie: SSATB *conc & cap*, 2V o 2Cttino, 2Va o 2Trb, Fag o Trb, Vo, Org.

F-Pn Vm¹ 996   *WalkerSB   RISM G2621

  *Edition: SMd 2

GLUCK, Christoph Willibald (*b* Erasbach, Upper Palatinate, 1714; *d* Vienna, 1787)

In the opera *Orfeo ed Euridice*:
in Act I: Ah se in torno: SATB, Ctto, 3Trb, 2V, Va, Fag, Vo, Cemb.
in Act II: Deh placatevi con me: SATB, Ctto, 3Trb, 2V, Va, Fag, Vo, Cemb, Hp.
Misero Giovane: SATB, 2Ob, 2Ctto, 2V, Va, Fag, Vo, Cemb.
Ah quale incognito: SATB, 2Ob, 2Ctto, 2V, Va, Fag, Vo, Cemb.
A-Wn sig. mus. 17783 (dated 1762);[25] US-Eu (selections, ms from early 19th cent)
*Edition: DTÖ 44A   RISM AII 103476

GÖRNER, Johann Gottlieb (*b* Penig, Saxony, *bapt.* 1697; *d* Leipzig, 1778)

Missa brevis di J.G. Görner con 1 cornetto e 3 tromboni aggiunti da Harrer [Kyrie, Gloria]: SATB, Ctto, 3Trb, 2V & 2Ob, Va, Org.
D-BI Mus. ms. 30167 (score); -Kdma [2/2232]

GOSSWIN, Anton (see instrumental list)

GRANCINI, Michel'Angelo (Milan, 1605-1669)

Sacre fiori concertati à una, due, tre, quattro, cinque, sei, & sette voci, con alcuni concerti in sinfonia d'Istromenti, & due canzoni à 4. opera sesta . . . libro quarto. Milan: Giorgio Rolla, 1631.
    33. Trium puerorum cantemus hymnû: SSS o 3V o 3Ctto, Bc.
    36. Exultate Christo adiutori nostro: TT, 2V o 2Ctto, Bc.
The print also includes two canzonas à 4 with no specific instrumentation.
I-Mb (SB,Org), -Mcap (SATB,5,Org), -VCd (B,Org)   SartMS 1631; RISM G3401

GRANDI, Alessandro (*b ca* 1575/80; *d* Bergamo, 1630)

Raccolta Terza di Leonardo Simonetti . . . de messa et salmi del sig. Alessandro Grandi et Gio Croce Chiozzotto a 2, 3, 4, con basso continuo, aggiontovi li ripieni à bene placito. . . . Venice: Bartolomeo Magni, †1630 (and 1632),[26] ∞1636.
    Sinfonia avanti il Gloria: Ctto o V, Trb, Bc
    Gloria: SSAT *conc* o (SSA, Trb); SABB *rip*, o (V, Ctto, 2Trb); Bc.
    Confitebor . . . in consilio: TTB *conc*; AATTB *rip*, Ctto o V, s (one T *rip* part says "C. a 3. voci con cornetti se piace"), Bc.
†I-Bc; ∞A-Wgm; GB-Ge (C); PL-WRu (C, Org)   RISM G3460/3461

Factum est silentium a 7: S & Ctto, A & Trb, T & Trb, B & Bomb, Chit (missing 3 parts).
PL-WRu (Bohn collection Ms. mus. 145a, now in D-BI, parts)

---

[25] The cornett parts were superseded by clarinet parts in a source dated 1764, but the cornett instrumentation appears again in a 19th-century source in US-Eu.

[26] The following partbooks were published in 1630: C o T, T, A, T o B, Bc. All others (six partbooks with *ripieno* vocal parts and instrumental parts) were published in 1632.

GRIMM, Heinrich (*b* Holeminden, 1592/93; *d* Brunswick, 1637)

Wie schön leuchtet der Morgenstern[?], 1622.
Ch pro org SSATB; Ch fidicinus SATB; Ch tubicinus SATTB; 2Ctto o 2Tpt, Org.
PL-WRu ms. mus. 46 (lost; the print is missing the title page)   *BohnH, *BohnD

GRUNDE, Adalbert

De uno confessore a 10 voc: SSATTB, V o Ctto, Ctto, 3Trb, Org.
Quare fremuerunt gentes a 15 voc: SSAATTBB, V, V o Ctto, Ctto, Tpt, 4Trb, Org.
A-KR L 13 (ms from 1633-39)   *RISM AII 600153421, 600153423

HALLMANN, Andreas

Mutteto â 15. Voc: è 6.Instr: 9.Voc: Omnium sanctorum festum celebrate / Singet
all dem Herren lobet seinen Nahmen: SATTB *conc*, SSATB *cap*, 2V, Ctto, 4Trb,
Org.
PL-WRu (Bohn collection Ms. mus. 148, now in **D-BI**, contains two sets of parts: one
with German and one with Latin text)

HAMMERSCHMIDT, Andreas (*b* Brüx, Bohemia, 1611/12; *d* Zittau, 1675)

Vierdter Theil, musicalischer Andachten, geistlicher Moteten, und Concerten, mit
5,6,7,8,9,10,12, und mehr Stimmen, nebenst einem gedoppelten General-Baß.
Freiburg: Georg Beuther, †1646, ∞1654, ‡1669.
    7. Wer waltzet uns den Stein, Dialogus à 6, 12 o 14 voc: SSAB *conc*, SSATTB
        cap, 2Tpt, 3 Trb, Bc (preceded by a symphonia à 5: 2Ctto, 3Trb, Bc).
    15. Herr höre und sey mir gnädig: TB, 2Ctto, 3Trb, Org, Bc.
    28. Laudate servi Domini: STB *conc*, SSATB *cap*, Org, Bc (with a symphonia:
        2Ctto, 3Trb, Bc).
    34. Verleih uns Friede genädiglich: STB *conc*, SSATTB *cap*, Org, Bc (with a
        symphonia à 5: 2Ctto, 3Trb, Bc).
    37. Veni Sancte Spiritus: ATB *conc*, SSATB *cap*, 2Ctto, 2Tpt, Bc (with a
        symphonia à 3: 2Ctto, Bc).
    38. Alleluia lobet den Herren in seinem Heiligthumb: TT *conc*; SSATB *cap*; 2Ctto,
        3Trb *ad plac*; Bc.
    39. Singet dem Herren: ChI&II SATB; 2Tpt, 2Ctto, 2Trb, Bc.
†**A-Wgm** (missing 10); **B-Bc**; **CH-Zz** (1); **D-BI** (1,2,9), -BD, -Dl (1-8), -DlP (6,9,10),
-GRu (missing 10), -HAmk (missing 10), -Kl, -MÜG, -Rp (missing 4,9), -UDa (3,7),
-W (1), -WF (3,7); **GB-Lbl** (2,3,4,5,6,8,9), -Lcm (incompl); **PL-GD** (4), -WRu
(3,5,6,7,8); **S-L** (missing 6,9), -STr, -Uu (1), -V; **US-MSu**, -NYp (missing 1,2,7,8), -R;
∞**CH-Zz** (missing 1); **D-BÜ**, -JE (2), -W (missing 1,4,5); **GB-Lbl** (8); **S-Uu** (2-10);
‡**D-B**; **D-WA** (1-5,7,9), -PR (2); **GB-Lbl** (3,4); †∞**D-B** (now in **PL-Kj**); **S-VX** (2,3,5)
*MitUB   RISM H1931/1932/1933

Musicalische Gespräche über die Evangelia, mit 4. 5. 6. und 7. Stimmen nebenst den
basso continuo. Dresden: Christian Bergen [W. Seyffert, Georg Beuther], 1655.
    1. Freue dich, du Tochter Zion à 6: SSTB, 2Cttino, Bc.
    5. O, ihr lieben Hirten à 6: SATB, 2Cttino, Bc.

6. Was meinestu, wil aus dem Kindlein werden à 5: ATB, 2Cttino, Bc.
16. Gelobet sey der Herr à 4: AB, 2Cttino, Bc.
27. Warlich ich sage euch à 7: SSSTB, 2Cttino, Bc.

The specification *cornettino* is found only in the headings of the individual parts. The *Register* always gives *violin* or *viol*.

A-Wgm, -Wn; **B**-Br; **CH**-Zz; **D**-Dl, -HAmk, -SAh, -ZI; **GB**-Lbl; **R**-Sb; **S**-V; **US**-R, -U
Edition: Harold Mueller, "The *Musicalische Gespräche über die Evangelia* of Andreas Hammerschmidt," Ph.D. dissertation, University of Rochester, 1956   RISM H1948

Ander Theil Geistlicher Gespräche über die Evangelia, mit 5. 6. 7. & 8. Stimmen nebenst den Basso continuo. Dresden: Christian Bergen (Wolfgang Seyffert), 1656.
1. Heileg ist der Herr à 7: SSATB, 2Cttino, Bc.
6. Gelobet sey der Herr à 7: SSATB, 2Cttino, Bc.
7. Mein Seele erhebt den Herren à 7: SSATB, 2Cttino, Bc.
13. Mein Haus ist ein Behthaus à 7: SSATB, 2Cttino, Bc.
14. Ich danke dir, Gott: ATB, 2Cttino, Bc.
25. Du Schlacksknecht à 7: STTTB, 2Cttino, 3Trb, Bc.
26. Und es erhub sich ein Streit: SATB, 2Tpt, 2Cttino, Bc.

A-Wgm, -Wn; **B**-Br; **D**-BD (missing part 7), -Dl, -DT, -HAmk, -LUC (missing part 9), -SAh (7 parts incompl), -ZI; **GB**-Lbl (missing part 9); **PL**-V (8 parts incompl)
Edition: Mueller, *op. cit.*   RISM H1949

Missae, V. VI. VII. IIX. IX. X. XI. XII. et Plurium Vocum, tam vivae voci quam instrumentis varijs accomodatae. Dresden: Christian Bergen (Wolfgang Seyffert), 1663.
15. [Missa] Pro organo à 12: SSATB, 2V, 2Ctto, 3Trb, "2 tubis & tympanis cum sanctus ad praefationem" (with 2 symphonie).

A-Wgm (missing part 6); **CH**-Zz; **D**-B (now in **PL**-Kj), -BD; **F**-Pn; **GB**-Lbl (parts 3,4,5,6,11,12); **S**-Uu (missing part 13)   *MitUB   RISM H1953

Ms with 43 works in large settings specifying Ctto.
1. Frewe dich du Töchter Zion: [S]SAATB, 2[?]Ctto, 4Trb, Org.
2. Himmel und Erden vergehen: SSATB, 2Ctto, 2Trb, Bomb.
3. Da aber Johannes im Gefängnüss die Werck: SSATB, 2Ctto, V, 3Trb, Bomb, Org.
4. Und diß ist daß Zeugniss Johannis: SSATB, 2Ctto, V, 3Trb, Org.
5. O Ihr lieben Hirten: SATB, Ctto, 3Trb, Org.
6. Waß meinstu wil auß kindlein werden: SSATTB, 2Ctto, 4Trb, Org.
7. Und da acht Tage umb waren: SATB, Ctto, 2Trb, Bomb, Org.
8. Wo ist der newgeborne Konig: S[S]ATTB, 2?Ctto, 3Trb, Bomb, Org.
9. Mein Sohn warumb hast du unß daß gethan: SSATTB, 2Ctto, 4Trb, Org.
10. Herr sie haben nicht Wein: STB *conc*; SATB; SSA, 2Ctto, Trb, Org.
11. Herr ich bin nicht werth, daß du unter mein Dach: SSATTB, 2Ctto, 3Trb, Bomb, Org.
12. O Herr hilff wir verderben: TB *conc*; SSATTB *cap*, 2Ctto, 3Trb, Bomb; Org.
13. Herr hastu nicht gutten Saamen: SSATTB, 2Ctto, 4Trb, Org.

14. Herr diese letzten haben nur eine Stunde: SSATTB, 2Ctto, 4Trb, Org.
15. Höret zue, Es gieng ein Seeman: SSATTB, 2Ctto, 3Trb, Bomb, Org.
16. Gelobet sey der Herr Jesu: SSAT[T]B, 2Ctto, 4Trb, Org.
18. Ach Herr du Sohn David erbarme dich mein: SSA[T]TBB, 2Ctto, 4Trb, Org [T1, Trb1 presumed missing].
21. Gott fähret auff mit Jauchtzen: S[S]ATB, 2Ctto, 3Trb [S2, Ctto2 presumed missing].
27. Frewet euch mit mir: S *conc*; [S]SATTB, Ctto, Trb; Org.
28. Seyd barmhertzig, wie auch ewer Vater: ST; SAATB, 2Trb; 2Ctto; Org [Ctto1 presumed missing].
29. Gelobet sey der Herr Gott Israel: [S]SAT[T]B, 2Ctto, 3Trb, Org (the tab version has 2C and 2Ctto; S1 & Ctto1 presumed missing).
30. Meine Seele erhebet den Herren: [SS]ATB, [2Ctto], 3Trb, Org (soprano and cornett parts only in tab version).
31. Simon fahre auff die Höhe: SSATB, 2Ctto, 3Trb, Org.
32. Wer mit seinem Bruder zürnet: SSATB, 2Ctto, 3Trb, Org.
33. Sehet euch vor für den falschen Propheten: S[S][A]A[B]B, 2?Ctto, 4?Trb, Org [S2, A1, B1, Ctto2, 2Trb presumed missing].
34. Wie hör ich daß von dir: SS[A]A[T]TB, Ctto, Trb, Org [A1, T1, presumed missing; tab version has 2Trb].
35. Mein Hauss ist ein Bethauss: S[S]ATB, 2Ctto, 3Trb [S2, Ctto2 presumed missing].
36. Ich dancke dir Gott daß ich nicht bin: S[S][A]A[T]TB, [2]Ctto, [5]Trb, Org.
37. O mein Jesu, du hast alles wolgemacht: SATB, Ctto, 2Trb, Org.
38. Meister wass muß ich thun: S[S]ATB, [2]Ctto, 3Trb, Org.
39. Jesu lieber Meister erbarme dich vnser: [S]SATB, [2]Ctto, 3Trb, Org.
40. Herr woher nehmen wir Brodt: [S]SATTB, [2]Ctto, 3Trb, Bomb, Org.
41. Und es erhub sich ein Streit im Himmel: SATTB, Ctto, 3Trb, Bomb; 2Ctto; Org.
42. Jüngling ich sage dir stehe auff: SS[AB], 2Ctto, [3Trb], Org.
43. Wer sich selbst erhöhet der sol erniedriget werden: SSATB, 2Ctto, 2Trb, Bomb, Org.
44. Wende dich Herr: SSATTB, 2Ctto, 4Trb, Org.
45. Viel sind beruffen, aber wenig außerwehlt: [S]S[A]ATT[B]B, [2]Ctto, [4?]Trb, [2?]Bomb, Org.
47. Du Schalcksknecht du: SSA[A]TT[B]B, 2Ctto, [6?]Trb, Org.
48. O Jesu wir wissen: SSATB, 2Ctto, 3Trb; TT, 2Trb; Org.
50. Es wird eine grosse Trübsal sein: S[S]ATB, [2]Ctto, 3Trb, Org.
53. O Vater aller Augen: SSAAT, 2Ctto, 3Trb; 2Ctto; B, Trb; Org.
55. Friede sey mit euch: S[S]AATBB, [2]Ctto, 4Trb.
56. O Jesu mein Jesu selig ist der Leib: S[S]ATB, [2]Ctto, 3Trb, Org.
PL-WRu (Bohn collection Ms. mus. 150, now in **D-Bl**, parts and tab)   *BohnH

Ach wie flüchtig ach wie nichtig à 5: 5v (with 2Ctto, 3Trb); Bc.
PL-WRu (Bohn collection Ms. mus. 150a, now in **D-Bl**, tab)   *BohnH

HANDEL, George Frideric (*b* Halle, 1685; *d* London, 1759)

In the opera *Il Tamerlano*:
pastoral air – Par che mi nascha: S, 2Ctto, 2V, Va, Bc.
D-Hs
Edition: HändelW 69

HASSLER, Hans Leo (*b* Nürnberg, *bapt.* 1562; *d* Frankfurt a. M., 1612)

Verbum caro factum est à 16 voc.: ChI SSTB; ChII ATTB; ChIII 2V, Va, Vo; ChIV
Ctto, 4Trb; Bc.
PL-WRu (Bohn collection Ms. mus. 151, now in **D**-BI, parts and tab)

HERBST, Johann Andreas (*b* Nürnberg, *bapt.* 1588; *d* Frankfurt a. M., 1666)

Lob- und Danck-Lied auss dem 34. Psalm, deß Königlichen Propheten Davids, sampt
einen Ritornello, auss dem 92. Psalm . . . mit 13 Stimmen uff drey Chör zu Musicieren:
Zwo Violino oder Cornetto und Fagott; Fünff Stimmen Vocaliter, in Concerto, und
Fünff Stimmen vocaliter und Instrument: in Ripieno. . . . Nürnberg: Johann Friederich
Sartorio, 1637.
ChI SATTB; ChII SSATB *cap* with instruments; ChIII 2V o 2Ctto, Vo o Fag; Bc.
D-B (12 partbooks: C,A,T1,T2,B,C*rip*,A*rip*,T1*rip*,T2*rip*,B*rip*,V o Ctto1,V o Ctto2,Vo
o Fag, now in **PL**-Kj)

Treifelt ihr Himmel von oben: SSATB, 2V, 2Ctto, 2Fl, Fag, Bc.
D-BI Mus. ms. 30378   *SamuelN

(A.) Es ist ein köstlich ding. (B.) Da ich den Herren suchte: 5v *conc & cap*, 2V o
Ctto, Fag, Org.
D-BI (dated 1637, now housed in **PL**-Furstenstein)   *SamuelN

Danck- und Lobgesang auss dem 107. Psalm: ChI B, 3V o 3Ctto, Trb, b; ChII SATB
conc; ChIII SATB, 4Trb o 4VaG; "Clarini", Timp, Org.
D-BII (present location uncertain) (dated 1649)
*Edition EdM

Preatio regis Josaphat: ChI 2V, 2Ctto, VaBr, T, Vo o Fag; ChII SSB, 2V; ChIII AB,
5Trb; Org.
D-F ms. Ff. mus. 261 (ms dated 1650)   RISM AII 23504
*Edition: EdM

Dancket dem Herrn, denn Er ist freundlich: ChI SSSB, 3V, 2Ctto, Fl, Trb; ChII
SATB "favoriti"; ChIII ATTB, 4Trb; Org.
D-Tu (dated 1649)   *SamuelN
Edition: LD 1

Domine Dominus noster. (Herr unser Herscher.): ChI&II SSATTB *conc & cap*; 3Ctto, 3Trb, Bc.
D-Tu (dated 1651)   *SamuelN
Edition: LD 1

HILDEBRAND, [Johann Heinrich or Johann ?]

Wie lieblich sind deine Wohnungen: SSATB, 2V, 2Va, 2Ctto, 3Tpt, Vo, Bc.
D-Gs Cod. ms. philos. 84E   *WalkerSB

HILLEMEYER, Johann Bernhard

Salve Regina: B, V, Va, Vo, [Ctto], Org.
D-DO Mus. ms. 750 (ms dated 1711)   *RISM AII 74237

HOFER, Andreas (*b* Reichenhall, 1629; *d* Salzburg, 1684)

Missa Archiepiscopalis: ChI&II SATB, 2V, 2Va, 2Ctto, 2Tpt, 3Trb, Bc.
A-KR C/7/653 (dated 1699)   *WalkerSB

Missa valete: SSATB, 2V, 2Va, 2Tpt, 2Ctto *ad lib*, 3Trb, Org, Vo.
CS-KRa B I 158; **D**-BII ms. 10698 (copied by Theodor Beer)

Dextera Domini à 17: ChI&II SATB, 2Ctto, 3Trb, 4VaBr, [Org].
CS-KRa B II 34   OttoS

Fundata est Domus (De Dedicatione). à 12: SSATTB *conc & rip*, 2V, 2Va, 2Ctto, Org [with opening sonata].
CS-KRa B II 36   OttoS

Gaudeamus exultemus à 15: ChI&II SATB, 4VaBr, 2Ctto, 3Trb, Org.
CS-KRa B II 198   OttoS

Estote fortes in bello à 15: ChI&II SATB, 2V, 2Ctto, 3Trb, Org.
CS-KRa B II 292   OttoS

Dixit Dominus: ChI&II SATB *conc & rip*, 2V o 2Ctto, 3 Va o 3Trb, Org.
CS-KRa B III 77   OttoS

Magnificat à 17 (with Sonata): ChI&II SATB; 4Va, 2Ctto, 3Trb, [Org].
CS-KRa B III 81   OttoS
Edition: Univ. of Missouri Press no. 10

Te Deum laudamus à 23: ChI&II SATB; 2V, 2Va, 5Tpt, 2Ctto, 3Trb, Timp, Org.
CS-KRa B XI 1 (missing Ctto1), & B XI 5   OttoS
Edition: Univ. of Missouri Press no. 1

HOINECK, B[oras] (17th cent)

Nun danket alle Gott: SSB, 2V, 2Ctto "et Flöt," 2Fl, 3Tpt, Bc.
D-F ms. Ff. mus. 290   *SussKM

HORN, Johann Caspar (*b* Feldsberg, Lower Austria, *ca* 1630; *d* Dresden, *ca* 1685)

Geistliche Harmonien über die gewöhnlichen Evangelia . . . mit 4. Vocal-Stimmen und 2. Violinen auffgesetzet . . . der Sommer-Theil. Dresden: Johann Christoph Mieth (Christian Bergen), 1680 (and 1681).

   1. Jesus sprach zu seinen Jüngern: SATB *conc & cap*, 2V, 2Ctto, 2Va, 2Trb, Bc.
   2. Da der Tag: SATB *conc & cap*, 2V, 2Ctto, 2Va, 2Trb, Bc.
   9. Es naheten aber zu ihm: SATB *conc & cap*, 2V, 2Ctto, 2Va, 2Trb, Bc.
 12. Maria aber stund auf: SATB *conc & cap*, 2V, 2Ctto, 2Va, Bc.
 18. Und als er nahe: SATB *conc & cap*, 2V, 2Ctto, 2Va, 2Trb, Bc.
 21. Jesus wandte sich zu seinen Jüngern: SATB *conc & cap*, 2V, 2Ctto, 2Va, 2Trb, Bc.
 24. Zu der selbigen Stunde: SATB *conc & cap*, 2V, 2Ctto, 2Va, 2Trb, Bc.
 26. Und es begab sich: SATB *conc & cap*, 2V, 2Ctto, 2Va, Bc.
 34. Da Jesus solches: SATB *conc & cap*, 2V, 2Ctto muto, 2Ctto, 2Va, 2Trb, Bc.
 38. Und Jesus zog hinein: SATB *conc & cap*, 2V, 2Ctto o 2"Shalmeyen," 2Va, 2Trb, Bc.

The alto partbook contains the following passage: *"Daß auch vor Schalmeyen die Flöten und vor Trompeten die Cornetten & c. in Ermanglung zu gebrauchen solches und übriges alles, stellt man zu des Hn Directoris gefälliger Anordnung. . . ."*
A-Wgm, -Wn; **B**-Bc; **CH**-Zz; **D**-B (now in **PL**-Kj), -Dl (5 copies, 1 compl but S,T,B defective), -HAmk, -LEm, -W; **GB**-Lbl; **S**-Uu; **US**-BE (missing Va2; the soprano partbook is from 1681; all others are from 1680), -Wc   RISM H7419

Geistliche Harmonien . . . der Winter-Theil. Dresden: Johann Christoph Mieth (Christian Bergen), 1680.

   1. Da Sie nun nahe: SATB *conc & cap*, 2V, 2Ctto, 2Va, Bc.
   5. Es begab sich: SATB *conc & cap*, 2V, 2Ctto, 2"Schalmeyen," 2Va, Bc.
 12. Zu Jesus gebohren war: SATB *conc & cap*, 2V, 2Ctto, 2Va, 2Trb, Bc.
 29. Und da der Sabath: SATB *conc & cap*, 2V, 2Ctto, 2Va, 2Trb, Bc.
 37. Zulebt da die [H]ilfe: SATB *conc & cap*, 2V, 2Ctto o 2Tpt, 2Va, 2Trb, Bc.

In the partbooks for violin I & II, there are indications for cornett in works 1, 5, 12, 29, and 37. Cornett is absent from the tables of contents.
A-Wgm, -Wn; **B**-Bc; **CH**-Zz; **D**-Dl (5 copies, 1 compl but S,B defective), -HAmk, -LEm, -W; **GB**-Lbl; **S**-Uu; **US**-BE (missing Va2), -Wc   MitUB   RISM H7418

Musicalische Tugend- und Jugend-Gedichte . . . mit 1.2.3.4.5. und 6. Vocal-Stimmen nebenst 5. Violen oder auch Floeten, und dem Basso continu. . . . Frankfurt am Main: Balthasar Christoph Wust, 1678.

   Lasst uns aus spatzieren fahren: SS, 2Cttino, 2Va, Fag, Bc
S-STr (missing Va1), -Uu

HÜBER, Vendelini [Wendelin]

Missa pleno: ChI&II SATB, 2V, 2Ctto, 2Tpt, 3Trb, Vo, Org.
CS-KRa B I 69 (dated 4 May. 1665)   OttoS

JAHN, Martin (*b* Merseburg, *ca* 1620; *d* Ohlau, Silesia, *ca* 1682)

Ich frewe mich im Herren à 10 Voc: 5 Voc: è 5 Instrument: ChI SSATB; ChII 2Tpt
o 2Fl o 2Ctto o 2V, 3Trb; SATB*cap* (Cantus: Voce e Cornetto), V; Org.
PL-WRu (Bohn collection Ms. mus. 156, now in **D-BI**, parts and tab)

Nun dancket alle Gott: SSATB, 2Ctto, 2Tpt, 4Fl, 2V, 2Va, Vo, 3Trb, Fag, Bc.
The instrumentation is organized in the parts as follows: 2 parts with alternating instr.
Ctto, Tpt, Fl, V; 2 parts with alternating instr. Trb, Fl, Va; 1 part with alternating instr.
Trb, Vo, Fag.
PL-WRu (Bohn collection Ms. mus. 156a, now in **D-BI**, parts)

JENNERICH, Hieronymus

Es sind die Hörner in der Welt.   Stettin: Samuel Höpffners Witwe, 1683.
S, 2Ctto, 3"Corno torto," Bc.
D-GRu   *RISM JJ530a

KAINZ, Joseph (1738-1810)

Missa ex B fa a 4 voci in pieno: SATB, 2V, 2Tpt, Ctto, 2Trb, Timp, Vc, Vo, Org.
A-Wa Sign. 531 (ms dated *ca* 1770)   *RISM AII 600054003

KERLE, Jacobus de (*b* Ypern, West Flanders, 1531; *d* Prague, 1591)

Te Deum laudamus: SATTB, Ctto, a, t, t, Org.
PL-WRu (Bohn collection Ms. mus. 158, now in **D-BI**, parts)

KERLL, Johann Kaspar (*b* Adorf, Saxony, 1627; *d* Munich, 1693)

Missa à 3 Chori: ChI,II&III SATB; 2V, 3Va, 2Tpt, 2Ctto, 3Trb, Vo, Org.
A-KR ms. Ser. C. Fasc. 14 no. 702
Edition: DTÖ 49

Justus ut palma: SSATB, 2V, 2Va, 2Ctto, Bc.
A-Sd ms. A209   *WalkerSB

Triumphate sidera: SSATTB, 2V, 3Va, 2Ctto, 4Trb, Vo, bVa o Fag, Bc.
A-Sd ms. A210   *WalkerSB

K[ERN], A[ndreas]

Dialogus Germanicus inter Mariam et Peccatorum: SA, 2V, VaG, 2Ctto muto o
2Va, Trb, [Bc].
CS-KRa B II 39   OttoS

KINDERMANN, Johann Erasmus (Nürnberg, 1616-1655)

Ich will singen von der Gnade des Herren: ChI SSATB, 2V, Va, Trb; ChII 2V, Ctto, 2Trb, Trb o Fag, Vo; Bc.

PL-WRu (Bohn collection Ms. mus. 159, now in **D-BI**, parts)

KLEIN, Henrik (*b* Rudelsdorf, Moravia, 1756; *d* Bratislava, 1832)

Libera me: SATB, 2V, Va, Vc, Ctto, 3Trb, Vo, Org.
The cornett is designated as *"Zinken."*
H-PH Mus.sacr.ant K 13 (ms dated after 1800)   *RISM AII 97766

KLÍMA, Benedikt (1701-1748)

Lytaniae Lauretanae: 4v, Ctto, 2Trb, Vo, Org.
A-HE VIII b 3   *RISM AII 600091686

KLINGENBERG, Friedrich Gottlieb (*ca* 1665-1720)

Der geschwinde Liebes-Postilion zur hochzeitlichen Ehren-Lust des . . . Georg Madeweisen . . . und der . . . Jgfr. Dorothea Elisabeth Cuntzmannin . . . den 14. Septembr. des 1699. Jahrs. . . . Stettin: Samuel Höpffners Witwe, 1699.
     Arie: Herr Bräutigam, wo seyd ihr doch: A, 4V, Ctto, Cemb.
D-GRu   *RISM KK909b

Der Hertz-Wurm der Liebe . . . dem . . . Berend OKern . . . und der Jgfr. Maria Elisabeth Wurmin am hochzeitlichen Cur-Tage, den 26. Septembr. des 1699. Jahrs. . . . Stettin: Samuel Höpffners Witwe, 1699.
     Arie: Es muß von heutger Welt ein jeder sagen und bekennen: S, 2V, 2Va, Ctto, Fag, Cemb.
D-GRu   *RISM KK909c

Da Braut-A, B, C am hochzeitlichen Ehren-Tage des . . . Herrn Egidius Borchers . . . und der Jungfer Barbara Elisabeth Blockin . . . den 4. Novembr. des 1700. Jahres. . . . Stettin: Samuel Höpffners Witwe, 1700.
     Arie: Ist es nicht poßierlich gnug: T, 2V, Ctto, Fag, Cemb.
D-GRu   *RISM KK909e

KNÜPFER, Sebastian (*b* Asch, Bavaria, 1633; *d* Leipzig, 1676)

     Herr, wer wird wohnen in deinen Hütten: SAB, 2Ctto, 3Va, Org.
 7. Es spricht der Unweisen Mund wohl: SSAATTBB, 2V, 3Va, 2Ctto, 3Trb, Fag, Org.
10. Herr Christ, der einig Gottes Sohn: SSATB, 2V, 3Va, 2Ctto, 3Trb, Fag, Org.
18. Wohl dem, der in der Gottesfurcht steht: SSATB, 2V, 3Va, 2Ctto, 3Trb, Bomb, Fag, Bc.
19. Was mein Gott will, daß gescheh alzeit: SSATTB, 2V, 3Va, 2Ctto, 3Trb, Fag, Bc.

D-BII Mus. ms. 11780 (Bokemeyer collection, score); -Kdma [3/821; 3/822; 3/826; 3/832; 3/835]; ("Herr, wer wird wohnen in deinen Hütten" also exists in **D**-Lr ms. 282 with setting: SAB, 2Ctto o 2V, 4VaG)   KümmerKB
Edition: DdT 58-59

Herr, ich habe lieb die Städte deines Hauses: ATB, 2Cttino, Trb, Bc.
D-BII Mus. ms. 11785[27] (Erfurt collection, parts dated 1682), 11780 no. 13 (Bokemeyer collection, score with parts unspecified)   *KümmerKB; NoackE

Christ lag in Todesbanden: ChI,II,&III SATB; 2Ctto *ad plac*, 2V, 2Va, Vo, Org.
D-BII Mus. ms. 12260 (dated 1693)   *DdT 58

Ach mein hertzliebes Jesulein à 15: SSATB, SSATB *rip*, 2V, 2Va, 2Ctto, 3Trb, 2Ob, 2Taille, Vo, Fag, Bc.
D-Dlb mus. ms. 1825 E 503 (Grimma U 179/V39, score dated 1692) and 1825 E 502 (Grimma U179/V40, parts); -Kdma [2/2245]   *GroveD; *WalkerSB

Ich habe dich zum Licht der Heiden gemacht à 16: SATTB *conc & rip*, 2V, 3Va, 2Cttino, 3Trb, Fag, Org.
D-Dlb Mus. ms. 1825 E 509 (Grimma U188/V46, parts dated 1690)   *BernC; *GroveD

Jauchzet dem Herrn alle Welt à 17: ChI&II SATB; SATB *rip*, 2V, 3Va, 2Tpt, 2Cttino, Ctto, 2Trb, Fag, Org.
D-Dlb mus. ms. 1825 E 510 (Grimma U187/V45, parts dated 1696)   *BernC; *GroveD

Machet die Thore weit: SSATB *conc & rip*, 2V, 4Va[G], 2Ctto o 2Bomb, 3Trb, Org.
D-Dlb mus. ms. 1825 E 512 (Grimma U191/V49, parts)
*Edition: DdT 58-59

O benignissime Jesu à 6, 10: ATB *conc*, SATB *rip*, 2V o 2Cttino, VaG o Bomb o Trb, Org.
D-Dlb mus. ms. 1825 E 513 (Grimma U174/V36, parts dated 1700)
Edition: KrauseK

Quare fremuerunt gentes: SSATTB *conc*, SATB *cap*, 2V, 3Va, 2Ctto muto, 4Trb, Fag, Org.
D-Dlb mus. ms. 1825 E 514 (Grimma U175/V35, parts dated 1672)   DdT 58-59

Super flumina Babylonis à 10, 15, 19: SATB *conc & cap*, 2V, 3Va, 2Cttino, 3Trb, Fag, Org, Bc.
The score specifies 2 *cornettini,* whereas the parts specify *cornettino primo* and *cornetto secondo.*

---

[27] The parts and title page indicate *cornetin*, while the score indicates *cornet*.

D-Dlb mus. ms. 1825 E 516 (Grimma U176/V34, score & parts dated 1683)
Edition: KrauseK

> Surgite, populi à 26, 34: ChI SATB *conc & cap*; ChII SATB *conc & cap*; 5Tpt, 2V,
> 3Va, 2Cttino, Ctto muto, 3Trb, Fag, Timp, Org.

The mute cornett and the trombones double the ripieno parts of choir II.
D-Dlb mus. ms. 1825 E 517 (Grimma U177/V33, score & parts dated 1688)
Edition: KrauseK

> Veni Sancte Spiritus à 20, 25, o 30: SSATB *conc & rip*, 4Tpt, 2V, 2Va, 2Cttino,
> 3Trb, Fag, Timp, Org, 5 instruments *rip*, Bc.

Five unspecified instruments are included as a ripieno group, although no parts exist
in the ms.
D-Dlb mus. ms. 1825 E 519 (Grimma U178/V32, score & parts dated 1676)
Edition: KrauseK

> Christ lag in Todesbanden à 19: SSATB *conc & cap*, Cttino, 3Bomb, V *piccolo*,
> V, 3Va, Bc.

D-Dlb ms. 1825 E 525 (Grimma U335/N34, parts)
*Friedhelm Krummacher, "Zur Sammlung Jacobi der ehemalige Fürstenschule
Grimma," *Die Musikforschung* 16, no. 4 (Oct.-Dec. 1963): 346

KÖLER, Martin (*b* Danzig, *ca* 1620; *d* Hamburg, 1703/04)

> 11. Alleluia, lobet den Herren: SSATB, 2Vo 2Ctto, 2Va o 2Trb, Trb o Fag, Bc.

D-BII Mus. ms. 3840 (Bokemeyer collection, score)   KümmerKB; *WalkerSB

KONWALYNKA, Paul

Musicalische Neu-Jahrs Beehrung. . . .   Brieg: Christoph Tschorn, 1671.

> O Jesu liebster Schatz: SS, V, Ctto, Trb o VaG, Fag, Org.

PL-WRu   RISM K1334

[KRESS], Johann Albrecht (*b* nr. Nürnberg, 1644; *d* Stuttgart, 1684)

> In te Domine speravi: A, Cttino, Bc.

D-BII Mus.ms. 4320 (Bokemeyer collection, score)   KümmerKB

KRIEGER, Johann (*b* Nürnberg, *bapt.* 1652; *d* Zittau, 1735)

Neue Musikalische Ergetzligkeit [Erster Theil]. . . .   Frankfurt-Leipzig: Christian
Weidmann (Zittau: Michael Hartmann), 1684.

> 11. Himmelfahrts-Andacht: Der Heyland fähret auff: A, 2Cttino, Fag, Bc.
> 14. Zu ende des Kirchen-Jahrs: Gott lob die Kirche Blüht: S, 2Tpt, 2Cttino, 2V,
>   2Va, 3Trb, Fag, Timp, Bc.
> 16. Auff ein Frieden-Fest: Ach du hoher Frieden-Fürst: S, Tpt, 2Cttino, V, Vo, Bc.

D-LEm, -Lr, -Mbs (missing *Hauptstimme*), -Z; **S**-Uu   RISM K2448, KK2448
MitUB; WelterRL

Hallelujah, Lobet den Herren in seinen Heiligthum à 32: ChI&II SATB *conc*; SATB *cap*; 2V, 2Va, Vc, 2Fl, 2Tpt, 2Cttino, 3Trb, Cemb, Fag, cymbals, Hp, Timp, 2Org.
D-Kdma [3/2136], -ZI ms. B140c (dated 1685)   *KriegerW

KRIEGER, Johann Philipp (*b* Nürnberg, *bapt.* 1649; *d* Weissenfels, 1725)

2. Cantate Domino canticum novum: SATB, Tpt o Ctto, 2V, 2Va, Fag, Bc.
D-BI Mus. ms. 30224 (Bokemeyer collection, score dated 1685); **GB**-Lbl R.M. 24.a.l. (no.7, score); **S**-Uu 84:100 (tab) 57:8 (parts)   *KümmerKB; *SamuelN; *KriegerW

Preise, Jerusalem, den Herren: SATB, 2Tpt, 2Cttino, 2V, 2Va, 3Trb, Fag, Timp, Bc.
D-BII Mus. ms. (Bokemeyer collection, score dated 1698)   *KümmerKB
Edition: DdT 53

KUHNAU, Johann (*b* Geising, Erzgebirge, 1660; *d* Leipzig, 1722)

Christ lag in Todesbanden (with symphonia): SATB *conc & cap*, 2Ctto *ad plac*, 2V, 2Va, Org (dated 1693).
Lobe den Herren meine Seele (with sonata): SSATB, 2V, 2Va, Fag, 2Ctto, 3Trb, Bc.
D-BII Mus. ms. 12260 (Bokemeyer collection, score)   KümmerKB
Edition: RimbachK

LANGE, Gregor (see instrumental list)

LAPPI, Pietro (*b* Florence, *ca* 1575; *d* Brescia, 1630)

Sacrae melodiae unica, duobus, tribus, quatuor, quinque, nec non et sex vocibus decantandae . . . liber primus. Venice: Ricciardo Amadino, †1614; Frankfurt: Nicholas Stein, ∞1621; Antwerpen: Pierre Phalèse, ‡1622.
    Incipite à 6: STB, 2V o 2Ctto, Trb o V[o], Org.
†**I**-Bc (missing S, 6, Org); ∞**D**-B (now in **PL**-Kj), ∞ -Dl (SATB, Org); ∞**US**-R (S); ‡**B**-Br (5); ‡**D**-F; **GB**-Lbl (T, B, Org); **NL**-At (A)   RISM L687/688/689

Messa secondo libro a 4, 5, 6 voci . . . opera 14. Venice: Bartolomeo Magni, 1624.
    ChI,II,III&IV SATB; [Ctto, V, Trb in ripieno]; Org.
Instrumentation according to the Brescia catalog is as follows: ChI SATB56(in organo); ChII ATB *rip*; ChIII SATB *ripieni per li cornetti ò violini*; ChIV SATB *ripieni per li tromboni.*
I-BRd   *RISM L694

LASSO, Orlando di (see instrumental list)

LASSUS, Rudolph de (Munich, *b ca* 1563; *d* 1625)

Virginalia Eucharistica, quae magnae Virgini, Virginisque filio vocibus singulis, II, III, IV, V, VI, VII, octonis cum basi continua memor gratusque concinuit. Munich: Nikolaus Heinrich, 1615.

Regina coeli: S, Ctto, 3Trb, Bc.

D-As (v1, v3, Bc), -Rp (ChI: v1-v4, Bc; ChII: v1-v4)   RISM L1040

LEMMLE, Sebastian [Lämblein, Agnelli]

Ms including 29 works with cornetts in large settings.

1.   Ach Gott von Himmel sih darein: ChI SSATB; ChII ATTTB; Ctto, [5?]Trb, Vo, Bc (parts and tab dated 16 July 1639).

3a. Allein Gott in der Höhe sey Ehr à 21 in Echo: ChI 2V, Va, Vo; ChII SSTTB, Fag o Trb; ChIII SATB; ChIV TT, 4Trb; Cap B, Ctto; Tior, Org (parts and tab dated 24 May 1632).

3b. Allein Gott in der Höhe sey Ehr à 22 in Echo: ChI 2V, 2Va, Vo; ChII SSATB; ChIII SATB; ChIV 2Ctto, 6Trb; SATB *cap*, Tior, Vo, Org (parts and tab dated 12 Sept. 1635).

5.   Alleluia. Wohl dem der den Herren fürchtet à 10: ChI SSATB, Tior; ChII 2Ctto, 3Trb; Org (parts and tab dated 1634).

6.   Dancket dem Herren unndt prediget seinen nahmen à 10 o 18: ChI S, 2V, 2Va, Vo; ChII SATTB; CapI SATB; CapII Ctto, 3Trb, Fag o Vo; v. *pro Org.*, SATB; Tior, Org (parts and tab dated 20 Jan. 1635).

7.   Dilectus meus loquitur mihi à 8: ChI SSAB, 3V [o?] 3Ctto; ChII SATB, 4Trb; Vo, Org (parts and tab dated 31 Dec.1634).

8.   Dilectus meus loquitur mihi à 10, 14, et 16: ChI SSATBB, 2V [o?] 2Ctto, Va, 2Vo; ChII T, 4Trb; CapI SAB, Va; CapII ATB, Ctto; Tior, Org (parts).

9.   Domine ad adjuvandum / Laudate pueri Dominum à 14: ChI SSS, 3V, Vo; ChII SATTTB; ChIII 2Ctto, 5Trb; SSATTB; SSATTB *pro org.*; Tior, Vo, Org (parts and tab dated 10 Jan. 1636) (cornetts only in Laudate).

10. Du Tochter Zion freue dich sehr à 25: ChI SS, Fag, Tior; ChII ST, 2V, Va, Vo; ChIII ATB, 2Ctto; ChIV AT, 4Trb; TT*cap*; Tior, Org (parts and tab dated 14 Dec. 1634).

13. Ein feste Burgk ist unser Gott à 17: ChI SSB, 2V, Va, Vo; ChII SATB; ChIII T, Ctto, 4Trb; Bc (parts and tab dated 28 June 1635).

14. Ein feste Burgk ist unser Gott: ChI SSSSSSB, [4?]V, Vo; ChII ATTB; ChIII T, 2Ctto, 4Trb; Org (parts and tab dated 2 Sept. 1639).

17. Exultate Deo salutari nostro à 16: ChI S, 3V, Vo, Tior; ChII SSATB, 2Ctto, Vo, Tior; ChIII ST, 4Trb; *cap ad* ChIII ATTB, 2Ctto; ATTB *pro org.*, Org (parts and tab dated 22 June 1634).

18. Herzliebste schaut die Kranckheit ahn: ChI T, 3V, Vo, Tior; ChII S, 2Ctto, 4Trb, Org (parts and tab dated 19 Nov. 1633).

20. Heut triumphiert Gottes Sohn à 20: ChI S, 2V, Va, Vo; ChII SATB, Ctto o Tpt; ChIII SATBB; ChIV Ctto o Tpt, 4Trb; SATB *cap*; Tior, Fag, Vo, Org (parts and tab dated 2 April 1632).

21. Hodie completi sunt dies Pentecostes à 12, 15, et 20: ChI SSSSATB, 5V, Va, Vo; ChII SATTB, Ctto, 4Trb [or 2Ctto, 3Trb?], Vo; ChIII SSATTB *cap*; Org (parts and tab dated 26 May 1635).

22. Ich suchte des Nachts in meinem Bette à 11: ChI SATB, Ctto, 4Trb; ChII "di liuti" S, Fag o Vo o Trb, 2Tior; ChIII 2V, 2Va, Vo, SSATB *cap*; Vo, Org (parts and tab dated 27 July 1634).

23. In dich hab ich gehoffet Herr à 15: ChI T, 2V, Va, Vo, Tior; ChII SSATB, 2Ctto; ChIII SATTB, 5Trb; Org (parts and tab dated 8 Jan. 1635).

24. Jauchzet dem Herren alle weldt à 27 o 45: ChI SSSATB; ChII S (3 parts missing); ChIII 2Ctto, 4Trb; ChIV T, 4VaG; ChV 6Tpt; Org (parts and tab).

25. Jauchzet Gott alle Lande, lobsinget zu ehren à 17: ChI S, 3V, Vo, Tior; ChII SATB, Ctto; ChIII ST, Ctto, 4Trb, SATB *cap*; Vo (parts and tab dated 26 Oct. 1632).

26. Jubila concinent gentes cum gaudio à 16: ChI S, 2V, Va, Vo; ChII SATB, Ctto, Vo; ChIII T, Ctto, 4Trb, Vo; CapI SATBB; CapII SAT (parts and tab dated 21 March 1636).

28. Magnificat V toni à 16: ChI SSSAB, 3V, Va, Vo, Tior; ChII SSATTB, 2Ctto; ChIII S, 4Trb; Org (parts and tab dated 19 Dec. 1634).

29. Magnificat VIII toni à 13: ChI SS, 2V, Va, Vo, Tior; ChII SATB, Ctto, Vo, Fag; ChIII SATTB, Ctto, 4Trb, ATTB *cap*; Org (parts and tab dated 3 June 1634).

30. Magnificat super: Heut Triumphieret à 17: ChI 3V; ChII SATB, Ctto o Tpt; ChIII SATB; ChIV Ctto o Tpt, 4Trb; Vo, Org (parts).

31. Nun kom der Heyden Heylandt: ChI SSB, 3V, Va; ChII T, Ctto, 4Trb; ChIII SATB; Vo, Org (parts and tab dated 30 Nov. 1635).

32. Sihe meine Freundin du bist schöne à 8: ChI 2V, Va, Vo; ChII STTB Fag, Tior; [S]SAA[T]TB *cap*; (Ctto, 4Trb) *cap*; Vo, Org (parts and tab).

33. Singet frölich Gott der unser stärke ist à 15 o à 20: ChI T, 2V, Va, Vo; ChII SATB, Fag o Tior; ChIII Ctto, 4Trb; ChIV SATTB *cap*; Tior, Vo, Org (with sinfonia: 2Ctto o 2V, 2Trb, Vo, Org) (parts and tab dated 13 Aug. 1632).

34. Singet frölich Gott der unser stärcke ist à 15 o à 20: ChI 2V, Va, Vo, Tior; ChII SATB, Vo, Tior; ChIII T, 2Ctto, 4Trb; SSATTB *cap*; Org (parts and tab dated 24 Sept. 1635).

35. Veni Sancte Spiritus, reple . . . Kom heiliger Geist Herre Gott à 21: ChI S, 2V, Va, Vo, Tior; ChII SATB, Ctto, Fag; ChIII SATB, Ctto, Bomb *piccolo* o Trb *piccolo*, Bomb; ChIV ST, 4Trb, Tior; Org (parts and tab dated 27 April 1632).

37. Wohl dehm, der den Herren fürchtet: ChI SATB, Ctto, 2Trb, SATB *cap*, Tior, Vo; ChII 2V, [3?]Va, SSATB *cap* (parts and tab dated 5 Aug. 1634).

PL-WRu (Bohn collection Ms. mus. 166, now in **D**-BI, dated 1632-1639)   *BohnH

LEONI, Leone (*b* Verona, *ca* 1560; *d* Vicenza, 1627)
Prima parte dell'aurea corona ingemmata d'armonici concerti, a dieci con quattro voci, & sei istromenti. . . . Venezia: Ricciardo Amadino, 1615.
  In hac die a 10: AATT, 2V, Ctto, t Trb, b, b, Org.
  Surgite mortui a 10: AATT, V o Ctto, V, s, a Violetta, b, b, Org.
  Ne reminiscaris a 10: SATTT; Ctto o V, V, s, (S1 sinfonia only), t, Va, b, Org.
D-B (C1,C2,A1,A2,T1,T2,Bar2,B1,B2,5,Org, now in **PL**-Kj), -Mbs (B1,Bar2); also survives in ms copy in **D**-F   RISM L2010

LEOPOLD I (Vienna, 1640-1705)

Parce mihi: SSATB *soli*, SSATB, 4Va, 2Ctto, 2Trb, Vo, Fag, Bc.
A-Wn ms. 15642 (dated 1676)   *WalkerSB

Stabat Mater: SATB *soli*, SATB, 2Va, Vtta, Vc, Ctto, 2Trb, Vo, Fag, Bc.
A-Wn ms. 15731 (score), -Wgm I 17562 (parts, dated 1678)   *WalkerSB

Heu! Heu! peccatores: SATB *soli*, SATB, 3Va, bVa, 3VaG, Ctto, 3Trb, Vo, Tior, Bc.
A-Wn ms. 15844 (score), 16053 (parts)   *WalkerSB

Salve Regina: S *solo,* SATB, 2Va, Vtta, Vc, Ctto, 2Trb, Vo, Fag, Bc.
A-Wn ms. 15848 (score), 16043 (parts)   *WalkerSB

Domine Jesu Christe: SSATTB *soli*, SSATTB, VaG, 3Vtta, 2Ctto, 2Trb, Vo, Fag, Bc.
A-Wn ms. 16041 (dated 1662)   *WalkerSB

Dixit Dominus: S *solo*, SATB, 2Va, Vtta, Vc, Ctto, Tpt, 2Trb, Vo, Fag, Bc.
A-Wn ms. 16044   *WalkerSB

Beatus vir: A *solo*, SATB, 2Va, Vtta, Vc, Ctto, Tpt, 2Trb, Vo, Fag, Bc.
A-Wn ms. 16045   *WalkerSB

Magnificat: SSATB *soli*, SSATB, 2V, 2Va, Vc, 2Ctto, 2Tpt, 2Trb, Vo, Fag, Bc.
A-Wn ms. 16046   *WalkerSB

Laudate Dominum, omnes gentes: S *solo,* SATB, 2V, Vtta, Vc, Ctto, Tpt, 2Trb, Vo, Fag, Bc.
A-Wn ms. 16047   *WalkerSB

Ave maris stella: SATB *soli*, SATB, 4Va, bVa, Ctto, 3Trb, Vo, Tior, Bc.
A-Wn ms. 16049   *WalkerSB

Confitebor: T *solo*, SATB, 2V, Vc, Ctto, Tpt, 3Trb, Vo, Bc.
A-Wn ms. 16050   *WalkerSB

Laudate pueri: B, Tpt, 2V, Fag, *conc*; SSSAB *cap,* 2Ctto; Vc, Vo, Org.
A-Wn ms. 16051
Edition: *AdlerMW

Litaniae Lauretanae: SATB *soli*, SATB, 2V, Vc, Ctto, 2Trb, Vo, Fag, Bc.
A-Wn ms. 16052   *WalkerSB

Sub tuum praesidium: S *conc;* SATB *cap,* Ctto, Vtta, 2Va, 2Trb, Fag; Vo, Org.
A-Wn ms. 16052
Edition: *AdlerM

Missa pro defunctis a 5 voci: SSATB *soli*, SSATB, 4Va, 2Ctto, 3Trb, Vo, Bc.
A-Wn ms. 16054 (dated 1673)   *SpielmannZ; WalkerSB

Dies Irae: SATB *soli*, SATB, 2V, Va o Ctto, 2Va o 2Trb, bVa o Fag, 2Tpt, Vo, Bc.
A-Wn ms. 16055 (dated 1673)   *WalkerSB

Sancte Wenceslae: SATB, Va, Vtta, Vc, Ctto, 2Trb, Vo, Fag, Bc.
A-Wn ms. 16056   *WalkerSB

Decora lux: SATB *soli*, SATB, 2V, Vc, Ctto, 2Trb, Vo, Fag, Bc.
A-Wn ms. 16057   *WalkerSB

Hymnus: De Sancto Josepho (Te Josephi): SATB *conc*, 2V; SATB *cap,* Ctto, 2Trb,
Fag; Vc, Vo, Org.
A-Wn ms. 16058
Edition: *AdlerMW

Te splendor: SATB *soli*, SATB, 2V, Vc, Ctto, 2Trb, Vo, Fag, Bc.
A-Wn ms. 16060   *WalkerSB

Ut queant laxis: SATB *soli*, SATB, 2V, Vc, Ctto, 2Trb, Vo, Fag, Bc.
A-Wn ms. 16061   *WalkerSB

Iste confessor Domini: SSATB *soli*, SSATB, 2V, 2Vtta, Vc, 2Ctto, 2Tpt, 2Trb, Vo,
Fag, Bc.
A-Wn ms. 16062   *WalkerSB

Hymnus: de Dedicatione Ecclesiae: Caelestis urbs Jerusalem: SSATTB *soli*,
SSATTB, 2V, tVa, aVtta, Vc, Ctto, 2Tpt, 2Trb, Vo, Fag, Org.
A-Wn ms. 16064   *WalkerSB
Edition: *AdlerMW

Salve decus Bohemiae: SATB *soli*, SATB, 2V, Vc, Ctto, 2Trb, Vo, Fag, Bc.
A-Wn ms. 16066   *WalkerSB

Motetto de septem doloribus beatae Mariae Virginis: Veratur in Luctum: SSATB,
4Va *conc*; SSATB *cap,* Ctto, 3Trb; Va, Fag, Vc, Vo, Tior, Org.
A-Wn mss 16070 & 16069 (missing opening section) (parts)
Edition: *AdlerMW

Tres Lectiones I. nocturni pro defunctis: SSATB *conc*, 2Ctto muto, 4Va; SSATB *cap,* 2Trb, Fag; Vo, Org.
A-Wn ms. 16596 (dated 1676)   *AdlerMW

Hymnus: Fortem virili pectore: SATB *conc*, 2V; SATB *cap*, (Ctto, 2Trb, Vo) *cap*; Tior, Org.
A-Wn ms. 16757; -Wgm I/17.563
Edition:*AdlerMW

"Il Sacrafizio d'Abramo" (sepolcro from 1660): Ctto is specified.
A-Wn   *SpielmannZ

[LÖWENSTERN], Matthiäus Apelles von (*b* Polnisch-Neustadt, 1594; *d* Breslau, 1648)

Die den Herren fürchten à 8 cum Symphonia: ChI SSSB, 3V, Vo; ChII SATB, Ctto, 3Trb; Org.
PL-WRu (Bohn collection Ms. mus. 63, now in **D-BI**, parts and tab)   *BohnH

 b. Dancket dem Herren, predigt seinen nahmen à 8 o 12: ChI SATB; ChII SATB; 3V; STB *cap,* Ctto, a,t; Bc.
 c. Deus misereatur nostri à 12: Ch I SATB, [3?]V; ChII: SATB; ChIII: SATB Ctto "e trombino," 3Trb; SSAB *cap*, "Bassgeige," Org.
 f. Kommet herzue, last uns dem Herren frolocken: ChI SATB; ChII SATTB, 4Trb; Symphonia: 3V, Vo, 2Ctto, Bc.
 h. Singet dem Herren ein neues Lied à 8: ChI SATB, [3?]Ctto, [4?]Tpt, Trb; ChII SAB, 2V, Ctto, 2Trb, 3Tpt, "violino grande."
PL-WRu (168 b,c,f in parts & tab; 168 h in tab. Bohn collection Ms. mus. 168, now in **D-BI**)   *BohnH

MALVEZZI, Cristofano (*b* Lucca, *bapt.* 1547; *d* Florence, 1599)
Intermedii et Concerti, fatti per la commedia rappresentata in Firenze nelle nozze del Serenissimo Don Ferdinando Medici, e Madama Christiana di Loreno, Gran Duchi di Toscana. Venice: Giacomo Vincenti, 1591.
Primo Intermedio di Christofano Malvezzi:
Sinfonia à 6: 5Viole, Ctto, 4Trb, 6Lt, Salterio, Cetra, Mandola, [2LiredaBr, 2Hp].
The following description of the "Sinfonia à 6" is contained in the 9th partbook, p. 7:
"*La seguente Sinfonia si fece con gli detti strumenti & in oltrie in cielo aperto con sei liuti tre grossi, tre piccoli, un salterio, un basso di viola, con tre tenori, quattro tromboni, un cornetto, una traversa, una cetra, una mandola, e un sopranino di viola sonato in ogni maggiore eccellenza da Alessandro Striggio.*"
Coppia gentil à 6: tutti voices and instruments.
The following description of "Coppia gentil" is contained in the 9th partbook, p. 7: "*Il seguente Madrigale a sei fù cantando e sonato con gli medesimi strumenti e voci radoppiando tutti le parte a proportione de l'altra con il quale si die fine al primo intermedio.*"
Terzo intermedio (see MARENZIO, Luca)
Sesto intermedio

[Chi con eterna legge: voices with viols, lutes, cetra, organi, lire, tromboni, cornetti, violini, flauti]

"Chi con eterna legge" is not in the Vincenti print but was described by Bastiano d'Rossi in *Descrizione dell'apparato* (Florence, 1589)   *BrownSCI

    O qual resplende nube à 6: SSATTB; 4Lt, 4VaG, 4Trb, 2Ctto, V, Lirone, Cetra, Salterio, Mandola.

The following description of "O qual resplende nube" is contained in the 9th partbook, p. 16: "*Il madrigale, che segue fù concertato con quatro liuti, quatro viole, due bassi, quatro tromboni, due cor netti, una cetra, un salterio, una mandola, l'arciviolata lira, un violino, con ventiquattro voci.*"

    O fortunato giorno à 30: 7 Choirs, tutti instruments.

The following description of "O fortunato giorno" is contained in the 9th partbook, p. 17: "*Il seguente madrigali a sette Chori si fece con gli primi sopranominati strumenti e tutti gli altri e le voci furono al numero di sessanta. . . .*"

    O che novo miracolo à 5 & à 3: tutti voices and instruments.

The following description of "O che novo miracolo" is contained in the 9th partbook, pp. 19-20: "*Questo ballo fu cantando da tutti gli strumenti sudetti.*"

A-Wn; **I**-Fn (5, 6, 8, 11); **GB**-Ckc (C)   RISM M262
BrownIM 1591; *BrownSCI   *SartMS I&II 1591a
Edition: D.P. Walker, ed., *Musique des intermèdes de "La Pellegrina"* (Paris: Editions du Centre Nationale de la Recherche Scientifique, 1962)

MARENZIO, Luca (*b* Coccaglio nr. Brescia, 1553/4; *d* Rome, 1599)

Intermedii et Concerti, fatti per la commedia rappresentata in Firenze. . . . Venice: Giacomo Vincenti, 1591 (see also: MALVEZZI, Cristofano)

    Terzo intermedio

    Combatimento di Apolline col Serpente; Qui di carne si sfama: 12v, V, Ctto, Trb, 4Lt, LiredaBr, Hp, bVa.

The following description of the "Combatimento" is contained in the 9th partbook, p. 10: "*Si fece questo concerto con un'arpa due lire due bassi de viola, quattro leuti un basso di trombone, un cornetto un violino e dodeci voci.*"

    O mille volte: ChI&II; [Liuti, arpi, tromboni, violini, cornetti]

The following description of "O mille volte" is contained in the 9th partbook, p. 10: "*In questo si tenne l'ordine medesimo dell'antecedente.*" The above instrumentation for "O mille volte" is not in the Vincenti print but was described by Bastiano d'Rossi in *Descrizione dell'apparato* (Florence, 1589)   *BrownSCI

A-Wn; **I**-Fn (6, 5, 8, 11); **GB**-Ckc (C)   RISM M262
BrownIM 1591; *BrownSCI   *SartMS I&II 1591a
Edition: D.P. Walker, *Musique des intermèdes de "La Pellegrina"* (Paris: Centre Nationale de la Recherche Scientifique, 1962).

MARINI, Biagio (*b* Brescia, *ca* 1587; *d* Venice, 1663)

Concerto terzo delle musiche da camera . . . a3, 4, 5, 6, e più voci con due violini, et altri stromenti opera XVI. Milan: Carlo Càmagno, 1649.

    Grotte ombrose. echo à 6: SSS o TTT, 3V o 3Ctto, Bc.

I-Fn   SartMS I 1649a; RISM M667

MATTEIS, Nicola II (*b* late 1670s; *d* Shrewsbury? *ca* 1749)
In the opera *Archelao re di Cappadocia* (by Francesco Conti):
    from Act 1 Ballet: aria with Ctto
A-Wn ms. 17283 (dated 1719)   *McCredieM

In the opera *Sirita* (by Caldara):
    Marcia burlesca in movement in *partcello*: "unisono con il cornetto."
A-Wn ms. 18093 (dated 1719)   *McCredieM

MATTHAEI, Conrad (*b* Brunswick, 1619; *d* Königsberg? 1667)
Hochzeit-Lied aus dem XVIII Psalm. Königsberg: Johann Reussner, 1657.
    Hertzlich lieb hab Ich dich Herr: ChI STB, 2Ctto; ChII SATB, Org.
L-KA (present location uncertain)   *MüllerK

MAYER, Martin (Breslau?, *d* 1707)
    9. Credidi propter quod locutus sum: ChI SSATTB; ChII SSATTB, 2V, Ctto &
       V, 4Trb, Bomb; Org.
   14. Gaudete omnes et exultate à 8: ChI&II SATB; ChIII S, 3Trb; ChIV Ctto, 3Trb;
       Org.
  27a. Magnificat III toni: Ch I&II: SATB; 3V, Ctto, 3Trb, Fag, Vo, Org.
  28a. Magnificat VI toni: ChI&II SATB; ChIII Ctto, 3Trb; ChIV Ctto, 2Trb, Fag; Bc.[28]
  28b. Magnificat VI toni: ChI&II SATB; ChIII Ctto, 3Trb; ChIV Ctto, 2Trb, Bomb;
       Bc (partially identical with 28a).
PL-WRu (Bohn collection Ms. mus. 170, now in **D-B**I, parts)   *BohnH

Ms contains 21 works with cornetti in large settings.
    1. Hosianna dem Sohne David à 13 o 18: SSATB *conc & cap*; 2V, 2Tpt o 2Ctto,
       3Trb, Vo, Org (dated 1674).
    5. Es wird dass Scepter von Juda à 12, 20, o 23: SSATB *conc & cap*; 2Tpt,
       2Ctto, 2V; 2Tpt, 3Trb, Timp *ad lib*, Vo (missing), Bc (dated 19 Dec. 1676).
  11. Schmecket und sehet wie freundlich à 9 o 16: SATB *conc & cap*; 2V, 2Ctto,
       3Trb o 2Va *ad plac*, Vo, Bc (dated 1676).
  13. Gott ist unser Zuversicht und stärcke à 7, 12, o 16: SATB *conc & cap*; 2V,
       2Ctto, 3Trb *ad plac*, Vo, Bc (dated 1677).
  25. Siehe, es kommt die Zeit, dass ich dem David à 11, 15, o 20: SSATB *conc &
       cap*; 2V, 2Tpt; 2Ctto, 3Trb *ad plac*; Vo (missing), Bc (dated 1679).
  26. Freude! Jesus ist erstanden à 9, 14, o 20: SSATB *conc & cap*; 2V, 2Tpt; 2Ctto,
       3Trb *ad plac*; Vo, Bc (dated 1677)
  33. Schaffe in mir Gott ein reines Hertz à 10, 15, o 20: SSATB *conc & cap*; 2V,
       2Tpt; 2Tpt, 2Ctto, 3Trb *ad plac*; Vo, Org (dated 17 March 1679).

---

[28] Apparently there are two sets of parts for this work, one of which has an extra basso continuo part along with a *bombarde* part in place of a *fagotto*.

34. Heylig ist der Herre Zebaoth à 14 o 22: SSATTB *conc & cap*; 2V, 2Ctto, 2Trb o Va, Trb; 2Tpt *ad plac*; Vo, Org (dated 1676).

36. Kommet her zu mir alle à 7, 9, o 16: SATB *conc & cap*; 2V; 2Ctto o 2Fl, 2Trb, Trb o Fag *ad plac*; Vo, Org (dated 1676).

39. Der segen dess Herren machet reich à 13 o 21: SSATB *conc & cap*; 2V, 2Tpt, 2Trb, Trb o Fag; 2Ctto, 2Tpt, Timp *ad plac*; Vo, Org (dated 27 Sept. 1675).

42. Ihr Lieben, gläubet nicht einem ieglichen Geiste à 12, 14, o 21: SSATB *conc & cap*; 2V, 3Trb; 2Ctto, 2Tpt, 2Tpt *ad plac*; Vo, Bc (dated 1677).

54. Ich wil mich mit dir verloben à 6, 10, o 17: SATB *conc* [missing *cap*]; 2V; 3Trb, 2Tpt *cum surdin ad plac* [missing 2Ctto, Vo]; Bc (dated 1676).

PL-WRu (Bohn collection Ms. mus. 171, now in **D-BI** [nos. 1-54], parts)   *BohnH

Pieces missing from **D-BI** mus. ms. 171:

60. Treuffelt jhr Himmel von oben: SSATB *conc & cap*; V, VaG, Fag *conc*; 2V, 2Ctto, 2Tpt, 3Trb *ad plac*, Vo, Bc (dated 1681).

61. Gloria in excelsis Deo, Ehre sey Gott in der Höhe et Verbum caro factum est, Daß Wort ward Fleisch: SSATB *conc & cap*; 2V, 2Ctto, 2Tpt, 2Tpt princ, 3Trb, Timp *ad plac*; Vo, Bc (dated 1677).

62. Mein Hertz tichtet ein feines Lied: SSATB *conc & cap*; 2V, 2Ctto, 2Tpt, 2Tpt princ, 3Trb, Timp *ad plac*; [missing Vo], Bc (dated 1680).

64. Alleluja. Auff mein Psalter und Harffenklang: SSATTB *conc & cap*; 3V, 2Va, Fag; 5VaG, Vo; 4Fl, Fl o Fag; 2Ctto, 4Trb; 2Tpt, 2Tpt princ.; Timp, 2Vo, Bc (dated 1675).

69. Dieses ist der Tag, den der Herr gemacht hat: SSATB *conc & cap*; 2V, [missing 2Ctto], 2Tpt, 3Trb *ad plac*; Bc (dated 1683).

75. Wie lieblich sind deine Wohnungen: SSATB *conc & cap*; 2V, 2Ctto, 3Trb *ad plac*; [missing Vo], Bc (dated 1679).

76. Christus ist aufgefahren über alle Himmel: SSATB *conc & cap*; 2V, 2Ctto, 2Tpt, 3Trb, [missing Vo], Bc (dated 1679).

77. Zu der Zeit Herodes, des Königs: SSTB *soli*; SSATB *cap*; 2V, 2Ctto, 2Tpt, 3Trb *ad plac*; [missing Vo], Org (dated 1679).

79. Wir gläuben alle durch die Gnade: SSA *soli*, TB *conc*; TBSSATB *cap*; 2V, 2Ctto, 2Tpt, 3Trb *ad plac*, Bc (dated 1679).

The location of nos. 60-79 has not been yet determined. It is possible that they may have become separated from the rest of the Bohn mss during or after WWII.
PL-WRu ms. mus. 171 (lost)   *BohnH

MAZÁK, Alberik (*b* Ratibor, Silesia, 1609; *d* Vienna, 1661)

Cultus harmonicus . . . vario concentuum vulgo mottettorum una, duabus, tribus, quatuor, quinque vocibus exprimendorum. . . . Vienna: Matthäus Cosmerovius, 1649.
    Michael pugnavit: B, Ctto, Bc.
A-Wn (S, B, Bassus generalis); D-W (compl)   RISM M1500

MAZZOCCHI, Virgilio (Civita Castellana, 1597-1646)

Beatum Franciscum à 16
Sinfonia "alla quarta bassa": 2Ctto, 2V, 2Trb, Vlo, Org.
Millia, Millium à 16: 4SATB, 4V, 4Ctto, 4Trb (Vl, Ctto, Trb *colla parte* in each choir).
I-Bc ms. Q45 ff. *73r-77r*

Opus musicum a. V. Mazochi magistro capelle pontificiae apud S:ma Petrum Romae, ad n:um concinnatum: in Aula Collegij Romani publice exhibitum, ac Sereniss:mi Ferdinandi Caroli Archiducis Aust:ae nonori dicatum; . . . Anno Dom. M: D: C.XXXX.
(Motet in 8 choirs): ChI,II,III,IV,V&VI SAATBQ; ChVII 2V, Ctto, Lt, Cetra, Tior, Spinetta; ChVIII 2V, Fl, Lt, Cetra, Tior, Spinetta; 4Org.
I-TRc ms

MEDER, Johann Valentin [Giov. Valentino] (*b* Wasungen, *bapt.* 1649; *d* Riga, 1719)

Trauen und Leiden soll Heute verschwunden: SSATB, 2Va, 2Ob o 2V, 2Ctto, Vo, Bc.
D-LUC ms. 221A, -Kdma 2/512   *WalkerSB

Wüntschet Jerusalem Glück: ChI SATB, 2V, 2Va, Fag, Org; ChII SATB, 2Cttino, Org; ChIII 3Trb, Org.
PL-GD ms. 4038 (lost, dated 1687)   *Otto Gunther, *Die musikalischen Handschriften der Stadtbibliothek . . . Danzig*, Katalog der Handschriften der Danziger Stadtbibliothek, vol 4 (Danzig: Saunier, 1911).

In the opera *Die beständige Argenia*: for soloists, choir and instruments:
Ritornelli for 2Ctto & Bc (other instruments mentioned are 2V, 2VaG, Tior).
S-Sk Cod. Holm. S 164
Edition: EdM 268

MEGERLE, Abraham (*b* Wasserburg am Inn, 1607; *d* Altötting, 1680)

Ara musica solemni concertu ad veram et veterem formam redacta. . . . Salzburg: Christoph Katzenberger, 1647.
     14. Qui sequitur me: ATB, Va, 2Ctto, Bc.
     42. Justorum animae: SATB, SATB, SSATTB, 2Ctto, 4Trb, Bc.
     57. Homo quidam: SATTB *soli*, SATTB, 6Va, 2Ctto, 4Trb, Bc.
     58. O beatum virum: SATB, 2V o 2Ctto, 3Va, 5Trb o 5Va, 5Fag o 5Trb, Bc.
     59. O vere felix: SSATTB, SSATTB, SSATTB, 2V o 2Ctto, 4Trb, Bc.
     65. Justus ut palma: SSATTB, SSATTB, SATB, Ctto, Tpt, 4Tpt princ, 8Trb, Bc.
     71. Beatus vir qui inventus est: SSATTB, 2Ctto o 2V, 4Trb, Bc.
     72. Cantate populi: SATTB, 2Ctto o 2V, Bc.
     73. Magnificate Dominum mecum: SSATB, 2Ctto o 2V, 2Tpt, 3Trb, Bc.
     78. Vox caelestis: SSATTB, SSATTB, 2Ctto, 4Trb, 6Fag, Bc.

87. Afferentur regi virgines: SATB, SATB, SSATTB, 2Ctto, 3Tpt, 5Tpt princ, 4Trb, Bc.
88. Diffusa est gratia: TB *soli*, 10v, 3Ctto o 3V, 3Trb, Bc.
95. Filiae regum: SSATTB, SSATTB, 2V o 2Ctto, 4Trb, Bc.
98. Laudemus Deum nostrum: SSATB, 2V o 2Ctto, 3Trb, Bc.
104. Domine Deus: SATB, 2V o 2Ctto, 3Trb, Bc.
105. Domine Deus: SSATB, 2Ctto o 2V, 2Tpt, 4Tpt princ, 3Trb, Bc.
106. Domus mea: SSATTB, SSATTB, 2Ctto o 2V, 4Trb, Bc.

A-Wn (3,6,8,20,Bc, partitura); D-Mbs (partitura); -Rp (2,3,4,6,9,10,12,13,14,15,16, 20,Bc[3Ex.], partitura)   RISM M1749

MELANI, Jacopo (Pistoia, 1623-1676)

In the opera *Ercole in Tebe* (performed in Venice, 1671):
Act 3 scene VII, Plutone, Proserpina, Aletto, Choro di Mostri: Ritornello "Cornetti e Tromboni": 2Ctto, 2Trb (followed by "Terribile horribile" a 3: ATB).
Act 3 scene XI, Ritornello "Cornetti": 2Ctto, 2Trb (preceded by a trio "Si si si savventura": Plutone, Radamanto, and Minosso.
Act 3 scene XIII, Ritornello "Cornetti e Tromboni": 2Ctto, 2Trb (followed by the "Choro di Mostri": ATB, then a repeat of the sinfonia).
Act 5 Balletto: "violini" 2V, [Va, Vc]; 2Ctto, 2Trb.
Act 5 [Balletto]: "violini" 2V, [Va, Vc]; 2Ctto, 2Trb.
Act 5 [Balletto]: "violini e cornetti insieme" 2V, [Va, Vc]; 3Ctto, Trb.
Act 5 Vaghe sfauillano (with ritornelli): SATB, tutti instruments 2V, [Va, Vc]; 2Ctto, 2Trb.
I-Rvat ms. Chigi Q. IV. 59.

MERULA, Tarquinio (Cremona, 1594/5-1665)

Missa à 12: SATTB *conc*, 2V, 4Trb, SATTB *rip* (S of *rip* may be doubled by Ctto), 2Cttino, 2Va, Basso Va, Bomb, Fag, Org.
PL-GD ms. 406 vol 6 no. 10 (recopied by Cantor Gottfried Nauwerck, 1689)   *BernC

MICHAEL, Samuel (*b* Dresden, *ca* 1597; *d* Leipzig, 1632)

Psalmodia Regia, das ist: Außerlesene Sprüche aus den ersten 25. Psalmen . . . mit 2. 3. 4. und 5 Stimmen beydes Vocaliter und auch Instrumentaliter zu gebrauchen . . . erster Theil. Leipzig: Samuel Scheiben & Johann Franckens Erben (Gregor Ritzch), 1632.
9. Ich dancke dem Herrn von gantzem Hertzen à 5: TT, 2Ctto, Fag, Org.
20. Der Herr erhöre dich in der Noth: ST, Ctto, 2Trb, Org.
A-Wgm; D-B(now in PL-Kj), -Dl (AB), -HAmk, -MÜG (missing A); DK-Kk (missing Bc); GB-Lbl; S-Skma, -Uu (Bc)   MitUB   RISM M2631

MICHAEL, Tobias (*b* Dresden, 1592; *d* Leipzig, 1657)

Musicalischer Seelenlust Ander Theil Leipzig: Johann Franckens Erben & Samuel Scheiben, 1637.
37. Man sol dich nicht mehr: SSATB, 2V, 2Ctto, 3Trb, Bc.

46. Eins bitte sich vom Herrn: SSSSBB, with sinfonie: 2Ctto, 3Trb, Bc.
48. Mein Freund ist mein: SSATB, 2Tpt, 2Ctto o 2V, Trb, Bc.
A-Wn (2nd part); D-As (missing 5th part & Bc), -HAmk, -LEm, -LEt; GB-Lbl; S-V
*Edition: Kenneth Munson, "The Musicalischer Seelenlust of Tobias Michael" (Ph.D.
dissertation, University of Rochester, 1953)   RISM M2637

Wol dem der den Herren fürchtet à 5: SSATB *cap*; S, 2Ctto, 3Trb, Fag.
PL-WRu (Bohn collection Ms. mus. 173a, now in B-Bɪ, parts and tab)   *BohnH

MICHNA, Adam Václav (?Jindruichuov Hradec, *ca* 1600-1676)

Missa "Sancti Wenceslai": SSATTB *conc & cap*, 2Tpt, 2V o 2Ctto, 4Va, Org.
CS-KRa B I 109
Edition: MAB III, 1

Te Deum à 4-8v V, Va, [?]Ctto, [?]Trb, (Org) Bc.
*GroveD
Edition: *Dejiny ceské hudby v príkladech* (Prague: Státní nakladetelvtví krásné
literatury, hudby a umění, 1958), 77

MIELCZEWSKI, Marcin (*d* Warsaw, 1651)

Magnificat à 9 vel 13: SATB *conc & rip*, 2V, 2Cttino *ad plac*, 3Trb, b Va, Bomb
o Fag, Org *ad plac* (S *rip*: voce o Ctto).
PL-GD ms. 406 vol. 1 no. 1 (recopied by Cantor Gottfried Nauwerck, 1688)[29]

Missa Cerviensiana à 12 vel 18: SSATTB *conc & rip*, 2V, 2Cttino, 2Va, 4Trb, b
Va, Vo, Org (SS *rip* may be doubled with 2Ctto).
PL-GD ms. 406 vol. 7 no. 11 (recopied by Nauwerck, 1689), -Kj   *BernC

Missa Triumphalis à 14: Chɪ&ɪɪ SATB; 2V, 2Va, 2Cttino, 4Trb, Org *ad plac.*
PL-GD ms. 406 vol. 8 no. 14 (recopied by Nauwerck, 1689)   *BernC

M[ONARI], C[lemente] (*b* Bologna, *ca* 1660; *d* Forlí, in or after 1729)

Te Deum à 8 con concerti, e Stru:ti di C.M. Anno 1708 13 Maggio: Chɪ SATB, 2V;
Chɪɪ SATB, 2V; Ctto, Trb, Va, Vo, Bc.
I-Bof ms. 14 (parts)

MONN, [Matthias Georg] (Vienna, 1717-1750)

Dies Irae et Domine: SATB, 2V, 2Tpt, 2Trb, Ctto, Org.
H-P M 18 (ms from *ca* 1800)   *RISM AII 78853

---

[29] The same piece exists in CS-KRa without parts for bVa, Trb, Cttino, or Vo.

Requiem/Kyrie, Sanctus et Benedictus: SATB, 2V, 2Va, Vc, 2Tpt, 2Trb, Ctto, Org.
H-P M 19 (ms from *ca* 1800)   *RISM AII 78854

MONTE, Phillippe de (see instrumental list)

MONTEVERDI, Claudio (*b* Cremona, 1567; *d* Venice, 1643)

L'Orfeo favola in musica . . . rappresentata in Mantova l'anno 1607. Venice:
Ricciardo Amadino, †1609, ∞1615.
    Act 2-3. Sinfonia à 7: 2Ctto, 5Trb, "regali."
    Possente spirto: T, 2V, 4VaBr, "Contrabasso di viola," 2Ctto, Chit, "Organo di
    legno," Hp.
    Act 4. Sinfonia à 7: 2Ctto, 5Trb, "regali."
†**B-Br**; **I-Fn**, -Gu (incompl), -MOe, -Rsc; ∞**GB-Lbl**, -Och; **PL-WRu**
Facs. edition: BmB 6; Edition: Monteverdi, Op. 11   RISM M3449, M3450

*Sanctissimae Virgini missa senis vocibus, ac vesperae pluribus decantandae, cum
nonnullis sacris concentibus ad sacella sine principum cubicula accommodata.*
Venice: Ricciardo Amadino, 1610.
    1. Domine ad adiuvandum: SSATTB, 2V, 4VaBr, 3Ctto, 3Trb, Vc, Org.
    11. Sonata sopra Sancta Maria à 8: S, 2Ctto, 2V, 2Trb, VaBr oTrb, VaBr, Org.
    13. Magnificat à 7: SSATTBB, 2V, 3Ctto, 2Fl, 2"Fifari," 2VaBr, 2Trb, Org.
I-Bc, -BRd, -Ls (missing Bc), -Rc (T), -Rdp (A); **PL-WRu** (missing T, 5, 6, S incompl);
S-Sk (T)   SartMS I 1610b; RISM M3445
Edition: Monteverdi, Op. 14

MOVIUS, Caspar (*b* Lenzen ?, Brandenburg, *fl* 1633-59)
    5. Nun dancket alle Gott à 8: (only 3 surviving parts: Ctto, Vo, tab) (with 2 voices)
PL-WRu (Bohn collection Ms. mus. 51, now in **D-BI**, parts and tab)   *BohnH

MUFFAT, Georg *(b* Mégeve, Savoy, *bapt.* 1653; *d* Passau, 1704)
    Missa in labore requies à 20 (Kyrie I&II, Gloria, Credo): SATB *conc & rip*; SATB
    conc & rip; 5Tpt, Timp; 2Ctto, 3Trb, 2V, 2Va, bVa; 2Ctto, 3Trb, 2V, 2Va, bVa;
    Org.
This instrumentation remains the same throughout the work, with the exception of the
"Qui Tollis" section of the "Gloria" which has only one wind choir (2Ctto, 3Trb). The
mass is preceded by a sonata: 5Tpt, Timp; 2Ctto, 3Trb; 2Va, bVa; Org.
H-Bn   Edition: Ernst Hintermaier, *Denkmäler der Musik in Salzburg*, Bd. 5 (Bad
Reichenhall: Comes Verlag, 1994)

NIEDT, Nicolaus (*d* Sonderhausen, Thuringia, 1700)

*Musicalische Sonn- und Fest-Tags Lust, auf alle Sonn- und Fest-Tage durchs gantze
Jahr. . . .* Sonderhausen: Ludwig Heinrich Schönermarck, 1698.
    28 works in "Advent Theil": SSATB, 2V, 2Va, Vo, Bc. + ritornelli & sonatine with
    2Tpt (o 2Ctto – see below), 3Trb, Bc.
    45 works in "Oster Theil": SSATB, Bc.

"Sind in Advent-Theil auf alle hohe Fest-Tage, die Instrumenta durchaus mit Drometen und Posaunen gesetzet, in Ermangelung solcher können Cornetten, Flöten und dergleichen gebraucht werden, und so Frantzösische Schallmeyen genommen werden, so müssen solche eine Secund höher transponirt und aus dem d fis geblasen werden."
D-B (11 partbooks, now in **PL**-Kj); **F**-Pn; **GB**-Lbl (ParsI: S2,T,B,V2,Va1,Va2,Vo,Bc; ParsII: S1,S2,A,T,B,V1,Bc); **S**-Uu; **US**-R   *MitUB   RISM N683

OTTO, Stephan (*b* Freiberg, Saxony, *bapt.* 1603; *d* Schandau, Saxony, 1656)
Kronen Krönlein, Oder Musicalischer Vorläuffer auff geistliche Concert Madrigal-Dialog-Melod-Symphon-Motetische Manier, etc. mit 3. 4. 5. 6. 7. und 8. Stimmen sampt einem General Bass.   Freiburg: Georg Beuther, 1648.
    8. Sihe meine Freundin: SSATB, 2Ctto, 2V, "trombone picciolo," 2Trb, 3Va, Bc.
   13. O ihr lieben Hirten: SSATB, 2Ctto, "trombone picciolo," 2Trb, Tior, Bc (with symphonie for V, Va, Bc).
In the above works, the instruments always play together with the corresponding vocal parts, but cornetts and violins as well as trombones and violas play in different sections.
D-LEm, -Lr, -UDa, -WA; **GB**-Lbl (missing 1 part)   WelterRL   RISM O282

   12. Siehe meine Freundin du bist schön: SSATTB, 2Ctto, 4Trb, Org.
PL-WRu (Bohn collection Ms. mus. 52, now in **D**-BI; cf. *Kronen Krönlein*, no. 8, parts and tab)   *BohnH

   O ihr lieben Hirten fürchtet euch nicht à 6: ATTB *conc*; SSATT, 2Ctto, Trb, Vo; Org.
PL-WRu (Bohn collection Ms. mus. 180a, now in **D**-BI; cf. *Kronen Krönlein*, no. 13, parts and tab)   *BohnH

   Dialogus: Warlich, warlich, ich sage euch à 5: SAATB with Ctto, 2Trb, Bomb, 2V, Org.
PL-WRu (Bohn collection Ms. mus. 180b, now in **D**-BI, parts)   *BohnH

PACHELBEL, Johann Andreas (Nürnberg, 1653-1706)
   Kommt her zu mir: SATB, 2V, 2[Ctto], Bc.
The indication of instrumentation is unclear in this ms. Woodward interprets the headings: "V:i" and "C:i" as *Violino primo* and *Cornetto primo* respectively. The latter abbreviation could just as easily mean *Corno* or *Clarino*.
GB-T ms. 1209   *WoodwardP
Edition: Bärenreiter

   Magnificat: SSATB, 2V, 2Ctto o 2Ob, 3Va, Fag, Bc.
GB-T ms. 1208
Edition: WoodwardP

PALESTRINA, Giovanni (see Bach, J.S., Missa sine nomine)

PALLAVICINO, Carlo (*b* Salò, Lake Garda; *d* Dresden, 1688)

In the opera *Il Galieno*:
Aria: Ride il cielo e ride il mar: S, 2Ctto, Serpentone.
I-Rvat ms. chigi Q.V. 65   *BernS

PASSARINI, Francesco (Bologna, 1636-1694)

Laudate pueri à 8 [in Mi min.e] P. Passarini M.G.: 2SATB *cap*; TBBB, 4V, 2Va,
Ctto, Tpt, Bc.
I-Bc ms. BB 95 (dated 1693)

Motetto della Madonna a 16: "con vv. cornetti, tromba principiato in Venetia e
fornito à Bologna l'anno 1675"
I-Bc ms. BB100/3 (only Bc survives)

Te Deum a 8 "fatto in Venezia nel 1676 per l'incoronazione di Innocenzo XI":
2SATB; 2V, Ctto, Tpt, Org.
I-Bsf M. Passarini I-4

In campum o Duces: SB, 4V, 4Va, Ctto, Tpt, Org.
I-Bsf M. Passarini I-9

Ad montes ad colles ad nives: B, V, Va, Ctto, Tpt, Org.
I-Bsf M. Passarini I-10

Spargite lilia a 8: 2(SATB) *cap*; V, Va, Ctto, Tpt, Org.
I-Bsf M. Passarini I-11

PAUMANN, [Bernhard]

Missa in A minore a 4 Vocibu: 4v, Ctto, 2Trb, Vo, Org.
A-WIL ms. 714   *RISM AII 600077408

PEKIEL, Bartholomiej (*d* Kraków?, *ca* 1670)

Missa concertata la lombardesca à 13: ChI&II SATB; 2V, 2Va, 2Cttino, 3Trb, bVa,
Vo, Bomb, Org.
PL-GD Ms. 406 vol. 4 no. 7 (recopied by Nauwerck, 1689)
*Edition: WDMP 74

Missa à 15: ChI&II SATB; 2V, 2Cttino, 3Trb; 2Vtta, bVa [i.e., 3VaG] *ad plac*, Vo,
Bomb, Fag, Org.
PL-GD Ms. 406 vol. 5 no. 8 (recopied by Nauwerck, 1689)
*Edition: WDMP 69

PERANDA, Marco Giuseppe (*b* Rome or Macerata, *ca* 1625; *d* Dresden, 1675)

Missa Peranda: SSATB *conc & cap*, 2V, 2Va, VaG, 2Ctto, 2Tpt, 3Trb, Vo, Org.

The attribution of this work to Marco Giuseppe Peranda is based solely on the title "Missa Peranda."
CS-KRa B I 43 (dated 1672)   OttoS

Missa beatae Angelis: SSATTB *conc* SSATB *rip*; 2V, 2Va, 2Ctto, 3Trb, Vo, Org.
CS-KRa B I 44 (dated 1671)   OttoS

Factum est proetium magnum: SSATTB, 2V, 2Cttino, 2Va, 2Trb o 2Va, Vo, Tior, Bc.
D-BII Mus. ms. 17081 (Bokemeyer collection, score), -Dlb ms. 1738 D 1, -Kdma [22//37]; **S**-Uu Vok. Mus. i hs 61:16 parts.[30]

Repleti sunt omnes spiritu sancto à 8: AT o TB, 2V, 2Cttino o 2Ctto, Fag, Spinetto o Org.
D-Dlb mus. ms. 1738 E 501 (score & parts);[31] **D**-BII Mus. ms. 17081 (Bokemeyer collection, score)[32]   *KümmerKB; *BernC

Fasciculus Myrrhae est dilectus meus à 15: SSATB *conc*; SSATB *rip*; 2V, 2Va, 2Cttino [o Ctto], 3Trb, Fag, Org.
The score and parts specify *cornetto 1º* and *2º*, while the title page specifies *cornettin*.
D-Dlb mus. ms. 1738 E 509 (Grimma U235/U35, score and parts)   *BernC

Accurite gentes: ATB, 2Ctto [o 2V], Fag, Org.
The title page and heading specify *cornetti,* except for the vocal parts and one organ part which specify *violini.*
D-Dlb Mus. ms. 1738 E 510 (Grimma U233/O63, parts); **S**-Uu Vok. Mus. i hs 30:3 (parts) & 85:26b (tab) (dated 1666)

Veni Sancte Spiritus: SATB, 2V, 2Va, 2Ctto, 3Trb, Fag, Bc.
D-Dlb mus. ms. 1738 E 526 (Grimma U206/U7, parts missing Trb3)   *WalkerSB

Buccinate. Concerto ad Festum Michaelis à 13 et 18: SSATTB *conc* & 5vv *rip*; 2V, 2Cttino, 2Trb o 2Va, Fag, Org.
S-Uu Vok. Mus. i hs 61:14

Miserere mei Deus à 15, 20: SSSATB, 2V, 2Cttino *se piace*, 2Tpt *con sourdino*, 3Va, 3Trb *se piace*, bVa, Timp, Bc.
S-Uu Vok. Mus. i hs 61:18 (dated 1660; missing Cttino parts)

---

[30] This work is a shorter version of Vok. mus. i hs 61:14 (Buccinate).

[31] The cornettino parts are indicated by *"Cornetto 1º"* and *"Cornettino 2º"* in the score.

[32] In this ms *cornetto* is specified instead of cornettino, organ instead of *spinetto,* as well as the alternative: TB o AT.

PERTI, Giacomo Antonio (Bologna, 1661-1756)

In the opera *Penelope la casta*, Rome, 1696:
Aria in Act III Scene I: Va scherzando la speranza: S, Ctto, Bc.
GB-Ob Mus Sch E390

Messa à cinque CCATB con V.V.: SSATB *conc*, [S?]SATB *cap*, 2V, Va, Vo, Ob,
Ctto, Trb, Bc.
I-Bof ms. 20

Cantate cantate laeta. Motetto a 5 concert.to. con Trombe Cornetti Strom.ti.; e Rip:
SSATB *conc & cap*, 2Tpt, 2Ctto, 2V, Va, Vc "spezzato," Vo, Org.
I-Bsp ms. Lib. P. XIV

Gaudeamus omnes in Domino. Motetto a 8 con Trombe, Cornetti e Violini: Ch I&II
SATB *conc & cap*, 2Tpt, 2Ctto (o 2Ob), 2V, Vtta, Vc "spezzato," Org.
The indication *Cornetti* in the score has been crossed out and replaced with *Obuis* by
a later hand. The corresponding parts (in a different hand) are labelled *Tromba 3a and
4a*, while all of the other parts (in yet another hand) carry the heading "Motetto con
trombe, et Obuè e V.V."
I-Bsp ms. Lib. P. XIV (dated 1704)

Canite cives. Motetto à 5 Concertato con Tr.e, Cornetti: SSATB *conc & cap*, 2Tpt,
2Ctto (o 2Ob), 2V, Vtta, Vc "spezzato," Org.
The indication *Cornetti* on the parts and the score has been erased and replaced with
Obuè in a later hand.
I-Bsp ms. Lib. P. XV

In the opera *Nerone fatto Cesare*, Venice, 1693:
Aria in Act III Scene I: Chi trionfo dell'etra e servo à tua beltà (titled: "aria con
violoncelli e cornetto"): A, Ctto, 2Vc, Bc.
Source not given   *BernS

PETRUCCI, Santo

Liber primus missarum quator vocum cum Basso Generali. . . . Op. I. Venice:
Vincenti, 1621.
Missa sine nomine: SATB, Bc; with sinfonie V, Ctto, 2Trb, Bc.
The print also contains a "Missa Votiva S.M.V." with the same setting and sinfonias,
which do not have instruments specified.
I-Bc

PETSCH, Paul

*Jubilum Pentecostale . . . Das ist: eine geistliche Pfingst- Harmonia, und frölich
jauchzend musicalische Zusammenstimmung . . . so mit . . . T. & C. pro org. wie auch
zween absonderlichen Choren, un'Instrum. alter. Voce, nebenst denBasso Continuo,
und gegenwärtigen Instrumenten: Alß Clavicimbel, Spinett, Laut, Trompetten, Paucken,*

Dulcian, Cornetten, Posaunen, Geigen. und Flöten. . . . Greifswald: Mattaus Doischer, 1662.
S-Uu; D-Kdma [3/1951]   *RISM P1659

PEZEL, Johann Christoph (*b* Glatz, Silesia, 1639; *d* Bautzen, 1694)

Missa à 10 & 15: SSATB *conc & cap*, 2Ctto o 2V, 3Trb.
D-BI Mus. ms. 30171 (score dated 1669)   HowardL

PFENDNER, Heinrich (*b* Hollfeld, Franconia, *ca* 1590; *d* Würtzburg, *ca* 1631)

Motectorum binis, ternis, quaternis, quinis, senis, octonisque vocibus concinendorum liber secundus cum basso ad organum. . . . Würtzburg: Johann Volmar, 1623; †Michael Zinck, 1631.
    11. Ave virgo gloriosa à 6: SSB, 2Ctto o 2V, Fag o Va, Org.
The *Cantus* partbook specifies V o Ctto, whereas the *Altus* partbook specifies Ctto o V.
A-KR; D-B (2 partbooks now in PL-Kj), -F (T), -Rp, -Ru (S); F-Pc (Partitura); PL-Wn (A,B); S-Uu (missing partbook with S1 and Ctto1); †PL -WRu (missing partitura); S-Uu (missing S)   MitUB   RISM P1750, †P1751

PFLEGER, Augustin (Schlackenwerth nr. Carlsbad, Karlovy Vary, *ca* 1635-1686)

Veni Sancte Sancte Spiritus: ChI&II SATB, 2V, 3Va, 2Ctto, 2Trb, Vo, Fag, Bc.
S-Uu 86:71a (tab) 31:22 (parts)   *WalkerSB

PHENGIUS, Johannes

Frisch auff ietzt ist es Singens Zeit à 26: ChI 2V, Va, Vo, Lt o Tior; ChII SSAB; ChIII SSTTB *conc*; ChIV AATTB, Bc; ChV 2Tpt o 2Ctto, 5Trb; Bc.
The composer provides a page of detailed instructions regarding instrumentation and disposition of the choirs. He provides an optional division of the same instruments and voices into three choirs instead of five for the convenience of chapels where space would otherwise be insufficient.
PL-WRu (Bohn collection mus. ms. 183, now in D-BI, parts)   *BohnH

O meine Taub O Hertz O werthes Licht: SSTTB, 2V o 2Ctto, 2Va o 2Trb, Vo o Fag o Trb, Org.
PL-WRu (Bohn collection Ms. mus. 183c, now in D-BI, parts)   *BohnH

PICHELMAIR, Georg

Missa super. Dulcis Jesu: ChI&II SATB; 2Ctto, Bc.
Cornetto col soprano is indicated in the Kyrie and the beginning of the Gloria.
PL-WRu (Bohn collection Ms. mus. 184, now in D-BI, parts)   *BohnH

Erhalt uns Herr bey deinem Wort à 12: ChI: SSAB with V & Ctto, V; ChII SATB; ChIII ST with Ctto, 3Trb; Vo, Org.
PL-WRu (Bohn collection Ms. mus. 187c, now in D-BI, parts)   *BohnH

POHLE, David (*b* Marienberg, 1624; *d* Merseburg, 1695)

Der Engel deß Herrn lagert sich: SATB, V, Cttino, Trb, Fag, Bc.
D-BI Mus. ms. 30242, -Kdma [3/1273]; **S-U**u Vok. Mus. i hs 82:37   KümmerKB

Benedicam Dominum: SA, 2V o 2Cttino, Fag, Bc.
D-Kdma [2/520]; **S-U**u Vok. Mus. i hs 81:27

POLIDORI, Ortensio (*b* Camerino; *fl* 1621-54)

Messe a cinque, et a otto concertate . . . con doi violini ad libitum, & anche con ripieni di tromboni, ò di viole, ò voci ne passi, dove si trovarà segnata la dittone Tutti. Opera XIIII. Venice: Alessandro Vincenti, 1639.
    SATTB, 2V o 2Ctto, Org.
The violin parts indicate *violino o cornetto.*
I-Bc   RISM P5025

Salmi concertati a tre e cinque . . . con doi violini ad libitum & anche con ripieni di tromboni, ò di viole, ò voci ne 'passi, dove si trovarà segnata la dittione Tutti. Libro secondo, opera XV. Venice: Alessandro Vincenti, 1641.
    Dixit Domino: SATTB, 2V o 2Ctto, Bc (with ripieni "di tromboni, ò di viole, ò voci").
    Confitebor: SATTB, 2V o 2Ctto, Bc (with ripieni).
    Beatus vir: SATTB, 2V o 2Ctto, Bc (with ripieni).
    Laudate pueri: ATB, 2V o 2Ctto, Bc.
    Laudate Dominum: SATTB, 2V o 2Ctto, Bc (with ripieni).
    Laetatus sum: SATTB, 2V o 2Ctto, Bc (with ripieni).
    Nisi Dominus: SSB, 2V o 2Ctto, Bc.
    Credidi: SAB, 2V o 2Ctto, Bc.
    In convertendo: SATTB, 2V o 2Ctto, Bc (with ripieni).
    Magnificat: SATTB, 2V o 2Ctto, Bc (with ripieni).
D-B (now in **PL-**Kj); **I-**Bc   RISM P5026

POSCH, Isaac (*d* Carinthia? 1622/3)

Harmonia concertans. Id est: Cantiones sacrae (quas concertus itali vocant) I. II. III. IV. voc. tam vivae voci, quàm organo caeterisque instrumentis musicis accommodatae. Nürnberg: Simon Halbmayer, 1623.
    40. Alleluia resurrexit sicut dixit: TT, Ctto, Trb, Bc.
A-Wn; **D-B** (2 partbooks, now in **PL-**Kj), -Dl (SATB), -F, -SAh (A); **GB-**Lwa;
PL-WRu (ATB Partitur); **S-U**u   MitUB   RISM P5244
Edition: SEM 1

PRAETORIUS, Michael (*b* Creutzburg an der Werra, *ca*1571/3; *d* Wolfenbüttel, 1621)

Musae Sioniae, Geistliche Concert Gesange . . . Ander Theil. Jena: Autor (Christoph Lippold), 1607.
    1. Komm, heiliger Geist, Herr Gott: ChI&II SATB.
    2. Nun komm der Heiden Heiland: ChI&II STTB.
    3. Gelobet seist du, Jesu Christ: ChI&II STTB.

4. Puer natus in Bethlehem: ChI&II SATB.
5. In dulci Jubilo: ChI&II SATB.
6. Puer natus in Bethlehem: ChI&II SATB.
7. Puer natus in Bethlehem: ChI&II SATB.
8. An Wasserflüssen Babylon: ChI&II SATB.
9. Christ lag in Todesbanden: ChI&II SATB.
10. Jesus Christus, unser Heiland: ChI&II SATB.
11. Erstanden ist der heilige Christ: ChI&II SATB, Org/insts.
12. Wir danken dir, Herr Jesu Christ: ChI&II SATB.
13. Jesia dem Propheten das geschah: ChI&II SATB.
14. Heilig ist Gott der Herre: ChI&II SATB.
15. Wir gläuben all an einen Gott: ChI&II SATB.
16. Es ist gewißlich an der Zeit: ChI&II SSTB.
17. Wohl dem, der in Gottesfurchte steht: ChI&II SATB.
18. Wie lang willst du, o lieber Herr: ChI&II SATB.
19. Wie nach einer Wasserquelle: ChI&II SSTB.
20. Zu Gott in dem Himmel droben: ChI&II SSTB.
21. Selig ist der gepreiset: ChI&II SATB.
22. Durch Adams Fall ist ganz verderbt: ChI&II SATB.
23. Erhalt uns, Herr, bei deinem Wort: ChI&II SATB.
24. Verleih uns Friedn genädiglich: ChI SSTB, ChII SATB.
25. Es ist das Heil uns kommen her: ChI&II SATB.
26. Ich ruf zu dir, Herr Jesu Christ: ChI,II&II SATB.
27. Allein Gott in der Höh sei Ehr: ChI,II&II SATB.
28. Erbarm dich mein, o Herre Gott: ChI,II&II SATB.
29. Christe, der du bist Tag und Licht: ChI,II&II SATB.
30. In dich hab ich gehoffet, Herr: ChI,II&II SATB.

The preface gives various alternative combinations of instruments and voices for each choir in the above pieces; s,a,t,b instruments are: 3Ctto, bVa; or 3Va, bVa; or Ctto, [2]Va, bVa; and a,t,b instruments are: 3Trb, or 2Trb, bVa.
B-Br; **D**-B (SI incompl, ATBI, SATII), -BD (ATBI, SATBII), -BFa (SATII incompl), -BS, -Cm (S missing title page), -DS (BII), -GAU, -HAu (missing SII), -HVl, -LEm (BI), -Mbs (BI, ATBII), -NA (missing ABII), -NOk (ATI, SATBII); -SWsk (missing BI); **DK**-Kk; **F**-Pc (AI), -Ssp; **GB**-Lbl; **I**-Rsc (BI); **NL**-DHk; **PL**-Tu (BI,TII), -WRu (BII)
*Edition: PraetW 2   RISM P5349

Musae Sioniae . . . Fünffter Theil. Wolfenbüttel:Autor (Fürstliche Druckerei), 1607.
9. Nun bitten wir den heiligen Geist à 6: [o AT, with strings, Ctto/Trb, Org.]
11. Nun bitten wir den heiligen Geist à 6: [o SAT, with strings, Ctto/Trb, Org.]
54. Nun Komm der Heiden Heiland à 5: [o AT, with strings, Ctto/Trb, Org.]
151. Komm, Gott Schöpfer, heiliger Geist à 4: [o S, with strings, Ctto/Trb, Org.]
155. Gott der Vater wohn uns bei à 5: [o T, with strings, Ctto/Trb, Org.]
The above settings with instruments are suggested in the preface, part III.

B-Bc, -Br ; **D**-B (S incompl, T,B,6,7 incompl), -BD, -BFa (5,6,7), -BS, -Dl (S,A,5,6,7), -HAu (missing 5) -Hs, -HSk (S,B,5), -HVl, -Mbs (5,6), -NOk (incompl); -W; **F**-Pc; **GB**-Lbl; **US**-Pu (B)
*Edition: PraetW 5   RISM P5352

Eulogodia Sionia, continens cantiones sacras in ecclesia conclusionis loco ad dimissionem usitas. . . . Wolfenbüttel: Autor (Fürstliche Druckerei), 1611.

Contains 60 works à 2, 3, 4, 5, 6, 7, & 8:

In Adventu Domini:
1. Benedicamus: SS.
2. Benedicamus, Deo dicamus: SATB.
3. Deo dicamus: SSATB.
4. Deo dicamus: SSATTB.
Minus Summum:
5. Benedicamus: SS.
6. Deo dicamus: SATB.
7. Deo dicamus: SATTB.
Summum:
8. Benedicamus: SS.
9. Deo dicamus: SATB.
10. Deo dicamus: SATTB.
Feriale:
11. Benedicamus: SS.
12. Bendedicamus, Deo dicamus: SATB.
13. Deo dicamus: SSATB.
Angelicum:
14. Bendedicamus: SATB.
15. Deo dicamus: SATB.
16. Deo dicamus: SATB.
17. Deo dicamus: SSSTB.
In Festo Nativitatis Christi:
18. Bendedicamus: SS.
19. Deo dicamus: SATB.
20. Deo dicamus: SSSATTB.
21. Puer Natus in Bethlehem (pars 1): SST.
22. (pars 2): SSTB.
23. In natali Domini: SSTTB.
24. Angeli vigilibus: SSB.
25. Involutum fasciis: SSATB.
26. In obscuro stabulo: ST.
27. Lac sugit infantulus: SSB.
28. Hanc immensam gratiam. SSTTB.
29. Resonet in laudibus: SSSTTB.
30. Resonet in laudibus: SSSSATB.

Paschale Primum.:
31. Benedicamus: SS.
32. Deo dicamus: SSTB.
33. Benedicamus, Deo dicamus: SSSTTB.
34. Benedicamus, Deo dicamus: SSATTB.
Paschale Secundum:
35. Benedicamus: SS.
36. Benedicamus, Deo dicamus: SATB.
37. Deo dicamus: SATTB.
Paschale Tertium Paschale Primum:
38. Christus pro nobis passus est: SSTB.
In Festo Ascensionis:
39. Benedicamus: SS.
40. Benedicamus, Deo dicamus: SST.
41. Deo dicamus: SSSTTB.
In Festo Pentecostes:
42. Benedicamus: SSS.
43. Benedicamus, Deo dicamus: SSTB.
44. Deo dicamus: SSATTB.
Dominicale Primum:
45. Benedicamus: SS.
46. Benedicamus, Deo dicamus: SSTB.
47. Deo dicamus: SSATTB.
Dominicale Secundum:
48. Benedicamus: SS.
49. Benedicamus, Deo dicamus: SATB.
50. Deo dicamus: SATTB.
Apostolicum Primum:
51. Benedicamus: SS.
52. Deo dicamus: SATB.
Apostolicum Secundum:
53. Benedicamus: SS.
54. Benedicamus, Deo dicamus: SATB.
55. Deo dicamus: SSATTB.
Regina coeli Laetare:

56. Laetemur in Christo: SATB.
57. Laetemur: SATTB.
Aliud Regina coeli:

58: SSATTB.
Salve Regina.
59: SATB.

In the preface the following instrumentation is suggested to reinforce the soprano voices of the above vocal works: Discant 1: sVa; Discant 2: Ctto, Regal; Discant 3: Fl, Cemb; Discant 4: krummhorn o sVa; positif & Lt.
A-Wgm; **B**-Br (S); **D**-BD (A,T), -Dl, -LEm (S,A,5,6), -Mbs (missing A,5), -W; **GB**-Lbl; **PL**-WRu; **US**-Wc (A)
Edition: PraetW 13   RISM P5364

Megalynodia Sionia, continens canticum B. Mariae Virginis, Magnificat, 5.6. & 8 voc. Super Ut Re Mi Fa Sol La. . . . Wolfenbüttel: Autor (Fürstliche Druckerei), 1611.
Contains 14 Magnificats:
1. Magnificat super Angelus ad pastores: SATTB.
2. Magnificat super Ecce Maria: SSATB.
3. Magnificat super Surrexit pastor bonus: SSATB.
4. Magnificat super Gia lieto: SSATTB.
5. 6. Magnificat super Valle che lamenti: SSATTB.
7. Magnificat super Dolorosi martyr: SSATTB.
8. Magnificat super Elle est à vous: SSATTB.
9. Magnificat super Sel disse mai: SSATTB.
10. Magnificat super Mentre qual viva: SSATTB.
11. Magnificat super In te Domine speravi: SSATTB.
12. Magnificat super Chorale melos Germanicum: ChI&II SATB.
13. Magnificat: ChI SATB, ChII ATTB.
14. Magnificat per omnes versus super Ut Re Mi Fa Sol La: SSATTB.
The preface recommends the alternative use of violins, cornetts, and other instruments to reinforce the soprano parts. The preface also gives an alternative of cornetts and trombones, organ or regal with one soprano, or all voices.
A-Wgm; **B**-Br (S); **D**-BD (A,T), -Dl, -LEm (S,A,5,6), -Mbs (S,T,B,6), -W; **F**-Pc (missing 6); **GB**-Ge, -Lbl; **PL**-Wn (A,T,5), -Wu (missing B), -WRu (missing A,B); **US**-R, -Wc (A)
Edition: PraetW 14   RISM P5365

Urania, oder Urano-Chorodia. Wolfenbüttel: Autor (Fürstliche Druckerei), 1613.
13. Nun freuet euch: [ChI SSAT; ChII SSAT o (S o T); ChIII SSAT o (S o T, 2Ctto o 2V, 2Trb o 2Va); Org.]
14. Vom Himmel Hoch: [ChI SATB; ChII SATB o S; ChIII SATB o (S o T, Ctto o V, Ctto o V o Trb, 2Trb o Va; Org.]
15. Erstanden ist der heilige Christ: ChI SSTB; ChII STTB o S; ChIII ATTB o (A o T, Ctto o V, Ctto o V o Trb, 2Trb o Va; Org.]
25. Kommt her zu mir: [ChI SATB; ChII SATB o (S o A o T, 2Ctto, 2Trb); ChIII SATB o (S o A o T, 3Fl o 3crummhorns, Fag o crummhorn; ChIV SATB o (S o A o T, 4V o 4Va); Lt o Cemb, o Hp o Tior o Org.]

28. Jesus Christus, unser Heiland: [ChI SATB; ChII SATB o (S o A o T, 2Ctto, 2Trb); ChIII SATB o (S o A o T, 3Fl o 3crummhorns, Fag o crummhorn; ChIV STTB o (S o T, 4V o 4Va); Lt o Cemb, o Hp o Tior o Org.]
These and other alternative instrumentations are given in the preface.
D-Dl (SI, AI, SII, AII, TII, BII); **GB**-Ge, Lbl; **PL**-WRu (missing BII, AI incompl)
Edition: PraetW 16   RISM P5368

III. Polyhymnia cauduceatrix et panegyrica, . . .   Wolfenbüttel: Elias Holwein, 1619.
7. Das alte Jahr ist nun vergahn à 3.4.5.6.7.& 8: SSTB, [2V, Va, Vc], [Ctto o V], [4Lt], Trb o Fag, Bc.
17. Nun komm der Heiden Heiland: SSATTB; SATT *rip*; Cum symphonia & ritornelli à 6,7,10,11, &12: Ctto o V, a, t, Trb, bVa, Vo, Bc.
21. Wachet auf / ruft uns die Stimme: SSSAATTB, SATB *rip*, SATB *rip*, 2Ctto *in ecco*, 2V, Ctto, Va, 3Trb, Ctto o Fl o V o Trb, Vo, Org.
22. Christ unser Herr zum Jordan kam: V, "fiffaro," VaBr, Ctto muto, 3Trb, Fag, Bc.
23. Jubiliret frölich: SSSS; [4]Lt, [4]Va[G]; [2]Ctto, [2]Trb, SATB *cap*; Bc.
25. In dich hab ich gehoffet Herr: SSSTT *conc*, SATTB *cap*, Ctto, Fl, 3V, 2Va, 4Trb, Fag, Bc (Lt, Cemb, Org, Tior).
27. Als der gütige Gotte: SSSSTT, 4 Va[G], [4]Lt, (Fl o Trav, Ctto muto, Fag o Trb).
28. Lob sei dem allmächtigen Gott: ChI SATB, [4]Fl; ChII SATB, [4]Va; ChIII SATB, [4]Trb; (with 2"Cttino octava") Vo, Bc.
29. Erhalt uns Herr bei deinen Wort: SSSATBB, ChI "fiffaro" o V o Ctto muto; ChII 4VaG; ChIII 4Trb; SATB *cap*, Org.
34. In dulci jubilo: ChI S, 2Ctto o 2V, Fag; ChII S 2V o 2Fl, Fag; ChIII S Trb, 2Trb o 2Fag; SATB *rip*, 4Tpt; Bc.
36. Wenn wir in höchsten Nöten sein: ChI&II SATB; ChIII T, Ctto o V, 3Trb; ChIV A, 4VaG; ChV S, 2Fl o 2"fiffari," Fag; Bc.
38. Missa gantz Teudsch: Glory sei Gott: ChI SATB *conc & cap* (Fl o Ctto muto col sop); ChII SATB *conc & cap*; ChIII 3Va[G] o [3V][bVa], [4Lt], Org.
39. Herr Christ der einzig Gottes Sohn: ChI SSATTB *conc &rip*, Trb o Fag o Vo; ChII 2V o 2Ctto o 2Fl, 3Va o 3Trb; Org.

In no. 25. the instrumentation is varied using Ctto, Fl, V, and Trb. It is suggested that a mute cornett could be used in place of a third violin or the combination of Ctto, V, Fl. For no. 27. the following alternatives are given in the introduction to the piece: *Man kann aber anstatt der Lauten (darzu auch die Clavicymbel gehörig die Block= oder Querflöten / oder Stille Zinken / und Fagotten / oder Posaunen / nach den man sich bestimmet befindet werden).*
A-Wgm; **D**-B (now in **PL**-Kj), -BS; **DK**-Kk; **GB**-Lbl   RISM P5370
Editions: PraetW 17

V. Polyhymnia excercitatrix . . . Erster Theil.   Frankfurt: Simon Schamberger (Egenolff Emmel), 1619.
1. Jubilate Deo, omnis terra: TTT; t, b, b, Org o Regal Bc.
2. Sumite psalmum et date Tympanum: SS; a, t, b, b, Org o Regal Bc.
3. Laudate Dominum, laudate: SS; a, t, b, b, Org o Regal Bc.

4. Exultate, jubilate: SS; a, t, b, b, Org o Regal Bc.
5. Confitebor tibi, Deus: SS; a, t, b, b, Org o Regal Bc.
6. Exultemus adjutori nostro: SSS; t, b, b, Org o Regal Bc.
7. Venite cantate: SS; a, t, b, b, Org o Regal Bc.
8. Cantabo Domino semper: SS, a, t, b, b, Org o Regal Bc.
9. Gelobet seist du, Jesu Christ: SSTT; a, t, b, b, Org o Regal Bc.
10. Christ lag in Todesbanden: SS, a, t, b, b, Org o Regal Bc.
11. O Herre Gott, begnade mich: SS, a, t, b, b, Org o Regal Bc.
12. Durch Adams Fall ist ganz verderbt: SS, a,t,b,b, Org o Regal Bc.
13. Ach Gott, vom Himmel sieh darein: SS, a, t, b, b, Org o Regal Bc.
14. Wohl dem, der in Gottes Furcheten steht: SS, a, t, b, b, Org o Regal Bc.

The preface gives many suggested settings for the above pieces that include the alternative of reinforcing the soprano voices with Ctto, and alto and tenor voices with VaBr o Trb. In addition, the following alternatives are given for the instruments: 5Va; o 4Fl, Fag; o Ctto, 4Trb; o Ctto, [Va], t[Va], Trb, Trb o b[Va].
D-DS (S1S2,7/Bc); **PL-LEtpn** (6/b instrumentalis), **-Wn** (S1)   RISM P5371
*Edition: PraetW 18

Puericinium. Hoc est trium vel quatuor puerorum . . . cum basso generali & adjuncto canto continuo ad organum & theorbas. Frankfurt: Engenolff Emmel, 1621.
9. Komm heiliger Geist/ Herre Gott à 8 & 12: SATB *cap*, "fidicinia," Org; ChI puerorum: SSSS with V, Ctto, "Fiffaro" o V, Ctto; ChII ATTB with V o Fl, 2VaBr o 2Trb, Trb o Vo o Fag; Bc.
10. Wie schön leuchtet uns der Morgenstern: (same as no. 9. except that ChII has the Tenor I doubled with *flauto*).
D-B (13 partbooks, now in **PL-Kj**); **PL-Wn** (2,8,11), **-LEtpn** (7)   RISM P5272
*Edition: PraetW 19

Attolite portae capita vestra: ChI SSAT with 3V o 3Ctto; ChII SATBB with 2Trb, Trb o Vc o Sordun, *vel si placet etiam voce.*
Venite ad sanctarum Domini à 12: ChI SSAT with 2V o 2Ctto; ChII SATB; ChIII ATBB with 3Trb.
D-W
*Edition: PraetW 20

PRIULI, Giovanni (*b* Venice, *ca* 1575; *d* Vienna, 1629)

Missae . . . octo, novemq. vocibus, atque etiam instrumentis musicis concinendae. Venice: Bartolomeo Magni, 1624.
Missa quinta à 9: SAATTB, V, Ctto, Vo, Bc.
D-As   RISM P5479

Delicie musicali, part I. Venice: Bartholomeo Magni, 1625.
Il tempo fugge à 3 & à 6 se piace: STB, Ctto, V, bVa, Bc.
A duro stral à 4 et à 6 se piace: SATB, Ctto, V, bVa, Bc.
Non vedi tù: TT, Ctto, V, bVa, Bc (with ritornello).
Quando vuol sentir: SATB, V o Ctto, Bc.

Belle treccie: SSATB, Ctto, V, bVa, Bc.
Pastorella vaga: 3v, Ctto, V, bVa, Bc.
Quella bell'amor, à 6 & à 9: SSATB, V, Ctto, bVa, Bc.
O vezzosetta, à 6 & à 9: SSATBB, V, Ctto, bVa, Bc.
La violetta: SATB, Ctto, V, bVa, Bc.
Che ferai dolente: SATB, Ctto, V, bVa, Bc.
Hor destati: SATB, Ctto, V, bVa, Bc.
La violetta: SSATB, Ctto, V, bVa, Bc.
O regina de fiori: 6v, 2Ctto.
Perche t'en fuggi: SSATBB, Ctto, V, bVa, Bc.
Alla fiera: SSATTB, Ctto, V, bVa, Bc.
Presso un fiume tranquillo: SSATTB, Ctto, V, bVa, Bc.
Spiegate ò stelle: SS[ATTB], Ctto, V, bVa, Bc.
Chiudete l'orecchie: SSAATTBB, Ctto, V, bVa, Bc.
D-As, -Kl (6)   RISM P5483
Editions: MAM 45; DTÖ 77

Beatus vir à 12: ChI TT, Org; ChII B, Cttino [o Ctto], V, Org; ChIII SS, tiorba, Org; ChIV AB, Va, Vo, Org.
Pascha nostrum immolatus a 12: SAATTB, V, V o Ctto, Ctto, 3Trb, Org.
Laudate pueri a 12: SSATB, 2V, Ctto, 3Trb, Org.
In "Beatus vir," *cornetto* is specified on p. 129 of the ms, although *cornettino* is specified on p. 31. "Pascha nostrum immolatus" & "Laudate pueri" are arranged in choirs I,II&III.
A-KR Ms. L 13 (ms from 1633-39) *KellnerK *RISM AII 600153415, 600153372

RAUCH, Andreas (*b* Pottendorf, 1592; *d* Ödenburg, 1656)

Concentus votivus sub . . . Ferdinandi II. Vienna: Gregor Gelbharr, 1635.
Attolite portas principes: ChI&II SATB, 2 Ctto o 2V, 2Tpt, Trb, Org.
A-Wn; PL-WRu   *BohnD   RISM R340

Currus triumphalis musici, Imperatorum romanorum tredecim ex augustissima archiducali domo Austriaca . . . in quo selectiores iubilares, triumphales, ac solemnes festivales cantus, 8. 9. 10. 11. 12. pluriumque vocum. . . . Vienna: Matthäus Rictius, 1648.
13. Ferdinadus tertius, Te Deum laudamus Venezia à 10 & 14: ChI Ctto e S, S [e Ctto?]; ChII T, 3V; ChIII ATTB; ChIV SATB *cap*; VaG, Org.
The second cornett part is editorial because the second soprano part of ChI is incomplete in PL-WRu and does not contain this piece.
PL-WRu (vox 2 incompl, missing vox 5, 10, 11, 12)   RISM R342

RÈ, Benedetto

Sacrarum cantionum que duabus, tribus, ac quator vocibus concinuntur. . . . Venice, 1618.
Ostende Mihi a 3: S o T, V o Ctto, Vo o Trb, Org.
Tulerunt Dominum a 3: C o T, V o Ctto, Vo o Trb, Org.

Cornett is indicated only on the part of "Ostende Mihi."
D-B (S,A,T,B,B *ad organum*, now in **PL**-Kj)

REINA, Sisto (*b* Saronno, near Milan; *d* ?Modena after 1664)

Fiorita corona di melodia celeste a una, due, tre, e quattro voci con instrumenti, opera settima. . . . Milan: Giovanni Francesco & Fratelli Camagno, 1660.
    De profondis: B, 2Ctto, Org.
I-Bc, -Bsp   RISM R1017

REUSCHEL, Johann Georg (*fl* mid-17th cent)

Decas missarum sacra à 4. 5. 6. 7. 8. 10. 11. 12. 13. 14. 15. 16. 17. & 18. voc.
Freiburg: Georg Beuther, 1667.
    Missa quinta à 7, 11, e 12: SATB *conc & cap*; 2V o 2Ctto, Vo o Fag, Bc.
    Missa sexta ab 8, 13, e 14: SSATB *conc & cap*; 2V o 2Ctto, Vo o Fag, Bc.
    Missa septima ab 8, 13, e 14: SSATB *conc & cap*; 2V o 2Ctto, Vo o Fag, Bc.
    Missa decima ab 11 e 12: ChI&II SATB; 2V o 2Ctto, Vo o Fag, Bc.
In the headings of "Missa quinta," "sexta," and "septima," the indication *Violino o Cornetto* is used, whereas in "Missa decima" the heading indicates *Cornetto* only. In the table of contents only "Missa Decima" has the designation *Violino o Cornetto,* the others being designated *Violino* only.
A-Wgm, -Wn; **F**-Pn; **GB**-Lbl; **PL**-WRu   BohnD   RISM R1212

REUTTER, Georg (*bapt.* 1656; *d* Vienna, 1738)

    Mass: SATB, Ctto, 2V, 2Trb, Fag, Vo, Org.
A-Wa sign. 742   *RISM AII 600054185

    Requiem: SATB with Ctto, 2Trb, Fag; 2V, 2Va, Vo, Org.
A-Wn ms. HK 793
*Edition: DTÖ 88

    Ad te levavi: 4v [SATB], 2V*rip*, Va, Ctto, 2Trb, Fag, Vc, Vo, Org.
A-Wn ms. HK 833   *card catalog

    Ad te levavi animam meam: 4v [SATB], 2V, Va, Ctto, 2Trb, Fag, Vc, Vo, Org.
A-Wn ms. HK 834 (dated 1762)   *card catalog

    Dies sanctificatus illuxit nobis: 4v [SATB], 2V*unis*, Va, Ctto, 2Trb, Fag, Vc, Vo, Org.
A-Wn ms. HK 836   *card catalog

    Regis tharsis et insulae: 4v [SATB], 2V *conc*, Va *conc*, Ctto, 2Trb, Fag, Vc, Vo, Org solo.
A-Wn ms. HK 845   *card catalog

Christus factus est pro nobis (grad. ad festo exaltationis): 4v [SATB], 2V, Va, Ctto, 2Trb, Fag, Vc, Vo, Org.
A-Wn ms. HK 856   *card catalog

Haec dies quam fecit Dominus: 4v [SATB], 2V, Va, Ctto, 2Trb, 2Tpt, 2"Trombe," Timp, Fag, Vc, Vo, Org.
A-Wn ms. HK 859   *card catalog

Species tua et pulcritudine tua: 4v *rip* [SATB], 2V, Va, Ctto, 2Trb, Fag, Vc, Vo, Org.
A-Wn ms. HK 902   *card catalog

Steht angelus mixta aram templi: 4v [SATB], 2V, Va, Ctto, 2Trb, Fag, Vc, Vo, Org.
A-Wn ms. HK 903   *card catalog

Ergo plebs fidelis, de omni tempore: 4v [SATB], 2V, Va *conc*; Ctto, 2Trb, Fag, Vc, Vo, Org.
A-Wn ms. HK 910 (dated 1759)   *card catalog

Vesperae de Beata: 4v [SATB], 2V, Va, Ctto, 2Trb, Fag, Vc, Vo, Org.
A-Wn ms. HK 946   *card catalog

Succure rex coelorum: 4v [SATB], 2V, Va, Ctto, 2Trb, Fag, Vc, Vo, Org.
A-Wn ms. HK 971 (dated 1759)   *card catalog

Dei nomen magnificate: 4v [SATB], 2V *conc*, Va *conc*, Ctto, 2Trb, Fag, Vc, Vo, Org.
A-Wn ms. HK 974 (dated 1759)   *card catalog

Per mundi castra velox ad astra: 4v *rip* [SATB], 2V, Va, Ctto, 2Trb, Fag, Vc, Vo, Org.
A-Wn ms. HK 976 (dated 1757)   *card catalog

Quae festiva nobis lucet: 4v [SATB], 2V, Va, Ctto, 2Trb, Fag, Vc, Vo, Org.
A-Wn ms. HK 985 (dated 1761)   *card catalog

Justus ut palma florebit: 4v [SATB], 2V, Va, Ctto, 2Trb, Fag, Vc, Vo, Org.
A-Wn ms. HK 989   *card catalog

De manu insidiandum: 4v [SATB], 2V, Va, Ctto, 2Trb, Fag, Vc, Vo, Org.
A-Wn ms. HK 993   *card catalog

Deo sit laus: 4v [SATB], 2V *conc*, Va, Ctto, 2Trb, Fag, Vc, Vo, Org.
A-Wn ms. HK 994 (dated 1762)   *card catalog

Laudate Deum: 4v [SATB], 2V*unis*, Va, Ctto, 2Trb, Fag, Vc, Vo, Org.
A-Wn ms. HK 999 (dated 1761) *card catalog

De manu peccatorum: 4v [SATB], 2V, Va, Ctto, 2Trb, Fag, Vc, Vo, Org.
A-Wn ms. HK 1003 (dated 1762) *card catalog

Si observaveris iniquitates: 4v [SATB], 2V, Va, Ctto, 2Trb, Vc, Vo, Org.
A-Wn ms. HK 1004 (dated 1762) *card catalog

Veni Sancte Spiritus: Chor, V, Va, Ctto, Ob, 2Trb, Fag, [2Tpt], [Trb], Vc, Org.
A-Wn ms. HK 1147 *card catalog

Requiem excerpts: Domine Jesu Christe rex gloriae: SATB, 2V, Va, Vc, Fag,
2Horn, 2Trb, Ctto, Vo, Org.
H-Bb 46,207 (ms from *ca* 1800)   *RISM AII 30262

Requiem excerpts: Domine Jesu Christe rex gloriae: SATB, 2V, Va, Vc, Vo, [Fag],
2Trb *conc*; Ctto, Org.
H-Bb 47,156 (ms from *ca* 1800)   *RISM AII 30263

Requiem fragment: Hosanna: 4v, Ctto, 2Tpt, 2V, 2Trb, Fag, Vo, Org.
A-HE VIII b 1   *RISM AII 600091995

RITTER, Christian (*b* 1645/50; *d* after 1717)

  16. Gelobet sey der Name des Herren: ChI SATB, 2V, 2Va, Fag; ChII SATB,
    2Cttino, 3Trb; 4Tpt, Timp, Org.
D-BI Mus. ms. 30260 (Bokemeyer collection, score dated 1672) *KümmerKB

ROLLE, Christian Carl

*Das Herr Gott dich loben wir, wie solches bey den öffentlichen Gottesdienst auf der
Orgel mit der Gemeinde am übereinstimmigsten gespielt werden kann. Mit ausgesetzten
Trompeten und Paucken. Wie auch Zincken und Posaunen.* Berlin: Georg Ludwig
Winter, 1765.
  à 9 v with 3Tpt [o 3Ctto], 4Trb, Timp, Org.
In the score and the parts, the instruments indicated are 2 *Clarini, Principale, Paucken*,
and 4 trombones. The foreword suggests cornett, possibly as an alternative to the
clarini.
D-LEm, -Sl; **US**-Wc   RISM R2055

ROLLE, Johann Heinrich (*b* Quedlinburg, 1716; *d* Magdeburg, 1785)

  In the Oratorio *Lazarus* for 6 vocal roles, orchestra, and chorus: Largo non troppo,
  Ein Jungling, "Mein stille Abend ist gekommen": SA, T *solo*, B, Ctto, 3Trb, 2Fag,
  2V, Va, Bc.
US-Wc ms. M1500.R64 L3 (score, *ca* 1793); -Ws ms. XXXIV (score, after 1778; 1.
perf: 1778 in Magdeburg)   RISM AII 00107753, 00112868

ROSENMÜLLER, Johann (*b* Oelsnitz, nr. Zwickau, *ca* 1619; *d* Wolfenbüttel, 1684)

Credidi propter quod locutus sum: ChI&II SATB; 2V, 2Va, 2Ctto, 2Trb, Vo, Bc.
D-B[?] Berlin Stadtliche Akad. für Kirchen u. Schulmusik   *Hamel

Preise Jerusalem den Herrn: ChI SSAB; ChII ATTB; 2V, 2Ctto [??]
D-B[?] Mus. ms. 24860 (missing); L-KA [?]   *Hamel

2. Gloria in excelsis Deo à 19: ChI&II SSAATTBB, 2V, 2Va, Fag, Tpt, 2Ctto, 3Trb, Bc.
3. Gloria in excelsis Deo, Das Wort ward Fleisch à 14: SSATTB, 2V o 2 Cttino, 2Cttino, 4Trb, Bc (dated 1683).
6. Gloria in excelsis Deo à 10 et più: ChI SATB, 2V, 2Vtta; ChII SATB, 2Ctto; Bc.

In no. 3. the title page gives the instrumentation cited above, while the first page of the score gives 2 violins and 2 *cornetti*.
D-BII Mus. ms. 18880 (Bokemeyer collection, score)   KümmerKB

10. Dilexit quoniam exaudiet Dominus: ChI&II SATB; 2V, 2Vtta, 2Ctto, 3Trb, Vo.
11. Domino probasti me: ChI&II SATB; V, Ctto, Bc.
12. Estote fortes: BB, 2V o 2Ctto, 2Trb, Fag, Bc.

D-BII Mus. ms. 18881; GB-Lbl mus. ms. R.M. 24.a.4, no. 1 (nos. 10 & 11)
*KümmerKB

2. Laetatus sum in his: ChI SATB, 2V, 2Va, Fag; [ChII SATB] 2Ctto, 3Trb, Org.
4. Laudate Dominum omnes gentes: ChI SATB, 2V, 2Vtta, Va; ChII SATB, 2Ctto, 3Trb; Org.
6. Levavi oculos: ChI SATB, 2V, 2Vtta, Va; ChII SATB, 2Ctto, 3Trb, Org.
7. Nihil novum sub sole: SSATB *conc & rip*, 2V o 2Ctto, 3Trb o 3Va[G], Fag, Org, Bc.
15. Magnificat à 18: ChI SATB, 2V, 2Vtta, Va; ChII SATB, 2Ctto, 3Trb; Org.

D-BII Mus. ms. 18882 (Bokemeyer collection, score), -Kdma [2/1802 (no. 2), 2/1806 (no. 6), 2/1807 (no.7)]   KümmerKB

Laudate pueri Dominum: ChI&II SATB; 2V, 2Vtta, 2Ctto, 3Trb, Vo.
The existence of this piece is questionable. According to KümmerKB there is no "Laudate pueri" in D-BII Mus. ms. 18882. It may have been mistaken for "Laudate Dominum omnes gentes" (no. 4 in that ms).
D-BII Mus. ms. 18882 (score)   *Hamel

1. Bleibe bey unß, Herr Jesu Christ à 11, 16: SSATB *conc & cap*, 2V, 2Ctto, 3Trb, Bc.

D-BII Mus. ms. 18884 (Bokemeyer collection, score)   KümmerKB

9. Confitebor tibi Domine: ChI&II SATB; 2Ctto *se piace*
D-BII Mus. ms. 18886 (Bokemeyer collection, score)   *Hamel

3. Beatus vir qui timet Dominum: SATB, 2V [o] 2Ctto, 2Vtta [o] 2Trb, Bc.
The title page says *2 cornetti se piace; 2 violette overo tromboni.*
D-BII Mus. ms. 18887 (Bokemeyer collection, score)   *KümmerKB

4. Dixit Dominus: ChI&II SATB; 2V, 2Va, 2Ctto, 3Trb, Fag, Org.
D-BII Mus. ms. 18888 (Bokemeyer collection, score)   *KümmerKB

7. In te Domine speravi: ChI&II SATB; 2V, Va, Vtta, 2Ctto, 3Trb, Vo, Bc.
The above instrumentation differs from that given in KümmerKB (V, SATB, Ctto,
SATB, Bc).
D-BII Mus. ms. 18889 (score)   *Hamel; *KümmerKB

   1. Laudate pueri Dominum: SAB, 2V, 3Va, 2Ctto, Fag, Bc.
   2. Laudate pueri Dominum: SSB, 2V, 2Vtta, Tpt o Ctto, Ctto, Bc.
   10. Laudate pueri Dominum concertato con istromenti e tromba: SSSSAATTBB,
      2V, 2Vtta, Fag, Tpt, 2Ctto, 3Trb, Bc.
D-BII Mus. ms. 18890 (Bokemeyer collection, score); **GB**-Lbl mus. ms. R.M. 24.a.3,
no. 3 (score of no. 10)   *KümmerKB; WalkerSB

   Nun gibst du, Gott, einen gnädigen Regen: SSTTBB *conc*, SSATB *cap*; 2V, 2Va,
   2V o 2Cttino, 5Trb, Spinetto o Tior, Vo, Fag, Org.
D-BII Mus. ms. 18893 (Erfurt collection, parts)   *NoackE; *LeonardT

   Als der Tag der Pfingsten erfüllet: SSATTBB *conc*; SSATTB *cap*; 2V o 2Ctto,
   2Va, 5Trb, Vo, Bc.
D-BII Mus. ms. 18898 (Erfurt collection, score and parts dated 1678)   *NoackE

   Entsetze dich, Natur: SSATTB *conc & cap*; 2V, 2Ctto, 3Trb, Bc.
D-BII Mus. ms. 18902 (Erfurt collection, parts dated 1677)   *NoackE

   Wie lieblich sind deine Wohnungen à 9: SSTTB, 2V, 2Va, 2Cttino, 3Trb, Bc.
The *cornettini* are found only in the opening sonata.
D-Dlb Mus. ms. 1739 E 502 (Grimma U519/T33, parts), -Kdma [3/1293]   *BernC

   Seine Jünger kammen: [SS]ATB, SSATB *rip & cap*, 2V, 2Va, 2Ctto, 3Trb, Fag o
   Vo, Org, Bc.
D-Dlb Mus. ms. 1739 E 507 (Grimma U512/T46, parts), -Kdma [61/154]
*WalkerSB; *LeonardT

   Lauda Jerusalem Dominum: ChI&II SATB; 2V, 2Va, 2Ctto, Tpt, 3Trb, Fag, Org,
   Bc.
D-Dlb Mus. ms. 1739 E 519 (Grimma U 250/U 50, parts and tab dated 1704), -Kdma
[3/1285]; **GB**-Lbl Mus. ms. R.M. 24.a.3, no. 4 (score)   *Hamel

   Puer natus est nobis: SATB, 2V, 2Va, Tpt, Ctto, Bc.
D-Dlb Mus. ms. 1739 E 521 (Grimma U255/U56, parts); -Kdma [3/1290]

Daran ist erschienen die Liebe Gottes à 7: SAB *conc*; SATB *cap*, Ctto, 4Trb; V, Vo, Org.
PL-WRu (Bohn collection ms. 192, now in **D**-BI, parts)   *BohnH

ROSSI, [?]

Motetto. Beatus vir qui timet Dominum: ChI&II SATB; 2V, 2Va, 2Ctto o 2Ob, Fag, Bc.
D-BI Mus. ms. 30260 (Bokemeyer collection, score)   *KümmerKB

ROTHE, Wolf Ernst

Concert. nun dancket alle Gott . . . mit 4. Vocal- und 10. Instrumental-Stimmen sambt dem basso continuo. . . . Breslau: Gottfried Gründern Baumannischen Factor, n.d. [library catalog: 1650-1663].
SATB, 2V, 2Va, 2"Cornetin," 3Trb, Vo, Bc.
PL-WRu   RISM R2795

ROVETTA, Giovanni (Venice, *ca* 1595-1668)

Kyrie and Gloria (from *Messa et salmi,* 1639): SSATTB, 2Cttino, Bc.
S-Uu Vok. Mus. i hs 33:2 (dated 1671)

RÓŻYCKI, Jacek Hyacinth (*b*? Leczyca; *d ca* 1697)

4. Domine ad adjuvandum: SATTB *conc*; SATTB *rip*, Ctto, 3Trb; 2Cttino, 2V, bVa, Org.
In the cornett part and one of the trombone parts, the indications *voce ó cornetto* and *voce ó trombone* are found.
PL-GD ms. 406 vol. 2 (recopied by Nauwerck, 1688)
Edition: WDMP 54

4. Magnificat anima mea Dominum à 9 vel 13, 4. voci e 5. Instrom. con 4 Rip.: SATB *conc & rip* (SATB o Ctto, 3Trb), 2V, 2Vtta, Vo, Cttino (doubling V1 *ad plac*), Ctto (doubling V2 *ad plac*), Va b *ad plac* (doubling Vo), Bomb e Fag *ad plac* (doubling Vo), Bc per l'organo.
PL-GD ms. 406 vol. 3

6. Dixit Dominus Domino veo à 9 vel 13: SATB *conc & rip*; 2V, 2Va, 2Cttino; Ctto, Bomb o Fag, Vo *ad plac*, Bc (SB ripieno may be doubled by Ctto, Fag).
PL-GD ms. 406 vol. 3 (recopied by Nauwerck, 1688)   *BernC; *GroveD

RUBERT, Johann Martin (*b* Nürnberg, 1614; *d* Stralsund, 1680)

Musikalische Seelen-Erquickung. . . . Stralsund: Joachim Reuman, 1664.
3. Man muß die Sünd a 7: SS, 2V e 2Ctto*, 2Va, Bc.
5. Merck auff mein Hertz a 8: SSS, Ctto, 2V, Fag, Vo, Bc.
6. Gott ist mein a 8: SS, 2Ctto, 2V, Fag, Vo, Bc.
9. Wie Jonas der Prophet a 8 & 10: SSB, Ctto, V, Fag, Vo, a & tVa *si placet, 5. & 7.*, Bc.

D-B (3.Cant:Tenor:Voc/Ctto/t Va/b Fag, *a[33] Va, *tVa/bFag, tVa/bFag, 2V:Ctto2, tVa, bVo wie auch zu einem Clavi Cymbal, Harff, Theorba oder Pandor, zu gebrauchen, now in **PL**-Kj), -Dl, -W; **L**-KA   *MüllerK   RISM R3031

RUFFO, Vincenzo (see instrumental list)

SANCES, Giovanni Felice (*b* Rome, *ca* 1600; *d* Vienna, 1679)

Missa Praesentationis: 8v, 5Va, 2Ctto, 5Trb, 1"Galizone" (colacione), Org.
A-KR C 7, 652   *WebhoferS

Missa Requiem Ferdinandi III. "Imperatoris Augustissimi": 8v *cap*, 5Va, 2Ctto muto, 4Trb, Vo, Org.
A-KR E 2, 66   *WebhoferS

   2. Nativitas/Conceptio est hodie Sanctae Mariae: SATB, 2Va, Ctto, 2Trb, Fag, Vc, Vo, Bc.
      Nativitas gloriosae Virginis Mariae: SATB, 2Va, Ctto, 2Trb, Fag, Vo, Bc.
      Quando natus est: SATB, 3Va, Vc, Ctto, 2Trb, Vo, Fag, Bc.
   3. Regali ex progenie: SATB, 2Va, Ctto, 2Trb, Fag, Vc, Vo, Bc.
   4. Corde et animo Christo canamus: SATB, 2Va, Ctto, 2Trb, Fag, Vc, Vo, Bc.
   5. Cum jucunditate conceptionem: SATB, 2Va, Ctto, 2Trb, Fag, Vc, Vo, Bc.
   6. Gloriosae Virginis Mariae ortum: SATB, 2Va, Ctto, 2Trb, Fag, Vc, Vo, Bc.
A-Wn ms. 18997 (parts)   *WalkerSB

Antiphonae ad Vesperas. In circumcisione: SATB; 3Va, Ctto, 2Trb, Fag, Vc, Vo, Org.
A-Wn ms. 18998   *WeberhoferS

   1. O admirabile commercium: SATB, 3Va, Vc, Ctto, 2Trb, Vo, Fag, Bc.
   4. Germinavit radix Jesse: SATB, 3Va, Vc, Ctto, 2Trb, Vo, Fag, Bc.
   5. Ecce Maria genuit: SATB, 3Va, Vc, Ctto, 2Trb, Vo, Fag, Bc.
   6. Propter nimiam caritatem: SATB, 3Va, Vc, Ctto, 2Trb, Vo, Fag, Bc.
   7. Senex puerum portabat: SATB, 3Va, Vc, Ctto, 2Trb, Vo, Fag, Bc.
A-Wn ms. 18998 (parts)   *WalkerSB

Antiphonae ad Vesperas. In natale communi: SATB; Vtta, Va, Ctto, 2Trb, Fag, Vc, Vo, Org.
A-Wn ms. 18999   *WeberhoferS

   1. Hoc est praeceptum meum: SATB, Va, Vtta, Vc, Ctto, 2Trb, Vo, Fag, Bc.
   2. Majorem caritatem nemo habet: SATB, Va, Vtta, Vc, Ctto, 2Trb, Vo, Fag, Bc.

---

[33] The partbooks marked with an asterisk(*) are bound together with Constantin Dedekind, Königs Davids goldnes Kleinod (1675), sign. D100, and are cataloged only under the latter title.

3. Vos amici mei estis: SATB, Va, Vtta, Vc, Ctto, 2Trb, Vo, Fag, Bc.
4. Beati pacifici: SATB, Va, Vtta, Vc, Ctto, 2Trb, Vo, Fag, Bc.
5. In patientia vestra: SATB, Va, Vtta, Vc, Ctto, 2Trb, Vo, Fag, Bc.
6. Tradent enim vos: SATB, Va, Vtta, Vc, Ctto, 2Trb, Vo, Fag.
A-Wn ms. 18999 (parts)   *WalkerSB

Jubilate: SATB, Va, Vtta, Ctto o Vtta, Trb o Va, Vc, Vo, Org.
A-Wn H.K. 648 (parts)   *WebhoferS

Inclina Domine: SATB, Va, Vtta, Ctto o Vtta, 2Trb o 2Va, Vc, Vo, Org.
A-Wn H.K. 673 (parts)   *WebhoferS

Miserere mei, Domine: SATB, V o Va, Va, Vtta, Ctto o Vtta, Trb o Va, Trb, Vc, Vo, Org.
A-Wn H.K. 674 (parts)   *WebhoferS

Le lacrime de S. Pietro. Azzione sacra da rappresentati al santo sepolchro nella cesarea cappelle dell'anno MDCLXVI: SATBB, [2?]V, [2?]Ctto muto, [?]Fag, [?]Trb, Bc.
The surviving score contains only bass lines for the sections with instruments. Mute cornetts are indicated for one ritornello occurring twice.
A-Wn   *WebhoferS

Il trionfo della croce. Rappresentatione sacra al sepolcro di Christo, nella Cesarea cappella dell'Augustissimo Imperatore Leopoldo nella sera dell venerdi santo dell'anno MDCLXXI: SSSSATTBBBB, [2?]Va, [2?]Ctto muto, [?] "Pifari," [?]Trb, Bc.
The surviving score contains only the outer parts for the sections with instruments. Mute cornetts are indicated for one ritornello and one aria marked "Basso con Cornetti Muti."
A-Wn   *SpielmannZ; *WebhoferS

Missa Reminiscere: 8v *conc*, 2V, 4Vtta, 2Ctto, 4Trb, Vo, Org.
CS-KRa B I 19 (dated Jan 1672, all parts missing except C1, C2, A1, & Org)   OttoS

Cum Complerentur dies Pentecostes de S.Spiritu: SSATTB *conc & cap*, 2V, 4Trb *pro lib*, [3 Va, 2 Ctto], Vo, Org.
The Va and Ctto parts were added on the title page by another hand.
CS-KRa B II 32

Canzonetta à 6, "Nel regno d'amore": SSB; 2Ctto muto o 2VttaBr, Trb, *ad lib* (*alla Bastarda*); bVa, Cemb, "basso per la battuta."
D-Kl 2° ms. 57 m   *WebhoferS

There are also listed in an inventory of G.F. Sances over 100 works of large-scale forces using cornett (see Appendix).   *WebhoferS

SARTI, Benedetto (17th cent)

Domine adjuvandum: ChI,II&III SATB; Ctto, V, 2Va, 2Trb, Tior, Vo, Org Bc.
I-Baf capsa I, n. 13 (ms dated 1684)   *RISM AII 179443

SARTORIUS, Christian (*b* Querfurt; *d* Kulmbach, 1676)

Unterschiedlicher Teutscher nach der Himmelcron zielender Hoher Fest- und DanckAndachten Zusammenstimmung mit 1. 2. 3. 4. 5. 6. und 8. Nemblichen, einer, zwey, drey, auch fünff, Vocal-dann zweyen und meher Instrumental-Stimmen als Violinen oder Corneten, auch Posaunen. Sampt gedoppelten Basso continuo. Nürnberg: Christoph Gerhard, 1658.
   24. Alleluja, lobet ihr Himmel den Herrn à 8: SSTTB, 2V o 2Ctto, 2Trb, Vo, Org.
D-BI, -B (5 partbooks, now in **PL-Kj**), -ERu; **GB-Lbl** (missing b, Org); **PL-WRu** (S1/T1, S2/T2, V1, Org); S-Uu   *MitUB   RISM S1076

SCACCHI, Marco (*b* Gallese nr. Viterbo, *ca* 1600; *d* Gallese, 1681/87)

Missa pacis. Kyrie & Gloria: S *conc;* SS *cap* & 2Ctto (only these parts survive).
PL-WRu (Bohn collection Ms. mus. 197c, now in **D-BI**)   *BohnH

SCARLATTI, Alessandro (*b* Palermo, 1660; *d* Naples, 1725)

In the opera *Il Comodo Antonio*, Naples, 1696:
   9. Coronata di Laura: S, Ctto, Bc.
   10. Son lo scherzo di sorte rubella: S, Ctto, Bc.
   11. Cara e dolce rimembranza: S, Ctto, Bc.
*Gloria Rose, "Two Operas by Scarlatti Rediscovered," *The Musical Quarterly* 58, no. 2 (July 1972): 420-428.
Edition: In Henry Prunières, ed., *Les Maîtres du chant (*Paris: Heugel, 1927)

In the opera *Marco Attilio Regolo*:
   2. Choro e Ballo: SAT, 2Ob, 2Ctto, 2V, Va, Bc.
   3. Coro: SAT, 2Ob, 2Ctto, 2Corno da Caccia, 2V, Va, Bc.
GB-Lbl Add 14171
*Edition: D.J. Grout, ed., *The Operas of Alessandro Scarlatti,* vol II (Cambridge, MA: Harvard University Press, 1975)

SCHÄFFER, Paul (*fl* Guhrau & Breslau, 1617-1645)

Jauchzet dem Herrn alle Welt: ChI SATB, 3V, Va, Bc; ChII SATB, 2Ctto, 2Trb, Bc.
PL-WRu (Bohn collection Ms. mus. 198b, dated 1645, now in **D-BI**)   BohnH

Siehe wie fein und lieblich: ChI SA o 2Ctto, TB, Bc; ChII SATB, Bc.
PL-WRu (Bohn collection Ms. mus. 198c, now in **D-BI**)   BohnH

SCHEIDT, Samuel (Halle, *ca* 1587-1654)

Pars prima concertuum sacrorum II. III. IV. V./ VIII. et XII. vocum adiectis symphoniis et choris instrumentalibus, cum basso continuo seu generali pro organo. Hamburg: (Michael Hering; Laurentius Pfeiffer), 1622.

> Concertus III. Cantate Domino 2.3.4.& 5 vocum cum Symphonia variorum instrumentorum. versus 1: TT, Ctto, VaBr, 3Trb, Org (with symphonia); versus 5: SSATTB, Ctto, VaBr, 3Trb, Org.

> Concertus XII. Magnificat à 12 vocum cum symphonia. 5 versus: ChI B, 3Ctto o 3V; ChII SATB; ChIII S, 3Trb; Org.

A-Wgm (compl); **D**-B (17 partbooks, now in **PL**-Kj); **US**-R, -Wc (11 partbooks)
Edition: ScheidtW XIV & XV   RISM S1350

> Nun Danket alle Gott, der grosse Dinge tut: SSAATB, 2Ctto, 4Trb; SSAATB, 2Ctto, 2V, 4Fl, 5Fag, 2Va, Vo, Trb, SSAT, SATB, ATTB, Bc.
L-K Univ. i. Pr. Ms 13160   *LeonardT

> Nun lob, mein Seel, den Herren: SATB, 4Va[G], SATB, Ctto, 3Trb, Bc.
PL-WRu (Bohn collection Ms. mus. 319, now in **D**-BI)   BohnH; *LeonardT

SCHEIN, Johann Hermann (*b* Grünhain nr. Annaberg, 1586; *d* Leipzig, 1630)

Das Te Deum Laudamus. . . . Leipzig: Johann Glück, 1618.

> Herr Gott dich loben wir: ChI SATB, V, Va; ChII SATB, Tpt o Ctto, 2Trb; ChIII SATB, Ctto, Trb; ChIV SATB, Fl, Fag; CapellaI&II SATB.
PL-WRu, (lost; possibly the same piece as in ms. mus. 200d)   *BohnD

Lyrica Davidica. . . . Leipzig: Johann Glück, 1620.

> Beati omnes qui timent Dominum: ChI S & Ctto, A & Ctto, T, B & Fag; ChII S, A & Trb, T, B; Bc.
The alto part with which the cornett is paired is marked *"alto"* but is really a second soprano in treble clef.
PL-WRu   BohnD   RISM S1412

Der 23. Psalm Davids . . . mit 3, 11, 8, und 22 Stimmen auf 3. 5. oder 6. Chore abzutheilen componiert. . . . Leipzig: Gregor Ritsch, 1625.

> ChI SSBB, 2"Piffaro," 2Ctto, Bomb; ChII SATB, V, 2Va, Vo; Bc.
D-LEsm   *RISM S1421

Opella Nova ander Theil geistlicher Concerten mit 3, 4, 5, & 6 Stimmen zusampt dem General-Baß. . . . Leipzig: autor (Freiberg: Georg Hoffmann), 1626.

> 8. Mach dich auf, werde Licht: ST, 5v *cap*, 2V, 2Ctto, 2Fl, 3Trb, Bc.

> 9. Herr, nun läßt du deinen Diener: B, 2V o 2Ctto, Vc o Fag, Bc.

> 18. Vater unser: SSATB, V o Ctto, Trav o Ctto, 2Va o 2Trb, Bc.

> 28. Nun ist das Heil und die Kraft: SSAATB, Tpt, Ctto, 3Trb, Bc.

> 29. Selig sind die, da gleich arm sind: SSATB, Ctto, Trav, 3Trb, Bc.

A-Wgm; **D**-B (5 partbooks, now in **PL**-Kj); **GB**-Lbl; **PL**-WRu; **US**-NH

Edition: Paul Horn, ed., *Das Chorwerk alter Meister IV*, 12 (Stuttgart: Hänssler Verlag, 1964)   RISM S1388

1. Freuet euch des Herren ihr gerechten à 9, 13, et 18: ChI SSATB, Ctto, 3Trb; ChII SATB; SATB *cap*, Trb; 2Ctto, 3V, Va; Bc.
2. Der Herr ist mein Hirtt, mir wird nichts mangeln: ChI SSATB, 2"Piffari," 2Ctto, 3Bomb; ChII SATB, 4V; SB, 2Bomb, Bc.

PL-WRu (Bohn collection Ms. mus. 200b, now in **D**-BI, parts)   *BohnH

Herr Gott dich loben wir à 24: ChI T, "Violino soprano," "Violino alto," "Viola bassetto"; ChII A, Trb o "Cornetto soprano," 2Trb; ChIII "Cornetto soprano," "Cornetto alto," "Trombone bassetto"; ChIV A, Fl; CapI SATB; CapII SATB (missing CapIII T; CapIV Trb, Fag)

PL-WRu (Bohn collection Ms. mus. 200d, now in **D**-BI, parts)   *BohnH

Ich frewe mich deß, das mir geredt ist à 14 o 26: ChI SSTB; ChII SATB; ChIII SAT, 4Trb; ChIV 3V; 2Tpt, 2Ctto; Vo, Org.

PL-WRu (Bohn collection Ms. mus. 200e, now in **D**-BI, parts and tab)   *BohnH

Mache dich auff werde Licht: STB, 2Ctto, 3Trb, SAT *cap*, Vo, Org (with symphonia).

PL-WRu (Bohn collection Ms. mus. 200f, now in **D**-BI, parts and tab)   *BohnH

SCHELLE, Johann (*b* Geising, Thuringia, 1648; *d* Leipzig, 1701)

1. Herr, deine Augen sehen nach dem Glauben à 12: SSATB *conc & cap*, 2V, 2Cttino, 3Trb, Fag, Bc.
5. Lobe den Herrn, meine Seele à 26: ChI SSATB *conc*; ChII SSATB *cap*; 2V, 2Vtta, 2Cttino, 3Trb, 4Tpt, Fag, Timp, Org.
8. Vom Himmel kam der Engel Schar: SSATB, 2V, 2Vtta, 2Tpt, 2Ctto [o 2Cttino], 3Trb, Fag, Timp, Org.
11. Schaffe in mir, Gott: SATB, 2V, 2Vtta, 2V*piccolo* o 2Cttino, Tpt *con sordino*, Vc, Org.

Another setting of No. 8, "Vom Himmel kam der Engel Schar," in **F**-Pc does not specify trombones, and specifies *cornettini* instead of *cornetti*.
D-BII Mus. ms. 19781 (Bokemeyer collection, score); -Kdma [1/1643, 1/1646]; **F**-Pc ms. vm¹ 1180 (of No. 8)   *KümmerKB; *MGG
Edition: DdT 58-59

Alleluia, man singet mit Freuden: SSATB, 2V, 2Va, 2Ctto, Fag, Bc.
D-Dl ms. 19780
Edition: *Die Kantate* 39 (Stuttgart: Hänssler Verlag, 1966)

Ich lebe, und ihr sollt auch Leben à 9 cum sonata: B, 2V, 2Cttino, 2Fl, 2Tpt, Bc.
D-Dlb mus. ms. 1857 E 502

Eructavit cor meum à 20: ChI&II SSATB; 2V, 2Va, 2Cttino, 3Trb, Fag o Vo, Org (dated 1696).
D-Dlb mus. ms. 1857 E 505 (parts)   *GraupnerF

Actus Musicus auf Weyh-Nachten: Vom Himmel hoch: SSATTB, SSATB *rip*, 2V, 2Va, Ctto, schreier, Fl, Trb, Fag, Bc.
D-LUC Ms. 236   *GraupnerF
Edition: Kassel: Bärenreiter, 1965; Friedrich Wanek, ed. Mainz: Schott, 1969

Durch Adams Fall conc. à 14: SSATB, 2V, 2Va, Cttino, Ctto, 3Trb, Org.
GB-Ob mus. ms. sch. c. 31 (parts)

Magnificat à 10 & 20: SSATB *conc & cap*; 2V, 2Cttino, 2Va, Org.
Salve solis orientis: SSATTB *conc & cap*; 2V, 2Va, 2Cttino, Tpt, 3Trb, Org.
GB-Ob mus. ms. sch. c. 31 (parts)

SCHMELZER, Johann Heinrich (*b* Scheibbs, L. Austria, *ca* 1620/3; *d* Prague, 1680)

Compieta [including] Cum invocarem; In te Domine, Qui habitat in adjutorio, Ecce nunc benedicte, Te Lucis ante terminum, & Nunc dimitis: SATB, 2V, Vc, Ctto, 2Trb, Vo, Fag, Bc.
A-Wn 17328 (parts)   *WalkerSB

Vesperae brevissimae de beatissimae virgine et de apostolis: SATB, 2V, Vc, Ctto, 2Trb, Vo, Fag, Bc.
A-Wn 17329 (parts)   *WalkerSB

Missa S. Spiritus: SSATTB, 2V, 2Va, 2Ctto, 2Tpt, 4Trb, [Org].
CS-KRa B I 23 (parts)   OttoS

Missa Mater purissima: SATB *conc & cap*, Ctto, 3Trb, 3Va, Vo, Org.
CS-KRa B I 29 (score & parts, dated Jan. 1677)

Missa tarde venientium: SATB *conc & cap*, 2V, [Ctto, 2Trb *ad lib*], Vo, Org.
CS-KRa B I 30 (parts, dated 1671)   OttoS

Missa peregrina in honorem S. Rochi: SATB *conc &* [*rip* with instruments *ad lib*]; 2V, 3Va, 2Ctto, 3Trb, [Vo, Org].
CS-KRa B I 141, 242 (dated 1679; two copies)   OttoS

Ad concentus o mortales ad triumphos: SSATTB *conc & rip*, 2V, 3Va, 2Ctto, 2Tpt, 4Trb, Vo, Org, Bc.
CS-KRa B II 62 (dated 1676)   *OttoS

Vesperae Solennes: SSAATTBB *conc & cap*, 7Va, 2Ctto, 3Trb, 2Tpt, Vo, Bc.
The work is scored for strings with the exception of the "Laudate pueri Dominum" and
"Magnificat" sections, the former calling for 2Ctto, 3Trb and the latter for 2Tpt, 2V,
3Va.
CS-KRa B III 92 (parts)   OttoS

SCHMIDT, Johann Christoph (*b* Hohnstein nr. Pirna, 1664; *d* Dresden, 1728)
> 9. Sie ist fest gegründet: ChI SATB, Tpt, 2V, 2Va; ChII SATB, Tpt, 2Ctto, 2Trb;
> Bc.

D-BII Mus. ms. 30268 (score)   *KümmerKB

SCHMIEDT

> Lobe den Herrn, meine Seele: SATB, 2V, Va, Ob, 2Ctto, Bc.

D-Gs Cod, ms. philos. 84e (score & parts, dated 1723)   *WalkerSB

SCHNEIDER, Martin (*b* Silesia; *fl* 1667)

*Erster Theil: Neuer geistlicher Lieder. Ariaetten, Canto solo cum Sonatella a 5. Violin.
doi violini. doi viola da braccio è violone cum basso continuo.* Leignitz: Zacharias
Schneider, 1667.
> 2. Nun ist dein Feind zerstört sein Macht: S, 2Cttino o 2V o 2Tpt, aTrb, tTrb, Vo
>   o Trb, Bc.
> 4. Wo wiltdu hin weiß Abend ist: S, 2Cttino o 2V o 2Tpt, aTrb, tTrb, Vo o Trb,
>   Bc.
> 5. Ach was stehstu auff der Au: S, 2Cttino o 2V o 2Tpt, aTrb, tTrb, Vo o Trb, Bc.
> 6. Gutter Hirte willtu nicht: S, 2Cttino o 2V o 2Tpt, aTrb, tTrb, Vo o Trb, Bc.
> 10. Komm liebster komm in deinen Garten: S, 2Ctto o 2V, aTrb, tTrb, Vo o Trb,
>   Bc.

The print contains 40 *arietten* for soprano and strings of which Nos. 2, 4, 5, 6, and 10,
called inconsistently in the various partbooks "Sonata à 5" or "Sonatella à 5," indicate
cornett or *cornettino*.
D-Dl; PL-WRu (S, tVa); **S-Uu**   *MitUB   RISM S1892

SCHOP, Johann (*d* Hamburg, 1667)
> 16. Nu lob mein Seel den Herren à 8: T[T]B, [3]Trb; ATB *cap*, 2Ctto; Org.
> 17. Wol dem der den Herren fürchtet a 8: S, 2V o 2Ctto, 2Trb; SSATTB, 2Ctto;
>   Org.

PL-WRu (Bohn collection Ms. mus. 52, now in **D-BI**, parts and tab)   *BohnH

> 1. O Trawrigkeit, o Hertzeleid à 4: SATB, 2V o 2Ctto, Vo, Org.

PL-WRu (Bohn collection Ms. mus. 70, now in **D-BI**, parts and tab)

SCHULZE, Christian Andreas (*b* Dresden, *ca* 1660; *d* Meissen, 1699)
> Duo seraphim stabant et clamabant: ChI SSATB; 2V, 2Va, Fag; ChII SSATB,
> 2Cttino, 3Trb; Org, Bc.

D-Dl mus. ms. 1696 E 501 (Grimma U272/V79, parts)   *MGG

Laetatus sum: SSATB *conc & rip*, 2V, 3Va, 2"Piffari" & 2 Ctto, 3Trb, Org, Bc.
D-Dl mus. ms. 1696 E 507 (Grimma U279/U72, parts)   *LeonardT

Heut triumphiret Gottes Sohn: B, 2V, 2Va, 2Cttino, 2Trb, Fag, Vo, Org.
D-Dl mus. ms. 1696 E 509 (Grimma)   *GroveD

Also heilig ist der Tag: ChI SSATB; 2V, 2Va, Fag; ChII SSATB, 2Ctto 2Trb, Org, Bc.
D-Dl mus. ms. 1696 E 510 (Grimma U282/U75, parts)   *MGG

Als der Tag der Pfingsten erfüllet war: SAB, V, Ctto, Trb, Fag, Org.
D-Dl mus. ms. 1696 E 512 (Grimma U369/N57, parts incompl)

Der Gott Abraham à 20: ChI SSATB *conc*, 2V, 2Va, 2Cttino, 3Trb, Fag; ChII SSATB *cap*; Bc.
D-Kdma [2/1845]; **F**-Ssp ms. 102

Missa alla breve: SSATB, 2Ctto, 2V, 2Va, Fag, Bc.
F-Ssp   *GroveD

SCHÜRMANN, Georg Caspar (*b* Idensen nr. Hanover, 1672/3; *d* Wolfenbüttel, 1751)

Salomon, singspiel: aria with 3Ctto, Bc.
D-SWl (dated 1701)   *McCredieM

SCHÜTZ, Heinrich (*b* Köstritz nr. Gera, *bapt.* 1585; *d* Dresden, 1672)

Concert mit 11 Stimmen. . . . Dresden: Gimel Bergen, 1618.
Haus und Güter erbet man von Eltern: ChI T, 2Trb, Fag; ChII T, 3Ctto o 2V, Va; ChIII SSB, Lt; Org, Cemb [?].
For the wedding of Michael Thomes and Anna Schultes, Leipzig, 15 June 1618.
D-Kl   SWV 21   RISM S2274
Edition: SchützGA 14

Die Wort Jesus Syrach. . . . Dresden: Gimel Bergen, 1618.
Wohl dem, der ein tugendsam Weib hat: ChI T, 3Ctto; ChII SATB; Org.
D-Kl   SWV 20   RISM S2273
Edition: SchützGA 14

Der 133 Psalm. . . . Leipzig: Lorenz Kober, 1619.
SSATB, Ctto muto, V, Vo; o V, Fl, Fag; Org.
SWV 48 (lost in WWII)
*Edition: SchützGA 14

Psalmen Davids Sampt Etlichen Motetten und Concerten mit acht und mehr Stimmen . . . Wie auch mit beygefügten Basso Continuo vor die Orgel, Lauten, Chitaron, etc. Dresden: Gimel Bergen, 1619.

6. Herr unser Herrscher [SWV 27]: ChI SSAT o (1v, 4Ctto) o (2V, 2Va); ChII ATBB o (1v, 4Trb) o other; Capella SATB *ad lib*, Vo, Org.

11. Alleluia, Lobet den Herren in seinem Heiligthumb [SWV 38]: ChI SATB *conc & cap*, 3Ctto o 3V, Trb o Fag; ChII SATB *conc & cap*, Ctto o Fl, 2Trb, Trb o Fag; Vo, Org.

19. Ist nicht Ephraim mein theurer Sohn [SWV 40]: ChI SS o 2 Ctto, T o Ctto, Ctto o Trb, SATB *cap*; ChII A *conc,* 3Trb; SATB *cap*; Vo, Org.

20. Nun lob mein Seel den Herren [SWV 41]: ChI&II SATB; 2V, 2Va, 4Ctto, Trb, Vo.

22. Nicht uns, Herr, sondern deinem Namen gib Ehre [SWV 43]: ChI T *conc*, 3Ctto; ChII SATB; ChIII A *conc*; Org.

23. Wohl dem, der den Herren fürchtet [SWV 44]: ChI T *conc*, 4Ctto, SATB *cap*; ChII A *conc*, V, 3Trb, SATB *cap*; Vo, Org.

25. Zion spricht, der Herr hat mich Verlassen [SWV 46]: ChI ST *conc*, 2Ctto, Fag, SATB *cap*; ChII ST *conc*; 4Trb, SATB *cap*; Vo, Org.

26. Jauchzet dem Herren alle Welt [SWV 47]: ChI AT, 2Trav & 2Ctto, Fag; ChII ST "Coro di Liuti"; ChIII S, V, 3Va, SSATB *cap*; Vo, Org.

For no. 19, "Ist nicht Ephraim," in the first choir all parts are texted and have the following clefs and instrumental designations: *Cantus: C1 Cornetto o voce*; *Altus: C2 Cornetto o voce*; *Tenor: A Cornetto o trombone; Bassus: T Cornetto o voce.*
A-Wgm; **B**-Br; **GB**-Lbl; **US**-R　　　　　　　　　　　　　　RISM S2275
Editions: SchützGA 1-2; SchützW 23-24

Syncharma Musicum tribus choris adornatum. . . . Bratslava: Georg Baumann, 1621.
En novus Elysiis; Wo Gott nicht selbst bey uns were:[34] ChI T, 3Ctto o 2Ctto, Trb; ChII T, 3Fag; ChIII SSSB; Org.
D-Kl　　SWV49　　　　　　　　　　　　　　　　　　　　　RISM S2276
Editions: SchützGA 15; SchützW 38

Symphoniae Sacrae . . . varijs vocibus & instrumentis accomodatae A 3. 4. 5. 6. Novissimae in lucem editae . . . opus ecclesiasticum secundum. Venice: Bartolomeo Magni, 1629.

7. Anima mea (1. pars) [SWV 263]: TT, 2Cttino o 2Fiffari, Bc.

8. Adjuro vos (2. pars) [SWV 264]: TT, 2Cttino o 2Fiffari, Bc.

11. Benedicam Dominum (1. pars) [SWV 267]: STB, Ctto o V, Bc.

12. Exquisivi Dominum (2. pars) [SWV 268]: STB, Ctto o V, Bc.

15. Domine, labia mea aperies [SWV 271]: ST, Ctto o V, Trb, Fag, Bc.

19. Buccinate. . . (1. pars) [SWV 275]: TTB, Ctto, Tpt o Ctto, Fag, Bc.

20. Jubilate Deo (2. pars) [SWV 276]:TTB, Ctto, Tpt o Ctto, Fag, Bc.

Cornett is not specified in the index for nos. 15 & 20.
D-BI, -Bhm, -W; **GB**-Och; **PL**-WRu　　　　　　　　　　　　RISM S2287
Editions: SchützGA 5; SchützW 13-14

---

[34] The second text was added later in another hand.

Symphoniae Sacrae secunda pars Worinnen zubefinden sind Deutsche Concerten mit 3. 4. 5. nehmlich einer, zwo, dreyen Vocal, und zweyen Instrumental-Stimmen, Alß Violinen oder derogleichen, Sambt beygefügtem geduppelten Basso Continuo Den einen fur den Organisten, den andern fur den Violon . . . Opus decimum. Dresden: Johann Klemm, Alexander Hering (Gimel Bergen), 1647.
    4. Meine Seele erhebt den Herren: S, 2V, 2Ctto o 2Tpt, 2Fl, 2Cttino o 2V, 2Va o 2Trb, Org.
D-Bi, -Bhm, -Dl, -Kl, -Mbs, -W; **GB**-Lbl; **US**-BE (2, Vii, Org)   SWV344
Editions: SchützGA 7; SchützW 15   RISM S2292

Symphoniae Sacrae tertia pars Worinnen zubefinden sind Deutsche Concerten mit 5. 6. 7. 8. Nehmlich, Dreyen, Vieren, Fünffen, Sechs Vocal- und zweyen Instrumental-Stimmen, alß Violinen oder derogleichen, Sambt etlichen Complementen . . . Opus Duodecimum. Dresden: Christian & Melchior Bergen, 1650.
    Wo der Herr nicht das Haus bauet: ChI V, Cttino o V; ChII SSB *conc*; ChIII SATB *cap*, with 4 unspecified insts *ad plac*; Vo, Org.
A-Wgm; **D**-Bi, -Bii, -Bhm, -HAmk, -LEm, -WA   SWV400   RISM S2295
Edition: SchützGA 10

Historia . . . Geburth Gottes und Marien Sohnes, Jesu Christi. Dresden: Wolfgang Seyffert, 1664.
    13. Intermedium 6. Herodes. Ziehet hin und forschet: B, 2Tpt o 2Ctto, Bc.
D-Bii (The printed version contains music only for the Evangelist sections. In addition, there are two incomplete manuscript versions: an earlier one in **S**-Uu Vok. Mus. i hs 71, and a later one from *ca* 1671 in **D**-Bii ms. w39,52,95,96, which specifies *clarini o cornettini*.)   SWV435a
Editions: SchützGA 1; SchützW 1

    Herr Gott, dich loben wir: ChI SATB o S with Ctto, V, Trb *ad plac*; ChII SATB o S, 3Trb; 4Tpt, 2V o 2Ctto, Timp, Bc.
D-Bii Mus. ms. 20374   SWV472
Editions: SchützGA 18; SchützW 32

    Veni Sancte Spiritus: ChI SS, Fag; ChII B, 2Ctto o 2V; ChIII TT, 3Trb; ChIV AT, V o Ctto, Fl o Ctto, Vo; Org.
D-Kl mus. ms. 2° 49b   SWV475
Editions: SchützGA 14; SchützW 32

    Der 8 Psalm: Herr unser Herrscher: SSATB *conc & cap*; 2V o 2Ctto, 4Trb, Org. Cornettino and violin are also specified, but Schütz specifies *violini oder cornetti* in the organ part.
D-Kl 2° mus. 50d   SWV449
Editions: SchützGA 13; SchützW 27

    Freuet euch mit mir: SSAATTBB V, Ctto, Vo, Org.
D-Kl mus. ms. 2° 52t   SWV a6 (attrib. by Hans Engel)

Es erhub sich in der Streit im Himmel: ChI&II SATB; ChIII T, 3Ctto; ChIV T, Tpt, 3Fag; Vo, Org.
D-Kl mus. ms. 2° 53g   SWVal 1 (attrib. by Spitta)
Edition: SchützGA 18

Ach wie soll ich doch in Freuden Leben: ChI 3Lt; ChII 3Va; ChIII 3Trb; Capella ATB, V, Ctto; Org.
D-Kl mus. ms. 2° 56d   SWV474
Editions: SchützGA 18; SchützW 38

Der 7 Psalm: Auf dich Herr traue ich: ChI 2V, Va, Ctto, 3Trb; ChII SATB; ChIII SATB; Org.
D-Kl 49q   SWV462
Editions: SchützGA 13; SchützW 27

Der 24 Psalm: Domini est terra: ChI&II SATB; 2V, 2Ctto, 4Trb, 5Fag.
D-Kl   SWV476
Editions: SchützGA 13; SchützW 27

Gelobet seist du, Herr (Gesang der drei Männer im feurigen Ofen): SSATB *conc*, 2Cttino, 3Trb; SSATB *cap* with 2V, 2Va, Vo *ad plac*, Org.
L-Königsberg Gotthardischen Bib. (dated 1652)   SWV448
*Edition: SchützGA 13

Freue dich des Weibes deiner Jugend: SATB, 2Ctto, 3Trb, Org.
SeiffertL lists a piece with identical name and setting but it specifies *"Trombett, Corn."* instead of 2 *Cornetti*.
L-KA   SWV453
Edition: SchützGA 14

SCHWEMMER, Heinrich (*b* in Lower Franconia, 1621; *d* Nürnberg, 1696)
Jauchtzet Gott alle Land: SSATB *conc & rip*; 2V, 2Ctto, 2Va, 3Trb, Fag, Bc.
D-BII Mus. ms. 20555 (dated 1682)   *SamuelN

2. Victoria, plaudite coelites: SSATB, 2Ctto, 2Tpt, 2Trb, Fag, Timp, Bc.
4. Surgite, populi, clangite, buccina: SSATTB, 2Ctto, 3Trb, Bc.
D-BII Mus. ms. 20556 (parts, no. 2 is dated 1689)   *SamuelN
Edition (of no. 2): DTB 10 (Jg. VI)

Deus, in nomine tuo à 12: SSATB, 2V, 2Ctto, 3Trb, Bc.
Halleluja. Hodie Christus natus est: SSATB, 2V, 2Ctto, 3Trb, Bc.
D-Kdma [2/1398]; **S-Uu** 83:24 (tab) 35:2 & 66:7 (parts)
*DTB 10 (Jg. VI)

SEBASTIANI, Johann (*b* nr. Weimar, 1622; *d* Königsberg, 1683)

Hochzeitlichen Ehrengesang. Königsberg: Johann Reusner, 1664.
   Freuet euch ihr Gerechten des Herrn: ChI SATB; ChII SATB; V, Ctto, Bc.
L-KA (present location uncertain)   *MüllerK

   Motetto concertato. Promite laetifico: ChI&II SATB; 2V, 2Cttino, 2Trb, 2Fag, Bc.
   Nun danket alle Gott: ChI,II&III SATB; 2V o 2Ctto o 2Tpt, Va o Trb, Fag o Vo,
   Timp, Bc.
D-BI Mus. ms. 30272   *KümmerKB

SELICH, Daniel (*b* Wittenberg, *bapt.* 1581; *d* Wolfenbüttel, 1626)

Christlicher Wundsch aus dem 85 Psalm deß Koniglichen Propheten Davids. . . .
Wolfenbüttel: Elias Holwein, 1623.
   SATB, 2Ctto, v with Ctto o v, 4Trb, 4Fag, Bc.
D-W   *RISM S2742

SELLE, Thomas (*b* Zörbig nr. Bitterfeld, 1599; *d* Hamburg, 1663)

*Deliciarum Juvenilium decas harmonico-bivocalis. Hoc est Zehen lustige amorosische
Liedlein mit nur einer Vocal- und Instrumental-Stimme.* . . . Hamburg: Jakob
Rebenlein, 1634.
   All: S o T, V o Cittern o Fl o Ctto muto, Bc.

1. Wir wollen singen.	6. Erweich O Venus.
2. O liebes Hertze.	7. Wol auff Jungfräwlein wol gemuth.
3. Geselle mein.	8. Frisch auff mein Hertz.
4. Ade du edles Mündlein.	9. O Unglück.
5. Wie ich letzt mal spazierte.	10. Nach dem Ring.

D-Hs (S/T, S/T instrumentalis, Bc)   RISM S 2753

Thomas Selle, Gesammelte Werke, Motetten Geistliche Concerte u. Passionem,
Madrigale. . . .
II. Concertuum latino-sacrorum 6.8.9.10.12.13.&14. vocibus ad bassum continuum
concinendorum Liber Secundus. Authore Thoma Sellio . . . imprimebat [n.p., n.d.]
   10. Jubilate Deo à 10 in concerto & choro alternatim: Cap *fidicinium* SS, V, t, Vo;
      Ch *di tromboni*: SSATB, 2Ctto, 3Trb, Bc.
   11. Spiritus Domini à 12 per 3 choros concertantes: Cap *fidicinium* SB, ssb; Ch
      pro organo SSAB, 3Ctto, Trb; Ch *vocalis* ATTB; Bc.
*III.*Concertum Latino-sacrorum de praecipuis festis anniversariis à 2-17 vocibus
ad bassum contin. concinnendorum Liber Tertius. Authore Thomâ Sellio.
   1. Non auferetur sceptrum à 4.5.9.10.15.: ChI SSBB; Cap *fidicinum* 3V, Va, Vo;
      Rit.: SSATB, 2Ctto, 3Trb; Bc.
   2. Verbum Caro Factum est à 4.5.9.10. & 13.: ChI SSBB; *Rit.*: SSATB, 2Ctto,
      3Trb; 2V; Bc.
   3. Hodie Christus natus est à 3.5.8.10. & 11.: ChI SSB, 2V, Fag; *Rit.*: SSATBB,
      2Ctto, 3Trb, Vo; Bc.

4. Hodie nobis coelorum Rex à 2.4.6.11. & 15.: TTTTBB, bb; *Rit.*: SSATB, 2Ctto, 3Trb; Ch *di tromboni* 4Trb (attb); Bc.
5. In principio erat verbum: à 5.10.12. & 13.: ChI SSB, 2V, Fag; *Rit.*: SSATB, 2Ctto, Trb, t, b; 2Tpt, b; Bc.
10. Videntes stellam magi à 14.: ChI SSB, Ctto; Cap *fidicinum* sssa, Fag; *Rit.* SSATB.
20. Apparuerunt Apostolis à 14.: ChI SSB; Cap *fidicium* sssab; *Rit.* SSATB, V o Ctto, ssatb; Bc.

[*V.*] Erster Theil Teutscher Geistlicher Concerten, Madrigalien und moteten mit 3.4.5.6.7.8.9.10.11.12.14. und 16. Stimmen, zum basso continuo vox in Orgel, Regal, Clavicymbel, Spinet, Theorben und Lauten zu 1.2.3. & 4. Chören und allerhand Musicalischen besaiteten und blasenden Instrumenten und manschen Stimmen; auf trombetten & c. in Kirchen und sonsten zu gebrauchen componiert von Thomâ Selliô. . . .

2. Du großer König Gott und Herr à 3 vel 5: SSATB, [2]Ctto, Fag, Bc.
10. Stehe auf, meine Freundin à 5: SSATB, 2Ctto, 3Trb, 2V, 2Va, Vo, Fag, Bc.
22. Herr, wer ist dir gleich à 6: Ch *vocalis* SSB; Ch *instrumentalis* 2V, 2Ctto, 2Tpt, Trb; Bc.
23. Dies ist der Tag à 6: SSATTB, 2Tpt o 2Ctto, 4Trb, Bc.
24. Ich will Dich erhöhen à 6: AATB, 2Tpt o 2Ctto, 3Trb, Bc.
29. Gott, es ist mein rechter ernst à 7: SSAATBB, 2Tpt o 2Ctto, 2Tpt o 2Ctto, 5Trb, Bc.
30. Es war ein Mensch ab 8: Ch *instrumentalis* 3V, 3Ctto, 2Trb, Fag; Ch *vocalis* SSTB; Bc.
41. Das is mir lieb à 9: Ch *vocalis* SATB, Ctto, 3Trb; Ch *instrumentalis* SSATB, ssatb; Bc.
43. Es begab sich aber zu der Zeit à 10: Ch *vocalis* SSSTB, 2Ctto o 2Fl, 2V, Trb, Fag; Ch *instrumentalis* SSATB, 2Ctto, 2V, 3Trb, Fag; Bc.
45. Frohlocket mit Händen. Moteta ab 11: ChI SATB, 2Tpt, Ctto, 3Trb; ChII SATTB, Ctto, 4Trb; Bc.
46. Singet dem Herren. Moteta ab 12: ChI SATB, 2Tpt, Ctto, 3Trb; ChII SATTB, Ctto, 4Trb; Bc.
50. Lobet den Herren in seinem Heiligtum ab 11. 15. et 21: 2V, 2Ctto, 2Tpt, 3Trb; Ch *vocalis* STB, Trb, Vo; ChII SATB, V; Cap SATB, Ctto, 3Trb; Bc.
51. Und da die [?] ab 8: Ch *superioris* SSAB, 2Ctto, 2V, 2Trb; Ch *inferioris* ATTB, 4Trb; Bc.

[6.] Ander Theil Teutscher Geistlicher Concerten, Madrigalien und Moteten mit 1.2.3.-10. und 12. Stimmen zum basso continuo . . . componiert von Thomâ Selliô. . . .

58. Herr wer ist Dir gleich a 12: Cap *fidicinum* SSATB, 2V, 2Ctto, at, Trb, 2Tpt, Vo; Ch *di tromboni* TTB, 2Ctto, 2Tpt, 3Trb; Bc.
59. Du bist der schönste à 12: Ch *pro organo* SSTTBB; ChII SSATB, Ctto o V; Bc.
60. Jauchze fein Töchterlein à 12: Cap *fidicinum* CC, V, s; Ch *pro regalis* SAB, V, Va, Vo; Ch *pro organo* SSATB, 2Ctto, V, Trb; 2Tpt; Bc.

[*VII.*] Dritter Theil teutscher geistlicher Concerten &c. darinnen. . . .

2. Wol dem der in Gottes Furcht steht: SSB, Ctto, Bc.
19. Wie schön leuchtet der Morgenstern ab 6: SATB, 2Tpt, Ctto, 3Trb, Bc.
20. Christum wir sollen loben schon a 7: SSB, V, 2Ctto, Fag; ChII SATB; Bc.
21. Herr Gott Dich loben wir a 7: S, V, Ctto, Fag o Vo; ChII SATB; Bc.
23. Kyrie summum cum intermedio et sinfonia ab 8: Ch *pro organo* SSTB, Ctto, Fag; Ch *fidicinum* SATB, sssb; Bc.
36. Nun lob mein Seel den Herren a 9: Ch *pro organo* SSB, 2V, 2Ctto, Fag, Vo; Cap SATB; Bc.
39. Gelobet seistu Jesus Christ a 9: Ch *pro organo* SSST; Cap *fidicinum* SSATB, 2V, 2Ctto, 2Va, a, Trb, Fag; Bc.
53. Jesus Christ unser Heiland a 9: Ch *pro organo* SSTTB, Ctto *in echo*, 3Trb, Fag, Vo; Cap *fidicinum* SSATB, 3V, 3Ctto, 3Trb; Bc.
61. In dulci Jubilo ab 11: ChI SSSTB, 2V, Fag; ChII SSATTB, 2Ctto, 4Trb; ChIII SS; Bc.
68. Gen Himmel zu dem Vater ab 18: ChI SSTTB, Vo; Cap *fidicinum* SATB, V, Va; Ch *di tromboni* SB [missing 1 or 2 parts], Ctto, Trb; Cap SATB.
69. Nun lobet mein Seel a 20: Ch *pro organo* SSATB, Fag; Cap *fidicinum* SATB, 2V, Va, t, Vo; ChIII SSATB, ss [missing 1st page], 2Ctto, 3Trb; Bc.
70. Wie schön leuchtet der Morgenstern a 20: Cap *fidicinum* SATB, 2V, 2Ctto, 2Va, Ctto o Trb, Trb, Vo, Fag; Ch *di tromboni* SATTB, 4Trb; Ch *di cornetti* SSB, 2Ctto, Fag; Ch *di trombetti* 2Tpt; Bc.
71. Ach Herr mich armen Sünder a 13: Ch *fidicinum* SB, 2V, Va, Vo; Ch*pro organo* SSATTB, 2Ctto, 4Trb; Cap SATB; Bc.
72. Christ lag in Todes Banden a 22: Cap *fidicinum* S, 2V, Va, Vo o Fag; Ch *di tromboni* ATB, 2Ctto, 4Trb; Ch *pro organo* SSAT, 2Trb; Cap SAABB, Trb; Bc.
73. Wie schön leuchtet der Morgenstern a 23: Cap *fid* S, a, 2V (with an alternative of 2Fl in one section), 2Ctto, Fag; Ch *pro regalis* SSAB, Fag; Ch *vocalis* SATTB, Trb, Fl, Fag; Cap SATTB; Ch *di trombetti* 2Tpt, 2Trb; Bc.
74. Erschienen ist der Herrliche Tag a 21 per 4 choros: ChI 2V, Trb; Ch *voc* SSSSSA; Ch *di Flauti* SA, 3Fl, Trb; ChIV à 7 SATTB, ss, 2Ctto; Bc.

The ms consists of over 400 works in 20 folio volumes, partly in the hand of Thomas Selle and partly in those of his students. 43 of these works specify cornett. It also contains 16 partbooks and three corresponding volumes of organ tablature.
D-Hs Cod. scrin. 251, Bd. 1-16 (ms dated 1653)
Edition of no. 23, "Kyrie Summum," in Klaus Vetter, ed., *Ausgewählte Kirchenmusik, Geistliche Chormusik,* Reihe IV, 7 (Stuttgart: Hänssler Verlag, 1965)

Passion secundum Johannem a 6 mit 6. Vocal- und 5. Instrumental Stimmen. . . : SAATTB *soli*; SAATTB *cap*; 2Fl (accomp. Petrus); V solo; 3V (accomp. Magdeline & Jesus); 2Ctto, Trb (accomp. Pilatus); 2Fag (accomp. Evang.); Cemb, Org, Regal.
D-Hs Cod. scrin 251. Bd. 19 (ms dated 1643)   RISM AII 81590
*Edition: Rudolf Gerber, ed., *Das Chorwerk,* 26 (Wolfenbüttel: Möseler, 1933)

Die Aufferstehung Christi nach den 4. Evangelisten. . . . :
Es bagab sich aber zu der Zeit: ST *conc*; ChI&II SSATB; instruments.
Sinfonia III: 2V, 2Ctto, Trb, Bc.
Sinfonia VI: 3Fl o 3Ctto, Fag, 4Trb, Bc.
Choro alternatim: ChI SSATB, 3V, Fag; ChII SSATB, 2Ctto, 3Trb, Bc.
D-Hs Cod. scrin 251. Bd. 20
Edition: Klaus Vetter, ed., *Die Kantate,* 155 (Stuttgart: Hänssler Verlag, 1963)

SIEFERT, Paul (Danzig, 1586-1666)

Psalmorum Davidicorum, ad Gallicam melodiam arte compositorum musicali, qui diversis sistuntur partibus, à 4. 5. 6. 7. 8. vocibus . . . pars secunda. . . . Danzig: Typgrapheo Rhetiano, 1651.

1. Psalm XXX à 4: SATB, with Symphonia à 3; 2V o 2Ctto, "Violino di braccia o Storto," Bc.
3. Psalm XXXII à 4: SATB, with Symphonia à 3: 2V o 2Ctto, VaG o Trb, Bc.
4. Psalm CXII à 4: SATB, with Symphonia à 3: 2V o 2Ctto, VaG o Trb, Bc.
7. Psalm II à 5: SATTB, with Symphonia à 3: 2V o 2Ctto, VaG o Trb, Bc.
8. Psalm XCII à 5: SSATB, with Symphonia à 3: 2V o 2Ctto, VaBr o Trb, Bc.
9. Psalm CIIII à 5: SATTB, with Symphonia à 3: 2V o 2Ctto, VaBr o Trb, Bc.
10. Psalm XII à 5: SATTB, with Symphonia à 3: 2V o 2Ctto, VaBr o Trb, Bc.
11. Psalm XXVIII à 5: SATTB, with Symphonia à 3: SATTB, 2V o 2Ctto, b, Bc.
12. Psalm CXI à 5: SSATB, with Symphonia à 3: 2V o 2Ctto, VaBr o Trb, Org.
13. Psalm CXXXVI à 6: SSAATB, with Symphonia à 3: 2V o 2Ctto, VaBr o Trb, Bc.
14. Psalm CIII à 7 voc concertato: SATB, 2V o 2Ctto, VaBr o Trb, Bc.
15. Psalm CXXVIII: Ch I&II SATB, with Symphonia à 3: 2V o 2Ctto, VaBr o Trb, Org.

The print also contains a "Canzon à 8" specifying cornett (see instrumental list).
S-Uu　MitUB
Edition (of No. 13): in: Franz Kessler, ed., *Danziger Kirchen-Musik* (Neuhausen-Stuttgart: Hänssler, 1973)

SILVANI, Giuseppe Antonio (Bologna, 1672 - *ca* 1727)

3. Messa III brevis a 14 . . . coll'Accompagnamento fatto da Harrer: SATB, Ctto, 3Trb, 3Ob, 2V, Va, Bc (unfigured), "Basso ripieno," Cemb, Org.
D-BII Mus. ms. 20870 (parts), -Kdma [2/2288]

STADLMAYR, Johann (*b* Bavaria, *ca* 1575; *d* Innsbruck, 1648)

Cantici Mariani septies variati, Liber quartus. Innsbruck: Daniel Agricola, 1618.
2. Magnificat octavi toni à 12: ChI SSATB *conc*, ChII SATBB *cap*, 2Ctto o 2V, Org.
A-KR; **D**-Mbs, -Rp (missing A1 and T2)　　　　　　　　RISM S4288
Edition: Hilde Junkermann, "The Magnificats of Johann Stadlmayr," Ph.D. dissertation, Ohio State University, 1966

Missa concertante a VI, adiuncto choro secundo sive ripieni, ut vocant. . . . Innsbruck: Johann Gäch, 1631.
    ChI SSATTB *conc*; ChII SSATTB *cap*; 2Ctto o 2V, 4Trb, Org.
D-B (2 partbooks, now in **PL-Kj**), -Mbs, -Rp   RISM S4294

Antiphonae Vespertinae, alma redemptoris, ave regina, regina coeli, salve regina. . . . Innsbruck: Johann Gäch, 1636.
    Regina coeli: SSB, 2V o 2Ctto, Org.
A-KR; **D-B** (1 partbook, now in **PL-Kj**), -Mbs (T)   RISM S4295

Salmi a due, e tre voce con due violini, o cornetti. Innsbruck: Michael Wagner, 1640.
    SSB, 2V o 2Ctto, Tior.
D-Bi (compl), **-B** (2 partbooks, now in **PL-Kj**), -LA (B, Va/Tior), -Mbs (S1,S2, V2), -Mu (V2)   *RISM S4297

Psalmi integri a quatuor vocibus concertantibus, quatuor aliis accessorijs ad libitum accinendis cum 2. Cornet. sive Violin. Innsbruck: Michael Wagner, 1641.
    1. Nisi Dominus aedificaverit: ChI&II SATB; 2Ctto o 2V, Org.
    2. Confitebor tibi Domini: ChI&II SATB; 2Ctto o 2V, Org.
    3. Dixit Dominus meo: ChI&II SATB; 2Ctto o 2V, Org.
    4. Laetatus sum: ChI&II SATB; 2Ctto o 2V, Org.
    5. Laudate pueri Dominum: ChI&iI SATB; 2Ctto o 2V, Org.
    6. Laudati puiss Dominum: ChI&II SATB; 2Ctto o 2V, Org.
    7. Laudate Dominum omnes gentes: ChI&II SATB; 2Ctto o 2V, Org.
    Magnificat super Magnificat Orlandi à 5: SSATB; 2Ctto, Vo, Org.
A-KR; **B-Br**; **D-Kdma** [1/1478], -Lr; **F-Pn**   RISM S4301

Missae concertatae a X. et XII. vocibus et instrumentis cum quatuor partibus pro secondo choro. Innsbruck: Michael Wagner, 1642.
    Missae coelo rores à 10 : SSATB; SSATB, 2Ctto o 2V, 3Trb o 3Va, Org, Bc.
The print also contains "Jesu omnes à 12," "Quasi arcus à 10," and "Missa à 12" that may specify cornett.
A-KR; **D-LA**, -Rp, -Mbs; **F-Pn** (missing Vo, Org)   RISM S4302

Missae IX vocum, primo choro concertante a 5 v secundo pleno et necessario cum symphoniis ad libitum. Antwerp: Pierre Phalèse, 1643.
    Missa Dulcis Jesu: ChI SSATB; ChII SATB; 3Ctto o 3V, 3Trb o 3Va, Bc.
The print also contains two other Masses à 12 that may specify cornett.
A-Wgm   RISM S4303

    Hymn in Festo SS.mi Corporis Chri: SSAT, 2V, Ctto, Org.
A-KR L 13 (ms from 1633-39)   *RISM AII 600153015

    Beatus vir qui timet Dominum: ChI&II SATB; 2Ctto o 2V, Bc.
    Magnificat à 5: ChI&II SATB; 2V o 2Ctto, Vo, Bc.
    Magnificat: ChI&II SATB; 2Ctto o 2V, Vo, Bc.
D-Lr KN206   *WelterRL

STARCK

Missa Solemnis ex D.del Sgre Starck [word crossed out] 1754: SATB, 2V, 2Tpt, 2"Lituis," Timp (Incarnatus: TB, 2Tpt *pro ecco*; Quoniam with Trav, Vc; Qui tollis with Ctto, bTrb; Benedictus with Fl, V) bVa o Trb, Org.
D-EB (ms from *ca* 1754)   *RISM AII 19668

STOBAEUS, Johann (*b* Graudenz, 1580; *d* Königsberg, 1646)

Fürstlicher Ruhm und Schluß auß dem 20 Psalm Davids gennommen . . . Königsberg: Johann Reusner, 1645.
    Der Herr erhöre: [SSATTB], 3Tpt o 3Ctto.
L-KA (present location uncertain)   *MüllerK

STRADELLA, Alessandro (*b* Rome, 1644; *d* Genoa, 1682)

"Il Barcheggio": Serenata in due parte cum sinfonia: SAB, Ctto o Tpt, 2V, Bc.
Instrumentations occur throughout the work, but the two ms versions conflict frequently as to whether the wind instrument is cornett, trumpet, or either as alternatives. For more details on the structure and instrumentation of this work see BernS.
I-MOe mus. f. 1146 (dated 1681); **US-BE** ms. (Turin ms)
Edition: BernS

STRATTNER, Georg Christoph (*b* Gols nr. Pressburg, *ca* 1644; *d* Weimar, 1704)

Erstanden ist des Todes Tod: SATB; 2V, 2Va o 2Trb, bVa o Fag, 2Fl o 2Ctto [o Cttino], Org.
The second cornett part designates *cornettino* as the alternative.
D-F, ms. Pf. mus. 522 (parts)

STRAUSS, Christoph (*b* ?Vienna, *ca* 1575/80; *d* Vienna, 1631)

Nova ac diversi moda sacrarum cantionum compositio, seu motetae, 5.6.7.8.9.& 10. tàm vocibus quàm instrumentis varijs (ut adillas superius ac in indice annotatum est maxime accommodatae . . . liber primus, editio prima. Vienna: Johannem Fidler, 1613.
    Deus laudem meam à 8: ChI 2Trb, Trb "grande"; ChII 2Ctto, Ctto muto[C3], AT;
    Paratum cor meum à 8: ChI 3Trb; ChII AA, 3Ctto.
    O sapientia à 8: ChI T, Fag "*comune*," Fag *piccolo* [F3], Fag *grande*; ChII A, 3Ctto.
    Haec est Dies à 9: ChI A, 3Trb, Trb "grande"; ChII T, 2 Ctto, Ctto muto [C3].
    O Rex gloriae Domine virtutum à 10: ChI T, 4Ctto, 2Trb; ChII S, Ctto muto [C3], Fag "grande."
    Hodie completi sunt à 10: Ch I S, Ctto muto [C3], 3Trb, Fag "grande"; ChII A, 3Ctto.
D-Mbs (missing 7), **-Rp; SL-Lu** (A, 5)   RISM S6395

Missae . . . octo, novem, decem, undecem, duodecem, tredecem, et viginiti, tam vocibus, quam variis instrumentis, et basso generali ad organum accommodato. Vienna: Mathias Formica, 1631.

5. Missa in echo 8. voc: concertata cum Symphonia 8. Instrum: & suo Choro adjuncto signato: ChI&II SATB, Ctto o V, Ctto o Trb, Trb, Trb "grosso"; Org e Vo.

7. Missa O sacrum, 9 voc: pleno Choro cum symphonia 7. Instrumentorum diversorum: ChI SSAT, 2Ctto o 2V, Ctto o Trb; ChII ATBBB, 3Trb, Trb "grosso" o Va; Vo, Org.

8. Missa Maria 9. voc: concertata cum Symphonia 5. Instrum. & suo Choro adjuncto signato: ChI SSTBB, 2Ctto o 2V, 2Trb, Trb "grosso"; ChII SATB, Ctto o V, Ctto o Trb, 2Trb; Org e Vo.

11. Missa concertata ad modum Tubarum, 11 Voc: concertata cum Symphonia 5. Instrument: & suo Choro adjuncto signato: ChI SSTBB, 2Ctto o 2V, 2Trb, Trb "grosso"; ChII SSATTB, Ctto, Ctto o V, Ctto o Trb, 2Trb; Org e Vo.

12. Missa Iubilate, 12 Voc: cum Symphonia 6. Instrum: in quatuor plenos Choros distributata: ChI SSA, 2Ctto o 2V; ChII TTTB, 3Trb; ChIII ATB, V, 2Va; ChIV TB, Vo, Vo, Org.

13. Missa Gratiosa, 12 Voc: cum Symphonia 6. Instr: duobus Choris plenis, & uno ad submissiora, cum Voce sola accommodato: ChI SATTB, Ctto o V, 3Trb; ChII SATB, 3Va; ChIII SAT, 2Ctto o 2V; Vo, Org.

14. Missa Corporis Christi, 12 Voc: in tres plenos Choros, cum Instrumentis divisa: ChI SSTBB, Ctto o V, 3Trb; ChII SST, 2Ctto o 2V; ChIII SATB, Ctto, 3Trb; Vo, Org.

15. Missa Veni sponsa Christi, 13 Voc: Cum Tympanis ac 5. Tubis campestribus & Symphonia, 7. Instrument: atque una Tuba sola, partim pleno partim concertato Choro ut in singulis partibus signatum: ChI SSTT, 2Ctto o 2V, Ctto o Trb, Trb; ChII ATB, Ctto o Trb, Trb; ChIII SS*, 6Tpt, Timp; Vo, Org. *One soprano part in ChIII has the indication "voce cum tubis"; the other is a texted part in treble clef with the indication "clarino."

16. Missa Spiritus Sancti, 20 Voc: cum Symphonia 16 instrum: in quatuor plenos Choros divisa: ChI TBBBB, Fag *piccolo* o Trb, Fag o Trb, Fag *"comune"* o Trb, Va o Fag *grande* o Trb; ChII SS o 2Ctto, SSA, 2Ctto; ChIII SBBBBB, 4Trb; ChIV SSSA, 4V; Vo, Org.

A-KR; H-Gc (A)   RISM S 6936

STRIGGIO, Alessandro (see instrumental list)

STRUNGK, Delphin (*b* 1600/01; *d* Brunswick, 1694)

Kommet und sehet die Wercke des Herren: SSATB, 2V o 2Ctto, 2Va o 2Trb, Bc.
D-W mus. ms. 252 (dated 1671)   *WalkerSB

TARDITI, Orazio (*b* Rome, 1602; *d* Forli, 1677)

Concerto musiche varie da chiesa motetti, salmi, è hinni, à una sove sola, à due è tre, concertaati parte con violini è tiorba, e parte senza istrumenti . . . opera XXX. Venice: Stampa de Gardano, 1650.
Beatus vir qui timet: S, s[V], V o Ctto, Vo, Org.
Laudate pueri: S, s[V], Ctto o V, Trb, Org.

The instrumentation for the soprano instrument (s[V]) is from the partbook called *Violino Primo*, though no instrumental specification is found in this partbook for these works.

The following indication for "Beatus vir qui timet" is found in the organ partbook: *Voce sola con due violini è tiorba.*

The following indication for "Laudate pueri" is found in the organ partbook: *Soprano solo con due violini è trombone.*

I-Bc; **PL-WRu** (A)

TARDITI, Paolo (*b* 2nd half 16th cent; *d* after 1649)

Psalmi, Magnif. cum quatuor antiphonis ad vesperas octo vocib. una cum basso ad organum decantandi . . . liber secundus. Rome: Luca Antonio Soldi, 1620.
   All: ChI SATB, V, Lt, Tior; ChII SATB, Ctto, Org.

Confitebor à 8	In convertendo à 8
Beatus vir à 8	Laetatus sum à 8
Laudate pueri à 8	Lauda Hyerusalem à 8
Credidi à 8	Magnificat à 8

D-MÜs; F-Pc; I-Bc   *RISM T225

TAVOLA, Antonio dalla (*d* Padua, 1674)

   Laudate pueri Dominum: SATB, 2Cttino, 2V, Bc.
D-BII Mus. ms. 730 (Bokemeyer collection, score) -Kdma [3/408]   KümmerKB

TELEMANN, Georg Philipp (*b* Magdeburg, 1681; *d* Hamburg, 1767)

   Erhöre mich, wenn ich rufe: TB *conc*, 2V, Va, 2Ob, Cttino, 3Trb, Vc, Vo, "calcedon" (colascione), Org; SATB *rip* (chorale).
The cornettino and trombone parts are written one tone lower.
D-F ms. Ffm mus. 965 (dated 1717)

   Ich halte aber dafür: SATB *conc*, 2V, Va, Trav, 2Ob, Cttino, "calcedon" (colascione), Org; SATB *rip*.
The cornettino part is indicated only in the score; the music is that of the *traverso* part.
D-F ms. Ffm mus. 1155 (dated 1721)

   Jesu, wirst du bald erscheinen: STB *conc*, 2V, Va, Ob, Ctto, 3Trb, Vc, "calcedon" (colascione), Org; SATB *rip*.
There exists an alternative part *cornettino vel clarinetto* which is identical except that in the *cornetto* part a few notes are transposed down. However, the highest note in the cornettino part is only b♭".
D-F ms. Ffm mus. 1187 (dated 1719)   RISM AII 19990

   Sehet an die Exempel der Alten: SATB *conc*, 2V, Va, 2Ob, Cttino, 3Trb, "calcedon" (colasione), Vc, Org; SATB *rip*.
The cornettino and trombone parts are written in *A* since these instruments are pitched a semitone above the organ. The organ parts are in *B♭* and *C*.
D-F ms. Ffm mus. 1323 (dated 1721)

THEILE, Johann (Naumberg, 1646-1724)

9. Missa: [SSATB], 2V, 2Va, 2Ctto, Bc.
The third and fourth staves of the score are marked "oboe I and II"; however, no music appears on these staves except five measures in the second page of the "Gloria." This music is the same as that of the cornett parts and appears to have been a copyist's mistake.
D-BI Mus. ms. 30172

4. Herr unser Herrscher: SSATB, 2V, 2Va, Tpt, 2Ctto, 3Trb, Fag, Timp, Bc.
D-BII Mus. ms. 21823   KümmerKB

Tröstet mein Volk: SSATB, 2Tpt, 2V o 2Ctto, 3Trb, Bc.
D-BII Mus. ms. 21823 (dated 1679; scribe Francisco Gunther)   *MackeyT

TOLAR, Jan Křtitel [Dolar, Janez Krstnik] (*fl* Bohemia/Moravia, 2nd half 17th cent)

Miserere mei Deus: 8v *conc* & *cap*, 2V, 2Va, 2Tpt, 2Ctto muto, 3Trb, Vo, Org.
CS-KRa B XII 7   OttoS

Missa Viennensis: SSSSAAAATTTTBBBB *conc*, SATB *cap*; 2Ctto, 2Tpt, 4Trb, Fag, 3V, 2Va, Vc, Vo, Org.
SL-Lsa II 14898/996 C / LX/2607
Edition: Ljubljana: Edicije Drustva Slovenskih Skladateljev Ljubljana, 1981 (Ed. DSS 996)

USPER, Francesco [SPONGA] (*b* Parenzo, Istria, before 1570; *d* Venice, 1641)

Compositioni armoniche nelle quali si contengono motetti, sinfonie, sonate, canzoni, & capricci a 1.2.3.4.5.6.7.& 8. voci . . . opera terza. . . . Venice: Bartolomeo Magni, 1619.
Beatus qui intelligit à 8: T, 2Trb, Trombone Grosso; T, 3Ctto; Bc.
Ego dormio à 8: A, 2Trb, bTrb; T, V o Ctto, Ctto, Trb; Bc.
The print also contains a Sonata à 8 specifying cornett (see instrumental list).
PL-Kj (S,A,T,B,5,6,7,8,Bc)   SartMS I&II 1619a

VALENTINI, Giovanni (*b* Venice, 1582/3; *d* Vienna, 1649)

Secondo libro de madrigali a 4,5,8,9,10 & 11. concertate con voci & istromenti. Venice: Giacomo Vincenti, 1616.
Ecco maggio seren à 8: (has parts for V and V o Cttino)
Guerra guerra la brami à 11: (has parts for 2Cttino o 2V)
GB-Och 249-55   *BernC   RISM V88

Musiche concertante con voci, & istromenti a 6,7,8,9,10, con basso continuo. Venice: Gardano, 1619.
Deh fuggite gl'amori a 9: (Ctto solo indicated in Bc).
Only the partbooks in PL-Kj were examined, so a full determination of the instrumentation was not possible.
D-B (A,Bc, now in **PL-**Kj); **GB-**Lbl (S,A,T,B,5,7,8,9,Bc)   RISM V91

Dixit Dominus: ChI&III SATB, V, 3Vc; ChII Ctto, 6Trb, Fag; Org.
A-KR L 13 (ms from 1633-39)   *RISM AII 600153161

Missa coronationis: SSATTB, 2V, 2Va, 2Ctto, 3Tpt, 4Trb, Bc.
CS-KRa B I 1   OttoS

Missa S. Bernardi: 8v, 2V, 2Va, 2Ctto, 3Trb, Bc.
CS-KRa B I 2   OttoS

Gelobet sey der Herr der Herrligkeit à 17: ChI 2Ctto o 2V, V, Trb; ChII SSATB
conc; ChIII SATB *cap*, Ctto, 3Trb; ChIV 3Trb; Bc.
PL-WRu (Bohn collection Ms. mus. 204a, now in **D-BI**, parts)   *BohnH

Magnificat III toni super beata viscera à 17: ChI 2V, Trb, Fag; ChII SSATB *conc*;
ChIII SATB, Ctto, 3Trb; ChIV 4Trb, Vo, Bc.
PL-WRu (Bohn collection Ms. mus. 204b, now in **D-BI**, parts and tab)   *BohnH

Missa I toni: ChI&II: SATB; 2V, Cap: SS, Ctto; Org.
PL-WRu (Bohn collection Ms. mus. 204c, now in **D-BI**, parts)   *BohnH

Motet: Cantate gentes (1647): 7v; 2Ctto, Piffaro o Ctto, aTrb o Vtta, Va o Trb, Org.
S-Uu vok mus i hdskr. cap. 66:15
*Steven Saunders, "The Hapsburg Court of Ferdinand II and the *Messa, Magnificat et
Iubilate Deo a sette chori concertati con le trombe* (1621) of Giovanni Valentini,"
Journal of the American Musicological Society 44, no. 3 (Fall 1991): 383.

VALENTINI, Pietro Francesco (Rome, *b ca* 1570; *d* 1654)
Letanie e concerti a due, tre, e quattro voci . . . libro quinto.   Rome: Mauritzio
Balmonti, 1654.
    2-4v SATB, V, Ctto, Lt o Tior, Bc.
I-Ras   *GroveD   RISM V132

"Son pur passati," Aria Romanesca a 5 con sinfonia: SSATB, V, Ctto, Lt, Tior.
"Questa piaga c'ho nel core," Aria di Florenza a 5 con Sinfonie: SSATB, V, Ctto,
Lt, Tior.
I-Ras ms. 369   *RISM AII 35053

VARGAS, [Urbán de] (*b* Falces, Navarre, 1606; *d* Valencia, 1656)
    Al arma A la Resurreccion a 13: ChI&II SATB, ChIII ATB; ChIV Ctto; 2Hp Bc.
E-Zac B-13/260 (ms from *ca* 1645)   *RISM AII 101000097

VERDINI, Pietro [Verdina] (*b* Verona, *ca* 1600; *d* Vienna?, 1643)
    Missa S. Georgij: SATB *conc & rip*; 2V o 2Ctto, 3Trb, Org.

Cornetts are omitted from the title page, however, the parts are marked "*Violino ò Cornetto 1mo 2do*".

CS-KRa B I 141   OttoS

VETTER, Daniel (*b* Breslau, 1657/58; *d* Leipzig, 1721)

Alleluia, Christus von den Toden aufferwecket: SSATB *conc & rip*, 2V, 2Ctto, 4Tpt, 3Trb, Timp, Bc.
D-Dlb 1918 E 500 (Grimma U300/N8, score & parts)   WalkerSB; *LeonardT

Veni Sancte Spiritus: SSATB *conc & rip*, 2V o 2Ctto, 3Va o 3Trb, 4Tpt, Timp, Org, Bc.
D-Dlb 1918 E 501 (Grimma U301/N9, parts, Tpt lacking)   WalkerSB; *LeonardT

VIADANA, Lodovico (*b* Viadana nr Parma, *ca* 1560; *d* Gualtieri nr Parma, 1627)

Salmi a quattro chori per cantare, e concertare nelle gran Solennità di tutto l'Anno, con il basso continuo per sonar nell'Organo . . . Opera XXVII. Venice: Vincenti, 1612.

Domine ad adiuvandum	Laetatus sum
Dixit Dominus	Nisi Dominus
Confitebor tibi	Lauda Hierusalem
Beatus vir qui timet	Magnificat primi toni
Laudate pueri Dominum	Magnificat sexti toni
Laudate Dominum omnes	

Following the instructions in Viadana's preface all of these pieces will have the following instrumentation: ChI SATTB *conc*, Tior *ad plac*, Org; ChII SATB *cap*; ChIII Ctto o V, S, A(with V e Ctto "storto"), T(with Trb e Vo), Org; ChIV A(with V "all' ottava" e Ctto "storto"), T(with Trb), T(with Trb e V), B(with Trb e Vo, e Fag), Org. The author also comments that the cappella of ChII should have at least 16 singers and will sound even better with 20 to 30 singers and instrumentalists. In addition, he recommends multiple voices for the "solo" vocal parts of ChIII and ChIV and uses the plural for instrumental indications as well (e.g., *con violini e cornetti storti*).
B-Gu (BI); **D**-BAs (AI); **GB**-Lbl (AI, SII, TIV); **I**-Bc (compl), -CEc (TI), -FEc, -PIp (BII incompl, BIV)   RISM V1400

VIERDANCK, Johann (*b ca* 1605; *d* Stralsund, 1646)

Ander Theil geistlicher Concerten. . . . Rostock: Joh. Richel (Johann Hallerword), 1643.
    44. Freue dich des Weibes deiner Jugend: SATB, 3V o 3Ctto, Bc.
    45. Der Herr Zebaoth: SSTT, 2V o 2Cttino, 3Trb, Bc.
D-Bi
*Edition: EdM Sonderreihe, Bd. 7

    14. Ey du frommer und getrewer Knecht à 7: SSTT *conc*; SSATTB *cap*, Ctto; Org.
    18. Der Herr Zebaoth ist mit uns à 9: ChI T *conc*, ATB; ChII AB *cap*, Ctto; Org. [incomplete?]
PL-WRu (Bohn collection Ms. mus. 52, now in **D**-Bi, parts)

Der Herr hat seinen Engeln befohlen: SATB, 2V, 2"Flautini," 2Ctto, 3Trb, Bc.
S-Uu Vok. mus. i.hs 37:12
*Edition: EdM Sonderreihe, Bd. 6

VINTZIJ, Georg

17. Missa super Nun dancket alle Gott (S. Scheidt) à 8: Ctto, Bc.
PL-WRu (Bohn collection Ms. mus. 105, now in **D**-BI, only 2 parts survive)   *BohnH

VISMARRI, Filippo (*b* before 1635; *d* Vienna, *ca* 1706)

Dixit Dominus: SSATB, 2V, 3Va, 2Vtta, 2Ctto, 3Trb, Tior, Vo, Org, Bc.
CS-KRa B III 49 (parts)   OttoS

WAGENSEIL, Georg Christoph (Vienna, 1715-1777)

Missa Gratias agimus tibi: SATB *conc & rip*; 2V *conc*; (Ctto, 2Trb, Fag) *rip*; Vc,
Vo, Org.
A-Wn ms. 16994 (dated 1742)
*Edition: SKMB 3

WALTER, Johann Samuel [WELTER?] (nr. Schwäbisch Hall, 1650-1720)

Gott sey uns gnädig à 5 voc. et 7 inst: SSATB, 2V, Vo, 2Ctto, 3Trb, Org.
D-F Ms. Ff. Mus. 597 (2 sets of parts, 1 partially destroyed)   SüssKM

WECKER, Georg Caspar (Nürnberg, 1632-1695)

Allein Gott in der Höh sey Ehr: SSATTB, 2V, 2Va, 2Ctto, 2Trb, Fag, Bc.
D-BII Mus. ms. 22830 (parts), -BI Mus. ms. anon. 1037 (parts), -B Furstenstein ms.
40129 (tab, dated 1656, now in **PL**-Kj)   *WalkerSB
*Edition: DTB 10 (Jg. VI)

WEICHMANN, Johann (*b* Wolgast, Pomerania, 1620; *d* Königsberg, 1652)

Der CXXXIII Psalm auff H. Johann Welhorns und J. Anna Koesins Hochzeit. . . .
Königsberg: Johann Reusner, 1649.
      à 5, 10, 14 Stimmen: SSATB *conc & rip*, 2V, 2Tpt o 2Ctto, 3Trb o 3Fag *se piace*,
Org (begins with a sinfonia à 5).
D-Mbs; S-Uu   *MitUB   RISM W508

Psalmus CXVII. . . . Königsberg [?] 1648.
      SSATB, [2]Ctto, 3Trb, Bc.
L-KA   *MüllerK

WEILAND, Julius Johann (*d* Wolfenbüttel, 1663)

Lob- und Danck-Lied aus dem 89. Psalm. Wolfenbüttel: "gedruckt durch die Sternen,"
1661.

Ich wil singen von der Gnade des Herren ewiglich: SSATB, 2Cttino, 2VaBr, Fag, Bc.
PL-WRu (incompl)   *BohnD

WERNER, Christoph (*b* Gottleuba, 1617/8; *d* Danzig, 1650)

Es erhub sich ein Streit à 12 con li trombe tamburo e cornettis: ChI,II&III[4v]; 2Tpt, 2Ctto, Timp, Vo, Bc (dated 1648).
Exulta filia Jerusalem: A, 2V o 2Ctto, Bc (dated 1647).
O lux beata trinitas: A, 2V o 2Cttino, Bc (dated 1647).
D-Lr ms. K N 206 (dated 1648)   *WelterRL

WILHELMI, Johann Heinrich

Miserere mei, Deus: SSATTB, 2V, 2Va, 2Ctto, Fag, Bc.
D-Dlb 1799 E 500 (Grimma U307/N15, score & parts, dated 1682)   *WalkerSB

WÜLFER, Daniel

Daniel Wuelffers Kurtzer Historischer Bericht von Kirchen- und Tempel-Gebaewen . . .
Da ist gewesen 1. Posaun so vorher allein angefangen und aufgemahnet, darein sind
kommen 2. Viol: Voc: 2. Cant: 2. Alt: 2. Ten: 2. Bass. mit einer Rip: von 3 Choeren als
Cornet: Fagotten etc. . . . Nürnberg: Wolffgang und Johann Andreas Endter, 1652.
D-Nst (S,B)   *RISM W2185

ZACHER, Johann Michael (Vienna, 1651-1712)

Gaudeamus omnes [Festival introit]: SATB, 4Va, Vtta, Ctto, Fag, 2Trb, Vo, Org.
Spiritus Domini replevit [Festival introit]: SATB, 4Va, Vtta, Ctto, Fag, 2Trb, Vo, Org.
A-Ws (parts, dated 1712)   *GroveD; *WalkerSB

ZACHOW, Friedrich Wilhelm (*b* Leipzig, 1663; *d* Halle, 1712)

Siehe, das ist Gottes Lamm à 13: SATB *conc & cap*, 2V, 3Va, 2Cttino, Fag, Bc.
D-LUC ms. 139

Helft mir Gottes Güte preisen à 17: SATB *conc & cap*, 2V, 2Va, Tpt, Cttino, 3Trb, Org.
D-LUC ms. 367; **D-Dl** Mus. F 437 (parts for 2V, Va, Trb, Org)   *LeonardT

ZEUTSCHNER, Tobias (*b* Neurode, 1621; *d* Breslau, 1675)

Der Herr gebe euch vom Taw des Himmels à 18 o 23: ChI SSAB; ChII STTB; SSATB *cap*; 2V, Va, 2Ctto, 4Trb, Vo, Bc (dated 15 May 1656).
PL-WRu (Bohn collection Ms. mus. 210, now in **D-Bl**, parts)   *BohnH

Halleluja. Höret an die Geburt à 18: SSAATTTB, 2V, 2Tpt, 2Ctto, 2Fl, 3Trb, 2VaG, Org, Bc.
PL-WRu (Bohn collection Ms. mus. 210a, now in **D-Bl**, parts)   *BohnH

In suis Deus profecto fit: SATBB, 2V, 2VaBr, 2Ctto, 3Trb, Vo, Bc (dated 8 Feb. 1668).
PL-WRu (Bohn collection Ms. mus. 210b, now in **D**-BI, parts)   *BohnH

Te Deum laudamus à 15 o 20: Ch *vocalis* SSATB; Ch *fidicinium* S, 2V, Va, Vo o Fag; Ch *di tromboni* A, 4[Trb]; SSATB cap, 2 Ctto; Org, Bc.
PL-WRu (Bohn collection Ms. mus. 210d, now in **D**-BI, parts)   *BohnH

ZIANI, Marc'Antonio (*b* Venice, *ca* 1653; *d* Vienna, 1715)

Laudate Dominum: 4v [SATB], 4Va, bVa, Vo, Vc, Ctto, Fag, 2Trb, Org.
A-Wn ms. 17441   *card catalog

Laudate Dominum: 4v [SATB], 4Va[G], Vo, Vc, Ctto, Fag, 2Trb, Org.
A-Wn ms. 17442   *card catalog

Laudate Dominum: 4v [SATB], 2V, 3Va(atb), Vc, Vo, Ctto, Fag, 2Trb, Org.
A-Wn ms. 17443   *card catalog

Laudate Dominum: 4v [SATB], 3Va, Vc, Vo, Ctto, Fag, Trb, Org.
A-Wn ms. 17444   *card catalog

Laudate Dominum: 4v [SATB], 2V, Va, Vc, Vo, Ctto, Fag, 2Trb, Org.
A-Wn ms. 17445   *card catalog

Missa S. Placidi Martyr à16: SATB *conc & rip*; 2V, 2Trb *conc*, Ctto *rip*, Vc, [bVa], Vo, Org.
D-OB ms. 1089 (missing Vc)   *HaberOB

ZIEGLER, Johann Christoph

Laudate pueri, Dominum: SATB, 2V, 3Va, 2Ctto, Fag, Bc.
D-Dlb mus. 1916 E 500 (Grimma U322/N27, parts)   *WalkerSB

APPENDIX
Works with Unknown Location or Source

AGRICOLA, Georg Ludwig (*b* Grossfurra, Thuringia, 1643; *d* Gotha, 1676)

21. Höre Gott mein Geschrey: 5v, 2Tpt, Ctto, 3Trb, Fag, [Bc].
From an inventory: "Musikalienverzeichnis St. Magni (KapV.1, V.2) StaBS GII,6, Nr.6.O.S. um 1700"   *GreveBR

ANONYMOUS

Gott segne diß vertraute Paar: SSATB *conc & cap*, 2V o 2Ctto, 3Trb o Va, 3Tpt, Tamb, [Bc].
Kyrie eleison: SSAATTBB 2V, 2Ctto, [Bc].
Lobet den Herrn in seinen Heiligthumb: SSATBB *conc & cap*, 4Va, Fag, 2Ctto, 3Trb, [Bc].
Mein freundt ist mein ver ich bin sein: SSATB *conc & cap*, 2Tpt, 2Ctto, [2]V, 3Trb, 3Va, [Bc].
Magnificat: SSATB *conc & cap*, 4Va, 2Ctto, 3Trb, [Bc].
Nun dancket alle Gott: ChI&II SATB, SATB *cap*, 5Va, 2Tpt, 2Ctto, 3Trb, Timp, [Bc].
Venite celebrate festum splendidum: SSATTB *conc & cap*, 2Tpt, 2V, 2Ctto, 2Fl, 2Trb, [Bc].
From an inventory of the St. Michaelisschule in Lüneburg (17th cent.)   *SeiffertL

32. Kom H. Geist zeuch: SSAT, 2Cttino, [Bc.]?
204. Freuet euch des Herren: SSATTB, 2Vo, 3Va, 2Ctto, 3Trb, [Bc].
From an inventory: "Musikalienverzeichnis St. Magni (KapV.1, V.2) StaBS GII,6, Nr.6.O.S. um 1700"   *GreveBR

In the opera *I Santi Didimo e Teodora* with insts: 3V, Lira, 2Lt, Tior, Ctto, 2Vo. I-Catania Biblioteca Civica (dated 1635; music lost); instrumentation from a description of the cast in: **I-Rvat** Arch. Barberini Ristretto # 2468   *Margaret Murata, *Operas for the Papal Court, 1631-1668* (Ann Arbor: UMI Research Press, 1981).

BATI, Lucca (Florence, *ca* 1550-1608)

In a description by [Giovanni Maria] Cecci of the intermedii *L'esaltazione della croce,* 1592:
Tremendo e questo loco: A, 4Trb, 2Ctto muto, V, 2bLt, Org.
Grazie rendiamo à Dio à 8: ChI&II; Ctto muto, Flauti, Tromboni, Org, V, 2Lt.
?? à 24: 24v, Fl, V, Lironi, 2Lt, Tromboni, Ctto muto, Org.
Ecco l'arca sempre statta: Voices, Cornetti, Cornetti muti.
*BrownSCI

BARDI, Giovanni de' (*b* Florence, 1534; *d* 1612)

In a description of the intermedii *L'Amico fado,* 1586:

O noi lieti e felice: ChI&II, Lts, Hps, dolziani, zampogne, 3VaG, Flauti, Traversi, Tromboni, Cornetti muti, Cornetti diritti, ribecchini, Flauti grossi, Torti.
*BrownSCI

BUONAVITA, Antonio (*d* after 1606, in Pisa)

Intermedi (lost) a 52: with 6Trb, 4Ctto, & spinetto.
*GroveD

CAPRICORNUS, Samuel Friedrich (*b* Schertitz, 1628; *d* Stuttgart, 1665)

Bonum est confiteri: B, 2Ctto o 2V, [Bc].
Congregati sunt à 6: 2v, 2V, 2Ctto, Bc.
*KriegerW (dated 1684)

Das Wort wardt Fleisch: SSATTB *conc & cap*; 2Ctto, 4Trb, Fag, [Bc].
Heilig ist Gott der Herr Zebaoth: SSSATTB *conc & cap*; 2Ctto, 3Trb, Fag, 4Tpt, Timp, [Bc].
Kyrie Gott aller Welt: SATB *conc*, 2V, Fag; SATB *cap,* 3Va, 3Ctto, 3Trb; [Bc].
(Joachim Gerstenbüttel is also given as the composer)
From an inventory of the St. Michaelisschule in Lüneburg (17th cent)   *SeiffertL

COLER, Martin

Wohl dem der den Herrn fürchtet: SSATB, 2V, 2Ctto, 3Trb o 3Viol, [Bc].
From an inventory of the St. Michaelisschule in Lüneburg (17th cent)   *SeiffertL

CORTECCIA, Francesco (Florence, 1502-1571)

In a description of the intermedii *La Confanaria* by Domenico Mellini, 1565:
S'amor vinto e prigion posto à 6: SSATTB, Ctto muto, 5Crummhorns.
In bando iteme vili à 6: SSATTB, 2Ctto, dolziana, Ctto grosso, 2Trb, Timp.
Dal bel monte Helicon à 4: SATB, 2Ctto muto, Lira, ribecchino, 2Lt, dolziana, s"Stortina," Lyrone.
*BrownSCI

GERSTENBÜTTEL, Joachim (*ca* 1650-1721)

Ein Tag in deinen Vorhöffen: SSATTB *conc & cap*; 2Ctto, 4Trb, Fag, [Bc].
Herr Gott dich loben wir: SSATB *conc*, 4Va, 2Ctto, 3Trb, Fag, 2Tpt, Timp; ChI&II SSATB; [Bc].
Ich freue mich des, das: SSATB *conc*; 5V, 2Ctto, 4Trb, Fag, 2Tpt, Timp; ChI&II SSATB; [Bc].
Kyrie Gott aller Welt: (see Capricornus)
Meine Seel erhebt den Herrn: SSATB *conc*; 4Va, 2Ctto, 3Trb, Fag; ChI&II SSATB; [Bc].
Triumph! Triumph! Es hat überwunden der Löwe vom Stam Juda: SSATB *conc & cap*; 4Va, 2Ctto, 3Trb, Fag, 2Tpt, Timp, [Bc].

Wie lieblich sindt deine Wohnungen: SSATB *conc & cap*; 4Va, 2Ctto, 3Trb, Fag, [Bc].
From an inventory of the St. Michaelisschule in Lüneburg (17th cent)   *SeiffertL

HAHN, Michael

Heut triumphiret Gottes Sohn: ATB *conc*, SSATB *cap*, 2V, 2Ctto o 2Fl, 2Trb, 2Tpt, [Bc].
From an inventory of the St. Michaelisschule in Lüneburg (17th cent)   *SeiffertL

HILDEBRAND, Johann Heinrich

Stehe auff meine Freundin: ChI T(Sponsus), 2Ctto, 3Trb; ChII S(Sponsa), 5V; ChIII(ch. gratulans); [Bc].
From an inventory of the St. Michaelisschule in Lüneburg (17th cent)   *SeiffertL

KNÜPFER, Sebastian (*b* Asch, Bavaria, 1633; *d* Leipzig, 1676)

117. Ich freue mich in Dir: SSATB, 2V, VaBr, Vo, 2Ctto, 3Trb, [Bc].
From an inventory: "Musikalienverzeichnis St. Magni (KapV.1, V.2) StaBS GII,6, Nr.6.O.S. um 1700"   *GreveBR

KRIEGER, Adam (*b* Driesden nr. Frankfurt, 1634; *d* Dresden, 1666)

Meister, wir wissen: TB *conc*, SATB *cap*, V, Ctto, Trb, Bc.
D-Berlin (lost after 1945)   *MGG; GroveD

KRIEGER, Johann Philipp (*b* Nürnberg, *bapt.* 1649; *d* Weissenfels, 1725)

Der Christen Müt besteht à 6: SAB, V, Ctto, Trb, [Bc].
Heut ist der armen Heiden fest à 5: SAB, V, Ctto, [Bc].
Ich freue mich deß à 14: 4v, 3Tpt, 2Ctto, 5 *rip*. Timp, [Bc] (1688).
Magnificat à 23: 8v, 2Ctto, 3Trb, Timp, [Bc].
Missae à 22: 8v, 8Va[G], 2Ctto, 3Trb, Timp, [Bc].
Veni creatos à 20: 7v, 2Ctto, Trb, [Bc].
*KriegerW

LAWES, William

An antheme with verses for cornetts & Sagbutts set to Psalm XC
GB-Lbl Harleian 6346 titled: The Anthems used in Kings Chapel (contains no music)
*Murray Lefkowitz, *William Lawes* (London: Routledge & Kegan Paul, 1960).

LOCKE, Matthew (*b* Devon, 1621/2; *d* London, 1677)

In a description from Thomas Shadwell: *Psyche: A Tragedy, Acted at the Dukes Theater*. London, 1675:
"Voices, Flagotets, Violin, Cornets, Sackbuts, Hoaboys: all join in chorus: How happy are those that inhabit this place."

There are no wind instruments indicated in the 1675 edition of the work. This description indicates the possibility that a ms version, now lost, may have had more elaborate instrumentations.

*HardML   Edition: MB

MANUCCI, Piero

In a description of the intermedii *La Calandvia* for Bernardo Dovizi contained in *La Magnifica et triumphale entrata. . . .* Lyons, 1548.

L'eta mi Chiamo Aarato e venga à 5: SSATB, 2Ctto, 3Trb.

*BrownSCI

PASSARINI, Francesco (Bologna, 1636-1694)

Chirie à otto; instrumenti, tromba et cornetti: in D fatto in Bo/.ª 1683

Gloria à otto con tromba; Cornetti, et instrumenti in D con terza mag.ʳᵉ fatta in Bolª l'anno 1672

Gloria in D al terza mag.ʳᵉ à otto con Tromba, Cornetti, et Instrumentⁱ fatta in Venezia l'anno 1674

Motetto à 16 pr la Madª con trombe e cornetti in G sol re ut

Motetto pieno à 12 con tromba, e cornettj per L'Inocentj Bolª 1666

Dixit in G Sol fa ut à otto con tromba; cornetti, et Instromenti

Dixit à otto con Tromba; cornettj, e v.v. obligatj

Jubilate mei à dieci con Instromenti, tromba, cornetti. Venetia 1679

Laudate à otto con Instromenti, et cornetti in [?]

Nisi à otto con 6 v.v. e tre cornettj in [?]. Venetia 1674

Letatus à trè Chori con Trombe, e Cornettj. Venetia 1677

Letatus à 3 Chori con Trombe, Cornetti. Venetia 1677

From an inventory of his own works made by Francesco Passarini in the year of his death and preserved in Bologna.

I-Bc Ms. H67

PERANDA, Marco Giuseppe (*b* Rome, *ca* 1625; *d* Dresden, 1675)

Fremite as arma currite: SSATB *conc & cap*, 4Va, 2Ctto, 3Trb, Fag, [Bc].

Kyrie eleison: SSATB *conc & cap*, 4Va, 2Ctto, 3Trb, Fag, [Bc].

Kyrie eleison: SSATB *conc & cap*, 4Va, 2Ctto, 3Trb, Fag, [Bc].

Magnificat: ChI&II SSATB; SSATB *cap*; 4Va, 2Ctto, 3Trb, Fag, [Bc].

From an inventory of the St. Michaelisschule in Lüneburg (17th cent.)   *SeiffertL

PEZEL, Johann Christoph (*b* 1639 in Glatz, Silesia; *d* 1694 in Bautzen)

Decas Sonatarum, 1669: 2Ctto, 4Trb.

Intraden 1676: Ctto, 3Trb.

PFLEGER, Augustin (*ca*1635-1686 in Schlackenwerth, Karlovy Vary)

Ich habe di Schlüssel der Höllen: SSTB *conc & cap*, 4Va, 2Ctto, 2Tpt, Fag, [Bc].

From an inventory of the St. Michaelisschule in Lüneburg (17th cent.)   *SeiffertL

POHLE, David (*b*1624 in Marienberg; *d*1695 in Merseburg)

Gott sey unß gnädig: ChI,II&III SSATB; 2V, 2Va, 2Ctto, 3Trb, Fag, [Bc].
From an inventory of the St. Michaelisschule in Lüneburg (17th cent.) *SeiffertL

ROSENMÜLLER, Johann (*b* Oelsnitz, nr. Zwickau, 1619; *d* Wolfenbüttel, 1684)

Es erhube sich ein Streit: SATB *conc & cap*, 2Ctto, 2Trb, Fag, [Bc].
In dulci jubilo: SSATB *conc & cap*, 4Va, 2Ctto, 3Trb, 2Tpt, Timp, Fag, [Bc].
Quem vidistis pastores: SSATTB *conc & cap*, 2Ctto, 5Va, 5Trb, [Bc].
From an inventory of the St. Michaelisschule in Lüneburg (17th cent.)   *SeiffertL

148. Steh auf meine freundin: SSATB, 2V, 2Va, Vo, 2Ctto, 3Trb, [Bc].
From an inventory: "Musikalienverzeichnis St. Magni (KapV.1, V.2) StaBS GII,6, Nr.
6.O.S. um 1700"   *GreveBR

SANCES, Giovanni Felice (*b* Rome *ca* 1600; *d* Vienna, 1679)

Ave Regina: BBB, 2V, 4Va, 2Ctto muto, [Bc].
Beatus: ATB, 2Ctto muto, [Bc].
Beatus: 6v, 2Ctto muto, [Bc].
Beatus: T, 2Ctto muto; B, 2V; 4v *cap*, [Bc].
Confitebor: 4v, 2Va, 2Ctto, 4Trb, [Bc].
Confitebor: 4v, 2Vtta o 2Ctto, [Bc].
Confitebor: 6v, 4Va, 2Ctto muto, 4Trb, [Bc].
Confitebor: 6v, 2Ctto muto, 4Trb, [Bc].
Confitebor: 4v, 2Va, 2Ctto muto, 4Trb, [Bc].
Confitebor: ATB, 4Va, 2Ctto, 4Trb, *senza rip*, [Bc].
Cum Invocarnem: 4v, 2V, 4Va, 2Ctto muto, 4Trb, [Bc].
De Profondis: 5v, 2Ctto muto, 4Trb, [Bc].
De Profondis: BBB, 2Vtta, 2Ctto muto, 2Trb, [Bc].
Dies Irae: 8v, 4Va, 2Ctto muto, 4Trb, [Bc].
Dies Irae: 6v, 2Tpt, 5Va, 2Ctto muto, 4Trb, [Bc].
Dies Irae: 6v, 2Tpt *sordini*, 5Va, 2Ctto muto, 4Trb, [Bc].
Dies Irae: 6v, 2Tpt *sordini*, 5Va, 2Ctto muto, 4Trb, [Bc].
Domine Jesu Christe: 8v, 5Va, 2Ctto muto, 4Trb, [Bc].
Domine Jesu Christe: AB, ?Trb, 2Ctto, [Bc].
Ecce Nunc: SSATTB, 2Vtta, 2Ctto muto, [Bc].
In te Domine: 8v, 2Va, 2Ctto muto, [Bc].
In te Domine: 4v, 2V, 4Va, 2Ctto muto, 4Trb, [Bc].
In convertendo: AT, 2Ctto muto, 4Trb, [Bc].
In convertendo: BB, 2V o 2Ctto, 2Trb o 2Va, [Bc].
Laetatus sum: 6v, 2Ctto muto, 4Trb, [Bc].
Laetatus sum: 6v, 2Ctto muto o 2Va, [Bc].
Laetatus sum Nisi Lauda Jerusalem: 6v, 2Vtta, 3Va, 2Ctto, 4Trb, [Bc].
Lauda Jerusalem: 6v, 2Ctto muto, 4Trb, [Bc].
Lauda Jerusalem: 6v, 2Va, 2Ctto muto, 4Trb, [Bc].
Lauda Jerusalem: 4v, 2Ctto muto, 4Trb o 4Va, [Bc].

Laudate Pueri: 6v, 2Ctto muto, 4Trb, [Bc].
Laudate Pueri: BB, 2V, 2Ctto, [Bc].
Laudate Pueri: 6v, 2Ctto muto, 4Trb, [Bc].
Laudate Pueri: SSB, 2Vtta, 2Ctto muto, *senza rip*, [Bc].
Lettioni: 8v, 6Va, 2Ctto muto, 4Trb, [Bc].
Litanie: 6v, 2V o 2Ctto, 4Trb o 4Va, [Bc].
Litanie: 8v, 2V, 5Va, 2Ctto, 4Trb, 2Tpt, [Bc].
Litanie: 8v, 2V, 4Va, 2Ctto, 4Trb, 2Tpt, [Bc].
Litanie: 6v, 2Ctto muto, 4Trb, [Bc].
Litanie Cesare: ChI&II, 2V, 4Va, 2Ctto, 4Trb, 2Tpt, [Bc].
Litanie in afflicione: 5v, 2Va o 2Ctto, [Bc].
Litanie per la Visitat. di B.M.V.: 6v, 2Ctto, 4Trb, 5Va, 2Tpt, Fag, [Bc].
Magnificat: 5v, 2Ctto muto, 4Trb, [Bc].
Magnificat: 6v, 5Va, 2Ctto muto, 4Trb, [Bc].
Magnificat: 2v, 2V, 4Va, 2Ctto, 4Trb, [Bc].
Magnificat: 6v, 2Ctto muto, 4Trb, [Bc].
Magnificat: 5v, 5Va, 2Ctto, [Bc].
Magnificat: 6v, 2Tpt, 6Va, 2Ctto muto, 4Trb, [Bc].
Magnificat: 6v, 2Ctto muto, 4Trb, [Bc].
Miserere: 6v, 6Va, 2Ctto, 4Trb, [Bc].
Missa B: M: Magdelena: SSATTB *conc*, 2V, 4Vtta, 2Ctto, 4Trb, [Bc].
Missa Felicitas: ChI SSATTB, 2V, 4Va; ChII: SSATTB *rip*, 2Ctto, 4Trb, [Bc].
Missa Pro Infirmis: 6v, 2Ctto o 2V, 5Va, 4Trb, [Bc].
Missa St. Liborij: 4v, 4Va, 2Ctto muto, 4Trb, [Bc].
Motetto: SSAATTB, 4Va, 2Ctto, 4Trb, [Bc].
Motetto de B.M.V: 6v, 2V o 2Ctto, 5Va, 5Trb, [Bc].
Motetto de B.M.V.: 6v, 2V, 4Va, 2Ctto, 4Trb, [Bc].
Motetto de B.M.V. Virgo Clementissima: 6v, V, 5Va, 2Ctto, 5Trb, [Bc].
Motetto di S. Leopoldo: 6v, 2Ctto o 2V, 4Va, 4Trb, [Bc].
Motetto Per Martire e Per Apostoli: 8v, 2V, 4Va, 2Ctto, 4Trb, [Bc].
Motetto Per la Ressuretione: 8v, 2V, 4Va, 2Ctto, 4Trb, [Bc].
Motetto Per St. Leopoldo o altro Conf.: 6v, 2Tpt, 5Va, 2Ctto, 4Trb, [Bc].
Motetto Tu Michael Tu Spiritus: 5v, 4Va, 2Ctto, Trb, [Bc].
Nisi Dominus: 6v, 2Ctto muto, 4Trb, [Bc].
Nisi Dominus: SAB, 2Ctto muto o 2Va, [Bc].
Nunc dimittis: 8v, 2V, 2Ctto, [Bc].
Qui Habitat: BB, 2V, 2Ctto, [Bc].
Regina Caeli: 8v, 2V, 4Va, 2Ctto, 4Trb, 2Tpt, Fag, [Bc].
Regina Caeli: 6v, 2V, 4Va, 2Ctto, 4Trb, 2Tpt, [Bc].
Regina Caeli: 6v, 2V, 2Ctto, 4Trb, 2Tpt, [Bc].
Regina Caeli: SSB, 2Ctto muto, [Bc].
Regina Caeli: 6v, 2V, 5Va, 2Ctto, 4Trb, 2Tpt, [Bc].
Requiem: 6v, 2Ctto muto o 2Vtta, 6Va, 4Trb, [Bc].
Requiem Pro Defuncta Imperatice Margarita: 5v, 2Ctto muto, 5Va, 4Trb, [Bc].
Requiem: 5v, 2Ctto mut, 5Va, 4Trb, [Bc].
Requiem: 8v, 2Ctto muto o 2Vtta, 4Va, 4Trb, Fag, [Bc].

Requiem: 8v, 2Ctto muto o 2Vtta, 6Va, 4Trb, Fag, [Bc].

Responsorij: BB, 2Ctto muto, 2Vtta, [Bc].

Salmi. Dixit: 8v, 2V, 4Va, 2Ctto, 4Trb, [Bc].

Salmi. Dixit: 8v, 2V, 4Va, 2Ctto, 4Trb, [Bc].

Salmi. Dixit: 4v, 2V, 4Va, 2Ctto, 4Trb, [Bc].

Salmi. Dixit: 6v, 2V, 4Va, 2Ctto, 4Trb, [Bc].

Salmi. Dixit: 6v, 2V, 4Va, 2Ctto, 4Trb, [Bc].

Salmi. Dixit: 6v, 2Ctto muto, 4Trb, [Bc].

Salve Regina: SSB, 2Ctto muto, [Bc].

Salve Regina: 4v, 2V, 2Ctto muto, 4Va, 4Trb. [Bc].

Salve Regina: 8v, 2V, 2Ctto, 4Va, 4Trb. [Bc].

Salve Regina: 6v, 2Ctto muto, [Bc].

Salve Regina: 4v, 2Ctto muto, [Bc].

Spunta da l'orizonte: SATB, 2Ctto o 2V, [Bc].

Sub tuum presidium: 5v, 2Tpt, 2Ctto, 4Va, 4Trb, [Bc].

Te Deum laudamus: 6v, 2V, 4Va, 2Ctto, 4Trb, 2Tpt, [Bc].

Te Deum laudamus: 6v, 2V, 4Va, 2Ctto, 4Trb, 2Tpt, [Bc].

Te Deum laudamus: 6v, 6Va, 2Ctto, 4Trb, Tpt, [Bc].

Te Deum laudamus: 8v, 2V, 4Va, 2Ctto, 4Trb, [Bc].

Te Deum laudamus: SSATB, 5Va, 2Ctto o 2V, 4Trb, 2Tpt, [Bc].

Te lucis et nunc dimittis: 4v, 2V, 4Va, 2Ctto, 4Trb, [Bc].

Te lucis: SSB, 2Ctto, Fag, [Bc].

Te lucis: SS, 2Va o 2Ctto muto, [Bc].

Te lucis: SSB, 2Ctto, Fag, [Bc].

Vespro Interio Dixit: 6v, 2V, 2Ctto muto o 2Vtta, 4Trb, [Bc].

From an inventory of Giovanni Felice Sances   *WebhoferS

SCHELLE, Johann (*b* Geising, Thuringia, 1648; *d* Leipzig, 1701)

An den Waßern zu Babel saßen wir: SSATB *conc & cap*, 4Va, Fag, 2Ctto, 3Trb, [Bc].

Der Herr hat seinen Engeln befohlen über dir: SSATB *conc & cap*, 4Va, Fag, 2Ctto, 3Trb, 2Tpt, Timp, [Bc].

Ich dancke dir Gott: SATB *conc & cap*, 4[Va], Fag, 2Ctto, 4Trb, [Bc].

Unß ist ein Kindt geboren: SSATB *conc & cap*, 4Va, Fag, 2Ctto, 3Trb, 2Tpt, Timp, [Bc].

From an inventory of the St. Michaelisschule in Lüneburg (17th cent)   *SeiffertL

SCHIMROCK, J.

Lobet den Herrn alle Heiden: SSATB, 2V, 2Va, Fag, 2Tpt, 2Ctto, Timp, 3Trb, [Bc].

From an inventory of the St. Michaelisschule in Lüneburg (17th cent)   *SeiffertL

SCHULZE, Christian Andreas (*b* Dresden, *ca* 1660; *d* Meissen, 1699)

Ach daß die Hülffe aus Zion: 5v *conc & cap*, 4Va, Fag, 2Ctto, 3Trb, [Bc].
The author is listed as C. A. Sag[ittarius] in this inventory.
From an inventory of the St. Michaelisschule in Lüneburg (17th cent)   *SeiffertL

SEBASTIANI, Johann (*b* nr. Weimar, 1622; *d* Königsberg, 1683)

Nun dancket alle Gott: 8v *conc*, 4v *cap,* 2Tpt, [2]Ctto, 4Va, Timp, [Bc].
From an inventory of the St. Michaelisschule in Lüneburg (17th cent)   *SeiffertL

STRIGGIO, Alessandro

In a description by Alessandro Creccarelli of the Florentine intermedio *I Fabi,* for
the baptism of Leonora de Medici, 1567:
D'ogn'altra furia e peste à 5: SSATB, 2Ctto muto, 2Trb, bStorta.
Ecco dal ciel le nove à 5: SSATB, Ctto muto, 3VaG, 2Trb, Lt.
Se d'un medesmo germe à 6: SSATBB, Ctto muto, Lira, 4Trb, 3Fl, 3VaG, Lt.
O lieto ò vago Aprile à 6: 6v, 2Ctto, 4Trb, 6Lt, 2VaG, 2Fl, 2Trav.
*BrownSCI

In a description by Domenico Mellini of the Florentine intermedio *La Confernaria,*
for Francesco Ambra, 1565:
O altero miracolo novello à 4: 4v, V, VaG, Lt, Lirone, tFl, Trav, Ctto muto, Trb.
Instrumental music before the prologue à 5: Ctto muto, Trav, 2Fl, 4VaG, 2Trb, 2Lt.
A me, che fatta son negletta, e sola à 8: SSATB, 2Fl, Ctto muto, Trb, 4"Violoni,"
aLt, 2Cemb.
*BrownSCI

STRUNCK, [N. A.]

Dixit Dominus: SSATTB *conc & cap*, 4Va, 2Ctto, 3Trb, Fag, [Bc].
From an inventory of the St. Michaelisschule in Lüneburg (17th cent)   *SeiffertL

THEILE, Johann (Naumberg, 1646-1724)

Magnificat: SSATB *conc & cap*, 2V, 2VaBr, 2Ctto, Fag, [Bc].
From an inventory of the St. Michaelisschule in Lüneburg (17th cent)   *SeiffertL

THIEME, Clemens

Ach Herr unsere Mißethaten habens ja verdienet: TTB, 2Ctto, o 2V, 2Trb, [Bc].
Komt her undt schauet: SSAATTB *conc & cap*, 2V, 2Ctto, 4Trb, [Bc].
Kyrie eleison: SSATB *conc & cap*, 5Va, 2Ctto, 2Tpt, Trb, Fag, [Bc].
From an inventory of the St. Michaelisschule in Lüneburg (17th cent)   *SeiffertL

WECKMANN, Matthias (*b* Niederdorla nr. Mühlhausen, *ca* 1619; *d* Hamburg, 1674)

Gratia tibi ago: S o T, 2V, Ctto, [Bc].
From an inventory of the St. Michaelisschule in Lüneburg (17th cent)   *SeiffertL

WERNER, Christoph (*b* Gottleuba, 1617/8; *d* Danzig, 1650)

Ich bin eine blume von Saron: SSATB *conc & cap*, 2V, 2Ctto, Fag, Vo Tior.
From an inventory of the St. Michaelisschule in Lüneburg (17th cent)   *SeiffertL

ZEUTSCHNER, Tobias (*b* Neurode, 1621; *d* Breslau, 1675)

Stehe auf meine Freundin: SATB, 2V, 2Ctto, 4Trb, [Bc].
From an inventory of the St. Michaelisschule in Lüneburg (17th cent)   *SeiffertL

186.   Historia Nativitatis Christi: SSAATTT, 2V; SSBB, Ctto, 2Tpt, 5Trb, B & timp, 2VaG, [Bc].
From an inventory: "Musikalienverzeichnis St. Magni (KapV.1, V.2) StaBS GII,6, Nr. 6.O.S. um 1700"   *GreveBR

COMPOSER INDEX

TEXT INCIPIT INDEX

Michael Collver is an instructor of voice and cornett at the Longy School of Music in Cambridge, MA. He concertizes and records both as a cornettist and as a tenor-countertenor.

Bruce Dickey teaches cornett at the Schola Cantorum Basiliensis and is an active concert and recording artist. He is author of many articles on the cornett and on early music performance practices.